Second Edition

APPLIED FORTRAN IV PROGRAMMING

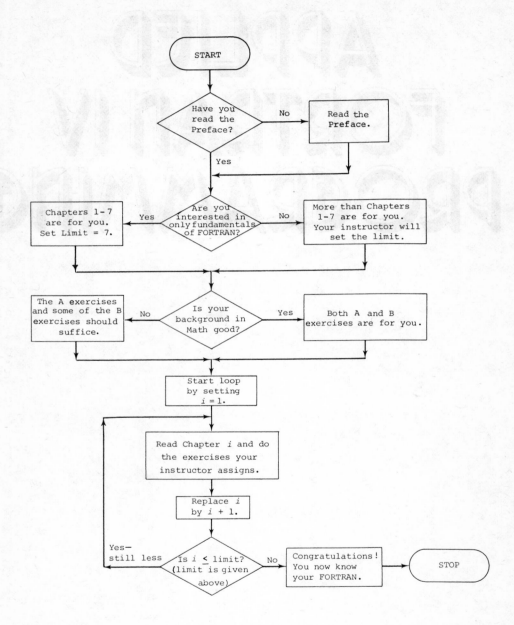

Second Edition

APPLIED FORTRAN IV PROGRAMMING

John R. Sturgul
Michael J. Merchant

The University of Arizona

Wadsworth Publishing Company, Inc.
Belmont, California

Designer: Dare Porter
Computer Science Editor: Don Dellen
Production Editor: Phyllis Niklas
Technical Illustrator: Carl Brown

ISBN-0-534-00440-7

L.C. Cat. Card No. 75-35463

Printed in the United States of America

1 2 3 4 5 6 7 8 9 10---80 79 78 77 76

CONTENTS

to the Second Edition

We have tried to incorporate many of the suggestions, comments, and criticisms of the teachers who used the first edition while still keeping the FORTRAN free from dependency on any one machine. Several of the examples in Part One have been modified and others added. It is our hope that the examples we have selected illustrate the logic in constructing a computer program and are representative of the types of problems solved using the FORTRAN language, without being so involved that the student becomes bogged down in problem-solving per se. The logical IF statement is now introduced in Chapter 3, where most teachers prefer to cover it. A detailed treatment of logical variables has been retained in Chapter 9. An appendix containing the common FORTRAN-supplied functions has also been added.

We wish to thank James Sasser of Oregon State University for his review of the manuscript and further suggestions to improve this edition.

Tucson, Arizona

John R. Sturgul
Michael J. Merchant

PREFACE

to the First Edition

The use of electronic computers has become so common that a
basic knowledge of programming has become virtually essential in
most branches of science and engineering. Programming courses are
required early in the engineering and science curricula of most
universities today, and the subject is being taught in many high
schools to third- and fourth-year students.

A common and widely applicable language used for programming
is FORTRAN. This is the language with which many students normally
become first acquainted, and for many students (those in the sci-
ences in particular) it is the only programming language they will
ever use to any extent.

The object of this book is to present a self-contained, thorough
treatment of FORTRAN which presupposes no prior knowledge of computers
and which will show the student not only how to write programs in
FORTRAN, but how to set up and solve problems using FORTRAN programming.

This book will probably find its optimum application as a text
for a one-semester first course in FORTRAN programming. However, it
is not restricted to such a course. For example, the first seven
chapters, which make up Part One, Introduction to FORTRAN, would be
quite suitable in themselves for use in a short course of the type
that is often presented by computing facilities to acquaint users
with FORTRAN. Also, when Part Two, Additional FORTRAN, is combined
with Part One, sufficient material is available to be used for a
two-semester course, especially at the high school or junior college
level.

The authors firmly believe in the value of demonstrating each
aspect of the material covered by applying it to typical examples,
and this method has been followed throughout the book. Most of these
examples presuppose nothing more than a basic knowledge of high school
algebra, and great care has been taken, particularly in the first six
chapters, to present examples which are simple and relevant, yet in-
teresting and typical of the sort of problems one encounters in programming. However, for students interested in slightly more sophisti-
cated applications of FORTRAN programming, there are examples in later
chapters of how FORTRAN can be used to solve problems involving cal-
culus, advanced algebra, and matrix algebra. Even these, however, do
not really require any previous knowledge of the subject.

There are several shortcomings in existing books on FORTRAN which
this book attempts to overcome. Many books present the subject without motivating it, without emphasizing the basic logical nature of
computer programming, and without clearly showing how to solve problems on the computer using FORTRAN. In this book, the student is
immediately introduced to the idea of the flowchart as a method of
graphically describing a program. In Chapter 1, we describe what a
computer can and cannot do, and how to write a flowchart for a program.
The examples illustrate basic techniques of programming such as
decision statements and iterative procedures, and the emphasis is on
how to solve simple problems by making a flowchart to represent a
method of solution which could be performed by a computer.

The authors feel that the use of flowcharts for setting up solutions to problems is a valuable instructive aid, and this method has
been used throughout the text.

Another problem with many existing texts is the sequence in
which the material is presented. For example, double-precision and
complex variables are of rather little importance to a beginning
student, and to include a discussion of these topics in an early
chapter (for example, along with fixed- and floating-point variables)
would either confuse the student or necessitate an unduly cursory
treatment. This has been handled by treating this topic separately
in a later chapter.

Similarly, there are some statements in FORTRAN (such as the
PAUSE and assigned GO TO) which are primarily of use only to an advanced student or professional programmer, and these topics have been
deferred to Chapter 13 rather than included in the early chapters.

The philosophy throughout has been to have the student write
flowcharts and programs as soon as possible to encourage an under-
standing of what FORTRAN programming is about before getting into
details which may obscure an overview of the subject. For this
reason, input and output statements are introduced in Chapter 4—
after the student has already written some programs. This chapter
is kept as simple as possible, since at this point the main problem
facing the student is in writing and successfully running a complete
program. Later, in Chapter 7, more detailed features of input-output
operations are discussed. This arrangement allows the student to run
programs at an early stage without having to first master the complex-
ities of the different types of FORMAT statements.

The exercises at the ends of the chapters have been chosen to
provide the student with a review of the subject matter just covered
and to give samples of the types of problems that can be solved with
the material learned to that point. The first chapters in the book
contain more exercises than those near the end of the book; as FOR-
TRAN is learned, fewer review problems and more actual problems
requiring complete programs for solution are needed. For the first
eight chapters, the exercises are in two parts, A and B. The A
exercises are rather straightforward and require no special training
or background; the B exercises may require either more background or
some originality to solve.

Another feature of this book is a detailed treatment of magnetic tape and disk operations. This subject is of great importance to anyone who works with a medium- or large-scale computer, and basic techniques such as sorting a tape are discussed here.

Logical variables and conditional statements are treated in Chapter 9 and alphameric data are treated in Chapter 10. A knowledge of this material is essential for anyone who is interested in acquiring a real proficiency in programming. The material in Chapters 11-13 is more advanced, but was found worthy of more consideration than it is generally given in introductory texts.

Another reason for this particular organization of the material is that many small computers (such as the IBM 1130) do not allow the use of logical or complex variables or magnetic tape operations in their versions of FORTRAN. For use with such a computer, Chapters 1-8 and 10 would be a complete treatment of the subject. Chapters 9 and 11-13 complete the introduction to FORTRAN. Beyond this, it is expected that a student will be able to read the reference manuals supplied for each computer system for descriptions of other permissible statements.

Finally, a few words about the FORTRAN used in this book. We have tried to present an introduction to the language in Part One that is general enough to be used on nearly any computer that handles FORTRAN, but not oriented toward any one specific machine. Part Two is strictly FORTRAN IV. In general, we have tried to present the FORTRAN in Part Two based on what is given as standard FORTRAN IV by the American National Standards Institute (ANSI). This also includes flowcharts, symbols, and computer terminology. We have made several deviations which are either noted or indicated by a footnote. In one case, for instance, we chose to use the terminology "statement number" instead of ANSI's "statement label," since the former seems to be much more widely accepted.

We are deeply grateful for the assistance furnished by the University of Arizona Computer Center in providing us with their computer facilities. Loren P. Meissner of the University of California at Berkeley and John D. Stevens of Iowa State University reviewed portions of the manuscript and did an excellent job of showing us what a complex subject computer language really is. Responsibility with the final choice of subject matter lies solely with us.

The manuscript was typed and retyped numerous times by Alison Odell. Finally, special thanks for their patience to our wives, Nancy and Alison.

Tucson, Arizona   John R. Sturgul
                                                      Michael J. Merchant

DEFINITIONS

FORTRAN Statements

Field Specifications

Operations

PART ONE

Introduction to FORTRAN

Chapter

Programs and Flowcharts

The design of electronic computers has advanced to such a level of complexity and sophistication that only a small number of individuals are familiar with all the details of the construction of any particular computer. Advances in this field have been so rapid that it is quite probable that the computers of today will seem slow and almost obsolete in 10 or 15 years. Fortunately, it is not necessary to understand the design of computers in order to program them, any more than it is necessary to understand the design of a television set in order to operate one. What concerns us is not how a computer operates as an electronic device, but rather how it behaves as a logical device.

A computer is a mechanism capable of manipulating numbers and symbols according to a well-defined program. For example,

1. input a number,
2. input another number,
3. add the two numbers,
4. output the result,

is the sort of program a computer can perform. Obviously, a computer would not be particularly useful if this were all it could do; a computer is useful because it can be programmed to do many different jobs.

Roughly speaking, a program is a process described in terms of instructions a computer can understand. Computers, of course, do not really *understand* anything; they can only perform certain basic operations (such as addition). So a program is a sequence of instructions; and each instruction describes one basic operation. Since each instruction tells the computer to do something, the order in which the instructions are performed is important, and it must also be specified by the program.

Specifically, a program is a sequence of instructions and a set of rules for performing them such that

1. only one instruction at a time is performed;

2. after performing any given instruction, it must be clear which instruction is to be performed next.

■ Instructions

A program consists of instructions. Not all instructions, however, are meaningful to a computer. The familiar command "Wipe your feet," for example, is not the kind of instruction a computer can obey. Actually, only four basic types of operations can be performed:

1. input-output,
2. storing,
3. computation,
4. simple decisions.

Input-Output. The input and output of data is obviously necessary. To add 3 and 5 on an adding machine, we must first "input" the 3 and then the 5 by pushing buttons on the keyboard. These keyboard entries correspond to two input operations. The answer must subsequently be displayed ("output") in some legible form.

On a computer we shall be able to handle large amounts of data; to input and output this data, more efficient means than pushing buttons have been developed. But whether punched cards, high-speed printers, magnetic tapes, or other devices are used, the purpose is the same—to read in or write out data.

Storing. Every item of data that is read into a computer has to be stored somewhere, and we must have some way of finding each item again. This is the purpose of the memory of the computer. The memory is a sort of electronic filing cabinet in which thousands of numbers can be stored and referenced. This enables us to work with many numbers and to keep intermediate results in the computer.

The computer refers to each location in its memory by an address. Thus, the memory may be thought of as many mailboxes; the address specifies a particular mailbox, and the contents of the mailbox is the number that is stored.

In FORTRAN programming, we do not actually use the internal address itself; for convenience, we use a name that has some meaning in the problem at hand. The machine will associate each name we use with the address of an empty mailbox; each time we want to refer to the contents of that mailbox, we use the same name. For example, to read in a number and store it at a location which we shall refer to by the name A, we could have an instruction like INPUT A. Then the instruction OUTPUT A would refer to that same location.

Computation. Arithmetic computation is performed electronically in a computer, but it is programmed in a very straightforward way. When a computation is performed, the result must be stored somewhere. For example, we cannot just say, "Add *A* and *B*." We must say, "Add *A* and *B* and store the result at *C*." We write C = A + B. This does not mean the same thing in a program as it does in algebra. In algebra it is an equation; in a program it is an instruction specifying that the computation on the right of the equals sign be performed and the result stored in the location named C. Consider the instruction X = X + 1. In algebra it is false; as a program instruction, however, it means to take the number at address X, add 1 to it, and put the result back at address X.

Simple Decisions. A computer can make decisions only in an elementary way. Given two numbers, it can compare them to determine whether the first is less than (<), equal to (=), or greater than (>) the second. Then, it can transfer control to another statement, which simply means that the next instruction to be executed is determined by the outcome of the comparison. For example, we might have the following procedure to print the larger of two numbers, *A* and *B*:

If $A < B$, output *B*.
If $A \geq B$, output *A*.

The ability of the computer to perform this very elementary operation is one of the most important tools of programming.

These four types of operations—input-output, storing, computation, and simple decisions—form the basis of programming. This is all a computer can do. The job of the programmer, then, is to formulate a given problem in terms of these instructions.

Languages

To tell a computer what to do, we must write our instructions in a language the machine understands. Each computer has its own language, called *machine language*. The various machine languages are difficult to use because they consist solely of numeric codes. Furthermore, a program written in a machine language for one computer would not necessarily run on a different model computer. To make it easier to use computers, several standardized languages have been developed. FORTRAN is such a language. When a program written in one of the standardized languages is input to a computer, a translator program (called a *compiler*) converts the instructions in the standardized language to instructions in the machine's own language. The computer then executes the program using the machine language instructions.

FORTRAN (from FORmula TRANslation) is widely used because it is logical and similar to familiar algebraic symbols. It is particularly useful in coding problems of engineering and mathematics, although it is also often used for business applications.

Before we examine FORTRAN itself, we should learn the basic method used to represent a program by a flowchart.

■ Flowcharts

A flowchart is simply a way to diagram a program. The idea is to represent what is going on in a form that is easy to read and work with. It is most helpful to flowchart a problem before trying to write a program to solve it. This procedure is almost indispensable for programs that are lengthy or complex.

Various shapes are used to represent different types of operations. For example, an input operation is represented by a parallelogram. To read in values for A and B, we would use the following diagram:

Input:
A, B

A parallelogram is also used for output operations. This is not as confusing as it may seem, since a programmer always writes either Input or Output at the top of the box to indicate which is meant. Thus, our output operations are represented by the following:

Output:
A, B

The next most important box is where we do our actual work. This is represented by a rectangle, and the instructions for what is to be done are written inside it:

$C = A + B$

To indicate the order in which the operations are to be performed, the boxes are connected with arrows that point in the direction of flow. For example, to read in two numbers, add them, and write out the result, we could use the flowchart shown in Fig. 1-1.

The Start and Stop terminals are an essential part of every flowchart. The Start terminal indicates the first instruction to

be performed, and the Stop terminal indicates that no more instructions should be processed after reaching it.

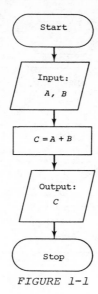

FIGURE 1-1

A decision statement is represented by a diamond-shaped box.
For the present, we shall write every decision in the form of a
question; later we shall introduce notation to simplify this procedure:

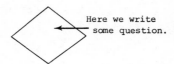

We shall now construct a few problems (two of which would not
normally be solved by a computer) that illustrate the applications
of flowcharts.

Problem 1

Suppose you are the president of company *X*. Two of your
employees, *A* and *B*, come into your office. You look at them and
decide to give the better-looking one a pay raise. Then they leave.
How would you flowchart this decision?

Solution. We must, of course, use a Start box. This might
correspond to your arrival at the office in the morning. The next
part of the flowchart is the Input box, representing when the two
employees enter your office. The Decision box comes next. This is
where you make the decision: "Is employee *B* better-looking than
employee *A*?" You then do the actual "arithmetic"—this is when you

give *A* or *B* the raise. The next step is the output, when the employees leave your office. Your flowchart would be the one shown in Fig. 1-2.

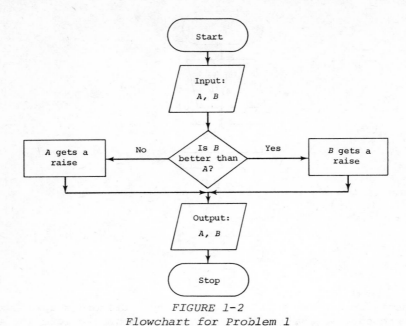

FIGURE 1-2
Flowchart for Problem 1

Problem 2

This is the same as Problem 1, except now you must apply the process to many pairs of employees.

Solution. We can use the flowchart for Problem 1, but this time we must add a Decision box after the Output box, and we must test to see if we are done. For now, let us just ask the question: "Are we done?" If so, we shall terminate. If not, we shall want to input two more employees; so we draw a line of flow back to the Input box to indicate that this is the next instruction.

Note that every employee in the flowchart in Fig. 1-3 is called *A* or *B*. This is alright because we have the Output box in our loop that allows the old pair to leave. If we had put the Output box *after* the last Decision box, we would eventually fill the office with people!

Problem 3

Input three unequal numbers and output the largest one.

Solution. Since we can compare only two numbers at a time, we shall need three Decision boxes to compare *A* to *B*, *B* to *C*, and *A* to *C*. The flowchart would be the one shown in Fig. 1-4.

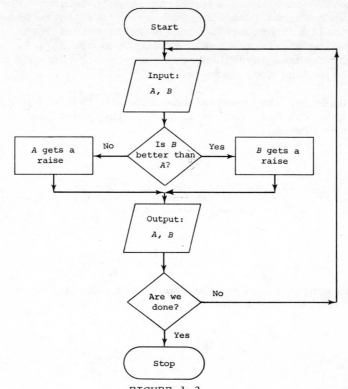

FIGURE 1-3
Flowchart for Problem 2

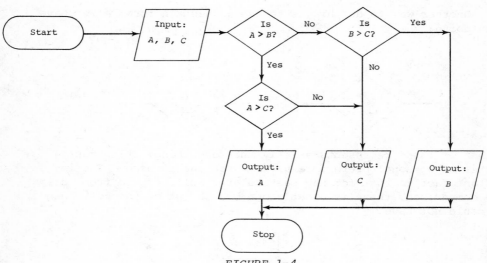

FIGURE 1-4
Flowchart for Problem 3

Convince yourself of the validity of this solution by assigning values to *A*, *B*, and *C*, and tracing these through the flowchart.

We have been placing a question in each Decision box and extending two branches from each, one for a Yes answer and one for a No. Actually, there are several ways to make a Decision box. We could write $A:B$ in the box, meaning "compare A to B," and then put a greater than, less than, or equal to sign on each of three branches extending from the box.

For example, the Decision box shown in the following diagram means to take the left branch if $A < B$, the right branch if $A > B$, or the lower branch if $A = B$:

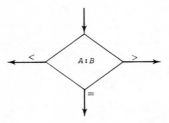

If we wanted to go to the same place when $A = B$ as we do when $A > B$, we could combine the two branches and put

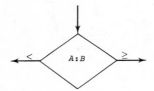

Another way to do this is to use a question form, as we have been doing:

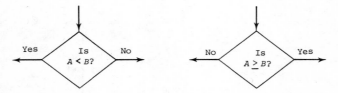

Either of these represents exactly the same thing; it is just a matter of personal preference as to which one is used. The important fact is that for any particular result derived from making the comparison, there is exactly one branch out of the box. Hence, we could *not* have

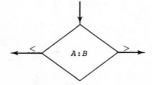

because if $A = B$, there would be no place to go. Even if we knew
in a particular problem that A would never be equal to B, we would
have to construct something like

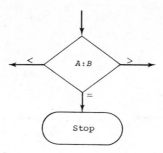

By now it should be clear how a flowchart represents an actual
program: The boxes are the instructions, and the lines of flow specify the order in which the instructions are to be processed. Furthermore, flowcharts visually illustrate the principle that after
one instruction is performed it must be clear which instruction is
to be performed next, and that only one instruction at a time can be
performed.

The flowchart should be a flexible and useful tool. In a
completed flowchart, the differently shaped boxes help to identify
types of instructions, and the lines of flow are easy to follow to
determine what actually happens and when.

A few conventions involved in writing flowcharts should be
mentioned. Usually, lines of flow are drawn either vertically or
horizontally. It is often convenient to have the main line of flow
proceed vertically from the top of the page to the bottom. The only
purpose of these restrictions is to improve legibility.

When a program loop is represented (that is, when the program
returns to a group of instructions in order to perform them more
than once), the line of flow can return to the box representing the
first instruction in the loop, as shown in Fig. 1-5.

In some situations it is inconvenient to draw a line of flow
to an instruction, so a connector (a small circle with an identi-
fier unit) can be used. This indicates that the next instruction
to be performed is identified by a similar connector rather than by
a line of flow. Figure 1-6 gives an example of a situation where
the use of a connector is called for to avoid crossing lines. If a
flowchart requires more than one page, a connector can be used to
indicate that the next instruction is on a different page.

The purpose of the flowchart is to help the programmer. In
the end, clarity and convenience should be the governing factors
when a flowchart is prepared. Flowcharts also help us construct
the program as we go along. Usually, a flowchart is not drawn from
start to finish; the main instructions are done first and then the

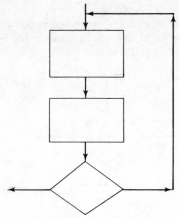

FIGURE 1-5
Method of showing a program loop

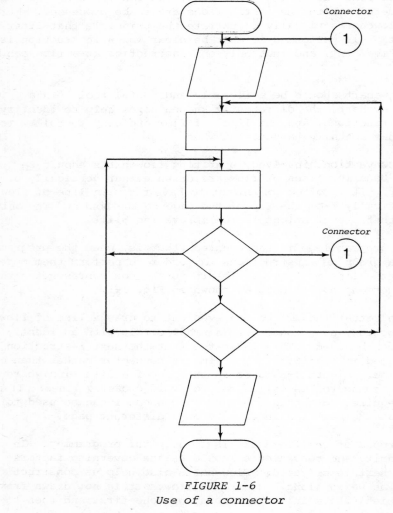

FIGURE 1-6
Use of a connector

rest is filled in. Even an experienced programmer may make several false starts before a satisfactory flowchart is mapped out. A little practice will give you a feeling for the method.

Example 1

Suppose we want to compute the sum of the integers from 1 to N [and suppose we do not remember the formula $S = N(N + 1)/2$]. We shall use the method, not uncommon in programming, of taking a partial sum; that is, at some step we have a location called SUM which contains $1 + 2 + \cdots + (I - 1)$. To the contents of this location, we shall add I. So the main instruction is:[1]

$$\boxed{\begin{array}{c} \text{SUM =} \\ \text{SUM} + I \end{array}}$$

After that, we must test to see if we are finished; so we compare I to N. If $I = N$, we output the answer SUM. If not, we add 1 to I and go back to the computation. So far, our flowchart, which represents the essential part of the program, looks like Fig. 1-7.

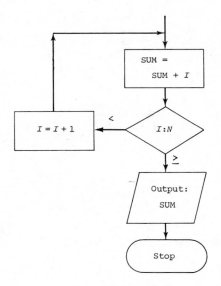

FIGURE 1-7

---

[1]Notice the equals sign in the instruction SUM = SUM + I. This obviously cannot have the normal arithmetic meaning. Instead, it has the computer meaning "is replaced by." We can read the statement as follows: "replace the value of the variable SUM by the old value plus I." Some authors use the symbol ← to indicate replacement.

But the flowchart of Fig. 1-7 is incomplete—the quantities SUM and *I* need to be initialized (that is, they must be given starting values). For this purpose, we use the instructions SUM = 0 and *I* = 1. Finally, we want an Input box to read in a value for *N* so we can use the same procedure for any value of *N*. The completed flowchart is shown in Fig. 1-8.

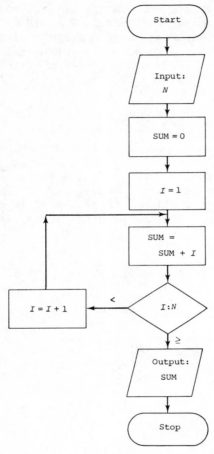

FIGURE 1-8
Flowchart for Example 1

■ Averaging Numbers

Let us now consider a simple problem of a practical nature.

Example 2

Suppose we have a sequence of items and we want to read them in one at a time, sum them, and find their average. To do this, we need to know how many numbers there are and to find their sum. One way to handle this is to read in the number of items, *N*, and then follow a procedure similar to that of Example 1. In this case, we would input *N*, and then input the items and find their sum by performing a loop *N* times. After this is done, we would compute the average and then output this average. The exact procedure is given by the flowchart in Fig. 1-9, where each number in turn is called *X*.

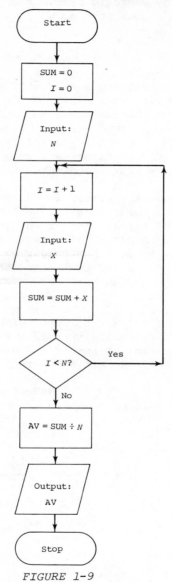

FIGURE 1-9
Flowchart for Example 2

In this example, notice that one work box has been used to represent the two instructions SUM = 0 and *I* = 0. This is occasionally done to conserve space when the two (or more) instructions are not separated by a Decision or other box affecting the flow.

Note that if we wish to set a value for *N* before reading *N* in, it is necessary to count the number of items to be averaged. This might be inconvenient if there were many items. Actually, we can modify the program so that the machine will do the counting for us. To do this, we first choose some value that we know will not occur among the items to be averaged and we read this in as an extra item. Example 3 illustrates this procedure.

Example 3

Suppose we are averaging a student's semester grades. Each grade is one of the numbers 4, 3, 2, 1, or 0. For the last item to be read in, let us put the value 999. In the program we begin by reading in a grade *X*. We then test to see if we have read in 999. If not, we add 1 to *N* and add *X* to SUM. Then we begin again by reading another grade. If we have read 999, however, we compute the average, AV = SUM/*N*, and output this result.

We might go one step further in this example by writing a program to find the averages of several sets of items. For example, we might want to find the average of the semester grades of each student in a school. After the last set of grades, we would put the value 9999. So, if John has grades 1, 2, 3, 4, and 4, and Fred has grades 4, 4, 3, and 4, we could find both averages by running the program once with the data 1, 2, 3, 4, 4, 999, 4, 4, 3, 4, 999, and 9999.

To construct a flowchart for this problem, let us begin with the Decision boxes. We shall first test the value of *X* to see if *X* = 999. If not, we want to see if *X* = 9999, and if it does, we stop. So we have the flowchart shown in Fig. 1-10.

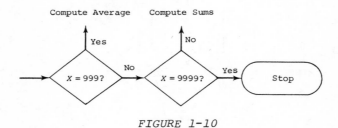

FIGURE 1-10

Now, if the value of *X* is neither 999 nor 9999, we add *X* to SUM, add 1 to *N*, again input *X*, and test. A partial flowchart showing these steps is given in Fig. 1-11.

If, on the first test, *X* = 999, we compute the average and output it. Then we initialize the quantities *N* and SUM and begin again. Finally, we must remember to include a Start terminal and to initialize *N* and SUM before the first time through. The completed flowchart is shown in Fig. 1-12.

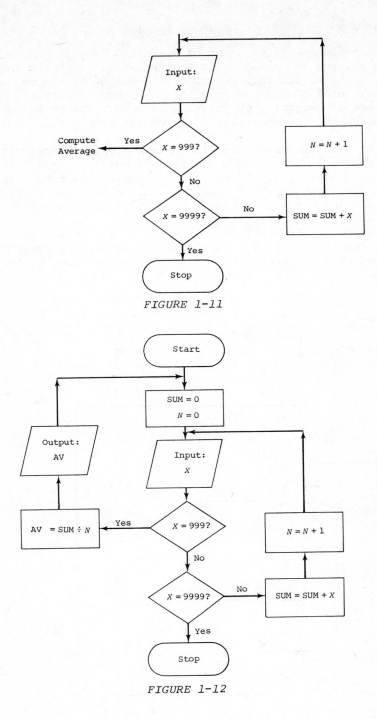

FIGURE 1-11

FIGURE 1-12

■ Sorting Numbers

A frequently encountered problem is that of sorting data into
an ascending (or descending) sequence.

Example 4

Assume you are given a set of n storage locations named X_1, X_2, $\ldots$, X_n, and you are asked to rearrange them so that the location named X_1 contains the smallest numerical value, X_2 the next smallest, etc., until the numbers are all in the desired order. We shall present one of several ways this can be done. The method presented here, though not the fastest, is one of the simplest to understand.

Start with the first location named X_1, and compare its value with that of X_2. If $X_1 \leq X_2$, do nothing, but if $X_1 \geq X_2$, interchange the values of X_1 and X_2. Next, compare the number in the X_1 position with that in the X_3 position and do the same as before. After finishing with all n numbers, we shall have succeeded in placing the smallest number in the first position. Next, compare the number in the second position, X_2, with X_3 and either leave them alone or interchange them. Continuing as before, we eventually have the second smallest number in the X_2 position. Next, go to the X_3

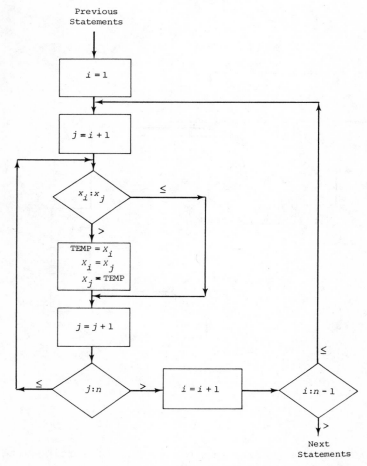

FIGURE 1-13

position and continue as before. When we reach the $n - 1$ position, we are through. The flowchart in Fig. 1-13 shows these steps (it assumes that the X_n values are already stored in the computer).

Notice that a new variable, called TEMP, has been introduced. This is necessary because if we only had the operation $X_i = X_j$ followed by $X_j = X_i$, we would not accomplish what we need to do. The first operation *replaces* X_i by X_j instead of *interchanging* them. By introducing the variable TEMP, we accomplish the interchange.

■ A Exercises

1. According to the accompanying flowchart, what is the final value of Y if $I = 1$? What happens if $I = 2$? How would you guard against this possibility?

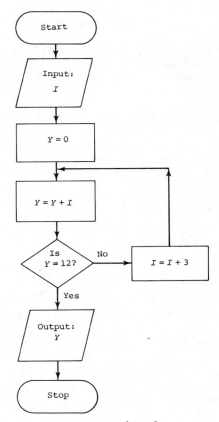

Flowchart for Exercise 1

Construct a flowchart to illustrate a solution to each of Exercises 2-9.

2. Read in the radius R of a circle and output the diameter D, the circumference C, and the area A.

3. Read in two numbers P and Q and output the quotient $X = P/Q$. Include a test to stop if $Q = 0$.

4. Input an integer N and output the sum of all even integers less than N.

5. Input X and output the absolute value ABS of X (that is, ABS = X if $X \geq 0$; ABS = $-X$ if $X < 0$).

6. Input A and B. Set $C = 1$ if $A = B = 1$. Set $C = 2$ if A or B, but not both, equals 1. Set $C = 3$ if neither A nor B equals 1. Output C.

7. Compute $y = x^2 + 5x - 3$ for values of $x = 0.0, 0.1, 0.2, \cdots, 5.0$. Output x and y for each value of x.

8. Input three numbers I, J, and K. If they are all different, set $N = 1$. If any two of them (but not all three) are the same, set $N = 2$. If all three are the same, set $N = 3$.

9. Input an integer N between 1 and 20 and determine whether it is even or odd by subtracting 2 repeatedly until either 0 or a negative number is reached. If N is even, set $M = 0$; if N is odd, set $M = 1$.

10. The accompanying flowchart (page 21) is supposed to count the number of elements of a doubly subscripted variable that are equal to 0. There is an error in the flowchart. Correct the error and trace through the flowchart with the following data:

    $n = 4$ $m = 2$

    $a_{11} = 2.0$ $a_{12} = 3.1$ $a_{13} = 2.0$ $a_{14} = 0.0$

    $a_{21} = 0.0$ $a_{22} = 5.0$ $a_{23} = 0.0$ $a_{24} = 6.1$

■ B Exercises

1. The general quadratic equation has the form $ax^2 + bx + c = 0$. It has two solutions, x_1 and x_2, given by

   $$x_1 = \frac{-b + \sqrt{b^2 - 4ac}}{2a} \qquad x_2 = \frac{-b - \sqrt{b^2 - 4ac}}{2a}$$

   Write a flowchart to read in three values a, b, and c and output x_1 and x_2. Since we cannot take the square root of a negative number, include a test to make the program stop if $b^2 - 4ac < 0$.

2. Write a flowchart to input a positive integer N and output $X = 2^N$.

3. Write a flowchart to input a positive integer N and output $Z = 1 + 1/2 + 1/3 + \cdots + 1/N$.

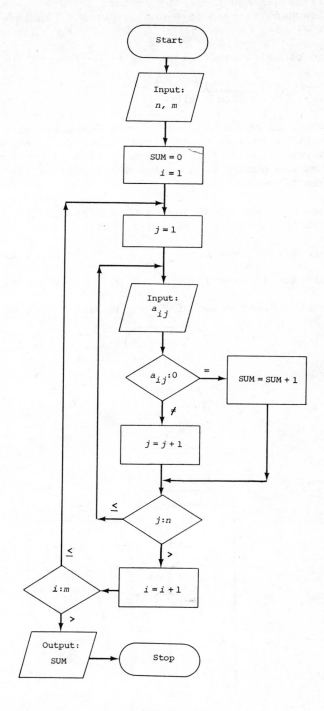

Flowchart for Exercise 10

4. If *M* is any positive integer, the number *M* factorial (written *M!*) is defined to be the product 1 × 2 × ··· × *M*. Write a flowchart to read in *M* and output *M!*. Include a test to stop if *M* < 1.

5. The binomial coefficient C_{nk} is defined by

$$C_{nk} = \frac{n!}{k!\,(n - k)!}$$

(where *n!* means *n* factorial—see Exercise 4). Write a flowchart to read in *n* and *k* and output C_{nk}. What would happen in your flowchart if the number read in for *k* were greater than the number read in for *n*? Include a test to stop if this happens.

6. What does the accompanying flowchart do? Find the value of *Z* that is output if the values read in are

(a) *X* = 0, *N* = 1, (c) *X* = 1, *N* = -2,

(b) *X* = 1, *N* = 2, (d) *X* = 2, *N* = 3.

Can the final value of *Z* ever be 0? Can it be less than 0?

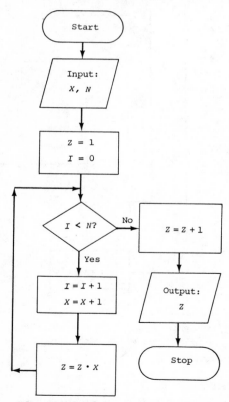

Flowchart for Exercise 6

7. Given a set T_1, T_2, $\cdots$, T_N of test scores, write a flowchart to read them in and determine:

   (a) *NA*   number of scores from 90 to 100,

   (b) *NB*   number of scores from 80 to 89,

   (c) *NC*   number of scores from 70 to 79,

   (d) *ND*   number of scores from 60 to 69,

   (e) *NF*   number of scores from 0 to 59.

8. In solving differential equations, it is sometimes necessary to compute with what are called the *Legendre polynomials*. The first six of these are given by

$$P_0(x) = 1 \quad \text{(for all } x\text{)} \qquad P_3(x) = 1/2(5x^3 - 3x)$$

$$P_1(x) = x \qquad\qquad\qquad P_4(x) = 1/8(35x^4 - 30x^2 + 3)$$

$$P_2(x) = 1/2(3x^2 - 1) \qquad P_5(x) = 1/8(63x^5 - 70x^3 + 15x)$$

   Write a flowchart to read in a number x and an integer $0 \leq N \leq 5$ and output $P = P_N(x)$.

Chapter

2

Constants, Variables, and Arithmetic Expressions

In an algebraic expression we are familiar with seeing numbers and variables used together. The numbers are referred to as *constants*. In general, any quantity that does not change in value is a constant. A quantity that can (or might) change in value is called a *variable* and is written in the form of a symbol. Quite commonly, the symbol used is a letter, but sometimes it may be a name, depending on what we happen to choose. For example, the formula for the area of a circle is often stated as

$$A = \pi r^2$$

Here the constant is π. The variables are A (area) and r (radius). Alternately, we could have written the formula as

$$\text{Area} = \pi (\text{Radius})^2$$

or, for that matter, in any form, as long as we know what the variables represent and we understand what arithmetic operations are implied.

A computer has the property of being able to evaluate a formula for certain values and then, at a later time, to evaluate the same formula for different values. This is done, in part, because as in algebra, we can use both constants and variables in our computer programs. We shall now learn what restrictions are imposed when writing the variables and constants in FORTRAN. We have only a few, but since a computer requires absolutely precise information, they must be followed exactly.

■ Constants

In FORTRAN, a constant is represented simply by a decimal number (that is, a string of decimal digits, possibly having a decimal point and a sign). This means that constants must be composed from the digits 0, 1, 2, 3, 4, 5, 6, 7, 8, and 9. Thus, a constant such as π, $\sqrt{2}$, or e must be represented by a decimal equivalent. Although it is often impossible to write the *exact* decimal equivalent of a desired constant, we can normally express it correctly to at least seven significant decimal places.

There are two different types of FORTRAN constants. (Remember that the same is also true for ordinary numbers.) For example, in an arithmetic examination each problem is given a sequence number, and then various real numbers are used in the problems. The computer, unfortunately, does not possess our common sense; we must be very careful to distinguish between the different types of constants. If we want to indicate a number that is to be used in a calculation to give us the correct arithmetic result, we simply write the number with a decimal point. This is called a *floating-point constant*. Some floating-point constants are listed in Table 2-1.

TABLE 2-1

Normal Arithmetic Constant	Floating-Point FORTRAN Constant
1	1.0 or 1. or 1.00, etc.
26	26.
1,000.2	1000.2
-16	-16.0 or -0016.0, etc.
1,000,000	1000000.
+2	+2. or +2.0 or 2.

The following rules are illustrated in Table 2-1 and *must be observed*:

Rule 1: Commas are not permitted in FORTRAN constants. Thus, the numbers in Table 2-1 that we normally write with commas must be written without them.

Rule 2: As in algebra, if a number has no sign it is taken to be positive. Negative numbers *must* be written with a minus sign.

Rule 3: Zeros in front of a number are not counted. One may thus place them there for convenience.

Rule 4: The size of a constant depends on the computer used. In general, one can assume that a computer can handle up to and including seven digits, not counting the sign or the decimal point.

We shall use numbers to keep track of what we are doing in the program. These numbers are called *counting numbers*; that is, they count the number of times operations are done, refer to various parts of the program, and so on. Such a number is called a *fixed-point constant*,[1] or simply an *integer*, and is distinguished from a

---

[1]Alternate terminology is *real* for floating-point and *integer* for fixed-point. Some authors prefer to use real and integer,

floating-point constant in that it has no decimal point. This means that no decimals or fractions are used as fixed-point constants. Thus, some programmers refer to them as integers. A fixed-point constant may have a minus sign, however, and later we shall learn under what circumstances this is helpful. Table 2-2 gives a few examples of fixed-point constants.

TABLE 2-2

Arithmetic Number	FORTRAN Fixed-Point Constant
31.3	31 or 313 (number must be written with no decimal)
-6.2	-6 or -62 (number must be written with no decimal)
1,000	1000 (no comma)
25	25 (number was already in fixed-point form)

The size of the fixed-point constant is more severely restricted than that of a floating-point constant. In some early computers it was as low as 32767. In modern computers, the size can be 4294967295 or even larger,[2] and in many systems up to eleven significant digits are acceptable.

There is a method of representing floating-point constants analogous to scientific notation. Often numbers arise that are either very large or very small, but that have only a few significant digits. For example, numbers such as those shown in Table 2-3 are frequently encountered in physics and engineering problems.

TABLE 2-3

Arithmetic Number	Scientific Notation
0.0000000666	6.66×10^{-8}
0.000000375	37.5×10^{-8}
8,000,000	8.0×10^{6}
0.000086	0.86×10^{-4}
50,000,000,000,000	5.0×10^{13}

---

especially because there are corresponding FORTRAN statements (see Chapter 13). Unfortunately, the words *real* and *integer* have other meanings. For example, a complex number is said to have a real and an imaginary part. To avoid ambiguity, we prefer the terms *floating-point* and *fixed-point*.

[2]The numbers 32767 and 4294967295 may seem to be strange limits. However, they are actually obtained by powers of 2, namely $2^{15} - 1$ and $2^{32} - 1$. Digital computers work on the binary number system and so they are indeed logical maximum sizes.

The method we use to represent these numbers as FORTRAN floating-point constants is known as the *E-form* (or *exponential form*). If we want to write 62,000 in E-form, we write

$$6.2 \quad E \quad + \quad 04$$

(a) (b) (c) (d)

Let us examine what this means:

(a) First, we wrote a floating-point constant. This, we recall, is a number with a decimal point. This *must* be a floating-point constant.

(b) Next, we put the letter E.

(c) Here we placed a plus sign to signify that the exponent is positive in our example. If we had, instead, 0.00062, we could have written 6.2 E - 04. If no sign appears here, the computer assumes it is positive.

(d) The last number is the exponent, or power, of 10. This *must* be a fixed-point constant. In fact, this illustrates one application of fixed-point constants. As mentioned before, they are used to count the operations being done. In, for example, 7.4×10^5, the number 5 counts the number of places the decimal is to be moved to the right and thus determines the number of zeros to be added to the number when converting back to an arithmetic representation. The zero before the 4 in E + 04 is not necessary but has been added to illustrate the point that, in general, leading zeros are not counted in FORTRAN. Table 2-4 provides further examples of the E-form.

TABLE 2-4

Arithmetic Number	E-Form
20,000	2.0E4 or 2.E4 or 2.E + 4 or 2.E + 04
-2	-2.0E + 0 or -.2E1 or -.002E03
0.00001	.1E - 4 or 1.E - 5 or 1.00E - 05
160,000,000,000,000	16.0E13

The limits on the sizes of such numbers vary with the computer. For some computers, the sizes may be between 10^{-77} and 10^{77}; other computers will accept even larger numbers. Most of the time, these limits will not concern us, as our numbers will be well within these ranges. However, if you wish to use very large numbers in a program, consult the reference manual for the particular computer to be used to determine what the actual limits are.

■ Variables

Several different types of variables are used in FORTRAN.
These types correspond to the different types of numbers used in
a program. In this chapter we shall confine our attention to the
two most commonly used types of variables: fixed-point and floating-point. You may wonder why it is necessary to make a distinction between these. The reason is that the different types of
numbers are stored differently in the computer and used differently
in the program. For example, we shall see in Chapter 5 that a
variable used to represent a subscript must be a fixed-point variable. We shall now see how these different types of variables are
formed.

Fixed-Point Variables. A fixed-point variable is defined by
the following:

Rule 1: It is represented by a name consisting of from one
to six characters.[3]

Rule 2: Each character must be a letter (A-Z) or a numeric
digit (0-9).

Rule 3: The first character *must* be one of the letters
I, J, K, L, M, or N.

This is how FORTRAN distinguishes fixed-point variable names
from floating-point variable names.

As long as we comply with the above rules, we can give a fixed-
point variable any name we choose. Usually, we choose variable
names to help us remember what the variables represent. For example, if a certain variable represents the sum of a group of numbers,
we might call the variable SUM. However, this is not a legal name
for a fixed-point variable, since it does not begin with a letter
I, J, K, L, M, or N. To comply with the rule, we could call the
variable NSUM.

The examples below show correct fixed-point variables:

I   JUMP   MASS   K1234   NNNNNN   L   LENGTH

A few examples of incorrect fixed-point variables are given in
Table 2-5.

---

[3]Most large computers will handle variables with names of
seven characters. For the sake of uniformity, we shall use names
with six or fewer characters.

TABLE 2-5.   Errors in fixed-point variables.

Variable	Reason for Error
I + J	*Illegal symbol (+)*
K1234567	*Too many characters*
HELLO	*Does not start with a letter I–N*
4HG	*Does not start with a letter I–N*
NAME$	*Illegal symbol ($)*

Floating-Point Variables.   The rules for naming floating-point variables are the same as for fixed-point variables—with one exception:

Rule 1: A floating-point variable is represented by a name consisting of from one to six characters.

Rule 2: Each character must be a letter (A–Z) or a numeric digit (0–9).

Rule 3: *The name of a floating-point variable must begin with some letter other than I, J, K, L, M, or N.*

Thus, we can determine the type of variable name by looking at the first letter. If it is I–N, the variable if fixed-point. A variable beginning with any other letter is floating-point. Below are some examples of valid floating-point variable names.

A   X   X1234   FORCE   ACCEL   OHM   ETC

Some examples of errors in floating-point variables are shown in Table 2-6.

TABLE 2-6.   Errors in floating-point variables.

Variable	Reason for Error
X + Y	*Illegal symbol (+)*
JUMP	*Starts with J*
1XY	*Starts with a number*
X$Y	*Illegal symbol ($)*
GOTOFOUR	*Too many characters*
DO3J = 1	*Illegal symbol (=)*

■ Arithmetic

Just as in algebra, in FORTRAN we must learn how to form expressions. To do this, in Table 2-7 we introduce the arithmetic operations performed in FORTRAN and the symbols used for each.

TABLE 2-7

Operation	FORTRAN Operator Symbol
Addition	+
Subtraction	-
Multiplication	*
Division	/
Exponentiation	**

FORTRAN constants or variables are combined in an operation to form an expression. Normally, the modes of all variables and constants in an expression will be the same, that is, they will all be fixed- or floating-point. If two or more different types of data appear in the same expression, the expression is said to be *mixed-mode*. Special rules apply to such expressions, and they may not be allowed in some versions of FORTRAN. Also, care must be taken to avoid having two arithmetic operators placed next to each other. Some FORTRAN expressions are listed in Table 2-8 together with their possible algebraic equivalents.

TABLE 2-8

FORTRAN	Algebra
X*Y	xy
A + (B - C)	$a + (b - c)$
DELP1 - DELP2	$\Delta P_1 - \Delta P_2$
3.14159*R**2	πr^2
.5*B*H	$\frac{1}{2} bh$

■ Order of Operations in FORTRAN

In complicated expressions it is important to know which of the operations should be performed first. The order in which the operations in an expression are evaluated is given by the following set of rules:

Rule 1: First, any part of the expression enclosed in parentheses is evaluated completely before proceeding to evaluate any part of the expression outside the parentheses. This rule applies to each set of parentheses. Thus, in the expression

$$6.*((A + B) + C) - D**2/E*F$$

A + B is evaluated first; and C is then added to this sum.

Rule 2: Next, each exponentiation is performed. This means that for the above expression, the term D**2 is evaluated.

Rule 3: Next, multiplication and/or division is performed from *left* to *right*. This means that the expression D**2/E*F has the algebraic equivalent of

$$\frac{d^2}{e} f$$

Rule 4: Finally, addition and/or subtraction is performed from *left* to *right*.

Example 1

Let us consider the FORTRAN expression

E/A**2 + B**3/(C + 6.*D**2)

First, the computer will evaluate the expression in parentheses, (C + 6.*D**2); it starts with the exponentiation, the value of D**2. The sequence of steps performed by the computer is shown below. (We have mixed together FORTRAN and algebra only to illustrate the above rules.)

Original expression   E/A**2 + B**3/(C + 6.*D**2)
After 1st operation   E/A**2 + B**3/(C + 6.*d^2)
After 2nd operation   E/A**2 + B**3/(C + 6d^2)
After 3rd operation   E/A**2 + B**3/(c + 6d^2)
After 4th operation   E/a^2 + B**3/(c + 6d^2)
After 5th operation   E/a^2 + b^3/(c + 6d^2)

After 6th operation $\frac{e}{a^2}$ + b^3/(c + 6d^2)

After 7th operation $\frac{e}{a^2}$ + $\frac{b^3}{c + 6d^2}$

Finally, the addition is performed.

It should be clear from the rules that

$$A/B*C \quad \text{means} \quad \frac{a}{b}c \quad \text{not} \quad \frac{a}{bc}$$

If *a/bc* is meant, be careful to insert parentheses, that is A/(B*C). Table 2-9 gives examples of the FORTRAN equivalents of some algebraic expressions. Notice how every constant is written with a

decimal point to keep the modes the same (except in the case of
exponentiation). These are all floating-point expressions.

TABLE 2-9

Algebra	FORTRAN Equivalent
$x^2 - y^2$	X**2 - Y**2
$\sqrt{b^2 - 4ac}$	(B**2 - 4.*A*C)**.5
$v_0 t - \frac{1}{2} g t^2$	VO*T - 0.5*G*T**2
$\dfrac{c q_1 q_2}{r^2}$	C*Q1*Q2/R**2
$\dfrac{\Delta g}{p^2 A + \dfrac{\Delta g}{AX}}$	DELG/(P**2*A + DELG/(A*X))

Every FORTRAN variable or constant has been written in the floating-
point mode in order to observe the rule of not mixing modes. In the
case of exponentiation, the modes may be mixed if a floating-point
variable (constant) is raised to a fixed-point power. In fact, this
is a more desirable programming practice, as it saves computer execution time. Some examples of this are listed in Table 2-10.

TABLE 2-10

Algebra	FORTRAN Equivalent
x^3	X**3
$\sqrt{x^2 + y^2}$	(X**2 + Y**2)**0.5
$\dfrac{a^4 b^3}{a^2 + b^2}$	A**4*B**3/(A**2 + B**2)
z^R	Z**R
$\sqrt[3]{w}$	W**(1./3.)

Table 2-11 lists several FORTRAN expressions that have at
least one error each.

TABLE 2-11

Expression	Error
A + I	*Mixed-modes*
C + -D	*Two operations next to each other*
A + (B - D/E*F*A((B))	*Parentheses do not match*
FORCE*MASS	*Mixed modes*
DELX/P(E + D)	*Operation missing*
Rl**Z/16 - A	*Mixed modes (decimal needed after 16)*

■ Fixed-Point Arithmetic

Most computer programs that involve arithmetic calculations are naturally done in the floating-point mode. This is so because the size of the numbers allowed is larger than in fixed-point arithmetic, and also because decimals are used. There are occasions, however, when a programmer will find it convenient to use the properties associated with fixed-point arithmetic.

The same operations are allowed in fixed-point expressions (+, -, *, /, **) as in floating-point expressions. The difference in this arithmetic lies in the fact that no decimals are permitted. As a computer evaluates a fixed-point expression, it will truncate all characters which would normally follow after the decimal. This means that the expression

4/3

would be evaluated as 1, the remaining .33333 having been truncated. Similarly,

50*(49/50)

is 0 and not 49.

■ The Equals Sign in FORTRAN

Remember that every time we compute an arithmetic expression, we have to store the result. This storing operation is denoted by an equals sign in FORTRAN. For instance, the FORTRAN statement

AREA = 3.1416*(DIAM/2.0)**2

tells the machine to evaluate the expression on the right of the equals sign and to store the result at the location named AREA.

Two rules govern the use of the equals sign in FORTRAN.

Rule 1: The quantity on the left of the equals sign must be a variable, not a constant or an expression.

Rule 2: If the expression and the variable are of different modes, the value of the expression on the right will be converted to the mode of the variable on the left before storing.

The first rule means that it is not allowable to have a statement like

A + 1.0 = B

It is always the expression on the *right* that is evaluated. The variable on the left simply tells where the result is to be stored. Thus, it is alright to have the statement

B = A + 1.0

For that matter, it is alright to have the statement

A = A + 1.0

as we have seen earlier.

The second rule may be illustrated by the following examples. In the statement

N = 7.0

the expression on the right is a floating-point constant (with a decimal point). The variable on the left is a fixed-point variable and as such must not have a decimal point. Rule 2 means simply that the floating-point constant 7.0 will be converted to the fixed-point number 7 before it is stored in N. If we had the statement

N = 7.9

the same process would occur. This time, since a fixed-point constant cannot have a decimal point, the .9 would be truncated, and N would again have the value 7.

If the expression on the right is a floating-point arithmetic expression and the variable on the left is a fixed-point variable, we would have the same situation. For example, suppose the variable ABC has the value 4.0. Then the statement

I2 = (ABC + 1.9)/2.0

would result in the following:

First, 1.9 is added to 4.0, to give 5.9.

This is divided by 2.0, to give 2.95.

Finally, this result is converted to a fixed-point number—so the decimal part is truncated, and we have I2 = 2. Note that no rounding occurs.

Similarly, if the expression on the right is a fixed-point expression and the variable on the left is a floating-point variable, a conversion from fixed-point to floating-point will occur before storing the result. For instance, if J has the value 5, then the statement

        X = (J - 1)**2

will cause the expression on the right to be evaluated (in this case the answer would be 16), and then a decimal point would be inserted so that X becomes 16.0.

This form, with an arithmetic expression on the right of the equals sign and a variable on the left, is called an *arithmetic assignment statement*. We say that the value of the expression is *assigned* to the variable when it is stored in the cell named by the variable.

Let us consider some examples involving the computation of some familiar formulas.

Example 2

Given the variables A, B, and C, write statements to compute the solutions X1 and X2 to the equation $AX^2 + BX + C = 0$.

There are two solutions to this equation, given by

$$\frac{-B \pm \sqrt{B^2 - 4AC}}{2A}$$

Now, if $(B^2 - 4AC) \leq 0$, we run into trouble, since then there will not be two real solutions. So, for this example, we shall assume that $(B^2 - 4AC) > 0$.

One way to write the program is by using the statements

        X1 = (-B + (B**2 - 4.0*A*C)**.5)/(2.0*A)
        X2 = (-B - (B**2 - 4.0*A*C)**.5)/(2.0*A)

Note that in this method, however, we are duplicating much of the work. For instance, $\sqrt{B^2 - 4AC}$ is computed twice, although, of course, the result will be the same both times. We want a more economical way to accomplish the same thing. Consider the statements

        TWOA = 2.*A
           D = (B**2 - 4.0*A*C)**.5
          X1 = (-B + D)/TWOA
          X2 = (-B - D)/TWOA

Here we have broken up the computation into parts. We have more statements, but less work is actually done since $\sqrt{B^2 - 4AC}$ is evaluated only once. This means the computer could compute X1 and X2 faster by the second method than by the first. While in this case the difference would be negligible, if we were to perform the computation for thousands of different values of *A*, *B*, and *C*, the difference might be considerable.

Example 3

Given the variables *A*, *B*, *C*, *D*, *E*, and *F*, find *X* and *Y* which satisfy

$$AX + BY = C$$
$$DX + EY = F$$

The solutions are given by

$$X = \frac{CE - BF}{AE - BD} \qquad Y = \frac{AF - CD}{AE - BD}$$

The real first step in solving this problem is to see if (*AE* - *BD*) = 0; if it is, we do not want to divide by it. This can be handled by a decision statement, which we shall learn how to program in Chapter 3. For now, we will ignore this possibility and write

$$X = (C*E - B*F)/(A*E - B*D)$$
$$Y = (A*F - C*D)/(A*E - B*D)$$

As before, we see that we would make the computation more efficient if we did not have to compute *AE* - *BD* twice, so let us introduce the variable DENOM and rewrite the computation as

$$DENOM = A*E - B*D$$
$$X = (C*E - B*F)/DENOM$$
$$Y = (A*F - C*D)/DENOM$$

Example 4

Consider the polynomial

$$Y = AX^4 + BX^3 + CX^2 + DX + E$$

One way to evaluate this would be to use the single statement

$$Y = A*X**4 + B*X**3 + C*X**2 + D*X + E$$

Following the rules on pages 31-32, let us see what actually happens when this expression is evaluated by the machine. First, the exponentiations are performed: *X* is multiplied by itself three times to give X**4, then multiplied by itself twice to give X**3, and so on; *X* is multiplied by itself six times in all. Then the terms are multiplied by the coefficients, requiring four more multiplications, and finally the terms are added to give Y. A total of ten multiplications and four additions is required for this computation.

Now, suppose we compute Y by the following method: We use the formula

$$Y = (((A*X + B)*X + C)*X + D)*X + E$$

The nested parentheses may make this formula seem unnecessarily complicated, but notice two things: First, we are really computing the same formula as before. That is, the above formula is equivalent to the polynomial, but the terms are grouped differently. This time, however, only four multiplications, instead of ten, are required. Thus, the above computation is more efficient than the first method. Furthermore, we can avoid the parentheses if we divide the formula into several statements:

```
Y = A*X + B
Y = Y*X + C
Y = Y*X + D
Y = Y*X + E
```

The first of these statements sets *Y* equal to the expression in the innermost pair of parentheses of the former statement. The second statement multiplies the *Y* calculated in the first statement by *X*, adds *C*, and stores the new result back in *Y*. After the fourth statement is performed, *Y* will have the desired value of the original polynomial.

■ Mixed-Mode Arithmetic

We said before that it is incorrect to use fixed-point and floating-point expressions in the same statement. While this is quite true on some compilers, other versions of FORTRAN will allow mixed modes to appear in the same expression. Consult the reference manual for your system to find out if mixed-mode arithmetic is allowed.

In its most general use, mixed-mode arithmetic provides a whole hierarchy of rules for mixing various types of numbers in the same expression. We shall see in later chapters how this applies to arithmetic using complex or double-precision numbers. For our purposes now, the function of mixed-mode arithmetic can be summarized by the following rule:

Rule: If an arithmetic operation involves both a fixed-point and a floating-point number, the result will be a floating-point number.

This means, for example, that it would be allowable to have the statement

```
Y = X + 2
```

which is a mixed-mode expression with X a floating-point variable and 2 a fixed-point constant, and the result of the addition will be a floating-point number, just as though the statement were

        Y = X + 2.0

As another example, suppose we want to add the variables X and K together to give W. One way to do this would be

        Y = K
        W = X + Y

Here we have used the statement Y = K to convert K from fixed-point to the floating-point variable Y. Using mixed-mode arithmetic, we could do this in one statement by writing simply

        W = X + K

As another example, the rule for mixed-mode arithmetic means that the statement[4]

        SQ2 = 2**0.5

would set SQ2 equal to the square root of 2 (that is, 1.414214 approximately) just as though the whole statement were written in floating-point form as

        SQ2 = 2.0**0.5

Note that although the above two expressions give the same result, they are not identical in terms of what the computer does. In the first case, one more operation must be performed: conversion of the fixed-point constant 2 to its floating-point equivalent 2.0. Thus, it is slightly more efficient to avoid mixed-mode expressions where possible. For this reason, and since not all FORTRAN compilers allow it, *we shall avoid mixed-mode arithmetic for the remainder of this book.*

■ FORTRAN-Supplied Functions

Many problems that are solved by using FORTRAN require the evaluation of certain common functions. These include the taking of a logarithm of a number, finding the sine or cosine of an angle, and using the absolute value of a number, to name only a few. The student usually finds values of these functions by means of tables that, in nearly every case, were originally constructed by using a lengthy long-hand process. One of the features of FORTRAN is that a great many of the commonly used functions are built-in, that is, they are an integral part of the programming system. For example,

---

[4]See page 33. This may not work on all systems.

to do a calculation involving the sine of an angle, a statement
might be

        Y = SIN(ANGLE)

   The effect of this statement is to take the sine of the variable ANGLE and then set the variable Y equal to this. The variable ANGLE must be given in radians; if it is originally given in degrees, it must be converted. In general, a FORTRAN-supplied function has the form

        NAME(argument)

   The exact form of the NAME part has to be looked up in a table, although in practice the names for the functions most commonly used are readily memorized. The argument will be either fixed- or floating-point, depending on the function. It may be an expression, and as such may even contain another built-in function. Table 2-12 lists a few of the more common built-in functions.

TABLE 2-12. FORTRAN-supplied functions.

Function	Definition	Type of Argument
ABS(X)	*Absolute value of X*	*Floating-point*
IABS(N)	*Absolute value of N*	*Fixed-point*
FLOAT(N)	*Convert to floating-point*	*Fixed-point*
INT(X)	*Convert to fixed-point by truncating*	*Floating-point*
IFIX(X)	*Same as INT(X)*	*Floating-point*
EXP(X)	*Exponential function, e^x*	*Floating-point*
SIN(X)	*Trigonometric sine, sin x, x is in radians*	*Floating-point*
COS(X)	*Trigonometric cosine, cos x, x is in radians*	*Floating-point*
SQRT(X)	*Square root, $x^{1/2}$*	*Floating-point*

   Several examples of using built-in functions are given below.

Example 5

        ANGLE = 45.0
        PI = 3.14159
        Y = SIN(PI*ANGLE/180.)

Example 6

        N = 4
        X = FLOAT(N)
        Y = SQRT(ABS(X - 29.0))

Example 7

```
Y = 100.0
X = SQRT(Y)*SIN(THETA)
```

In Example 5 the variable Y is set equal to the sine of 45°. The angle is first converted to radians by multiplying by $\pi/180$, and then the sine can be taken. Example 6 illustrates the use of a built-in function in an argument of another function. First N is defined as 4, then X is set equal to 4.0. Finally, after subtracting 29.0 from 4.0 and converting the result to +25.0, Y is set equal to 5.0. If the absolute value function had not been used, a FORTRAN error would have resulted. To avoid this, it is a common practice to include the absolute value function wherever one has to take the square root of an expression. Example 7 has two functions together in an arithmetic expression. Assuming the value of THETA has been previously defined, the effect of this statement is to set X equal to 10.0 times the sine of the angle THETA.

It is essential that the argument be the correct mode or an error will result. The examples below are all incorrect:

```
Y = SIN(1)
Z = 2. + SQRT(4)
W = Z + SQRT(-4.0)
```

The first two examples have arguments that are fixed-point numbers, which is not permissible. The third example has an argument that is the correct mode, but it is out of the permissible range. Notice that there are two functions for finding absolute values. The difference is the type of argument each takes. IABS takes a fixed-point argument and returns a fixed-point number (or variable). Thus, N = IABS(-3) would set N equal to the integer value of 3 (no decimal point). It is incorrect to write N = IABS(-3.0). To find the absolute value of the floating-point number -3.0, we would have to use the function ABS.

The function FLOAT converts an expression to floating-point form. If we wanted to add two variables, N and X, in floating-point form, we could use the statements

```
A = N
Y = A + X
```

or we could do this directly, using the function FLOAT, by writing

```
Y = X + FLOAT(N)
```

The counterpart of FLOAT is the function INT, which converts a floating-point expression to integer form by truncating the decimal part. For instance, the statement

```
N = INT(4.999)
```

would set N equal to the integer value 4 (no decimal).

There are a great many more functions, and in Chapter 8 this topic is covered in detail. The Appendix provides a table for quick reference to most of the built-in functions found in large computer systems.

■ Punched Cards

The FORTRAN statements we have just learned make up a portion of a complete program. Later, we shall learn other statements, and finally we shall learn what constitutes a complete program.

Now, we must consider a means for transmitting our FORTRAN program to a computer. Several are available, but we shall discuss only the most common one—punched cards. The standard punched card has 80 columns, numbered 1-80, into each of which a character can be punched. The color and printing on the cards are for identification purposes only; all that the computer senses are the holes punched in the card. (The card is punched by means of a keypunch machine.)

All the characters allowed in forming statements can be punched into the cards; these are:

         Alphabetic: A, B, C, D, ..., X, Y, Z

           Numeric: 0, 1, 2, ..., 8, 9

           Special: + Plus sign
                     - Minus sign
                     * Asterisk
                     / Slash
                     . Period
                     , Comma
                     (Left parenthesis
) Right parenthesis
                     = Equals sign
                     b Blank space
                     $ Dollar sign
                     ' Apostrophe

A FORTRAN statement must be punched only in columns 7-72. It need not start in column 7 but generally does. The first 6 columns are used, but not for the actual FORTRAN statement. Column 6 is used to allow a FORTRAN statement to be longer than 66 columns (see the explanation on page 44). The first 5 columns are used to make reference to the statement (this is explained in Chapter 3). The last 8 columns are not used for the FORTRAN statement; they may be used for whatever the programmer wishes—for example, to number the cards so that they may be kept in order.

Figure 2-1 illustrates these characters as they appear on a typical card. The punched code for numbers and letters is the same for all computer systems. However, the code for some of the other characters may vary.

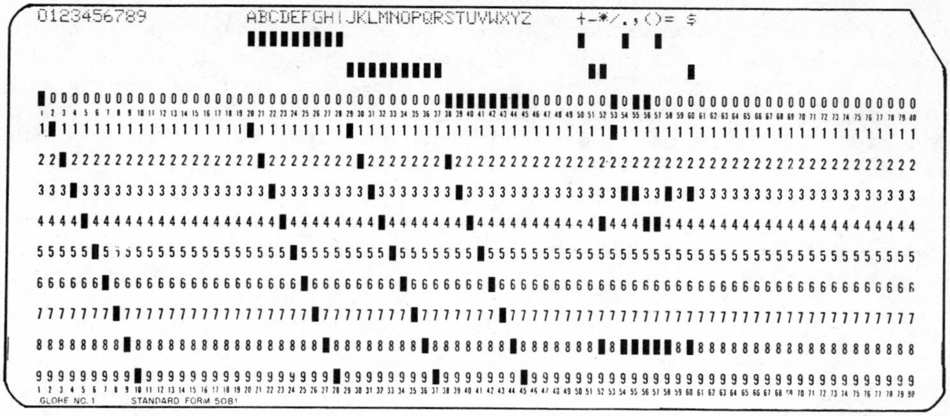

FIGURE 2-1
FORTRAN character code for punched cards

Figure 2-2 illustrates how the arithmetic statement

TAX = .2*AMT - 650.*DEP + COST/FACTOR

looks after it has been punched on a card. In this case, the statement begins in column 7, but it could have started in any column
after 7 up to and including column 42 and still be interpreted in
the same manner.

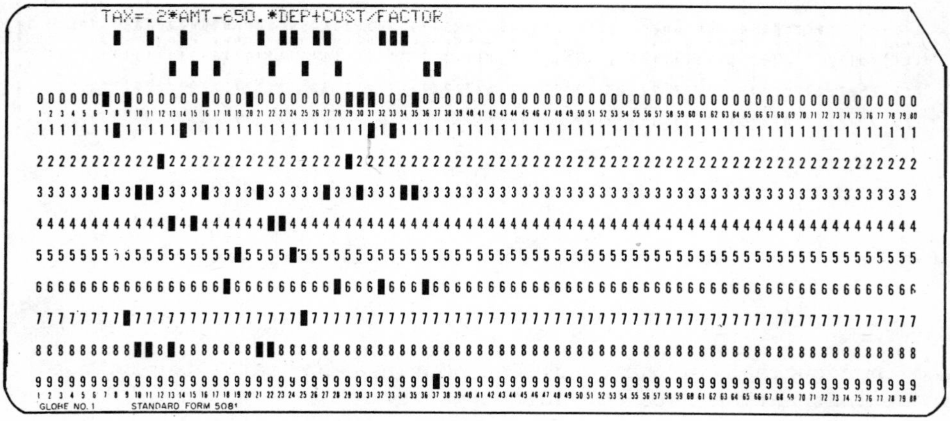

FIGURE 2-2

■ Continuation Cards

A FORTRAN statement can occupy more columns than the 66 allotted per card by using cards with numbers other than 0 punched in
column 6. The cards are called *continuation cards* and serve only
to continue the FORTRAN statement from one card to another. Any of
the digits 1-9 may be used to continue the statement. (Some computer
systems allow other FORTRAN symbols as well.) The number of allowable continuation cards for each statement varies with computers
from 9 to 19. In practice, only a few such cards are ever needed;
exceptionally long statements can be broken into two or more smaller
statements.

Example 8

When we write the FORTRAN statement

        Y = A + B + C/D +
        1E - F

it means that two cards are to be punched; the second card has a 1
in column 6. Thus, the two punched cards would look like those
shown in Fig. 2-3:

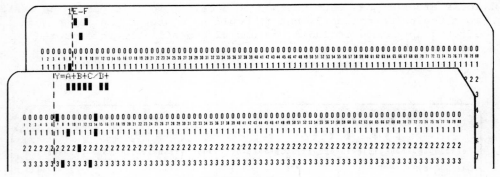

FIGURE 2-3
Example of a statement using one continuation card

Of course, the statement could just as well have been written

        Y = A + B + C/D + E - F

and then punched on one card, but continuation cards can be used to
break information into convenient parts.

Example 9

The following FORTRAN statement means that one statement will
occupy 5 punched cards. The first card has nothing punched in
column 6, the second, third, and fourth have a 2 in column 6, and

the fifth has a 1 in column 6:

```
        TEST = GRADE*SCORE
    2 - 4.0*OLD
    2 + CASE
    2 + TEACH
    1 - CLASS
```

The computer will interpret the statement the same as if it had been punched on one card as

```
    TEST = GRADE*SCORE - 4.0*OLD + CASE + TEACH - CLASS
```

Notice that the numbers in column 6 need not be in sequence and, in fact, can be repeated.

■ A Exercises

Write each number in E-form.

1. 6.2
2. 0.0017
3. 43.6×10^{-6}
4. 1 million
5. 10^{-10}

6. 12,345
7. 0.002×10^{5}
8. 0.002×10^{-5}
9. 300,000,000
10. 1/1,000

Write each number in decimal form with no exponent.

11. .1E - 1
12. .1E10
13. 100.0E - 2
14. 314.16E - 2
15. 0.0101E5

16. 14.14E - 1
17. 10.0E - 4
18. 111.1E - 4
19. 10000E2
20. .077E - 3

State whether or not each is a valid FORTRAN variable name. If it is, is it a fixed- or floating-point variable? If it is not, what is wrong with it?

21. I12
22. FICA
23. 7AB
24. YES
25. TWENTYFIVE
26. Q
27. ANS
28. K2K3
29. KK.KK
30. XXXXX

31. ABC - 1
32. 2UM
33. UM2
34. TANGO
35. NUMB
36. LETTER
37. P
38. MIKE
39. D/D
40. PLUS

For each FORTRAN expression, write the algebraic expression it represents.

41. A**B/C

42. A/B/C

43. A*B/C
44. A/B*C
45. A + B/C
46. ((A + B)/C) + D

47. A**B*C
48. A*B**C
49. (2.0**(2.0*X))/X**2
50. 4.0*3.1416*R**2*3.0**(-1)

For each algebraic formula, write a single FORTRAN statement to evaluate it, renaming variables where necessary to comply with the rules for naming floating-point variables in FORTRAN.

51. $A = R^2$

52. $W = (X_2 - X_1)Y^2$

53. $R = \dfrac{1}{1/R_1 + 1/R_2 + 1/R_3}$

54. $A = \dfrac{1}{3}Bh,$ where $B = \dfrac{d}{4}$

55. $v = \sqrt{x^2 + y^2}$

56. Area $= \sqrt{S(S-A)(S-B)(S-C)}$

57. Inner product =
$$x_1 y_1 + x_2 y_2 + x_3 y_3$$

58. Middle = minimum + $\dfrac{1}{2}$delta

59. $g = \dfrac{d}{b + \dfrac{c}{d + e/f}}$

60. $p = A(1 + r)^{-n}$

Check each FORTRAN statement to see whether or not it is correct. If it is not, why is it wrong (keep in mind the rules for naming variables and the rules for mixing fixed- and floating-point numbers in an expression)?

61. A = A
62. .A = I
63. 2 = M
64. Z = 123
65. K = ⁻1.06E2
66. 2ZX = A + 10.0**.04
67. Z1234 = A**R + FIN - Z1234
68. A = B/C**D*E
69. SMALLEST = LEAST*2*K
70. BHAT = (B1 - B2)/2

71. X1 = (Y + Z12 + C.X - W1 + 4.0)**I
72. Y = (X**2 + 2*X + 2)
73. J = H/I
74. Y = Z*-X
75. Y = -X*Z
76. Y = A*B/-C
77. X = X + 1
78. X + 1 = X
79. ABS = (X*X)**.5
80. REMAINDER = N - (N/M)*M

If $A = 3.0$, $B = 6.0$, and $C = 2.0$, find the value of D computed by each statement according to the rules for floating-point arithmetic.

81. D = (A - B) + C
82. D = A - (B + C)
83. D = -A**2 + C
84. D = A/B/C
85. D = A/B/(B/A)

86. D = (A*B)/B/A
87. D = A*B + C
88. D = A + B/B + A
89. D = A*A/A*A
90. D = A/A*A/A

If $I = 1$, $J = 2$, and $K = 3$, find the value of N computed by each statement according to the rules for fixed-point arithmetic.

91. N = I/J
92. N = J/I
93. N = J**K
94. N = I*K/2
95. N = K/J/J

96. N = K/(J/J)
97. N = K**I/J
98. N = I**J**K
99. N = J**I*K
100. N = J/J - 1

Rewrite each series of statements as a single statement. For
example,

```
M = N + 1
J = J + M
```

could be written as a single statement

```
J = J + N + 1
```

101. N = N + 1
     N = N + 1

102. M = N + 1
     M = M - 1
     N = N + M

103. Z = W1 - W2
     Y = W3 - W4
     X = 4.0*Y - Z

104. E = Y**2 + 1.0
     X = E*X
     X = E*X

105. K4B = K4B + 1
     K4B = K4B + 2
     K4B = K4B + 3

Try to simplify each statement by rewriting it as several statements which together accomplish the same thing. There will be more
than one correct way to do this, but try to make each statement as
simple as possible. For example,

```
Y = X + X**2 + X**3
```

could be written as three statements:

```
Y = X
Y = X + Y*X
Y = X + Y*X
```

106. E = (X1 - X2)**3 - (X1 - X2)**2
107. X = (C1*D - B*C2)/(C1*C4 - C2*C3)
108. E = ((A + B + C)/(B + C))*A*B
109. C = (A + B + C)/(1.0/A + 1.0/B + 1.0/C)
110. E = A*(A + B)*(A + B + C)

Determine the value of the variable *X* after each series of statements is executed.

111. X = 3.0
     X = X + 1.0
     X = SQRT(X)

112. X = 90.0
     X = X*3.14159/180.
     X = SIN(X)

113. I = 200
     X = FLOAT(2*I)
     X = SQRT(X)

114. Y = -1.0
     X = ABS(Y)
     X = 1. - X
     X = EXP(X)

■ B Exercises

Write the algebraic expression that corresponds to each FORTRAN statement.

1. C = X/(X**2 + Y**2 + Z**2)**.5
2. Y = X**3 + 4.0*X - X*X
3. A = (B + C/(D + (E/F)))
4. Y = 2.0*((A1 + A2)/3.0 + A)/X**N
5. AREA = 4.7*((X2 - X1)/2.0)**2 - 6.0*((X2 - X1)/2.0)

Write FORTRAN statements to evaluate each formula, giving suitable names to the variables to comply with FORTRAN rules. You may find it helpful to break up the computation into steps, as in Exercises 106-110.

6. $F = \left\{ \dfrac{(p_1 - p_2)^{1/3}}{1 + [R(q_1 - q_2)]} \right\} + \left\{ 10^5 + \dfrac{a}{b + c/d} \right\}$

7. $x = \dfrac{-b + \sqrt{b^2 - 4ac}}{2a}$

8. $w = \dfrac{e\left[\dfrac{(az + b)}{(cz + d)}\right] + f}{g\left[\dfrac{(az + b)}{(cz + d)}\right] + h}$

9. $G = \dfrac{(4/3)[(x - y)/(z - w)]^e [(a - b)/(c - d)]^f}{\sqrt[3]{p^2(r - s)}}$

10. $r = \dfrac{p_1 - \dfrac{p_2}{T} - 1 + \dfrac{2\pi y}{x}}{\left[v^2 a + \dfrac{x}{(A - B)}\right]^{3/2}}$

11. $z = \dfrac{\sin\left(\dfrac{2\pi x}{L}\right) \cos\left(\dfrac{2\pi x}{M}\right)}{\sin\left(\dfrac{2\pi x}{M}\right) \cos\left(\dfrac{2\pi x}{L}\right)}$

12. $S = (e^{-x/2} + e^{x/2}) \div 2$

Chapter

Control Statements

A program consists of a sequence of instructions and a set of rules specifying the order in which the instructions are to be performed. So far, we have seen how the FORTRAN statements (instructions) are formed. Now, we shall learn how to specify the order in which they are performed.

Unless otherwise specified, FORTRAN statements are performed in the order in which they are written. The statements

```
Y = 5.0*X + 2.0
Z = X*Y + 3.0
W = X*Z + 9.0
```

do the same thing that is indicated in the flowchart boxes shown in Fig. 3-1.

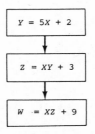

FIGURE 3-1

An obvious question arises: How do we change this one-after-another order? For instance, how can we go back to the beginning of a group of instructions and perform them again, and how can we represent a Decision box with a FORTRAN statement? These tasks are performed by control statements, so-called because they pass control of the program to something besides the next statement.

The three basic control statements we shall consider in this chapter are the STOP, GO TO, and IF statements.

■ The STOP Statement

The purpose of this statement is simply to terminate the operation of the program. In other words, the STOP statement is the FORTRAN equivalent of the Stop terminal in a flowchart. We mentioned in Chapter 1 that every flowchart must have one Start terminal and at least one Stop terminal. There is no such thing as a START statement in FORTRAN, because operation always begins with the first statement in the program. However, every complete FORTRAN program will normally have at least one STOP statement.

The following illustrates the use of the STOP statement:

```
X = X + 1.0
Y = 5.0*X
STOP
```

We can use more than one STOP statement in a program if necessary, and we shall see an example of such a situation when we discuss the IF statement.

■ The END Statement

The STOP statement terminates the running of the program. It can appear at any place in a program where the·programmer wishes to stop the operations. There is another statement, called the END statement, that *must* be used at the end of every FORTRAN program. This instructs the compiler that it has reached the end of the program. The form is simply

```
END
```

Later, when we write complete programs, we shall see more of this statement.

■ Statement Numbers[1]

Both the GO TO and IF statements make use of statement numbers, so we shall first look briefly at what a statement number is, and then we shall see how it is used in the discussion of the GO TO statement.

A statement number is just a number we put before a statement so we can refer to that statement in another part of the program. It is a label that is used to determine which statement we are talking about. We can give a number to any statement in a program simply by putting any number from 1 through 99999 in front of the

---

[1]The ANSI term for these is *statement labels*. Most programmers are more familiar with the notation *statement numbers* and so we have used this form.

statement. For instance, we could have the following four statements:

```
999   Y = X + 1.0
      Z = X
  3   W = 4.5*Z - 11.6
  7   X = W - Z
```

If we then referred to Statement 7, we would mean the statement

```
      X = W - Z
```

This does *not* mean the seventh statement in the program; it means the statement whose number is 7. Similarly, if we refer to Statement 999, we mean the statement whose number is 999, that is, the statement

```
      Y = X + 1.0
```

We can use any numbers, in any order, for any statements we choose. The only restriction is that *any given number may be used only once*. We cannot have two different statements with the same number.

Location of Statement Numbers on Punched Cards. We mentioned earlier that the first 5 columns of a punched card cannot be used for a FORTRAN statement and that column 6 is used to indicate continuation cards. The remaining columns 1-5 are reserved for the statement number. The number can be punched anywhere in these columns (although most programmers prefer to place them so that their last digits are in column 5). Thus, the three statements punched on cards as shown below are equivalent:

```
                    |  |  column 6
                    |  |/
(card 1)      100|  |X = 10.0
(card 2)      100 |  |X = 10.0
(card 3)      100 |  |        X = 10.0
```

■ The GO TO Statement

The general form of this statement is

```
      GO TO n
```

where *n* is a statement number. This statement causes the program to jump to the statement whose number is *n*. For example, if we had

```
 10   X = X + 1.0
      Y = 5.0*X
      Y = X*Y + 1.0
      GO TO 10
```

then, after performing the statement Y = X*Y + 1.0, the program
would go back and perform the statement X = X + 1.0. This program could also be represented by the flowchart shown in Fig. 3-2.

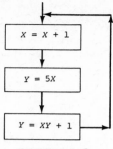

FIGURE 3-2

GO TO statements correspond to the lines of flow in the flowchart.
In this example, the statement GO TO 10 corresponds to the line of
flow returning to the first box.

Of course, we would never use exactly this procedure in a
real program because there is no way for it to stop. Usually, we
would have a Decision box which would cause the program to stop
after X got to a certain number.

■ The Arithmetic IF Statement

The arithmetic IF statement in FORTRAN corresponds to the
Decision box in a flowchart. The general form of this statement is

> IF(E) a, b, c

where E is any FORTRAN expression and a, b, and c are statement
numbers. This statement works in this way: If $E < 0$, the next
statement performed will be the statement whose number is a.
Similarly, if $E = 0$, the next statement performed will be the
statement whose number is b, or if $E > 0$, the next statement performed will be the statement whose number is c. So, depending on
whether the expression in parentheses is negative, 0, or positive,
the IF statement acts like the statement GO TO a, GO TO b, or GO
TO c:

$$\text{IF}(E)\ a,\ b,\ c \begin{cases} \text{If } E < 0,\ \text{then GO TO } a. \\ \text{If } E = 0,\ \text{then GO TO } b. \\ \text{If } E > 0,\ \text{then GO TO } c. \end{cases}$$

Example 1

If we were given the statements

```
       X = -10.0
10     X = X + 1.0
       Y = 10.0*X
       IF(X) 10, 20, 30
20     Y = 5.0
30     STOP
```

we would follow the procedure shown in the flowchart in Fig. 3-3.

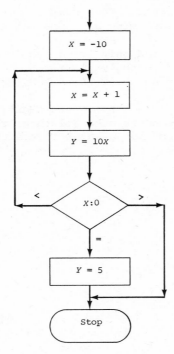

FIGURE 3-3
Flowchart for Example 1

In this example, the IF statement is executed 10 times. The first 9 times control is transferred back to Statement 10, but the last time, $X = 0$ and so control transfers to Statement 20. In this case, the IF statement never branches to Statement 30. Instead, Statement 30 is executed in normal sequence.

Example 2

Now suppose we want to compare two numbers, A and B, and we want to go to Statement 5 if $A < B$, to Statement 1 if $A = B$, or to Statement 900 if $A > B$. The flowchart box would be the following:

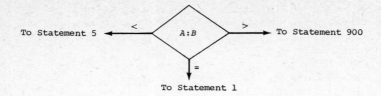

The corresponding IF statement would be

        IF(A - B) 5, 1, 900

In this statement, notice that we compare the expression $A - B$ to 0. This accomplishes the same thing as comparing A to B, for

        $A - B < 0$ if and only if $A < B$
        $A - B = 0$ if and only if $A = B$
        $A - B > 0$ if and only if $A > B$

We can also make any two of the statement numbers a, b, and c the same. (Actually, we could make all three the same, but, of course, that would be the same as a GO TO statement.) For example, the Decision box

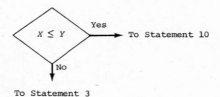

would be programmed as

        IF(X - Y) 10, 10, 3

Similarly, the Decision box

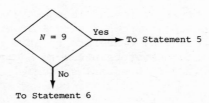

would be programmed as

        IF(N - 9) 6, 5, 6

Although the expression inside the parentheses of the IF statement is often a single variable or a difference of two variables, it can be any FORTRAN expression. If we want to go to either Statement 10 or 20, depending on whether or not $(5xy + 14)z = 0$, we can write

        IF((5.0*X*Y + 14.0)*Z) 20, 10, 20

To get a better idea of how control statements are used in a program, let us consider some simple examples.

Example 3

Write the statements that will set the value of Y equal to the value of X if Y > X and then stop; otherwise, Y will be set equal to 0 and then stop.

For this we need only one Decision box. If Y > X, we set Y = X; if Y ≤ X, we set Y = 0.0. This can be written in FORTRAN as

            IF(Y - X) 5, 5, 10
        5   Y = 0.0
            STOP
        10 Y = X
            STOP

Notice that two STOP statements are used. If the first of these were omitted, Y would always be equal to X when STOP was reached. Why? Rather than use two STOP statements, we could use a GO TO statement:

            IF(Y - X) 5, 5, 10
        5   Y = 0.0
            GO TO 15
        10 Y = X
        15 STOP

In this case, it really does not make any difference which way we do it. The flowchart for either method is shown in Fig. 3-4.

Example 4

Find the sum of the integers from 1 to *N*. For the moment, we shall ignore input and output statements. At the beginning of the program, let us set *N* = 20, and when we are done we shall stop, rather than writing out the answer. The flowchart will be as shown in Fig. 3-5.

Since we are dealing with integers, we use the integer variables N, I, and ISUM. We initialize these, and proceed to add I to ISUM:

```
N = 20
ISUM = 0
I = 1
ISUM = ISUM + I
```

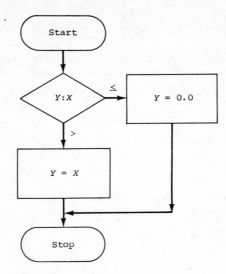

FIGURE 3-4
Flowchart for Example 3

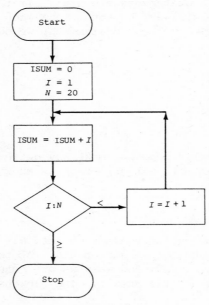

FIGURE 3-5
Flowchart for Example 4

Then, we use an IF statement to compare I to N. If I < N, we want
to add 1 to I, and the statement to do this will need a statement

number, say 10. If I ≥ N, we want to stop, and we shall give a statement number 20 to a STOP statement. So far, we have added the statements

```
        IF(I - N) 10, 20, 20
   10   I = I + 1
   20   STOP
```

This does not yet give us the total we want, however, for our program will always stop immediately after performing Statement 10. Actually, after performing this statement, we want to go back to the statement

```
        ISUM = ISUM + I
```

so we shall make this Statement 5, and after Statement 10 we shall use a GO TO statement to return. The completed program is

```
        N = 20
        ISUM = 0
        I = 1
    5   ISUM = ISUM + I
        IF(I - N) 10, 20, 20
   10   I = I + 1
        GO TO 5
   20   STOP
```

The set of statements below would be another way to accomplish the same thing:

```
        N = 20
        ISUM = 0
        I = 1
    5   ISUM = ISUM + I
        I = I + 1
        IF(I - N) 5, 5, 10
   10   STOP
```

Notice that the GO TO 5 statement has now been eliminated. This is a more desirable way to write the program, since it is more efficient.

Example 5

The problem is to determine whether an integer N is even or odd. This can be done using fixed-point arithmetic. Recall that if 2 does not divide N exactly, then the fixed-point division $N/2$ will be truncated. For example, $9/2 = 4$. Now consider $(9/2) \times 2$. This is $4 \times 2 = 8$. Since 2 divides 10, $(10/2) \times 2$ is $5 \times 2 = 10$. In general, if $(N/2) \times 2 = N$, then N must be even. If $(N/2) \times 2 \neq N$, then N must be odd.

Suppose we want to set $L = 0$ and go to Statement 100 if N is even, and we want to set $L = 1$ and go to Statement 200 if N is odd. This could be done using the procedure shown in the flowchart in Fig. 3-6.

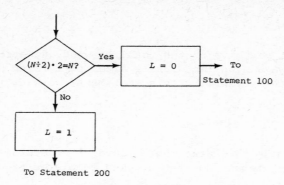

FIGURE 3-6
Flowchart for Example 5

This method can be programmed as follows:

```
      IF((N/2)*2 - N) 5, 10, 5
    5 L = 1
      GO TO 200
   10 L = 0
      GO TO 100
```

Each **IF** statement corresponds to a single decision. Frequently, however, we may want to perform some instruction only if both $A \leq B$ and $B \leq C$. This sort of situation may easily be treated by using a series of IF statements. Example 6 demonstrates this method.

Example 6

Given three numbers A, B, and C, we want to set D equal to 0, 1, or 2 according to the following rules:

If both $A \leq B$ and $B \leq C$, set $D = 0$.
If $A \leq B$ or $B \leq C$, but not both, set $D = 1$.
If neither $A \leq B$ nor $B \leq C$, set $D = 2$.

To solve this problem, we can first compare A to B. If $A \leq B$, then we compare B to C and then set D equal to 0 or 1, depending on whether $B \leq C$ or not. On the other hand, if $A > B$, we again compare B to C and then set D equal to 1 or 2, depending on whether $B \leq C$ or not. This process may be seen more clearly by referring to the flowchart in Fig. 3-7.

The FORTRAN program for this procedure uses three IF statements, that is, one for each Decision box in the flowchart. The final program reads

```
      IF (A - B) 10, 10, 20
10    IF (B - C) 30, 30, 40
20    IF (B - C) 40, 40, 50
30    D = 0.0
      GO TO 60
40    D = 1.0
      GO TO 60
50    D = 2.0
60    Next Statement
```

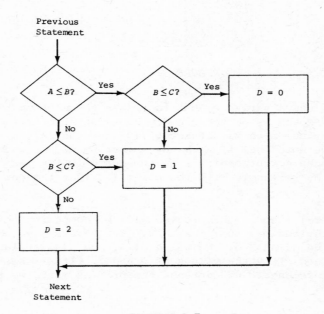

FIGURE 3-7
Flowchart for Example 6

Notice how the IF statements are interrelated. Notice also that two GO TO statements are used. Could we omit these two statements? Why not?

Example 7

A parcel of land is shown in Fig. 3-8. The boundaries are the x and y axes and a curve whose shape is described by the equation $Y = -4X^2 + 16$, where X and Y are in miles. You are asked to find the point P on the boundary for which the rectangle shown in the figure will have the maximum area.

You can solve this problem by writing a computer program in which you take values of X starting with $X = 0$ and going up to $X = 2$ in increments of 0.01.

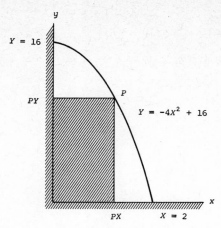

FIGURE 3-8

We shall use a variable AMAX to denote the maximum area, and we shall let *PX* and *PY* be the x and y coordinates of the point *P* where this maximum area is attained. To find the values of AMAX, *PX*, and *PY*, we note that if *X* is any number between 0 and 2, then the value of the corresponding *Y* on the curve is $Y = -4X^2 + 16$, and the area of the rectangle with the point (X,Y) at the corner is $A = XY$.

The central step in the program will be comparing this value *A* with the previous maximum area AMAX. If *A* > AMAX, we shall replace the value of AMAX by the value of *A*, and also replace the values of *PX* and *PY* by the values of *X* and *Y*. If *A* < AMAX, we shall just increment *X* and continue the process until we reach *X* = 2.

The complete process is shown in the flowchart in Fig. 3-9. This procedure can be programmed in FORTRAN using two IF statements, one for each Decision box in the flowchart. The program is

```
      AMAX = 0.0
      X = .01
10    Y = -4.0*X*X + 16.0
      A = X*Y
      IF(A - AMAX) 20, 20, 15
15    AMAX = A
      PX = X
      PY = Y
20    X = X + .01
      IF(X - 2.0) 10, 10, 30
30    Next Statement
```

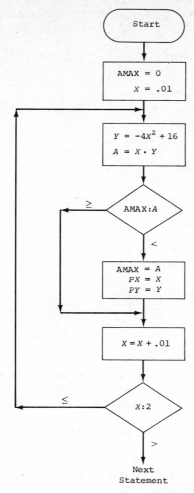

FIGURE 3-9
Flowchart for Example 7

■ Comment Cards

As our FORTRAN programs become longer, we shall need to check
back over the programs to determine what is being done and exactly
where it is happening. Comment cards help us find the parts of
the program we may want to single out. These cards have the letter C punched in column 1 together with whatever we want to write
on the cards. They are not processed by the FORTRAN translator,
but will be listed out when the whole program is printed. Thus,
we could write the previous program as follows:

```
COMMENT   THIS IS AN EXAMPLE OF A COMMENT CARD
C         PROGRAM TO FIND LARGEST RECTANGLE
C         THAT WILL FIT UNDER A GIVEN CURVE
C
C         AMAX WILL BE THE AREA OF THIS RECTANGLE
C         FIRST SET AMAX = 0.0
          AMAX = 0.0
C         START WITH X = .01
          X = .01
    10    Y = -4.0*X*X + 16.0
C         A IS USED AS AREA ALSO
          A = X*Y
          IF(A - AMAX) 20, 20, 15
    15    AMAX = A
          PX = X
          PY = Y
C         INCREMENT X
    20    X = X + .01
          IF(X - 2.0) 10, 10, 30
    30    Next Statement
C
C         WE ARE NOW THROUGH
C
```

A good programmer uses many comment cards. Some reasons for their use are the following:

1. Comment cards can be used to give an abstract of the program. This is especially helpful if another person will be using the program.

2. A listing of the variable names and what they represent is often made at the start of the program.

3. Special directions in the use of the program can be noted using comment cards.

■ Infinite Loops

When writing a program, be careful that the program eventually reaches a STOP statement. We could have a program containing the statements

```
    10   GO TO 20
    20   GO TO 10
```

In this case, no provision has been made to terminate the program. Such situations occur more often than one might expect, although the error is usually not so obvious.

In Example 8, we consider a numerical computation in which this problem could arise in a more subtle fashion.

Example 8

Several methods can be used to find the square root of a number in FORTRAN. In this example, we shall use the recursive method outlined below:

1. To begin, take any estimate X of the square root of Y, say $X = Y/2$.

2. Divide Y by X to obtain the quotient $Q = Y/X$.

3. For a new estimate of the square root of Y, take the average of X and Q.

It can be shown that this new estimate will be closer to the true square root than the original estimate. We continue the process to get better and better estimates until we have reached the desired degree of accuracy. The method is illustrated in Table 3-1, where $\sqrt{3}$ is calculated. (*Note*: The actual $\sqrt{3} = 1.73205080756 \ldots$.)

TABLE 3-1. Finding $\sqrt{3}$ ($Y = 3$).

Estimate X	Quotient Q = Y/X	New Estimate X = (X + Q)/2
1.5	2.0	1.75
1.75	1.7143	1.7321
1.7321	1.7319	1.7320

Now, consider the following FORTRAN program to set SQRTY equal to the square root of Y, using the above method:

```
        Y = 3.0
        X = Y/2.0
   10   Q = Y/X
        X = (X + Q)/2.0
        IF(X*X - Y) 10, 20, 10
   20   SQRTY = X
        Next Statement
```

The computation is straightforward. In the IF statement, we compare X^2 to Y. If they are equal, we go to Statement 20; otherwise, we repeat the process. At first glance, this seems reasonable enough. The trouble is that we are going to run into the problem mentioned earlier—the process will not necessarily terminate. The reason is this. Correct to five places, $\sqrt{3} = 1.73205$. But $(1.73025)^2 = 2.99999726250$, which, although very close, is not exactly 3. So, when we compare X^2 to Y, they will not be exactly equal, and the process will continue. Even if we have the best possible estimate of X correct to n places, the test may fail. Whether it actually does or does not depends on how many digits the particular machine can handle.

To avoid this problem, we shall test to see if X^2 is close enough to Y in absolute value. We shall test to see if $|X^2 - Y| <$ 0.0001. If this is true, then it can easily be shown that for $Y < 10,000$, X will be correct to eight places. Now, $|X^2 - Y| < 10^{-4}$ means that $X^2 - Y$ is very close to 0—in fact, it is between -10^{-4} and 10^{-4}.

We can use the ABS function to compute $|X^2 - Y|$. If this is less than 10^{-4}, we set SQRTY = X. Otherwise, we go back and find a better estimate. The final program is shown below, and the flowchart is given in Fig. 3-10.

```
      Y = 3.0
      X = Y/2.0
   10 Q = Y/X
      X = (X + Q)/2.0
      IF(ABS(X**2 - Y) - 1.0E - 4) 20, 10, 10
   20 SQRTY = X
      Next Statement
```

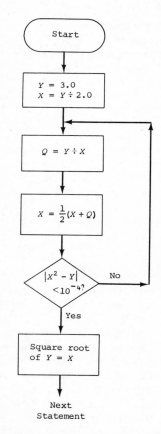

FIGURE 3-10
Flowchart for Example 8

■ The Logical IF Statement[2]

There is another type of IF statement that is much more powerful than the arithmetic IF—the logical IF statement. A complete treatment of this form of IF and related topics will be presented in Chapter 9, but several uses of it are so common that we shall consider them here. In Chapter 2 we learned how to construct arithmetic expressions using constants and variables together with the basic arithmetic operations that FORTRAN allows, and we learned to construct the arithmetic replacement statements. The procedure for constructing logical IF statements is analogous. First, we study the ways that constants and variables are related by means of expressions known as *relational expressions* and then how to incorporate these into the complete FORTRAN logical IF statement.

Relational Expressions. A relational expression is a type of logical expression used in FORTRAN to make comparisons between arithmetic quantities.

Such an expression consists of two arithmetic expressions connected by a relational operator. For example, one such relational operator is .EQ., which means "equal to."

A relational expression using this operator is A.EQ.9.0. This has a logical value: It is either true or false. These are actual FORTRAN expressions when written as .TRUE. and .FALSE. Even though we will not need to use them until Chapter 9, we shall write them this way. If A has a value of 9.0, then the expression is considered to have the value .TRUE.; otherwise, it has the value .FALSE..

Six relational operators may be used in FORTRAN. These are all listed in Table 3-2. The periods before and after each operator are considered to be part of the operator.

TABLE 3-2. Relational operators.

Operator	Meaning	Operator	Meaning
.EQ.	Equal to (=)	.LT.	Less than (<)
.NE.	Not equal to (≠)	.GE.	Greater than or equal to (≥)
.GT.	Greater than (>)	.LE.	Less than or equal to (≤)

The general form of a relational expression is

$A.R.B.$

---

[2]This is not available on some smaller computer systems.

where *.R.* is one of the six relational operators above, and *A* and *B* are arithmetic expressions which may be either fixed- or floating-point, but not mixed-mode. This expression is evaluated as follows:

1. The arithmetic expressions *A* and *B* are evaluated in the usual way.

2. The value of *A* is compared to the value of *B*.

3. If the values satisfy the relation, the relational expression takes on the value .TRUE.; otherwise, it takes on the value .FALSE..

For example, the expression

A.GT.ZED

will be .FALSE. if A has the value 4.0 and ZED has the same value or if ZED has any value less than 4.0. Some other examples of relational expressions are given in Table 3-3.

TABLE 3-3. *Some relational expressions and their values when A = 1.0, B = 2.0, and C = 3.0.*

Expression	Value	Expression	Value
A - 1.0.GE.0.0	.TRUE.	B.LT.C	.TRUE.
A - 1.0.LT.0.0	.FALSE.	1.5.LT.B	.TRUE.
3.0.LT.2.0*C	.TRUE.	B - 2.1.GT.C - 3.0	.FALSE.
(A - B)*C.EQ.B	.FALSE.	C.EQ.A + B	.TRUE.
A.NE.B	.TRUE.	5.2.NE.5.2	.FALSE.

The Logical IF Statement. The most important use of logical expressions is in connection with the logical IF statement. This statement has the same purpose as the arithmetic IF statement, but it has a different form that often is more convenient to use. In fact, many experienced programmers use the logical IF exclusively.

The general form of the logical IF statement is

IF(E)S

where *E* is any logical expression, and *S* is *any* executable FORTRAN statement *except* a DO statement or another IF statement. When this statement is executed, the logical expression *E* is evaluated. Then if *E* has the value .TRUE., statement *S* is performed, but if *E* has the value .FALSE., statement *S* is not executed.

Some examples are:

```
IF(NUM.EQ.0) STOP
IF(A.LE.B) GO TO 100
IF(ALPHA.GT.PI) ALPHA = 2.*PI
IF(X.NE.Y) Y = 10.0
```

In the first example, if the value of the variable NUM is 0, the command STOP is carried out, that is, execution of the program is terminated. In the second example, if the value of the variable A is less than or equal to the value of the variable B, control transfers to Statement 100. The examples below illustrate the use of arithmetic statements in conjunction with logical IF statements.

Example 9

An example of how a logical IF statement is used in place of an arithmetic IF statement is as follows: Consider the procedure shown in the flowchart of Fig. 3-11. This could be programmed with the statements

```
   IF(X - 3.0) 5, 10, 10
 5 M = M + 1
10 N = 2*M
```

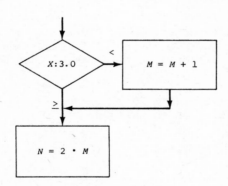

FIGURE 3-11
Flowchart for Example 9

Using a logical IF statement, this could be written

```
IF(X.LT.3.0) M = M + 1
N = 2*M
```

If the relational expression X.LT.3.0 has the value .TRUE., then the statement M = M + 1 will be performed before the statement N = 2*M. If X.LT.3.0 has the value .FALSE., then the statement M = M + 1 will be bypassed and the next statement performed will be N = 2*M.

Because any logical expression may be used within the parentheses, the logical IF statement can often be quite useful. Tests that require two or more arithmetic IF statements can often be combined into a single logical IF statement. For instance, the flowchart in Fig. 3-12 shows a procedure that will set $X = 0$ if $0 < X < 1$, leave the value of X unchanged otherwise, and then set $Y = X$. Using arithmetic IF statements, this could be programmed as

```
      IF(X - 1.0) 5, 20, 20
   5  IF(X) 20, 20, 10
  10  X = 0.0
  20  Y = X
```

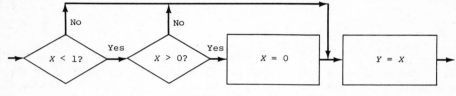

FIGURE 3-12

The same result can be obtained with the statements

```
      IF(X.GE.1.0) GO TO 20
      IF(X.GT.0.0) X = 0.0
  20  Y = X
```

Similarly, the flowchart in Fig. 3-13 shows a procedure that will set $X = 0$ if either $X > 1$ or $X < 0$. This would also require two arithmetic IF statements, but it can be done with logical IF statements:

```
      IF(X.GT.1.0) GO TO 10
      IF(X.GE.0.0) GO TO 20
  10  X = 0.0
  20  Y = X
```

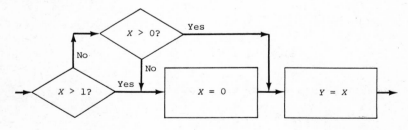

FIGURE 3-13

Anything that can be programmed using logical IF statements can be programmed with arithmetic IF statements. The logical form is quite versatile, however, and can sometimes make the program easier to write. Furthermore, the logical form reduces the proliferation of statement numbers, which can sometimes be confusing or make the program look messy.

There is actually more to logical IF statements, but this will be put off until Chapter 9 when the relevant additional subject matter is covered.

■ A Exercises

For each Decision box, write an arithmetic IF statement that will perform the test and go to the statement number indicated.

1.

6.

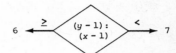

2.

7.

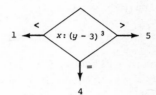

3.

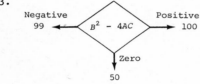

8.

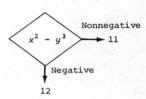

4.

9.

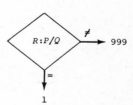

5.

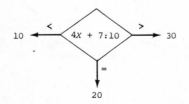

10.

For each arithmetic IF statement, draw the corresponding Decision box.

11. IF(X - Y) 5, 15, 10

12. IF(N - M*N) 1, 2, 3

13. IF(J) 5, 10, 5

14. IF(R*S - 1.0) 10, 10, 20

15. IF(M + N) 5, 1, 1

16. IF(M + N - 1) 3, 1, 2

17. IF(X - Y - R) 1, 90, 1

18. IF(3.0 - R + (X - S)) 99, 100, 101

19. IF(P/Q - R) 4, 5, 5

20. IF(B - C + D - E) 2, 1, 3

For each arithmetic IF statement, give the values of X for which control will pass to Statements 10, 20, and 30.

21. IF(X - 9.0) 10, 20, 30

22. IF(X*X - 9.0) 10, 20, 30

23. IF(X + 6.0) 10, 20, 30

24. IF(-X + 3.0) 10, 20, 30

25. IF(6.0 - (X*2.0 + 4.0)) 10, 20, 30

26. IF(X**2 - 2.0*X + 1.0) 10, 20, 30

27. IF(X*(X - 2)) 10, 20, 30

28. IF(X - X**2) 10, 20, 30

29. IF(X*X) 30, 20, 10

For each set of Decision boxes, write a set of arithmetic IF statements to accomplish what is indicated. An example follows:

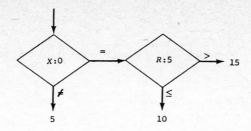

The information in this flowchart could be written in FORTRAN as two IF statements:

```
        IF(X) 5, 6, 5
    6   IF(R - 5.) 10, 10, 15
```

Notice that it was necessary to assign a statement number to the second IF statement.

30.

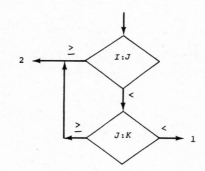

31.

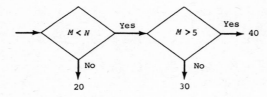

32.

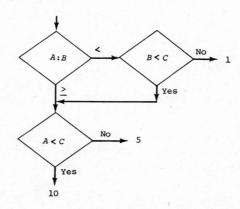

33.

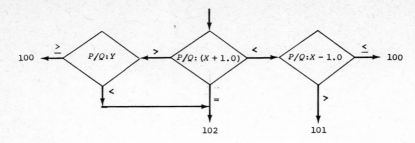

34. Redo Exercises 30-33 using logical IF statements.

For each set of IF statements, write Decision boxes to indicate what is being done.

35.   IF(A - B) 5, 10, 5
     10 IF(B - C) 5, 15, 5

36.   IF(M - N) 1, 1, 2
     1 IF(L - M) 3, 2, 2

37.   IF(M - N - 1) 5, 10, 10
     5 IF(N - 1 - M) 15, 10, 10

38.   IF(A - B) 5, 15, 10
     5 IF(B - C) 100, 15, 15
    10 IF(B - C) 15, 15, 100

39.   IF(X - Z) 10, 99, 99
    10 IF(Z - W) 100, 20, 20
    20 IF(W - X) 100, 99, 99

40.   IF(A.GE.B) GO TO 40

41.   IF(A.GE.B) STOP

■ B Exercises

Write a flowchart and a program for each of Exercises 1-5.

1. If I is even, set $J = 1$, and if I is odd, set $J = 2$.

2. Find the sum of the positive integers which are multiples of 3 and less than 100.

3. If I is 0 or 9, set $J = 10$. Otherwise, set $J = I$.

4. If neither I nor J is 0, set $K = 0$.
   If either I or J is 0, set $K = 1$.
   If both I and J are 0, set $K = 2$.

5. If the integer M is evenly divisible by the integer N, set $K = 0$. Otherwise, set $K = 1$.

6. The accompanying flowchart (page 73) shows how to set a variable called MAX equal to the maximum value of I, J, or K. Write the corresponding FORTRAN program.

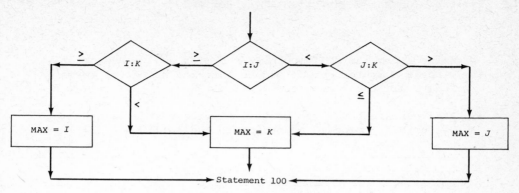

Flowchart for Exercise 6

7. What is the final value of ISUM in each example below? Draw a flowchart for each.

(a)
```
        I = 0
        ISUM = 0
   50   IF(I.EQ.4) STOP
        I = I + 1
        ISUM = ISUM + I
        GO TO 50
```

(b)
```
        I = 0
        ISUM = 0
   50   I = I + 1
        ISUM = ISUM + I
        IF(I.LE.4) GO TO 50
        STOP
```

8. In a certain country, income tax is computed according to the following schedule:

Income	Tax
Less than $200.00	No tax
$201.00–$500.00	2% tax
$501.00–$1000.00	3% tax
$1001.00 and up	4% tax

Write a program to compute the tax, TAX, from a given income, XINC.

9. Referring to Exercise B8, Chapter 1, write a program to compute the Legendre polynomial $P_N(x)$, where N is between 0 and 5, inclusive.

10. Referring to Exercise B5, Chapter 1, write a program to compute the binomial coefficient C_{nk}.

11. Write a program to average a set of numbers as in Chapter 1 (see pages 14-15).

12. The exponential function e^x is defined by

$$e^x = 1 + x + x^2/2! + x^3/3! + x^4/4! + \cdots$$

Write a program to compute EX = e^x for a given value of x. Since a computer cannot add an infinite number of terms, ignore all the terms from $x^7/7!$ on.

13. At a certain bank, the monthly service charge on checking accounts is computed according to the following table:

Charge	Number of Checks
$0.10 per check	First five checks
0.09 per check	Next five checks
0.08 per check	Next five checks
0.07 per check	All the rest of the checks for the month

The total monthly charge is the total charge for checks plus the monthly service charge. Write a program to compute the total charge for a given number of checks.

14. (The Euclidian Algorithm) The greatest common divisor (abbreviated GCD) of two integers M and N is defined to be the greatest number which divides both integers evenly. There is a classic method for finding this number (assume that N is greater than M):

Step 1: Divide N by M and find the remainder MR.

Step 2: If $MR = 0$, then M is the GCD of M and N, so output M and stop.

Step 3: If $MR \neq 0$, replace the value of N by the value of M, replace the value of M by the value of MR, and go back to Step 1.

It can be shown mathematically that the GCD of N and M is the same as the GCD of M and MR (unless $MR = 0$). Write a program to compute the GCD of two given numbers.

15. If $y = -2.0x^2 + 4.0x - 2.0$, find the maximum and minimum values of y for $-2.0 \leq x \leq 2.0$ by trying out values of x in this range, incrementing x by 0.1 each time.

16. Given three floating-point numbers A, B, and C, determine whether or not there is a triangle whose sides have lengths A, B, and C. If there is, set AREA equal to the area of the triangle. If there is no such triangle, set AREA = -1.0.

17. Each of the equations

$$y = Ax + B \qquad \text{and} \qquad y = Cx + D$$

has a graph that is a straight line. These lines might be the same, parallel, or intersecting at a point. You are given values for A, B, C, and D. If the lines intersect at a point, set $N = 1$ and set X and Y equal to the coordinates of the point. If the lines are the same, set $N = 0$ and set $X = Y = 0.0$. If the lines are parallel, set $N = -1$ and set $X = Y = 0.0$.

18. Since a computer is not perfectly accurate, small errors will exist in all floating-point arithmetic. Normally, these are negligible, but small errors can accumulate. To see this, write a routine to find the square root of a number. Using this routine, write a program to do the following:

    (a) Set $Y = \sqrt{X}$.
    (b) Set $X = Y^2$ and go back to Step a.
    (c) Do this 100 times.

19. The Ninth National Bank of Timbuktu pays 5% interest compounded quarterly on savings accounts. Inflation in Timbuktu amounts to about 3% per year (which means that $1.00 today will be worth only 97¢ a year from now). If Harvey Clyde puts $100.00 in a savings account, how many years will it take for his savings to grow to the equivalent (in today's money) of $1,000.00?

Chapter

Input and Output: Part I

Up to this point, we have learned how to do many manipulations in FORTRAN. However, we have tacitly assumed that the numbers were already stored in the computer. Actually, of course, we generally would want to read in data along with the program, and when we have calculated the results, we would want to present them in some manner so as to give us a permanent record. A number of different types of devices are used for input and output. Card readers, printers, card punches, magnetic tapes, magnetic disk units, paper tape readers, and remote terminals are all commonly used for this purpose. For the beginner, though, the card reader and the printer are probably the only machines that would be used, and so we shall confine our attention to these two devices in this chapter. Others will be treated in Chapter 12.

The card reader is a machine that reads punched cards by sensing the pattern of punched holes in the card. Each card consists of 80 columns, and the pattern of holes in each column represents 1 character. By a character, we mean the letters A-Z, any digit 0-9, or any other FORTRAN symbol, such as +, -, =, ., * (see page 42).

The printer is a machine that outputs results. The number of characters per line varies with the model of the printer. Nearly all printers can handle at least 120 characters per line, with some as many as 144. Each page of printed output usually has 66 possible lines. Here again, we are free to determine just what the output will look like; we may not know what values will be printed, but we can decide how many of them will be printed on each line, what headings will appear, and so forth. All of this information must be specified by the FORTRAN program.

Different input-output devices are distinguished by different unit numbers in FORTRAN. Unit 9 might be a magnetic tape unit and Unit 4 might be a card punch. The actual method of determining what number corresponds to what device varies among different computers. For the sake of being definite, we shall assume that

Unit 1 is a card reader;
Unit 2 is a printer.

In this chapter, we shall learn how to input data into the computer and output our results. There are many forms of FORTRAN statements that do these operations. This chapter gives the simplest forms of input and output so that complete FORTRAN programs can be run.

■ The READ Statement

Each input operation in FORTRAN involves two statements: a READ statement and a FORMAT statement. The READ statement tells three things about the input operation:

1. the device (unit) the data is to be read from (card reader, magnetic tape unit, etc.);

2. which storage locations are to receive the values of the numbers read;

3. which FORMAT statement is to be used to specify the arrangement of the numbers on the input record (this will be explained in more detail after the READ statement is introduced).

The general form of the READ statement is

$$\text{READ}(u, f) \text{ var}_1, \text{ var}_2, \text{ var}_3, \ldots, \text{ var}_n$$

where

u is the unit number of the device the data is to be read from—since we are assuming the number 1 designates a card reader, we would put 1 for u in order to read a card;[1]

f is the statement number of the FORMAT statement to be used for reading the data;

$\text{var}_1, \text{ var}_2, \text{ var}_3, \ldots, \text{ var}_n$ are the names of FORTRAN variables that are to receive the values read in.

Notice that the variables are separated by commas, but there is no comma before the first variable.

---

[1] The unit number can also be a fixed-point variable. Only certain values are allowed on some computers for these unit numbers: 5 for input, 6 for output, and 7 for punch.

Some examples of READ statements that illustrate this general rule are as follows:

        READ(1, 10) X

tells the computer to read in a value of the variable X;

        READ(1, 100) A, B, C

tells the computer to read in three values to be assigned to the variables A, B, and C;

        READ(1, 11) I, J, K, ABC

tells the computer to read in four values to be assigned to the variables I, J, K, and ABC.

The unit number 1 in the above three READ statements means that we are reading from the card reader. The numbers 10, 100, and 11 refer to FORMAT statements, which we will discuss below.

■ The FORMAT Statement

We are allowed a great deal of flexibility in deciding the format of our data, but unless we use a FORMAT statement, the computer has no way of knowing just what we want to do. For instance, we can read in values for two variables I and J by punching two numbers right next to each other on a card. Say that we want to punch 11 for the value to be read for I and 22 for the value to be read for J. The card could look like this:

```
1122
```

How is the computer to know that we mean that the two numbers are 11 and 22? If we had wanted the two numbers to be 112 and 2, or 1 and 122, we could have punched the same card. This is the kind of question that is answered by the FORMAT statement.

The FORMAT statement has the form

        FORMAT(desc 1, desc 2, ..., desc N)

where each of the desc 1, desc 2, ..., are field descriptors which specify the format of one data item on the card.

The FORMAT statement is a declaration, or nonexecutable statement, which means that it does not do anything in itself (that is, it causes no machine action); it is used only in conjunction with some executable statement, in this case the READ statement. The

FORMAT statement can appear anywhere in the program. In fact, some programmers like to put all the FORMAT statements together at the end of the program. Others prefer to put all of them at the beginning, or to put each one immediately following the first input or output statement that uses it. This does not make any difference, since the FORMAT statement is used only to describe the arrangement of data for an input or output statement. We now see how these two statements interact.

Every time a READ statement is performed, a new card is read from the card reader. The READ statement interacts with FORMAT statement number *f* and then uses the first field descriptor (desc 1) to determine the form of the first number. The number is then interpreted according to this descriptor and assigned to the first variable in the list of the READ statement (var 1). Likewise, the second field descriptor in the FORMAT statement determines where the second number on the card is, and how this number is interpreted to become the value of the second variable in the list; and so on for all the variables in the list. Notice that the list must consist entirely of variables. Constants and expressions are not allowed, because they cannot be assigned a value.

■ Field Lengths

There is a great deal of freedom in determining how data is to be punched onto a card. For instance, in writing a program to read in several numbers and find their average, we might want to punch one number per card, or to save cards, we might want to punch eight numbers on each card, right next to each other. In writing a program to do a company payroll, we might want to have one card for each employee containing employee number, the number of hours worked during a month, and wage rate.

We are at liberty to set up data in almost any way we choose, but once we decide how the data is to be punched, we must construct the FORMAT statements in a FORTRAN program to tell the machine how to read in the data correctly.

In the payroll program, suppose we have decided that an employee's card is going to have the following format:

          Columns 1-4   Employee number
          Columns 5-9   Wage rate
          Columns 10-13   Number of hours worked
          Columns 14-80   Blank

We call each group of columns containing one of these items a field on the card. A sample card for an employee might look like this:

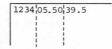

The numbers in the first field on this card (columns 1-4) indicate that the card is for employee number 1234. The numbers in the second field (columns 5-9) show that the employee earns $5.50 per hour. The numbers in the third field (columns 10-13) specify that the employee worked 39.5 hours. The FORTRAN program that reads this card would have to specify that the first field consists of the first 4 columns, rather than the first 3 or 5, and it would have to tell the machine where to store this number, that is, what variable receives the value read in. We shall see how this is done in FORTRAN a little later on in the chapter.

■ Field Descriptors

As mentioned before, the FORMAT statement consists of one or more field descriptors. The field descriptors we shall be using may be one of the following types:

> I to read or write fixed-point numbers;
> F to read or write floating-point numbers;
> E to read or write numbers in exponential form;
> X only for skipping spaces;
> H to print headings on a page of output.

The I Field Descriptor—Input. The I field descriptor, when used for input, means that we are reading a fixed-point number. The general form is

> In

where n is an unsigned fixed-point constant that tells how many characters long the field is. Thus, if a fixed-point number is punched in the first 7 columns of a card, to read in the number as a value for the fixed-point variable LIMIT, we would use the statements

> READ(1, 2) LIMIT
> 2 FORMAT(I7)

The number punched in the card can be preceded by blank spaces, and these will be treated as though they were zeros. So 0065 and 65 are considered to be the same number. Although it is not essential to use zeros this way, some programmers prefer to do it since it is much easier to count characters than blanks on a card. If the number is positive, we can either punch a plus sign (+) in front of the number or omit it, and the number will be read as positive. If the number is negative, we *must* punch a minus sign (-) in front of the number. Some examples of what would be read by the above two statements for various input are given in Table 4-1. The b's stand for blank spaces (we wrote in the b's here to make them easier to count).

In general, all blanks in a field on an input data card are processed exactly as if they were zeros. While blanks to the left of a digit are not significant, blanks which follow a digit *are* significant. These also are treated as zeros, with enough zeros being inserted to fill up the field.

TABLE 4-1

Characters in Columns 1-7	Resulting Value of the Variable LIMIT
bbb+100	+100
bbbb100	+100
0000100	+100
bb-5432	-5432
-bb5432	-5432
b-b5432	-5432
b+bbbbb	0
-bbbbbb	0
bbbbbbb	0

Table 4-2 shows what would happen for various input, using the statements

```
      READ(1, 97) J
 97   FORMAT(I5)
```

TABLE 4-2

Characters in Columns 1-5	Resulting Value of Variable J
bb5bb	+500
5bbbb	+50000
-bb32	-32
b-11b	-110
b+11b	+110
bbbbb	0
b1b1b	+1010

If we want to read several fixed-point numbers from the same card, we just use several I field descriptors, separated by commas, in the FORMAT statement. Then each of the fields will be read according to the above rules and the value will be stored in the corresponding variable in the list of the READ statement. If the first 19 columns of a card contain the characters shown below:

```
-12b1bb229-03330011
```

(where, again, the b's indicate blank spaces), then the statements

```
        READ(1, 77) JIG, JACK, MOM, N1, LEM
    77  FORMAT(I3, I2, I5, I5, I4)
```

result in the following values for the variables:

```
        JIG = -12
       JACK = 1
        MOM = 229
         N1 = -333
        LEM = 11
```

The F Field Descriptor—Input. In the preceding discussion, we talked only about fixed-point numbers. Floating-point numbers are handled similarly, but there is the additional consideration of where to put the decimal point. In reading floating-point numbers from a card, it is quite often convenient not to have to punch the decimal point. For example, if we were reading the amounts of purchases for a billing program, all the input might be in dollars and cents, and we would know that every number read is supposed to have a decimal point in front of the last two digits. Instead of punching the decimal point in the same place for each number read, we could leave it off the card. The F field descriptor will insert the decimal point and specify it automatically when reading the number.

The form of the F field descriptor is

$$F n.m$$

where n is the number of characters in the field to be read, and m is the number of decimal places that will be assumed if there is no decimal point punched in the number being read. If there is a decimal point punched, m will be ignored and the number will be read exactly as punched. If no decimal point is desired, m is 0 (*not blank*).

The n serves the same purpose here as it does in the I field descriptor; it tells how many columns wide the field is. This field width includes both the plus or minus sign, if there is one, and the decimal point, if there is one. *If the decimal point is punched, the m has no meaning, and is ignored*. It is used only if we want to omit actually punching the decimal point, but we want to insert it automatically during the reading process. In this case, the machine reads in the n characters which make up the field and puts a decimal point in front of the mth character from the right. For instance, if the characters 3333 were punched in the first 4 columns of a card, and if they were read in under an F4.2 format, they would be stored as the number +33.33. The 4 in the F4.2 means that 4 characters are to be read (that the field is 4 characters long), and the 2 means that a decimal point is to be placed in front of the second character from the right if there is no decimal point punched on the card. If there is a decimal point punched on the card, it overrides the assumed decimal point, and so it can be punched anywhere in the field. Thus, if .333 were read under an F4.2 format, it would be read as .333, not as 3.33. The number m can be 0, and in this case no decimal point is assumed if one is not punched. The characters b-456 read under an F5.0 format would be stored as -456.0.

Table 4-3 gives some examples of what the value of a floating-point variable T would be if the input shown were read with the statements

```
    READ(1, 6) T
6   FORMAT(F8.2)
```

TABLE 4-3

Characters in Columns 1-8	Resulting Value of T
bb44.600	+44.6
bbb-1231	-12.31
bb-12310	-123.1
-bbbb2.2	-2.2
-bbbb222	-2.22
-2.22bbb	-2.22
-222bbbb	-22200.0
bbbbb1bb	+1.0
bbbbbb1b	+0.1
bb-b101b	-10.1
bb-1.01b	-1.01

As the table indicates, the same rules apply for leading and trailing blank spaces as did for the I field descriptor; they are read as though they were zeros. Again, note the important rule: If a decimal point is punched in the data to be read, trailing blanks do not make any difference in the value that will be read in. Any zeros after a decimal point do not change the value of a number. In other words, 1.6 is the same number as 1.6000. If no decimal point is punched in the number read, trailing blanks will make a difference, since they are counted in determining where the assumed decimal point is to be placed. If 3bb is punched in the first 3 columns of a card, and it is read under an F3.1 format, the two blank spaces are assumed to be zeros, and the decimal point is assumed to be before the first character from the right. So the number would be read as +30.0.

The E Field Descriptor—Input. The E field descriptor is used to input floating-point numbers in the exponential form. Recall that a number in this form can be written as

      iii.fffEee

and this is interpreted by FORTRAN to mean the number

      $iii.fff \times 10^{ee}$

For example, the number -56.4E-3 means -56.4×10^{-3}, which is -0.0564.

    A number in exponential form is composed of three parts: the integer part, the fraction part, and the exponent. By the integer part, we mean the part of the number before the decimal point (the *iii* number above). Similarly, the fraction part is the part of the number after the decimal point (*fff*) but not including the exponent. The exponent is the number following the E (*ee*); it may be preceded by either a plus or minus sign, or no sign at all, in which case it is assumed to be positive. When punching a number in a field to be read by an E field descriptor, any of these parts may be omitted. If the integer part is omitted (that is, if no numbers are punched to the left of the decimal point), it is assumed to be 0. If the fraction part is omitted (that is, if no decimal point is punched), we can automatically put in an assumed decimal point with the E field descriptor just as we did with the F field descriptor. If the exponent is omitted (that is, if the E is not punched), the number is read just as it would be read by an F field descriptor.

    The general form of the E field descriptor is

      E*n.m*

where *n* is the field length, and *m* tells how many places to the left of the nonexponent part the decimal point is to be assumed if there is no decimal point punched.

    When a number is read under the specification of E*n.m*, the following takes place:

    1.   The *n* characters which comprise the field are read in.

    2.   If no decimal point is punched in the number read, a decimal point is assumed *m* places to the left of the last digit of the nonexponent part of the number.

    3.   This number is multiplied by 10 raised to the exponent read in. If the exponent read is *e*, this has the effect of shifting the decimal point *e* places to the right. If the exponent read is *-e*, this has the effect of shifting the decimal point *e* places to the left.

For example, if we read the data

    bb11.22E4

with an E9.3 specification, the number is read as 11.22E4, which is 112200.0. If we had left out the decimal point, though, and punched

 bbb1122E4

then the nonexponent part of this number is 1122, and this would be read as 1.122 because of the 3 in the E9.3, which means that there is to be an assumed decimal point before the third character from the right of the nonexponent part. Then after this is done, the resulting number is multiplied by 10^4, because the exponent read was 4. In other words, the decimal point is shifted four places to the right, so that the number is finally stored as 11220.0.

 As with the F and I field descriptors, any blanks in the field are considered as zeros. So the data

 b477bbE1

would be read under an E8.1 format as 04770.0 X 10^1, which is 47700, just as though the data

 047700E1

had been read. If the decimal point is punched in the data read, then leading or trailing blanks will have no effect. If no decimal point is punched in the data read, blanks may make a considerable difference in the way the number is read, just as zeros would.

 Table 4-4 gives some further examples of conversion in input data by the E field descriptor.

TABLE 4-4

Input Data	Field Description	Resulting Value
1111.11	E7.3	+1111.11
1111111	E7.3	+1111.111
4.7E2b	E6.0	+470.0
1234E-1b	E8.4	+0.01234
1234E+1b	E8.4	+1.234
1234bbbE+1	E10.4	+1234.0
2E1b	E4.0	+20.0
2bE1	E4.0	+200.0
-4.98	E5.1	-4.98
-b498	E5.1	-49.8
-498b	E5.1	-498.0
.3E+5	E5.2	+30000.0
.3E-3	E5.2	+0.0003
123E2	E5.1	+1230.0
123E-2	E6.1	+0.123
9E-1bb	E6.1	+0.09

■ The WRITE Statement

Output operations in FORTRAN are accomplished with the WRITE statement. This statement is quite similar to the READ statement. The general form is

WRITE(*u*, *f*) var 1, var 2, var 3, ..., var *N*

where

u is a unit that determines which device the data is to be written on;

f is the statement number of the FORMAT statement to be used;

var 1, var 2, var 3, ..., var *N* are the variables whose values are to be output.

We have assumed that the number 2 designates the printer, so to write on the printer, *u* would be 2.

When this statement is performed, the first variable in the list (var 1) is printed according to the first field descriptor in FORMAT statement number *f*, then the second variable in the list is printed according to the second field descriptor, and so forth for all the variables in the list.

The I Field Descriptor—Output. The I field descriptor, when used for output, means that we are printing the value of some integer variable. The form is the same as for input, namely, I*n*, where *n* is an unsigned integer constant. In this case, the *n* tells how big the output field is to be; I10, for instance, means that the number will occupy 10 print positions. This includes the minus sign if the number printed is negative. If the number to be printed is less than 10 characters long (including the minus sign if there is one), then it will be right-justified, which means that it will occupy the right-hand part of the 10 characters allotted, with the left-hand characters blank. A positive number will not be printed with a plus sign, but a negative number will have a minus sign preceding the first digit. Table 4-5 shows what would be printed for various values of an integer variable KAT, using the statements

```
      WRITE(2, 44) KAT
   44 FORMAT(I6)
```

We obviously cannot print a 7-digit number in 6 print spaces—the greatest value KAT could have would be 999999, and the most negative value KAT could have would be -99999, since if KAT were larger in magnitude there would be no room for the minus sign. What would

TABLE 4-5

Value of KAT	Number Printed
123	*bbb123*
-123	*bb-123*
0	*bbbbb0*
23344	*b23344*
-7777	*b-7777*

actually be printed if we tried to use the above statements to print a number outside these bounds would depend on the particular computer used. Some machines might print out asterisks instead of the number to indicate that the field length had been exceeded. Other machines might just truncate the number, leaving it to the programmer to figure out what happened. In still other machines, an error message would be printed out and execution of the program would be terminated. In any case, the result would not be the one desired, and care must be taken to make certain that the fields, as described in the FORMAT statement, are large enough to handle the data that will be printed. This is usually not a problem, however. By using an I12 field descriptor, virtually any integer one would normally encounter could easily be handled. If the number to be printed were actually small, the leading spaces would just be filled with blanks, and this would not cause a problem. Since printers normally provide 120 columns or more, plenty of space may be allowed for wide fields.

As with input, more than one variable can be printed with a single WRITE statement by using more than one field descriptor in the associated FORMAT statement. For example, if

```
I = 100
J = -545
K = 3
L = -888
```

then the statements

```
     WRITE(2, 2) I, J, K, L
  2  FORMAT(I4, I4, I2, I5)
```

would result in the output

```
     b100-545b3b-888
```

(where the b's again mean blank); the actual output would be

```
     100-545 3 -888
```

It is usually desirable to make the field large enough so that there will be some blank spaces printed. If

```
        N1 = 1
        N2 = 2
        N3 = 3
        N4 = 4
```

then the statements

```
        WRITE(2, 700) N1, N2, N3, N4
    700 FORMAT(I1, I1, I1, I1)
```

would result in the output

```
        1234
```

While this is legal, it would be more readable to use something like

```
    700 FORMAT(I3, I3, I3, I3)
```

which would print

```
        1   2   3   4
```

The F Field Descriptor—Output. When used for output, the F field descriptor determines how many decimal places the number printed will have, as well as how many characters of output the number will occupy. The form, F$n.m$, is the same as for input, where the n again tells how wide (how many characters) the output field is to be. The m in this case tells how many decimal places of the number are to be printed. Floating-point numbers are stored with more significant digits than we normally need to print. The number of significant digits printed is controlled by the m in the F$n.m$ specification. For example, suppose that we have computed a variable PI and that it has a value of 3.14159265. If we want to print this value, but we want only the first four decimal places, we can use the statements

```
        WRITE(2, 5) PI
    5   FORMAT(F9.4)
```

and this would result in the output

```
        bbb3.1416
```

The field length is nine characters, *including the blanks and the decimal point*, and four decimal places are printed. Notice that the number is rounded rather than truncated to 3.1415-. If we had used a field descriptor of F9.0 in the above FORMAT statement, the resulting output would have been

```
        bbbbbbbb3
```

with no places to the right of the decimal point. In this case the decimal point itself is also omitted on some systems. On other systems, the decimal point is included, and the output is bbbbbbb3..

Table 4-6 shows what numbers would be output for various values of the variable X, using the statements

```
       WRITE(2, 31) X
31     FORMAT(F8.3)
```

TABLE 4-6

Value of X	Output
+21.3	bb21.300
5.0	bbb5.000
-2.34567	bb-2.346
-0.01	bb-0.010
-50.0	b-50.000
-1234.0	Too big (results uncertain)
.0005	bbb0.001 (the 5 is rounded)
-0.0005	bb-0.001 (the 5 is rounded, but minus sign remains)

The E Field Descriptor—Output. When used for output, the E field descriptor has the same form, En.m, as it does for input, where the n is again the overall field width, and the m is the number of decimal places to be printed. The E field is very useful for printing numbers which may be quite large or quite small, because such numbers can be represented compactly in the exponential form. The number 100,000,000,000,000, for example, can be written as .1E+15.

A number written with an En.m format will always be printed as some number greater than or equal to 0.1 and less than 1.0, and it will have an exponent to show the scale factor. The first thing printed will be a blank if the number is positive, or a minus sign if the number is negative. Then a decimal point appears, preceded on some computers by a 0. This is followed by the first m significant digits of the number. Next comes the letter E, followed by a plus or minus sign, and finally the exponent, written as two digits.

For example, the number 100.0 would be written as b.10E+03 under an E8.2 format. If the field length is bigger than needed, the number is printed in the right-most positions, and the spaces on the left are printed as blanks. So, if 100.0 were printed using an E12.2 field description, the output would be bbbbb.10E+03. The number of decimal places, m, is the number of significant digits we want printed. Even if the number to be printed has more than m nonzero digits, only the first m digits will be printed, and the others will simply be rounded off. This means that if X = 614.753, for instance, then the statements

```
      WRITE(2, 91) X
   91 FORMAT(E8.2)
```

would result in the output

       b.61E+03

Since the E8.2 field specified that only two decimal places are to
be printed, the rest of the number is lost. In order to get six
significant digits printed, we would have to use a format of at
least E12.6. This would print the number as

       b.614753E+03

Notice that when using an E$n.m$ field descriptor on output, n
must be equal to at least $m + 6$. This is because 1 position is
required for the sign of the number; 1 for the decimal point; m
for the number itself; and 4 for the letter E, the sign of the
exponent, and the exponent itself. Thus, a field descriptor such
as E5.2 would be too small to print any number, and the result of
trying to print a number with such a format would be unpredictable
(on some machines, asterisks will be printed in the output field
to indicate that the data is too big; on others an error message
is printed).

Table 4-7 gives further examples of the use of the E$n.m$ output
conversion.

TABLE 4-7

Value of Variable	Field Description	Data Output
-10.4	E7.1	-.1E+02
-10.4	E8.2	-.10E+02
-10.4	E12.4	bb-.1040E+02
.0102	E8.2	b.10E-01
-.0001	E12.6	-.100000E-03
-.0001	E14.6	bb-.100000E-03
50000.0	E14.6	bbb.500000E+05
5000000.0	E14.6	bbb.500000E+07
143.7	E11.4	bb.1437E+03
-14.37	E11.4	b-.1437E+02

Let us look at an example showing how input and output statements are used in actual programs.

Example 1

A certain company is taking an inventory of the floor space in
their building. They have measured the dimensions of each room

(all of which are conveniently rectangular), and a program is
required which will give the area of each room and the total area
of all the rooms.

A simple way to prepare the data for this program would be to
use one card to input the data for each room. Each card will contain the length and the width of the room, and just to make sure
that every room is counted, it might also contain the room number.
The card for one room might then be punched in the following format:

    Columns 1-5   Room number
    Columns 6-10   Length (in feet)
    Columns 11-15 Width (in feet)

Since there is no room 0 in the building, we can put a blank
card after the last room card in the deck to be read in. Then in
the program, we test for a room number of 0, and when we find one,
we will know that all the cards have been read and it is time to
print out the total area.

For each room, we shall print out the room number, length,
width, and area. The flowchart for this program is shown in Fig.
4-1.

The FORTRAN program that does this is quite simple:

```
         TOTAR = 0.0
     2   READ(1, 5) NRM, ALEN, WID
     5   FORMAT(I5, F5.0, F5.0)
         IF(NRM) 10, 50, 10
    10   AREA = ALEN*WID
         TOTAR = TOTAR + AREA
         WRITE(2, 15) NRM, ALEN, WID, AREA
    15   FORMAT(I6, F10.1, F10.1, F12.2)
         GO TO 2
    50   WRITE(2, 55) TOTAR
    55   FORMAT(E12.6)
         STOP
         END
```

Notice that in FORMAT Statement 15,[2] an F10.1 field descriptor
is used to print out the length and width. The field length of 10
assures that there will be several spaces between each number
printed, so that they will be easy to read. The one decimal place
is all that is needed in this case, since 0.1 foot is accurate
enough for this purpose. The area is printed with an F12.2 field
descriptor because it will be larger than the length or width, and
we want to have it accurate to two decimal places. The total area
is printed in exponential form, just for illustrative purposes.

---

[2] In the FORMAT Statement 15, an additional space was specified
for the first variable to be output. The reason for this is given
on pages 96-97.

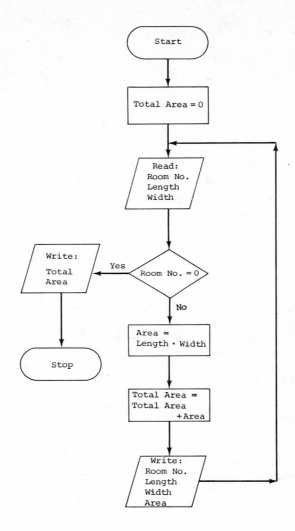

FIGURE 4-1
Flowchart for Example 1

The X Field Descriptor. In printing two numbers side-by-side on a print line, we would normally want to leave some spaces between them for legibility. We already know that this can be done by making the field specification large enough so that the number will not fill up the field. For example, if we are printing two integers M and N and we know that N has a maximum size of six characters (including minus sign), we can write these using the statements

```
      WRITE(2, 5) M, N
   5  FORMAT(I3, I10)
```

Then, since *N* will be right-justified in the I10 field, there will
be at least four blank spaces separating the two numbers printed.

There is an alternate way to skip spaces which is sometimes
more convenient. This is the purpose of the X field descriptor,
which has the form

```
      nX
```

where *n* is an unsigned integer. This field simply causes *n* spaces
to be skipped in the format.

Unlike the I, F, and E fields, the X field does *not* correspond
to a variable in the list of the READ or WRITE statements. For
example, the statements

```
      WRITE(2, 5) M, N
   5  FORMAT(I3, 4X, I6)
```

would print M under an I3 format, then skip four spaces on the
print line, and then print N under an I6 format.

When used for input, the X field functions in a similar way.
For instance, if we want to read an integer JOE punched in columns
1-10 of a card, and then skip 60 spaces and read a floating-point
number SAM which is punched in columns 71-80 of the same card, we
could use the statements

```
      READ(1, 1) JOE, SAM
   1  FORMAT(I10, 60X, F10.0)
```

The H Field Descriptor. Frequently, it is desirable to print
headings along with the results from a program. This can be done
using the Hollerith field descriptor (named for Herman Hollerith,
inventor of punch card equipment). This field descriptor is written

```
      nH
```

where *n* is an integer giving the total number of characters in the
field, *including blanks*. This field descriptor means that the succeeding *n* characters in the FORMAT statement will be printed
exactly as they are.

For example, if we were printing values of variables X and Y,
each of which we wanted to print with an F10.3 format, we could
label the numbers by using the statements

```
      WRITE(2, 12) X, Y
  12  FORMAT(10X, 3HX=b, F10.3, 5X, 3HY=b, F10.3)
```

The first three characters following the first H are X=b (b again means blank—blanks count in an H field just like any other character), and so these three characters would be the first things printed on the print line. Next, the value of the variable X is printed with an F10.3 field, then five blank spaces are printed by the 5X specification, the characters Y=b are printed by the H field, and finally the value of Y is printed in an F10.3 field. If the variable X had the value 20.6 and Y had the value of 100000.0, then the above statements would print out

        bbbbbbbbbbX=bbbbb20.600bbbbbY=b100000.000

Like the X field, the H field does not correspond to any variable in the list of the WRITE statement and is ignored in setting up that correspondence. In fact, it is not necessary to print out any data values if all that is wanted is a Hollerith field. In such a case, the list of variables in the WRITE statement is omitted altogether. For instance, to print out the message

        SIC TRANSIT GLORIA

we could use the statements

        WRITE(2, 44)
    44 FORMAT(19H SIC TRANSIT GLORIA)

Again, the 19H means that the next 19 characters are the Hollerith field to be printed. Remember that the number of characters includes the number of blank spaces. If we had forgotten to count the three blank spaces (one preceding SIC) and had put

    44 FORMAT(16H SIC TRANSIT GLORIA)

the computer would have taken only 16 characters as the H field and printed

        SIC TRANSIT GLO

Furthermore, since the computer would not know what to do with the leftover characters RIA, the results of trying to execute such a statement would be unpredictable, and we would not get the result desired. On most machines this would be caught during compilation and no attempt would even be made to execute the program.

As another example of the use of the H field, suppose that in some program MBOY and MGIRL are the numbers of boys and girls in the first 6 grades. These are punched on cards, with each card containing the number of boys in columns 1-4 and the number of girls in columns 5-8. We want to print these numbers in a column with column headings so that the output looks like this:

```
            bbbbbbGRADEbbbBOYSbbbbGIRLS

            1       423       432
            2       510       540
            3       411       450
            4       400       380
            5       396       377
            6      .390       400
```

We can do this with the statements

```
        WRITE(2, 50)
    50  FORMAT(5X, 6H GRADE, 2X, 5H BOYS, 3X, 6H GIRLS)
        I = 1
    80  READ(1, 60) MBOY, MGIRL
    60  FORMAT(I4, I4)
        WRITE(2, 70) I, MBOY, MGIRL
    70  FORMAT(I9, I8, I9)
        I = I + 1
        IF(I - 6) 80, 80, 90
    90  Next Statement
```

■ Carriage Control Characters

In all the examples of the WRITE statements presented so far, we have made sure that the first character printed is a blank. This is desirable for two main reasons. First, the printed output is easier to view if it does not occupy the left-most position. The second reason is very important to remember when writing FORTRAN. Most printers have a built-in feature that allows the programmer to control the vertical spacing on printing. The first character printed on any line is not really printed at all, but is used to instruct the printer to single-space, double-space, skip to the top of the next page, or suppress spacing. This first character is called the carriage control character; the code used for the carriage control is listed in Table 4-8.[3]

TABLE 4-8. *Carriage control characters.*

Character in First Print Position	Printer Action
Blank	Single space before printing
0	Double space before printing
1	Skip to the beginning of the next page before printing
+	Do not space before printing
Any other character	Single space before printing (same as blank)

[3]Some systems have additional carriage control characters. The reference manual for the system used should be consulted.

Normally, we would just want to leave this column blank. This could be done in several ways. For example, if we are printing an integer variable KOW and we know that KOW will never be greater than 9999, we could print KOW with an I5 format (or any greater field length) so that the first column would be blank. Another way is just to make the first output field an X field. These methods are both illustrated below.

```
         WRITE(2, 44) KOW
         WRITE(2, 55) KOW
    44   FORMAT(I5)
    55   FORMAT(1X, I4)     or     55  FORMAT(1Hb, I4)
```

Now, if we were using FORMAT Statement 44 and KOW happened to be 10000, the number printed would be 0000, and it would be printed at the top of a new page, since the 1 would be interpreted as a carriage control character (whether or not this is what we intended). Thus, (1X, I4) is safer than I5.

Suppose we wanted to print out students' numerical grade averages in Mathematics, English, and History. There is one data card for each student. The grades are punched on data cards as follows:

```
     Columns   1-5    Student identification number
     Columns   6-8    Mathematics grade
     Columns   9-11   English grade
     Columns   12-14  History grade
```

The last card in the data deck has a 99999 punched in the first 5 columns to assist in terminating the program. Each student is to be listed on a separate page of printer output. The FORTRAN program to do this is given as follows:

```
    C      ID IS STUDENT'S IDENTIFICATION NUMBER
    C      MATH IS STUDENT'S MATHEMATICS GRADE
    C      IENGL IS STUDENT'S ENGLISH GRADE
    C      IHIST IS STUDENT'S HISTORY GRADE

      1   WRITE(2, 100)
    100   FORMAT(1H1, 10X, 11HSTUDENT NO., 5X, 4HMATH, 3X,
          17HENGLISH, 3X, 7HHISTORY)
          READ(1, 101) ID, MATH, IENGL, IHIST
    101   FORMAT(I5, I3, I3, I3)
          IF(ID.GE.99999) GO TO 20
          WRITE(2, 102) ID, MATH, IENGL, IHIST
    102   FORMAT(13X, I5, 9X, I3, 6X, I3, 7X, I3)
          GO TO 1
     20   STOP
          END
```

A typical page of output would be the following:

STUDENT NO.	MATH	ENGLISH	HISTORY
1234	75	96	100

It is essential that we keep this carriage control in mind when
writing output statements.   Consider the statements

```
      I = 1
   1  WRITE(2, 10)
  10  FORMAT(1H1)
      I = I + 1
      IF(I.LE.1000) GO TO 1
      Next Statement
```

Their effect is to instruct the printer to skip 1,000 pages, which
would be a most spectacular sight if you consider the speed of
some printers. Such statements obviously should be avoided. In
fact, most computer centers wisely limit the amount of output to
only a small number of pages.

■ Location of Data Cards in a Program

     As we have learned, every time a READ statement is performed a
new data card is read. All the data cards for a particular program
are referred to as the *data deck*. These cards are not located in
the main program but immediately after the END statement is encountered. Figure 4-2 illustrates this.

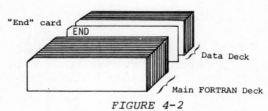

FIGURE 4-2
FORTRAN deck with data cards

     Actually, if you were to examine a complete FORTRAN program
that has just been submitted to a computer center to be run, you
would notice several more cards at various places in the deck.
These cards vary with the computer, but, in general, you might
expect the following:

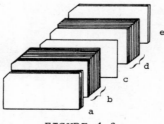

FIGURE 4-3

(a) The first few cards generally include a billing code to
     charge an account for computer time used, a code to

identify the program owner's special requests for when the job is to be run (large computer centers have several priorities for running programs), etc. Other cards in this group are needed to specify that the program is written in FORTRAN, and others may be needed for various purposes.

(b) The main FORTRAN deck, as shown in Fig. 4-2, follows. This is also called the *source program*. The END card is considered a part of this section.

(c) One or more separator cards follow the main program and precede the data deck.

(d) The data cards, if any, are placed next.

(e) Finally, one or more cards denote the end of the card deck. These are often specifically colored or labeled to ease identification by the people who run the program.

Figure 4-3 illustrates where these additional cards are located.

■ A Exercises

1. Below are examples of input and output statements. If the statement is valid, mark a V next to it; otherwise, make a suitable correction to make it valid.

    (a)   READ(1, 100), A, C, D, E
        100 FORMAT(F10.2, F10.3, F10.4, F10.0)

    (b)   READ(1, 1000) X, GO TO
       1000 FORMAT(F20.19, F7.2)

    (c)   WRITE(2, 2) I, J, ZZZ
          2 FORMAT(I1, I20, I30)

    (d)   WRITE(2, 20) A, AB, ABC, ABCD, E
         20 FORMAT(F10.0, F10.8, F10.4, F20.10, F30.20)

    (e)   READ(1, 6) X, Y, E, Z, I, K
          6 FORMAT(F6.2, F3.1, E8.4, F30.2, I3, I10)

2. Write the FORTRAN statements to correspond to the flowchart in Fig. 1-9.

3. Write the FORTRAN statements to correspond to the accompanying flowchart (page 100). The flowchart solves the problem of searching a deck of cards on which are punched grades for a class. There are *N* of these data cards, and the variable COUNT is used to determine how many are 90 or above.

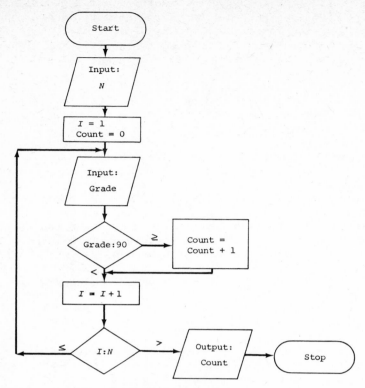

Flowchart for Exercise 3

4. Write the FORTRAN statements to correspond to the flowchart for Exercise Al, Chapter 1.

5. Write a program to input two numbers A and B. Set C = 1 if A and B are both equal to 1. Set C = 2 if A or B but not both equal 1. Set C = 3 otherwise. Output C.

6. (a) Add the necessary statements to Exercise 5 so that the program will work for *N* sets of numbers A and B.

   (b) Rather than count the sets of numbers A and B, suppose that we know that A is never larger than 1,000. After the last data card add a card with a 9999 punched in the same field that A occupied. Add the necessary statements to Exercise 5 to do this.

7. Write the FORTRAN statements to input a student's grades on three examinations, Tl, T2, and T3, and compute the final average as follows: Tl counts 19%, T2 counts 37%, and T3 counts 44%. Use Hollerith specifications to have the printer display the following above the scores:

        TEST1   TEST2   TEST3   FINAL AVG.

■ B Exercises

1. The equation of a circle with center at the origin is given by

$$x^2 + y^2 = r^2$$

where *r* is the radius of the circle. Write a program to input a card with three numbers punched on it as follows:

```
Columns  1-10   X
Columns 11-20   Y
Columns 21-30   R
```

Determine if the point (X,Y) is inside, on, or outside the circle. For your output include appropriate headings. Set up the program to work for any number of data cards.

2. Write a program that will print out your initials. First sketch your initials as you would like them to appear, and then write the program. A sample output may be as follows:

```
              XXXX              XXXXXXXXXX
              XXXX              XXXXXXXXXX
              XXXX              XXX
              XXXX              XXX
              XXXX              XXXXXXXXXX
              XXXX              XXXXXXXXXX
              XXXX                     XXX
     XX       XXXX                     XXX
     XXXXXXXXXXXX              XXXXXXXXXX
     XXXXXXXXXX               XXXXXXXXXX
```

Use any other symbol if you choose.

3. Write a program to draw the following axes, properly centered on your printer:

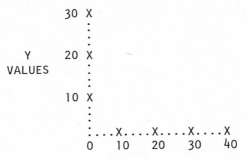

```
              30 X
                 :
                 :
                 :
        Y     20 X
     VALUES      :
                 :
                 :
              10 X
                 :
                 :
                 :...X....X....X....X
                 0   10   20   30   40
```

4. At the end of a grading period each student has his grades punched on two cards. The first card is punched as follows:

```
Columns 1-3  NUM          A 3-digit number for each student
Columns 4-8  M1, ..., M5  Numbers from 0 to 4 corresponding to
                            the student's grades for up to 5
                            courses (A = 4, B = 3, etc.)
```

The second card contains the credits or units for each course, punched in the first 5 columns. These are N1, ..., N5, with N1 corresponding to the grade M1, etc. A student's grade point average (GPA) is determined by the formula

$$GPA = \frac{N1 \cdot M1 + N2 \cdot M2 + N3 \cdot M3 + N4 \cdot M4 + N5 \cdot M5}{N1 + N2 + N3 + N4 + N5}$$

Write a program to determine the GPA for a single student.

5. Modify the program in Exercise 4 so that it will work for any number of students. Do this by including an appropriate test of input data.

6. Write a program to input a number representing an amount of money less than $100.00. The number can be read in with an F10.2 format. Then have the computer determine the amount and print out a message as follows:

```
BETWEEN $ 0.00 and $20.00
BETWEEN $20.00 and $40.00, etc.
```

7. Write a program to list the integers from 1 to 100. However, if an integer is divisible by 3 or contains the digit 3, an X is output. A sample output would be

```
1
2
X
4
5
X
etc.
```

Chapter

Arrays and Subscripted Variables

FORTRAN allows us to use subscripted variables. For example, if we had a program that involved, say, 100 variables, it would be tedious just to give them each a distinct name, such as A, B, ..., SUM, or PROD, and to keep all these names straight while working with the variables. Suppose, however, that we had 100 numbers written in a list:

$$
\begin{array}{rl}
1. & 1.3 \\
2. & 2.0 \\
3. & 6.1 \\
& \vdots \\
100. & 5.9
\end{array}
$$

If we were to talk about the third number in this list, it would be clear that we meant the number 6.1. This is the basic idea of subscripted variables. We give a name, say X, to a collection of storage locations or *array*, as it is more commonly called, and then to distinguish between the different locations in the array, we use the subscripted names:

$$X_1, X_2, X_3, \ldots, X_{100}$$

The array name, X, includes the whole collection of variables, and each of the names $X_1, \ldots, X_{100}$ is an individual variable referring to one of the elements of the array.

The chief advantage of using subscripts, however, is not just for naming variables. We can describe an operation that is to be performed on each of the variables in turn by including instructions in the program to manipulate the subscript itself. For instance, suppose we wanted to add up all the numbers in the above list. We certainly could do this explicitly by putting

$$Y = X_1 + X_2 + X_3 + X_4 + \cdots + X_{100}$$

if we were willing to spend the time to write out the whole expression. In algebra, however, we use the more compact notation

$$Y = \sum_{i=1}^{100} X_i$$

In a similar manner, as we shall soon see, the use of subscripts in FORTRAN can greatly facilitate many procedures.

■ Subscripts in FORTRAN

In FORTRAN, a subscripted variable is denoted by enclosing the subscript in parentheses after the array name. Thus, instead of A_1, A_2, ..., A_{99}, we would write A(1), A(2), ..., A(99). The same rules apply for naming arrays as applied for naming ordinary variables. The same considerations as to type also apply. Thus, an array named ABC would be a floating-point array. This simply means that each of the variables ABC(1), ABC(2), and ABC(3) is a floating-point variable. Likewise, an array named M123 would be a fixed-point array, so each of the variables M123(1), M123(2), M123(3), ..., would be a fixed-point variable.

The quantity in parentheses may be an unsigned integer, as above, or it may be a fixed-point variable, such as I, J, or NSUM. In this case, the reference is to the element of the array whose subscript is the value of the fixed-point variable. So if we had

        I = 6
        Y = A(I)

then Y would be set equal to A(6). Below are some examples of correct subscripted variables:

        ABC(94)
        ABC(INT)
        PRIME(1)
        N123(LOC)

While the subscript may be either a constant or a variable, its value must always be a positive integer; 0 and negative subscripts are not allowable, and neither are floating-point subscripts. Also, generally speaking, an arithmetic expression can be used as a subscript only in certain restricted cases. A subscript may be in any of the following forms:

        Constant
        Variable
        Variable ± Constant
        Constant*Variable
        Constant*Variable ± Constant

where the constant and the variable are both fixed-point. Thus,

        ARRAY(2*I)

is correct, but

          ARRAY(I*2)

is not. Table 5-1 shows some examples of incorrect subscripts.

TABLE 5-1

Incorrect Variable	Reason for Error
ABCDEFG(1)	*Too many characters in name*[1]
A(0)	*Subscript 0*
X(-1)	*Negative subscript*
X(1.5)	*Floating-point subscript*
M(X)	*Floating-point variable subscript*
Y2(N + M/2)	*Illegal arithmetic expression in subscript*
4L(J)	*Name does not begin with letter*

Some compilers allow more general subscript expressions. For
example, some allow any fixed-point expression as a subscript. Some
even allow floating-point subscripts. However, the forms listed in
the above rules will work on any system.

Care must be taken that the value of a variable or expression
used as a subscript is always positive. For instance, if we had
the statements

          J = 5
     6   J = J - 1
          Y = ALPHA(J)
          IF(J.GT.0) GO TO 6
          STOP

the result would be undefined, since an attempt is made to set
Y = ALPHA(0).

■ The DIMENSION Statement

Now that we have seen how subscripted variables are written in
FORTRAN, let us consider briefly what a subscripted variable does
in terms of the computer itself. Recall that an ordinary variable
is a name that corresponds to some memory location in the computer.
Each time we include the variable in the program, we are referring
to the contents of that memory location. If we are using a subscripted variable ALPHA, each of the variables ALPHA(1), ALPHA(2),
..., also refers to some memory location. In order to specify how
many memory locations are in the array, we must use a DIMENSION

---

[1]See footnote on page 29.

statement.   The DIMENSION statement is a declarative (nonexecutable) statement and it must appear at the beginning of any program in which subscripted variables are used.   This statement has the form

DIMENSION   name1(dim1), name2(dim2), ..., name*n*(dim*n*)

where name*I* is the name of an array and dim*I* is an unsigned integer constant giving the maximum value of the subscript for that array. For example, suppose in a program that we want to use an array named CAT, and we know that we shall not need a subscript for CAT greater than 100.   At the beginning of the program we would use the statement

DIMENSION   CAT(100)

This statement declares the existence of the array CAT consisting of the 100 variables

CAT(1), CAT(2), ..., CAT(100)

We could refer to any of these in the program.   It would be incorrect, however, to use CAT(101) in an expression.

Each array used in a program must appear in a DIMENSION statement at the beginning of the program to declare that the variable name is to be treated as a subscripted variable, and to specify the dimension, or size, of an array, that is, the number of subscripted variables it contains.   Note that it is not necessary to use a separate DIMENSION statement for every array.   If we want to use two arrays

CAT(1), CAT(2), ..., CAT(105)
DOG(1), DOG(2), ..., DOG(9)

in a program, we can use the single statement

DIMENSION   CAT(105), DOG(9)

Once we have used a DIMENSION statement to declare that a certain variable is an array name, that name should normally appear with a subscript when used in an expression.   If we used the above DIMENSION statement, it would be incorrect to have the statement

Y = CAT + 5.0

in the same program, because the variable CAT does not appear with a subscript.   [But not on all computers.   Some will actually treat the statement as Y = CAT(1) + 5.0.]

■ Use of Subscripted Variables

Example 1

As a simple example of how subscripted variables can save a considerable amount of effort, suppose we have N numbers stored in an array X, and suppose that $N \leq 100$.   To set Y equal to the sum of these numbers, we can use a procedure whereby we add X(I) to Y and then increment I until it is equal to N.   The complete procedure is shown in the flowchart in Fig. 5-1.

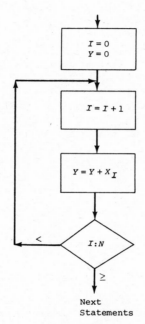

FIGURE 5-1
Flowchart for Example 1

This could be written in FORTRAN as

```
      DIMENSION  X(100)
         .
         .
         .
      Y = 0.0
      I = 0
    5 I = I + 1
      Y = Y + X(I)
      IF(I.LT.N) GO TO 5
      Next Statement
```

This program is the FORTRAN equivalent of the algebraic expression

$$Y = \sum_{i=1}^{N} X_i$$

Such procedures occur frequently in programming, and the use of the subscripted variables makes them easier to deal with. Note that the above program will work equally well for *N* equal to 1, 10, or 100.

Example 2

We want to tabulate values of the polynomial

$$Y = X^3 + 2X^2 - 3X + 1$$

for values of *X* from -1 to 1 in increments of 0.1. We want to store the *Y* values in an array Y.

First, note that there are 21 values in all: -1.0, -0.9, ..., 0.9, 1.0. So we can set up the array Y with 21 variables. The program to perform this job is as follows:

```
        DIMENSION  Y(21)
        I = 1
        X = -1.0
    1   Y(I) = ((X + 2.)*X - 3.)*X + 1.
        IF(I.GE.21) GO TO 2
        I = I + 1
        X = X + 0.1
        GO TO 1
    2   Next Statement
```

In some cases, we can perform a procedure either by using subscripted variables or not using them. For example, the flowchart in Fig. 3-5 gives a procedure for adding a list of numbers without using subscripted variables. Compare this with Example 1, where we do the same thing with subscripted variables. The difference is that in the first case, we did not store all the numbers internally (that is, not all at once). It is sometimes necessary to store a list of numbers internally, rather than to read them in and work with them one at a time. In such a case, the use of subscripts is a practical necessity.

Example 3

In statistics, it is frequently necessary to find the mean and variance of a set of measurements. The mean, or average, is defined by

$$\bar{x} = \frac{\sum_{i=1}^{n} x_i}{n}$$

where n is the number of measurements x_1, x_2, $\cdots$, x_n. (The symbol $\bar{x}$ is pronounced "x bar" and is commonly used to denote the mean.) The variance (var) is given by the formula

$$\text{var} = \frac{1}{n-1} \sum_{i=1}^{n} (x_i - \bar{x})^2$$

It appears that a program to compute the mean and variance would require two loops: one to compute the mean and a second to compute the variance, since the formula for the variance uses the mean. However, it can be shown by algebra that the variance is also given by the formula

$$\text{var} = \frac{\displaystyle\sum_{i=1}^{n} x_i^2 - n\bar{x}^2}{n-1}$$

so it is not necessary to have two loops. We merely accumulate the sum of the measurements and the sum of the squares of the measurements in a single loop. Both the mean and the variance can then be computed.

Suppose that the measurements have been read into an array X declared by the statement

        DIMENSION X(100)

(so we assume that $n \leq 100$). The following statements will find the mean, XBAR, and the variance, VAR:

```
        I = 1
        SUM = 0.0
        SSQ = 0.0
   10   SUM = SUM + X(I)
        SSQ = SSQ + X(I)**2
        I = I + 1
        IF(I.LE.N) GO TO 10
        XBAR = SUM/FLOAT(N)
        VAR = (SSQ - FLOAT(N)*XBAR**2)/FLOAT(N - 1)
```

In fact, it is not really necessary to use an array to solve this problem if the values of X(I) can be computed or read into the loop that accumulates the values SUM and SSQ.

Example 4

Suppose we have N numbers X(1), X(2), ..., X(N) and we want to set XMAX equal to the maximum of these numbers. To accomplish this, we begin by setting XMAX = X(1). Then we compare each X(I), starting with X(2), to XMAX and, if X(I) is greater, we replace the value of XMAX by X(I). The flowchart for the procedure is shown in Fig. 5-2. When a STOP terminal is reached, XMAX will be equal to the maximum of the given numbers.

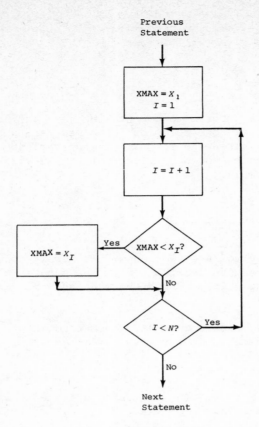

FIGURE 5-2
Flowchart for Example 4

This procedure could be performed with the following FORTRAN statements:

```
DIMENSION  X(100)
    .
    .
    .
XMAX = X(1)
I = 1
5  I = I + 1
   IF(XMAX.LT.X(I)) XMAX = X(I)
   IF(I.LT.N) GO TO 5
   Next Statement
```

Example 5

Let us carry the previous example one step further. Instead of just finding the maximum of $X(1)$, $X(2)$, ..., we shall rearrange these numbers in descending order, so that the greatest number is stored in $X(1)$ and the smallest in $X(N)$. There are many ways of

doing this, and when many numbers are to be stored, it is important
to use an efficient method. Some of the most efficient methods,
however, are also rather complicated, and for this example we shall
use a method which is really just an extension of the method used
in Example 4.

First, we find the maximum of $X(1)$, $X(2)$, ..., $X(N)$, just as
we did above. Suppose it is $X(J)$. We then interchange $X(1)$ and
$X(J)$. That is, the value of $X(J)$ is stored in $X(1)$, and the value
of $X(1)$ is stored in $X(J)$. The next step is to find the maximum
of $X(2)$, $X(3)$, ..., $X(N)$ and to interchange this value with $X(2)$.
In general, on the Mth step, we find the maximum of $X(M)$, $X(M + 1)$,
..., $X(N)$ and then we interchange this value with $X(M)$. (See
Fig. 1-13 for the flowchart showing the procedure for rearranging an
array in ascending order.) The statements would be

```
       DIMENSION  X(100)
          .
          .
          .
       I = 1
  10   J = I + 1
  20   IF(X(I).GT.X(J)) GO TO 40
       TEMP = X(I)
       X(I) = X(J)
       X(J) = TEMP
  40   J = J + 1
       IF(J.LE.N) GO TO 20
  50   I = I + 1
       IF(I.LE.(N - 1)) GO TO 10
       Next Statement
```

Example 6

In recent years there have been many applications of computers
in mathematics for testing hypotheses in number theory. A simple
example of this is using the computer to test whether or not a
particular number is prime. (A positive integer is called prime
if it is not divisible evenly by any integer except itself and 1.
For instance, 2, 5, 11, 19, and 23 are primes, while 4, 24, 50, and
99 are not.) It can be shown that a number is prime if and only if
it is not divisible evenly by any prime less than or equal to its
square root.

Suppose we are given an integer N, where $2 \leq N \leq 10^4$. We want
to set a variable L = 0 if N is not prime, and set L = 1 if N is
prime. Since $N \leq 10^4$, we need to test only the primes that are
less than or equal to 100. We may start by dividing N by 2. If 2
divides N evenly (with no remainder), then N is not prime, so we
set L = 0 and stop; if N is not divisible by 2, we try dividing
N by 3. If N is not divisible by 3 either, we try dividing by 5
and so on until we find a prime which divides N or we have tried
every prime less than or equal to the square root of N, in which
case we set L = 1 and stop.

Specifically, suppose we have an array called NPRM containing the primes from 2 to 100 (there are 25 of them in this range):

         NPRM(1) = 2
         NPRM(2) = 3
            .
            .
            .
         NPRM(25) = 97

Given any number N such that $2 \leq N \leq 10^4$, we first want to set an integer variable M equal to the integer part of the square root of N. We can do this with the statements

         AN = FLOAT(N)
         M = IFIX(SQRT(AN))

Note that we convert N to the floating-point variable AN before performing the square root function.

To test whether or not N is divisible by NPRM(I), we use integer arithmetic to compute

         J = (N/NPRM(I))*NPRM(I) - N

Then J = 0 if and only if NPRM(I) divides N. The final flowchart is shown in Fig. 5-3.

The FORTRAN program that performs this procedure reads

```
      DIMENSION  NPRM(25)
         .
         .
         .
C     ASSUME ALL VARIABLES ARE DEFINED PREVIOUSLY
      I = 0
      AN = FLOAT(N)
      M = IFIX(SQRT(AN))
    5 I = I + 1
      IF(NPRM(I).LE.M) GO TO 15
      L = 1
      GO TO 20
   15 J = (N/NPRM(I))*NPRM(I) - N
      IF(J.NE.0) GO TO 5
      L = 0
   20 WRITE(2, 30) L
   30 FORMAT(I10)
      STOP
      END
```

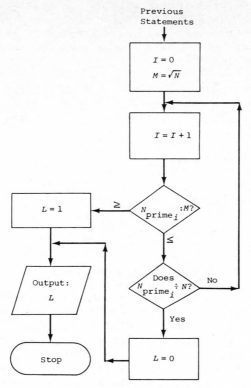

FIGURE 5-3
Flowchart for Example 6

■ Doubly and Triply Subscripted Arrays

All of the subscripted variables we have dealt with so far have had one subscript. It is also allowable in FORTRAN to have variables with two or three subscripts. These are handled in a similar manner. A doubly subscripted array (that is, a variable with two subscripts) is set up by using a DIMENSION declaration such as

        DIMENSION MATR(3,4)

This would declare that the array MATR consists of

        MATR(1,1), MATR(1,2), MATR(1,3), MATR(1,4)
        MATR(2,1), MATR(2,2), MATR(2,3), MATR(2,4)
        MATR(3,1), MATR(3,2), MATR(3,3), MATR(3,4)

In general, to specify a doubly subscripted array, we use a statement of the form

        DIMENSION name(m,n)

where name is the name of the array, *m* is an unsigned integer constant giving the maximum value of the first subscript, and *n* is an unsigned integer constant giving the maximum value of the second subscript. We can then refer to any of the variables name(I,J), where $1 \leq I \leq m$ and $1 \leq J \leq n$.

For instance, in an accounting job, we might want to know the amount of checks written on each day of the year, and it might be convenient to use two subscripts to do this. If we used the DIMENSION statement

        DIMENSION   CHECK(12,31)

then we could take CHECK(I,J) to mean the number of checks written on the *J*th day of the *I*th month of the year.

Example 7

Suppose there are *N* students in a class, and for the entire semester there are *M* test grades, where each grade is 0, 1, 2, 3, or 4. The grades are stored in a doubly subscripted array called GRADE, where GRADE(I,J) is the *I*th student's grade on the *J*th test. We want to compute the final grade, FINAL(I), for each student to be the average of all that student's test grades. We also want to compute the class average, CLSAV, which is the overall average of all the final grades. If we know that $N \leq 50$ and $M \leq 10$, we can use the following routine to do this (assume all variables have been read into the computer):

```
        DIMENSION   GRADE(50,10), FINAL(50)
        I = 0
        AM = FLOAT(M)
        CLSAV = 0.0
    1   I = I + 1
    5   J = 0
        FINAL(I) = 0.0
   10   J = J + 1
        FINAL(I) = FINAL(I) + GRADE(I,J)
        IF(J.LT.M) GO TO 10
        FINAL(I) = FINAL(I)/AM
        CLSAV = CLSAV + FINAL(I)
        IF(I.LT.N) GO TO 1
        AN = FLOAT(N)
        CLSAV = CLSAV/AN
        Next Statement
```

Example 8

Let us consider a routine for multiplying two 3 × 3 matrices *A* and *B* to give the product matrix *C*. If

$$A = \begin{bmatrix} a_{11} & a_{12} & a_{13} \\ a_{21} & a_{22} & a_{23} \\ a_{31} & a_{32} & a_{33} \end{bmatrix} \qquad B = \begin{bmatrix} b_{11} & b_{12} & b_{13} \\ b_{21} & b_{22} & b_{23} \\ b_{31} & b_{32} & b_{33} \end{bmatrix}$$

then, by definition, their product AB is

$$C = \begin{bmatrix} c_{11} & c_{12} & c_{13} \\ c_{21} & c_{22} & c_{23} \\ c_{31} & c_{32} & c_{33} \end{bmatrix}$$

where

$$c_{11} = a_{11}b_{11} + a_{12}b_{21} + a_{13}b_{31}$$
$$c_{12} = a_{11}b_{12} + a_{12}b_{22} + a_{13}b_{32}$$
$$\vdots \qquad \vdots \qquad \vdots \qquad \vdots$$
$$c_{mn} = a_{m1}b_{1n} + a_{m2}b_{2n} + a_{m3}b_{3n}$$

This multiplication could be accomplished with the following statements:

```
      DIMENSION  A(3,3), B(3,3), C(3,3)
      I = 0
   5  I = I + 1
      J = 0
  10  J = J + 1
      C(I, J) = A(I, 1)*B(1, J) + A(I, 2)*B(2, J) + A(I,3)*B(3, J)
      IF(J.LT.3) GO TO 10
      IF(I.LT.3) GO TO 5
  20  Next Statement
```

In a similar manner, we can use a triply subscripted array by giving a DIMENSION statement such as

    DIMENSION name(a,b,c)

where a, b, and c are unsigned integer constants and a is the maximum value of the first subscript, b is the maximum value of the second subscript, and c is the maximum value of the third subscript.

We shall see more examples of procedures involving the use of doubly and triply subscripted arrays after we learn about the DO statement, which facilitates such procedures.

Singly, doubly, and triply subscripted variables may be included in the same DIMENSION statement.

■ A Exercises

1. Below are examples of FORTRAN expressions and statements. Some are correct, others have errors. If the statement is valid, mark a V next to it. Otherwise, make a suitable correction to make it valid.

   (a) JACK(JUMP)
   (b) HELLO(5, I)
   (c) DIMENSION X(5), Y(J)
   (d) ARRAY(5*JOHN)
   (e) ZZZ(II45)
   (f) W(JJ - 60)
   (g) W(JJ - 60, KK)
   (h) X(2*LIM + 800)

   (i) DIMENSIONS X(10), ZZ(1000), Y(4)
   (j) AAA(IBB, KCC) = I
   (k) X = A(J - 5) + BB(I + J)
   (l) DIMENSION III(10000)
   (m) GO TO 5 = A(I, J)
   (n) PRES(MINE, NEVER)
   (o) B(IN, OUT)
   (p) VARY(IOU) = MONEY

For the following exercises, assume all variables are in storage in the computer, or else include appropriate READ and WRITE statements.

2. A list of 100 variables is called D. Write the FORTRAN statements to compute the elements of a new array named E where

$$E_i = D_{i+1} - D_i, \qquad i = 1, 2, \ldots, 99$$

3. Write the FORTRAN statements that will calculate an array consisting of the cube roots of the first ten integers. Call the array CBROOT.

4. Write the FORTRAN statements to correspond to the accompanying flowchart (page 117).

5. Write the FORTRAN statements to correspond to the following indicated sums:

```
SUM (1) = 1 + 2 + 3 + ··· + n
SUM (2) = 1 + 5 + 9 + ··· + (4n - 3)
SUM (3) = 1 + 3 + 5 + ··· + (2n - 1)
SUM (4) = 1² + 2² + 3² + ··· + n²
SUM (5) = 1³ + 2³ + 3³ + ··· + n³
```

6. Make any necessary corrections in the following sequences of statements:

```
(a)     N = 6
        DIMENSION X(N)
    2   Y = X(I)**2
        I = I + 1
        IF(I.LE.6) GO TO 2
        Z = Y
```

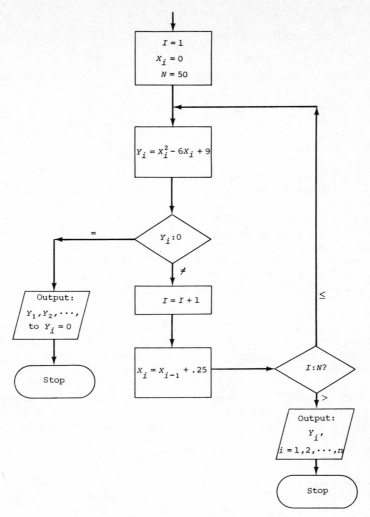

Flowchart for Exercise 4

6.—continued

(b)   DIMENSION X(5,5)
         I = 1
         J = 1
    1 X(I, J) = .25*(X(I + 1, J) + X(I, J - 1))
         J = J + 1
         IF(J.LE.4) GO TO 1
         I = I + 1
         IF(I.LE.4) GO TO 1
         Y = X(I,J)

6.—continued

(c)
```
        DIMENSION  A(10,10)
        I = 1
        J = 1
4       IF(I.NE.J) GO TO 1
2       A(I, J) = 1.0
        GO TO 3
1       A(I, J) = 0.0
3       J = J + 1
        IF(J.LE.10) GO TO 4
        I = I + 1
        IF(I.LE.10) GO TO 4
        Next Statement
```

(d)
```
        DIMENSION  ARRAY(20,20)
        DIMENSION  X(10), y(10)
        NUMB = 1
100     ARRAY(NUMB, NUMB + 1) = X(NUMB) - Y(NUMB + 5)
        NUMB = NUMB + 3
        IF(NUMB.LE.13) GO TO 100
        Next Statement
```

7. The test results of a large number of students who took both Mathematics and English examinations are stored in arrays TMATH and ENGL, respectively. The number of results is less than 1,000. Write the FORTRAN statements to fill up a new array called DIFF, where DIFF(N) = 0 if the difference between the Nth student's Mathematics and English scores is less than 20 points and DIFF(N) = 1 if it is 20 points or more. Let the variable COUNT be equal to the number of 1's in the array DIFF.

8. Draw a flowchart to correspond to Exercise 7.

9. Assume that you have two doubly subscripted arrays A(I, J) and B(I, J), where A and B have the same number of elements. Write the FORTRAN to construct a third array C(I, J), where each element of C is given by C(I, J) = A(I, J) + B(I, J). The maximum size of I and J is 10.

10. After the following FORTRAN statements have been executed, what is the value of B?

```
        DIMENSION  A(100)
        I = 1
3       X = I - 1
        A(I) = X**3 - X**2 - 10.*X - 8.0
        I = I + 1
        IF(A(I).EQ.0.0) GO TO 2
        IF(I.LE.100) GO TO 3
2       B = I
```

11. There are 1,000 test results stored in an array called SCORE. Write the FORTRAN statements to determine how many grades are equal to or greater than 90. Call this number A.

12. Write the FORTRAN statements for the flowchart in Fig. 1-13. Assume that there are 100 variables in the array.

■ B Exercises

1. The Alpha Alpha Alpha fraternity has interviewed every member of the Beta Beta Beta sorority and punched cards for the members as follows:

Columns	1-5	ID	Student's identification number
Columns	6-7	HT	Height in inches
Columns	8-10	WT	Weight in pounds
Column	11	IAVAIL	1 if available for blind dates; 0 otherwise
Columns	12-13	SCORE	0-99; the higher the number the better-looking the girl
Column	14	HAIR	Color of hair: 1 for blond, 2 for brunette, 3 for red, 4 for black
Column	15	SPORTS	0 if the girl likes sports, 1 if she hates sports, 2 if no opinion

(a) Write a program to find the average weight, height, and SCORE for the Beta Beta Beta sorority.

(b) Write a program to see how many Beta Beta Beta sorority members are available for a blind date with a person look-ing for a girl less than 5 feet 9 inches in height, weigh-ing more than 110 pounds (but less than 160), having a SCORE greater than 70, and who hates sports. As an exer-cise in running the program, punch typical cards for 50 sorority members.

2. In statistics, the rth moment about the mean, $\bar{X}$, of a set of data is defined as

$$m_r = \frac{\sum_{j=1}^{N} (X_j - \bar{X})^r}{N} \quad \text{where} \quad \bar{X} = \frac{\sum_{j=1}^{N} X_j}{N}$$

Assume that you have less than 1,000 of the variable X. Write the FORTRAN statements to find the mean of X and also the first five moments about the mean, and store these in an array called XMOM. Try to do this all in one pass, computing X, X^2, X^3, X^4, and X^5 as you go along.

3. Suppose that the following formula has been found to be an accurate index of pollution, P:

$$P = 0.01x^2 + 0.0001y^3 + 0.05z^2$$

where

x = number of particles of smog per million parts
y = number of particles of polluted water per million parts
z = number of particles of pollen per million parts of air

The index is set to be a maximum of 100 even if the value should be higher from the equation. Write a program to calculate P for the following data:

x	y	z
15	50	5
0	100	10
20	30	20
5	25	80
20	40	0
40	16	8
30	30	30
20	30	40

4. The projected growth of a country's population is given by the following equation:

$$A = A_0 \left(1 + t + \frac{t^2}{2} + \frac{t^3}{6} + \frac{t^4}{24} + \frac{t^5}{60}\right)$$

where

A = population present at any time
A_0 = population present at time $t = 0$
t = time in years divided by 10 (that is, for $t = 1$ year, use 0.1 in the formula)

Suppose that a country has 1 million people now. Write a program to predict the population for each of the next 10 years. How long will it be before the population is 10 million.

5. The standings for teams in a baseball league might be as listed in the accompanying table. Let $X(I)$ be the 6 team array; $W(I)$ be the number of wins for team I; and $XL(I)$ be the losses for team I. The games behind, GB, is given by

5.—continued

$$GB = \frac{(W(I) - XL(I)) - (W(J) - XL(J))}{2}$$

where *I* stands for the first team and *J* for any other team.

Team	Wins	Losses	Percent	Games Behind
6	10	2	0.833	0
2	9	3	0.750	1
1	8	3	0.727	$1\frac{1}{2}$
3	6	6	0.500	4
5	4	8	0.330	6
4	0	11	0.000	$9\frac{1}{2}$

Write a program to read in the team numbers, wins, and losses, and to output a table similar to the one above.

6. A ball is dropped from a building 200 feet high and bounces off the ground to 75% of its previous height. It continues bouncing 75% each bounce, until it comes to rest. In theory, this happens only after an infinite number of bounces. In practice, the ball will soon stop after a finite number of bounces. Write a program to print the height of the ball at the top of each bounce for up to 50 bounces. Give the distance traveled during each bounce as well as total distance traveled.

The DO Statement

A group of instructions which is performed over and over again is called a program *loop*. We have seen several examples of this before. For instance, the following instructions will add the integers from 1 to 20:

```
        NSUM = 0
        I = 0
    5   I = I + 1
        NSUM = NSUM + I
        IF(I.LT.20) GO TO 5
        STOP
```

In this procedure, notice that we are repeatedly performing the instruction

```
        NSUM = NSUM + I
```

while adding 1 to I each time until I = 20. This sort of situation arises so frequently in programming that a special statement—the DO statement—exists to make it easier.

In general, the DO statement has the form

$$DO \ y \ I = m_1, \ m_2, \ m_3$$

where y is some statement number; I is an integer variable, called the *control variable*, and m_1 (initial value), m_2 (terminal value), and m_3 (increment) are unsigned integer constants or variables.

Now this statement has the following effects:[1]

---

[1]The DO statement described here is known as a "one-pass" DO loop, that is, the statements in the DO loop are always executed at least one time. A "zero-pass" loop is one where the index is tested first. Certain new compilers may have this latter feature. In a one-pass DO loop, the statements associated with DO 10 I = 10, 1 are executed once; in a zero-pass loop, control passes out of the loop.

1. First, the value of I is set equal to m_1.

2. Then all the statements up to and including the statement number y are performed.

3. Then m_3 is added to I. This is compared to m_2. If the new value of I is greater than m_2, the next statement after the statement number y is performed. If the new value of I is equal to or less than m_2, control returns to the first statement after the DO statement. If m_3 is omitted, as it often is, it is assumed to be 1.

This procedure is shown in the flowchart in Fig. 6-1.

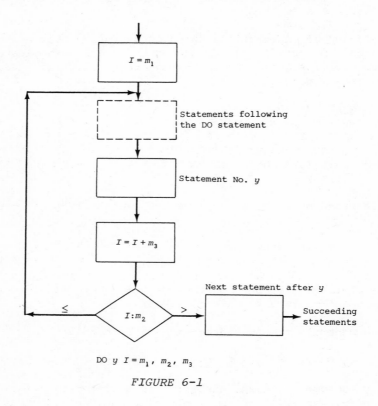

FIGURE 6-1

Example 1

To perform the program loop given earlier using the DO statement, we could have written

```
    NSUM = 0
    DO 7 I = 1, 20, 1
7   NSUM = NSUM + I
    Next Statement
```

In this case, the DO statement specifies that Statement 7 be performed, starting with I = 1 and that it be repeatedly performed adding 1 to I each time until I = 20.

Example 2

We know that if the increment m_3 is omitted from the DO statement, it is assumed to be 1. So in the above example, instead of

```
DO 7 I = 1, 20, 1
```

we could have put

```
DO 7 I = 1, 20
```

to gain the same effect.

Example 3

Suppose that at some point in a program we have computed a value for N and that we want to set $B = A^N$ without using exponentiation. We could accomplish this using the DO statement:

```
    B = 1.0
    DO 50 JOE = 1, N
50  B = B*A
```

The variable JOE is not used in the procedure itself, and in this case, the DO statement is used simply to perform Statement 50 N times.

Example 4

In Examples 1-3, we repeated only one statement in the DO loop. It is possible to have any number of statements in the DO loop. For instance, if we wanted to compute

$$NSUM = 1 + 2 + \cdots + 20$$
$$NSQU = 1^2 + 2^2 + \cdots + 20^2$$
$$NCUB = 1^3 + 2^3 + \cdots + 20^3$$

we could have the following statements:

```
    NSUM = 0
    NSQU = 0
    NCUB = 0
    DO 7 I = 1, 20
    NSUM = NSUM + I
    NSQU = NSQU + I**2
7   NCUB = NCUB + I**3
```

This would cause all three of the statements following the DO statement to be performed for I = 1, 2, ···, 20.

■ DO Loops in the Flowchart

Probably the most common way to represent a DO loop in a flowchart is to write out the entire process as shown in Fig. 6-1.
There is, however, an alternative method which shows the DO statement itself. For the DO statement, we use a box like this:

or

To show the range of the DO statement, we write the statement
number of the last statement in the DO loop in a small circle after
the last instruction box in the loop. Then, to indicate that the
loop is performed repeatedly, we use a dotted line to show the return path. In this notation, the statement

DO y I = a, b, c

would be flowcharted as shown in Fig. 6-2.

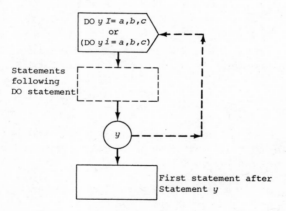

FIGURE 6-2

Compare this with Fig. 6-1. Figure 6-3 shows how this notation
could be used to draw the flowchart for Example 4.

■ Restrictions on the Use of the DO Statement

There are a few restrictions that must be observed when using the
DO statement. The purpose of these restrictions is to ensure that the
value of the control variable is controlled only by the DO statement.

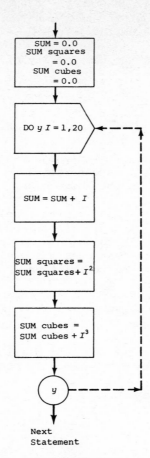

FIGURE 6-3
Flowchart for Example 4

Rule 1: We must not use any statements within the range of
the DO statement that alter the value of the control variable.

This would prevent us from writing statements such as

```
    DO 1 J = 5, 10
    J = 5
  1 M = M + 1
```

Of course, it is easy to see how this might lead to trouble if it
were allowable. In this example, the loop would never terminate
because the control variable never reaches the final value.

It is perfectly alright to use the control variable (as we did
in Example 1) as long as we do not have any statements in the DO
loop that alter its value.

Rule 2: We must not transfer control into the DO loop
from outside the loop.

This would exclude the possibility of such statements as

```
      GO TO 10
      DO 15 J = 1, 6
  10  N = N + J
  15  M = M*N
```

As before, this restriction simply ensures that the value of the
variable (J in this case) is controlled by the DO statement. It
obviously would not be in the above case.

The above restriction deals with transferring control *into* a
DO loop. Transferring control *out of* a DO loop is another matter.
It is frequently desirable to use control statements in a DO loop—
for performing a certain test over and over, for instance. This is
allowable, but there is one restriction which must be observed in
such instances:

Rule 3: The last statement in a DO loop must not be one
that causes transfer of control.[2]

This restriction causes no real difficulty, however, for it
may always be circumvented by using the CONTINUE statement.

The CONTINUE statement is a dummy statement which causes no
operation to occur, and consequently can be used anywhere in the
program without changing the effect of the program. Its real
usefulness, however, is for avoiding the situation described in
Rule 3 above. The form of the CONTINUE statement is simply

```
      CONTINUE
```

We shall use the following symbol to indicate this in a flowchart:

In many cases, the flowchart will not necessarily include the
CONTINUE box even though the computer program might have several
CONTINUE statements. This is because the programmer can often
write the flowchart, which gives the logic of the program, without
realizing that in FORTRAN such a statement will be needed. For
example, instead of using a control statement as the last statement
of a DO loop, we make it the second-to-last statement, and use a

---

[2]On some computers it is alright to have a logical IF statement as the last statement in a DO loop.

CONTINUE statement for the last statement. The CONTINUE statement corresponds merely to an arrow on the flowchart, rather than to a box.

Example 5

Suppose that we want to test to see if I is equal to 2, 5, 8, 11, 14, or 17, and suppose that we want to set J = I if I is one of the above numbers, and otherwise set J = 0.

Now, the restriction mentioned before would prevent the following from being acceptable, because an arithmetic IF statement would be the last statement in a DO loop:

```
 5   DO 10 J = 2, 17, 3
10   IF (J - I) 5, 15, 5
     J = 0
15   Next Statement
```

However, a slight modification using the CONTINUE statement resolves the problem:

```
     DO 10 J = 2, 17, 3
     IF (J - I) 10, 15, 10
10   CONTINUE
     J = 0
15   Next Statement
```

These statements perform the procedure indicated, and since the last statement in the DO loop is a CONTINUE statement, Rule 3 is not violated.

■ The DO Statement and Subscripted Variables

The DO statement is very useful in problems involving subscripted variables. Frequently, situations arise where we want to perform the same operation in some array, using all the elements in succession. The most common way to do this is to set up a program loop using the control variable of the DO loop as the subscript of an array. Thus, the loop will be performed repeatedly while the subscript is incremented.

Example 6

Suppose we have an array X consisting of the numbers X(1), X(2), ..., X(50). To set Y equal to the sum of these numbers using a DO statement, we could have

```
     Y = 0.0
     DO 1000 I = 1, 50
1000 Y = Y + X(I)
```

Example 7

In Chapter 5, we saw how to find the average and variance of
N numbers X(1), ..., X(N). This procedure can be somewhat simpli-
fied by using the DO statement:

```
        SSQ = 0.0
        SUM = 0.0
        DO 5 I = 1, N
        SUM = SUM + X(I)
     5  SSQ = SSQ + X(I)**2
        AN = FLOAT(N)
        AV = SUM/AN
```

After finding the sum of the numbers X by performing Statement 5 *N*
times, the average is obtained by dividing by *N* (remembering to
convert to a floating-point number). The variance can be computed:

```
        VAR = SSQ/AN - AV**2
```

Example 8

Another use of the DO statement in connection with subscripted
variables is for making repeated comparisons.

Suppose we want to see if the number *A* is equal to any of the
numbers B(1), B(2), ..., B(10). We shall set J = 1 if it is and
J = 0 if it is not. A flowchart for this procedure is shown in
Fig. 6-4. This important procedure is called *table lookup* or
linear search.

This could be programmed in FORTRAN as

```
        DIMENSION  B(10)
        DO 10 I = 1, 10
        IF (A.EQ.B(I)) GO TO 20
    10  CONTINUE
        J = 0
        GO TO 30
    20  J = 1
    30  Next Statement
```

Notice that we use a CONTINUE statement to avoid having the IF
statement as the last statement in the DO loop.

Example 9

We can use a similar method for the problem given in Example 4
of Chapter 5, where we set XMAX equal to the maximum of X(1), ...,
X(N). Using the DO statement, this could be written:

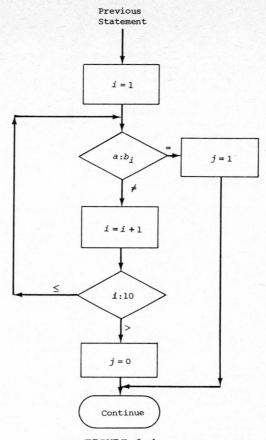

FIGURE 6-4
Flowchart for Example 8

```
       DIMENSION  X(100)
       XMAX = X(1)
       DO 10 I = 2, N
       IF (X(I).GT.XMAX) XMAX = X(I)
   10  CONTINUE
```

■ Nested DO Loops

    A DO statement involves a group of one or more other state-
ments that form the range of the DO loop. It is possible to have
among these statements another complete DO loop, making a DO loop
within a DO loop. This situation is known as *nested DO loops*.
Using a bracket to denote a DO loop, we can represent this pic-
torially as

```
Outer DO loop ──▶  ⌈ ⌈   ◀── Inner DO loop
```

Each time control passes once through the outer DO loop, the inner DO loop will be completely performed.

Example 10

Say that we have a doubly subscripted array X consisting of

```
X(1, 1)    X(1, 2)    ...    X(1, 5)
X(2, 1)    X(2, 2)    ...    X(2, 5)
  .
  .
  .
X(10, 1)   X(10, 2)   ...    X(10, 5)
```

Now, suppose we want to find the sum of the numbers in each row of the array and store the sum of the Ith row in Y(I). So,

$$Y(I) = X(I, 1) + X(I, 2) + \cdots + X(I, 5)$$

And suppose we also want to set Z equal to the sum of all the numbers in the array X. Then,

$$Z = Y(1) + Y(2) + \cdots + Y(10)$$

This problem may be solved as shown in Fig. 6-5 using nested DO loops. Notice that the loop containing the statement

$$Y(I) = Y(I) + X(I, J)$$

is performed five times every time the outer loop is performed once. This can be put into FORTRAN, using two DO statements:

```
        DIMENSION  X(10,5), Y(10)
        Z = 0.0
        DO 20 I = 1, 10
        Y(I) = 0.0
        DO 10 J = 1, 5
   10   Y(I) = Y(I) + X(I, J)
   20   Z = Z + Y(I)
```

The second DO statement corresponds to the inner loop in the flowchart. The first DO statement corresponds to the outer loop. Statement 10 will be performed first with I = 1 and J = 1, then with I = 1 and J = 2, and so on until I = 1 and J = 5. Then it will be performed for I = 2 and J = 1, I = 2 and J = 2, etc., until finally I = 10 and J = 5.

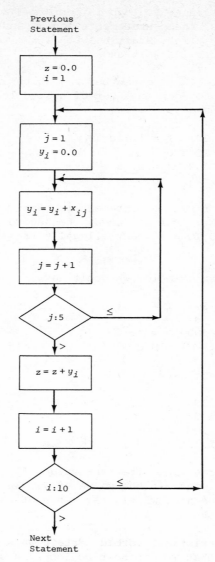

FIGURE 6-5
Flowchart for Example 10

Example 11

Two nested DO loops can end on the same statement. For instance, if we wanted to set each X(I, J) in the array of Example 10 equal to 0, we could have the statements

```
      DO 300 I = 1, 10
      DO 300 J = 1, 5
  300  X(I, J) = 0.0
```

As before, the inner DO loop is performed more often than the outer
DO loop. Thus, these statements would cause Statement 300 to be
executed fifty times, starting with I = 1 and J = 1, then I = 1 and
J = 2, etc., until I = 10 and J = 5.

The restrictions given before, which apply to single DO loops,
apply to *each* DO loop in a set of nested loops. So, for example,
we could not have

```
        DO 300  I = 1, 10
        GO TO 300
        DO 300  J = 1, 5
    300   X(I, J) = 0.0
```

As far as the first DO statement is concerned, the GO TO statement is alright. But as far as the second DO statement is concerned, the GO TO statement illegally transfers control to within
a DO loop.

As another example, we could have

```
        DO 300  I = 1, 10
        J = 0
        DO 300  J = 1, 5
    300   X(I, J) = 0.0
```

but we could not have

```
        DO 300  I = 1, 10
        I = 0
        DO 300  J = 1, 5
    300   X(I, J) = 0.0
```

In the first case, we alter the value of J *externally* through the
DO loop which controls the value of J. In the second case, we
alter the value of I *within the range* of the DO loop that varies I.
This violates Rule 1.

Such restrictions forbid certain ways of nesting DO loops.
We have seen that we can nest DO loops as shown in Fig. 6-6.

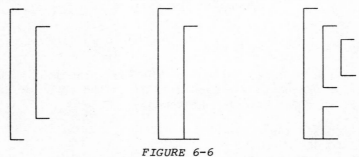

FIGURE 6-6
Some acceptable ways to nest DO loops

It is illegal, however, to try to nest DO loops as shown in Fig. 6-7. An attempt to execute such statements would amount to an illegal transfer of control into the range of a DO loop.

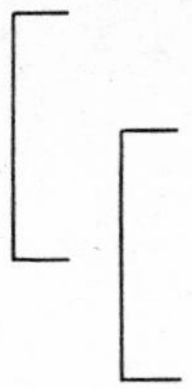

FIGURE 6-7
Unallowable "nested" DO loops

The following statements, then, would not be allowable

```
        DO 10 I = 1, 10
        DO 20 J = 1, 10
   10   A = A + 1.0
   20   B = B + 1.0
```

There is no sensible way to interpret the meaning of these statements. Of course, if we were to interchange Statements 10 and 20, there would be no problem of interpretation.

One final restriction is that we must use different control variables in DO statements forming nested DO loops. Actually, this is just to avoid the restriction that we cannot alter the variable of the DO statement within the DO loop. The following statements would be illegal:

```
        DO 5 I = 1, 5
        DO 5 I = 1, 10
    5   A = A + 1.0
```

■ A Exercises

1. Various FORTRAN statements are given below. Some are correct, but others violate a basic rule. If the statement is valid, mark a V next to it. Otherwise, make a suitable correction to make it valid.

   (a) DO 31 KXX = J, K, 3   (h) A(I, 3) = M2 + J
   (b) DO N K6 = S, J, 2   (i) DO 3 A = 1, N4A2, 2
   (c) DO 2 X = J, N, N   (j) DO 17 FEW = 1, N
   (d) DO 100 K = N, M, N   (k) DO 21 I = J, J, J
   (e) DO I = TWO TO 5   (l) DO 10 IX2 = N, N + M
   (f) DO 176 IJX2 = JC2K, LAST   (m) DO 3 IY = 10, 1
   (g) DO 21 I = 37   (n) DO 8 I = 1, 2, 3

2. Sequences of FORTRAN statements are given below. Some are valid and will be executed with no error. Others have errors.

2.—continued

If the statements are valid, mark a V next to them. Otherwise,
make the corrections necessary to make them valid.

(a)   DO 3 JIM = 1, 4, 2   (d)   DO 101 LIM = 1, N
```
        X = JIM                        X = A + B
        GO TO 4                        DO 9 LIM 2 = 1, M
      3 Y = X**2                  90   Y = X + Z
      4 Y = X**3/2.                9   CONTINUE
                                 101   A = 0.0
```

(b)   DO 100 J = 1, 10   (e)   DIMENSION X(100)
```
        X = J + 5                      DO 5 I = 1, 20
    100 GO TO 76                       ZZ = 5*I - 6
     76 CONTINUE                       J = ZZ
                                   5   X(J) = J - 4
```

(c)   DO 6 I = 1, 10   (f)   DO 22 K = 1, 20, 4
```
        DO 6 J = M, N, L               DO 22 L = 1, 16, 3
        X = J + I                      X = K
        Y = X**2                       Y = L - 8
      6 CONTINUE                       Z = X + Y
                                       IF(Z.GT.10.0) GO TO 12
                                  22   CONTINUE
                                  12   GO TO 9
```

3. After the following statements have been executed, what is the
value of K?

```
        DO 700 I = 1, 100
        X = I - 1
        DO 700 J = 1, 10
        Z = J + 4
        IF(X**2 - 2.0*X.EQ.Z) GO TO 600
    700 CONTINUE
        GO TO 800
    600 K = I + J
    800 CONTINUE
```

4. Write the FORTRAN statements to correspond to the accompanying
flowchart (page 137). Use a DO loop.

5. In the study of statistics, it is frequently necessary to calculate variance and standard deviation. We defined variance
on page 109. The standard deviation, S, is the square root of
the variance and is given by

$$S = \sqrt{\frac{\sum_{j=1}^{N} (X_j - \overline{X})^2}{N - 1}} = \sqrt{\frac{\sum_{j=1}^{N} X_j^2 - N\overline{X}^2}{N - 1}}$$

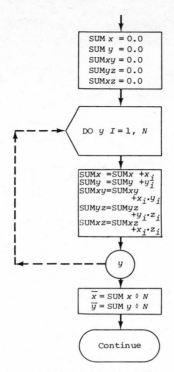

SUM x = 0.0
SUM y = 0.0
SUMxy = 0.0
SUMyz = 0.0
SUMxz = 0.0

DO y $I = 1$, N

SUMx = SUMx + x_i
SUMy = SUMy + y_i^i
SUMxy = SUMxy
    + $x_i \cdot y_i$
SUMyz = SUMyz
    + $y_i \cdot z_i$
SUMxz = SUMxz
    + $x_i \cdot z_i$

y

$\overline{x}$ = SUM $x \div N$
$\overline{y}$ = SUM $y \div N$

Continue

Flowchart for Exercise 4

5. —continued

where $\overline{X}$ is the mean. Write FORTRAN statements, using a DO
loop, which calculate the mean and standard deviation of an
array $X(1)$, ..., $X(N)$.

6. Assume that in 1975 the population figures for the United
States and Canada were 200,000,000 and 25,000,000, respectively. Assume also that the annual rate of growth for the
United States was 1.10% and for Canada 4.75%. If these growth
rates remain constant, will the population of Canada equal or
excel that of the United States in the next 100 years? In
what year will the population be equal? Construct a flowchart
to solve the problem. The flowchart should include a DO loop.

7. A deck of cards is punched with the following data:

Columns	1-5	ID	Student's identification number
Column	6	SEX	1 if male; 2 if female
Columns	7-8	HT	Height in inches
Columns	9-11	WT	Weight in pounds
Column	12	CLASS	1 if first year; 2 if second; etc.
Column	13	ATH	1-9; the higher the number, the greater the athletic ability

7.—continued

Write a program to determine how many prospective athletes
are in a school. A prospective football player must be a
male, of height greater than 60 inches, weight greater than
180 pounds, cannot be a freshman, and must have athletic
ability of 7 or more. Use a DO loop. Your output should
include a student's identification number.

8. Write a program to handle a person's bank checking account.
   Assume that for each deposit you have a card punched:

   Columns 1-3   NDEP   Deposit number starting with 001
   Columns 4-8   IDEP   5-digit number referring to the
                        depositer (does not change) as a
                        fixed-point constant
   Columns 9-16 DEP   Amount of deposit

   For each check you have a card punched:

   Columns 1-5   IDEP   Same as above
   Columns 6-9   NCHK   Check number
   Columns 10-17   AMT   Amount of check

   The first data card contains the following information:

   Columns 1-3   NUMDEP   Number of deposits to be read in
   Columns 4-6   NUMCHK   Number of checks to be read in
   Columns 7-14   BAL   Previous balance

   Write a program to input the above data and output the listing
   of your transactions. For sample input data, use your own
   checkbook and check records.

9. Modify the program written in Exercise 8 to handle not only
   your checks and deposits but also anyone else's. Rather
   than count the number of deposits and checks, add a test at
   the end of the data deck to stop the computer from reading
   cards. This can be done by assigning a number of 999 in the
   space on the last card where NUMDEP is and making a similar
   test for the checks.

■ B Exercises

1. The following results for the sum of the first *n* numbers, the
   sum of the squares of the first *n* numbers, and the sum of the
   cubes of the first *n* numbers are proven in nearly every elementary algebra text:

   $$1 + 2 + 3 + \cdots + n = 1/2\,[n(n + 1)]$$
   $$1^2 + 2^2 + 3^2 + \cdots + n^2 = 1/6\,[n(n + 1)(2n + 1)]$$
   $$1^3 + 2^3 + 3^3 + \cdots + n^3 = (1 + 2 + 3 + \cdots + n)^2$$

1.—continued

  Suppose, however, that we did not know this and we wanted to calculate the three sums. Write the FORTRAN statements to do this using a single DO loop.

2. Write a flowchart to correspond to the FORTRAN statements in Exercise 1.

3. Given the three sides of a triangle, a, b, c. The area is given by Heron's formula to be

$$AREA = \sqrt{s(s - a)(s - b)(s - c)}$$

  where $s = 1/2(a + b + c)$.

  (a) Write the flowchart to input three sides of a triangle, calculate the area, and output the answer.

  (b) Generalize your flowchart to calculate the areas for n triangles.

4. The atmospheric pressure, p, in inches of mercury, is given approximately by $p = 29.9(10)^{-0.093m}$, where m is the altitude in miles above sea level. Write a program to give the pressure at intervals of 1/4 mile starting from 1 mile below sea level to 10 miles above sea level.

5. A popular example of elementary probability theory is to determine the probability that 2 people out of a randomly selected group of m people have the same birthday. Ignoring leap years, the probability of any 2 people not having the same birthday is 364/365. The probability that a third person's birthday will differ from the first two is 363/365; a fourth person's is 362/365, etc. For 10 people we have 9 such fractions to be multiplied together to obtain the probability that all 10 birthdays are different. Write a program to generate the probabilities that 2 people out of a group of m people have the same birthday, where $m > 2$. (If you have never seen this problem, the results may surprise you.)

6. A deck of data cards is punched as follows:

Columns	1-5	IDEN	Student's identification number
Column	6	COLL	Student's college—6 colleges, numbered 1-6
Columns	7-11	GPA	Student's grade average as a number; 4.00 is the highest and 0.00 is the lowest
Column	12	CLASS	Class: 1 for freshman; 2 for sophomore; etc; student is a senior (graduating) if he is a fourth year or higher student

6.—continued

Write a program to input the above data and output the graduating students who are to graduate with honors (a GPA of 3.5 or more).

7. Modify Exercise 6 to output all the graduating seniors according to rank in class starting with the top GPA and going down.

8. An outdoor movie screen is 15 feet above eye level and is itself 40 feet high. The best spot to park your car is at the point P, where the angle (α) your eye makes with the screen is the largest. Let x be the distance measured from the screen. It can be shown that the tangent of α is given by the formula

$$\tan \alpha = \frac{40x}{x^2 + 825}$$

The value of x that maximizes $\tan \alpha$ also maximizes x. Write a program to find this value, starting with $x = 0$ and incrementing x by 1. For each increment of x, $\tan \alpha$ should increase until it reaches the desired maximum. When $\tan \alpha$ starts to decrease, the problem is solved, correct to the nearest foot.

Chapter

7

Input and Output: Part II

In this chapter, we shall present other forms of the READ, WRITE, and FORMAT statements. We shall also discuss other statements that may be used for obtaining input and output data from a computer.

■ Repeat Specifications in Field Descriptors

Consider the statements

```
      READ(2, 10) A, B, C, D
  10  FORMAT(F5.0, F5.0, F5.0, F5.0)
```

In this case, a series of identical field descriptors come one after another in the FORMAT statement. In such cases, there is a shorter way of writing the FORMAT statement. This consists of FORMAT statements using repeat specifications. In the statement

```
  10  FORMAT(4F5.0)
```

the number 4 is called a repeat count. It means that the F5.0 field descriptor which follows is to be repeated four times. So, both the above FORMAT statements mean exactly the same thing. The repeat specification may be used with any of the field descriptors we have mentioned. For example, the statements

```
      READ(1, 54) I1, I2, J, A1, A2, B1, B2, B3
  54  FORMAT(3I4, 2F10.0, 3E7.0)
```

mean that the first three fields read (I1, I2, J) are read with an I4 field descriptor, the following two fields (A1, A2) use an F10.0 field descriptor, and the last three fields (B1, B2, B3) use an E7.0 field descriptor. This form of the FORMAT statement is a shorthand way of writing

```
  54  FORMAT(I4, I4, I4, F10.0, F10.0, E7.0, E7.0, E7.0)
```

Suppose now that we have a whole group of field descriptors that is repeated. For instance, in the statement

```
5  FORMAT(I6, F10.2, I6, F10.2, I6, F10.2)
```

the group I6, F10.2 is repeated three times. This can also be
abbreviated, using a group repeat count. We place parentheses
around the whole group and then we write the repeat factor in
front of the parentheses to specify how many times the group is
to be repeated. This would be written

```
5  FORMAT(3(I6, F10.2))
```

The use of repeat counts in a FORMAT statement is quite general;
repeated descriptors of groups of descriptors can be used anywhere,
and the meaning will be the same as if the whole group were written
out the long way. The following are some further examples of repeat specifications:

```
12  FORMAT(I5, F5.2, 4(I3, E4.0))
55  FORMAT(3(I2, I4), 3F10.0)
 7  FORMAT(2(I3, F5.1, E8.0, I4), I2, 2(F5.0, I2))
14  FORMAT(F11.4, 2(I2, F6.0, I3), 3F5.2)
```

■ The Slash (/) in the FORMAT Statement

The slash (/) means division in an arithmetic FORTRAN expression. In a FORMAT statement, it has a different meaning—to skip
to the beginning of the next card (for input) or the next line (for
output). The slash can be used anywhere in the FORMAT statement.
Commas are used optionally around the slash to separate it from
adjacent field descriptors. Thus, the statements

```
    WRITE(2, 11) X, NED, ZAP
11  FORMAT(F10.1/I10/F10.1)
```

or

```
11  FORMAT(F10.1,/, I10,/, F10.0)
```

mean to write X with an F10.1 field, skip to the next line, write
NED with an I10 field, skip to the next line, and write ZAP with an
F10.1 field. So, if X = 12.2, NED = 100, and ZAP = 520.8, the
resulting output would be

```
12.2
 100
520.8
```

We can also skip more than one line, using the slash. There
are two ways to do this. The first way is just to write a series
of slashes in a row, such as ////. The second way is to use a
repeat factor and enclose the slash in parentheses: $n(/)$. For
instance, 4(/) means the same thing as ////. In both cases, each
time a slash is encountered it means to skip to the beginning of
the next line (or card). For example,

```
        WRITE(2, 3) M, L
    3   FORMAT(I5////I5)      or      3   FORMAT(I5,////,I5)
```

or

```
    3   FORMAT(I5, 4(/), I5)
```

means to write M under an I5 format, skip to the beginning of the
next line, skip to the beginning of the next line three more times,
then write L with an I5 format. Thus, three lines in all are
skipped between the two numbers printed. Notice that *n* slashes
means that *n* - 1 lines are skipped between the numbers printed.
This is because the slash means "skip to the beginning of the next
line," and not "skip a line." Note this difference. For example,
if N = 11 and M = 22,

```
        WRITE(2, 1) N, M
    1   FORMAT(I5/I5)
```

will print out

```
        11
        22
```

There is one slash, but no lines are skipped *between* the two numbers
printed; the second number is printed on the *next* line.

    When used for input, the slash means to skip to the beginning
of a new card. This enables us to read more than one card with a
single READ statement. For instance, suppose that A(I) and B(I)
are punched in columns 1-10 and 11-20 of a card. To read three
such cards and store the values read in the first three elements
of each array, we could use the statements

```
        READ(1, 7) A(1), B(1), A(2), B(2), A(3), B(3)
    7   FORMAT(2F10.0/2F10.0/2F10.0)
```

Then A(1) and B(1) are read from the first card, each with an F10.0
format. The slash means to ignore the rest of the first card and
go on to the beginning of the next card. Then A(2) and B(2) are
read from the second card, and A(3) and B(3) are read from the third
card. Actually, we can shorten this FORMAT statement somewhat, using
a repeat specification:

```
    7   FORMAT(2(2F10.2/), 2F10.2)
```

    Of course, we could do the same thing by performing the READ
statement three times, since each time the READ statement is executed, a new card is read. In this case, we could have put

```
        DO 10 I = 1, 3
    10  READ(1, 7) A(I), B(I)
    7   FORMAT(2F10.0)
```

In many cases, however, the use of the slash is more convenient.

■ Output on Punched Cards

We mentioned earlier that output from a computer can be in the form of punched cards. This is often very desirable since the data can then be immediately used in subsequent programs. Let us assume that the unit number in the WRITE statement for the punch is 7. The FORTRAN statements

```
        WRITE(7, 10) X
    10  FORMAT(10X, F10.4)
```

will result in a card being punched. This card will have the first 10 columns blank and the value of X punched in columns 11-20 with four decimal places. The rest of the card will be blank.

Since punched cards have only 80 columns, care must be taken not to exceed this field length. For example, the statements

```
        WRITE(2, 100) A, B, C
    100 FORMAT(3F40.8)
```

are correct, but the statement

```
        WRITE(7, 100) A, B, C
```

could not punch A, B, and C on a single card.

■ Alternate to the H Field Descriptor

One of the most time-consuming aspects of writing a program comes in the writing of the FORMAT statements using Hollerith specifications. At one time, this was the only way to obtain printed headings. This is still a satisfactory method and has the advantage that it will work in all FORTRAN systems. However, other convenient methods are now being used. Unfortunately, they are not uniform from computer to computer. One such method is to use single quote marks in the FORMAT statements. Everything between the quote marks is simply printed out as is. Other computer systems use aster-isks. Before attempting this, check the instruction manual for your computer.

For example,

```
        WRITE(2, 500)
    500 FORMAT(' THE ANSWER IS AS FOLLOWS')
```

results in the message

        THE ANSWER IS AS FOLLOWS

being printed out. But if one desires a quote mark to be printed, the H field must be used. *This is a superior method, since miscount of n in nH field is a very common error.* For the remainder of this book, we shall use quote marks for the majority of the output headings and messages.

■ Implied DO Loops in the Variable List

Consider the statement

READ(1, 5) X(1), X(2), X(3), X(4), X(5), X(6), X(7), X(8)

In this statement, we are reading in the first eight elements of the array X. Obviously, it is a bit tedious to have to explicitly write out each element of the array that is to be read. It would be considerably more tedious if we wanted to read the first 100 values of an array in a similar fashion. Fortunately, however, there is a method in FORTRAN that solves this problem. The notation is somewhat similar to the DO statement, and is called the *implied DO loop*. This is used only in the list of variables in a READ or WRITE statement (and in the DATA statement, which we shall discuss later). For a one-dimensional array, the form is

(Name(I), $I = m_1$, m_2, m_3)

where Name is any array name; I is any integer variable name; and m_1 (initial value), m_2 (terminal value), and m_3 (increment) are integer constants or variables. The last of these, m_3, can be omitted and assumed to be 1. When this form is encountered on the list of an input or output statement, the following occurs:

1. First, the variable I is set equal to m_1, and the array element Name (I) is read or written.

2. Second, m_3 is added to I.

3. Third, I is compared to m_2. If I is greater than m_2, the implied DO loop is finished. Otherwise, Name(I) is read or written, and then the process goes back to the second step.

In other words, writing (Name(I), $I = m_1$, m_2, m_3) in the list of variables of a READ or WRITE statement is like writing Name(m_1), Name$(m_1 + m_3)$, Name$(m_1 + 2m_3)$, ..., Name$(m_1 + nm_3)$, where $m_1 + nm_3 \geq m_2$.

Suppose we want to read in a value for a variable Z; then the values for the subscripted variables A(3), A(5), A(7), A(9), A(11), A(13), A(15), A(17); and finally the value of the variable Q. We could use the statement

READ(1, 87) Z, (A(IDEN), IDEN = 3, 18, 2), Q

After reading Z, the integer variable IDEN is set to 3 and A(3) is read. Then 2 is added to IDEN, and since IDEN is still less than 18, A(IDEN) [that is, A(5)] is read. IDEN is then incremented again

by 2, and A(7) is read, and so on until A(17) has been read. After
this, we are through reading values for A, and so Q is read. Of
course, an appropriate FORMAT statement must be used. In this case,
since ten values in all (Z, 8 A's, Q) are being read, if they were
all punched with an F5.0 format, we could use the statement

      87   FORMAT(10F5.0)

As always, there is one field descriptor for each variable.

    As mentioned before, if the increment m_3 is omitted from the
implied DO loop form, it is assumed to be 1, just as with the DO
statement. So, to rewrite the statement

      READ(1, 5) X(1), X(2), X(3), X(4), X(5), X(6), X(7), X(8)

using this form, it would suffice to put

      READ(1, 5) (X(JIK), JIK = 1, 8)

The limits in the implied DO loop can be integer variables as well
as constants, provided, of course, that their values are valid as
subscripts for the array involved. The above statement, for instance, is equivalent to

      L = 1
      LL = 8
      READ(1, 5) (X(JIK), JIK = L, LL)

    More than one variable name can appear in the implied DO loop.
In the more general case, the form is

      (Name1(I), Name2(I), ..., Name$N(I)$, $I = m_1$, m_2, m_3)

This form is equivalent to writing out Name1(m_1), Name2(m_1), ...,
Name$N(m_1)$, Name1$(m_1 + m_3)$, Name2$(m_1 + m_3)$, ... That is, the
implied DO loop is performed for all variables enclosed in parentheses. For instance, if A, B, and C are arrays, each with 7 elements, we can write out their values in the order A(1), B(1), C(1),
A(2), B(2), C(2), ..., C(7) by using the statement

      WRITE(2, 87) (A(I), B(I), C(I), I = 1, 7)

    There is one further simplification that is allowed in reading
or writing an array: If the whole array is to be read or written,
it is necessary to put only the name of the array in the variable
list. By the "whole array" we mean all the elements of the array,
as defined by the DIMENSION statement. If an array YYY is declared
by

      DIMENSION YYY(10)

then the whole array is the list of variables YYY(1), YYY(2), YYY(3),
..., YYY(10). In this case, the above rule means that putting just

the array name YYY in the list of an input or output statement is the same as writing out all the elements, or using an implied DO list which specified all the elements. Thus,

READ(1, 2) YYY

would mean the same thing as

READ(1, 2) (YYY(I), I = 1, 10)

Doubly subscripted arrays can also be handled with an implied DO loop. The general form in this case is

$$((\text{Name}(I, J), I = m_1, m_2, m_3), J = n_1, n_2, n_3)$$

where Name is the name of a two-dimensional array; I, J are integer variables; and m_1, m_2, m_3, n_1, n_2, n_3 are integer constants or variables. This form is similar to a pair of nested DO loops, with the innermost variable varying most rapidly. That is, the above form is equivalent to writing out

$$\text{Name}(m_1, n_1), \text{Name}(m_1 + m_3, n_1), \text{Name}(m_1 + 2m_3, n_1),$$
$$\dots, \text{Name}(m_2, n_1), \text{Name}(m_1, n_1 + n_3), \text{Name}(m_1 + m_3,$$
$$n_1 + n_3), \dots, \text{Name}(m_2, n_1 + n_3), \dots, \text{Name}(m_1, n_2),$$
$$\text{Name}(m_1 + m_3, n_2), \dots, \text{Name}(m_2, n_2)$$

In other words, J is first set to n_1, and then the whole inner loop is performed just as in the one-dimensional case. Then J is incremented by n_3, and if J is not greater than n_2, the inner implied DO loop is performed again, and so on until finally J is greater than n_2. If either m_3 or n_3 is omitted, it is assumed to be 1.

For example, the statement

READ(1, 3) ((A(N, M), N = 1, 2), M = 1, 3)

is equivalent to

READ(1, 3) A(1, 1), A(2, 1), A(1, 2), A(2, 2),
1   A(1, 3), A(2, 3)

An implied DO loop does not, however, have to apply to both subscripts of a two-dimensional array. We can vary only one subscript, if desired, while holding the other one fixed. For example,

WRITE(2, 17) (MAT(L, J), J = 2, 10, 2)

would write out the values of

MAT(L, 2), MAT(L, 4), MAT(L, 6), MAT(L, 8), MAT(L, 10)

(The variable L is understood to have been previously defined.)

As with singly subscripted arrays, if we put just the array
name of a doubly subscripted array in the variable list of a READ
or WRITE statement, this automatically specifies all the elements
of the array, as defined in the DIMENSION statement. In this case,
the first subscript varies the most rapidly. Thus, if XEL is a
doubly subscripted array defined by the statement

        DIMENSION XEL(2, 4)

then if we put just the name XEL in an input-output variable list,
it would mean the same thing as if we had written

        ((XEL(I, J), I = 1, 2), J = 1, 4)

So, if we had the statement

        READ(1, 4) XEL

it would read in all the elements of the array XEL in the order

            XEL(1, 1), XEL(2, 1), XEL(1, 2), XEL(2, 2), XEL(1, 3),
            ..., XEL(2, 4)

The implied DO loop notation can be used advantageously with
the slash and repeated field descriptors for reading or writing
subscripted variables. To see how this is done, suppose we want
to read in the values of a doubly subscripted array called Z. If
Z(1, 1), Z(2, 1), ..., Z(7, 1) are punched on the first card, each
with an F10.0 format, we can read these values with the statements

        READ(1, 5) (Z(I, 1), I = 1, 7)
      5 FORMAT(7F10.0)

If the next four cards are similarly punched, the second card containing the values of Z(1, 2), Z(2, 2), ..., Z(7, 2), the third
card containing the values of Z(1, 3), Z(2, 3), ..., Z(7, 3), and
so on, we could read all five cards with the statements

        READ(1, 5) ((Z(I, J), I = 1, 7), J = 1, 5)
      5 FORMAT(5(7F10.0/))

These statements mean that seven numbers are read from the first
card and stored in Z(1, 1), Z(2, 1), ..., Z(7, 1). Now there are
still ten blank columns left over on the first card, so the slash
means to go on and read the next number from the second card.
Notice that the group repeat count 5 repeats the slash as well as
the 7F10.0, so this process continues for all five cards. If the
array Z were dimensioned to be exactly 7 X 5, that is, if it were
declared by the statement

        DIMENSION Z(7, 5)

then we could omit the implied DO loops and just write the array
name Z in the READ statement

```
        READ(1, 5) Z
```

Since the whole array is being read, this would mean the same thing.

As another example, suppose that X, JOHN, and ZIP are one-dimensional arrays, and we want to print out X(1), JOHN(1), and ZIP(1) on the first print line, X(2), JOHN(2), and ZIP(2) on the second print line, and so on for all 20 values of each array. This can be done, using a DO statement:

```
        DO 23 I = 1, 20
   23   WRITE(2, 7) X(I), JOHN(I), ZIP(I)
    7   FORMAT(F10.5, I10, F10.5)
```

We could do this just as well using an implied DO loop notation:

```
        WRITE(2, 7) (X(I), JOHN(I), ZIP(I), I = 1, 20)
    7   FORMAT(F10.5, I10, F10.5)
```

In this example, the number of field specifications (3) and the number of variables (20) are not the same. The rules governing this situation are given next.

When the list is shorter than the FORMAT specifications, the additional numeric field specifications are ignored. But any field specifications that are not numeric are executed up to either the last right-hand parenthesis or the next numeric field specification, whichever comes first. The statements

```
        WRITE(2, 8) A, B
    8   FORMAT(F20.4,/,F20.4,//,F20.4)
```

will result in the following output: The value of A is printed out according to the field specification of F20.4; the printer skips to the next line; the value of B is printed in an identical field; and then the printer skips to a new line twice (leaving one actual line skipped) before execution of the original input or output statement is terminated. The DO loop

```
        DO 100 I = 1, 20
  100   WRITE(2, 101) X(I)
  100   FORMAT(2F15.4)
```

is another example of having more field specifications than variables. In this case, there will be 20 lines of print, with one value of X on each line.

If there are more variables in the list than specifications in the FORMAT statement, the format control will revert to one of two places determined as follows:

Case 1: If there are no nested parentheses, control reverts to the start of the FORMAT statement.

Case 2: If there are nested parentheses, control reverts
to the right-most left parenthesis.

In both of these cases, every time the control reverts to a
new position, the system demands a new record start (that is, read
another card, print on a new line).

The statements written as the implied DO loop

```
      WRITE(2, 101) (X(I), I = 1, 20)
  101 FORMAT(2F10.5)
```

will now result in 10 lines of printed output. The statements

```
      WRITE(2, 200) I, A, B, C, D, E
  200 FORMAT(I10, (F10.3))
```

will print the value of I according to the field specification I10
and then the values of A, B, C, D, and E according to the field
specification F10.3. The value of A will be on the same line as
the value of I, but the other values will be on separate lines.
Note that A will be in columns 11-20 while B, C, D, and E will be
in columns 1-10.

■ Other Forms of Input-Output[1]

There are several other statements that can be used for input
and output. These vary with the computer and so care must be
exercised before attempting to use them. If you understand the
principle behind the READ and WRITE statements discussed in the
preceding sections, there will be no difficulty in adapting the
statements to be presented here.

The READ Statement. Another form of READ statement can also
be used to read data into the computer. Its general form is

```
      READ f, var₁, var₂, ..., varₙ
```

where f is a number referring to a FORMAT statement and var_1,
var_2, ..., var_n are a list of n variables. Notice that a comma
is inserted between the format number and the first variable name.
No unit number is specified—the card reader is implied by the
form of the statement. Several examples of this statement together with a FORMAT statement are listed in Table 7-1.

---

[1]The statements presented here are not necessarily ANSI standard FORTRAN. They are, however, still very commonly used and will
work on most computer systems.

TABLE 7-1. Examples of READ Statements.

Statement	Explanation
READ 6, A 6 FORMAT(10X, F10.2)	*A variable A is read into the computer. The variable is punched on a card in columns 11-20.*
READ 100, YES, NO 100 FORMAT(F20.8/I3)	*Two variables YES and NO are read into the computer. YES is on the first card in columns 1-20 and NO is on the next card in columns 1-3.*
READ 20, (ARRAY (I), I = 1, 40) 20 FORMAT(7F10.3)	*Forty values of the variable ARRAY are read in. They are punched 7 to a card with field widths of 10. A total of 6 cards are read, 7 values from each of the first 5 cards and 5 from the last card.*
DO 20 I = 1, 40 20 READ 30, ARRAY (I) 30 FORMAT(7F10.3)	*Again, 40 values of the variable ARRAY are read. This time 40 data cards are needed. (Why?)*

The PRINT Statement. For output, the PRINT statement can sometimes be used. It is analogous to the WRITE statement we learned before; however, the unit is assumed to be the printer, and hence need not be specified in the statement. Its general form is

$$\text{PRINT } f, \text{ var}_1, \text{ var}_2, \ldots, \text{ var}_n$$

where f is a statement number referring to a FORMAT statement and var_1, var_2, $\ldots$, var_n are a list of variables to be printed out. A few examples of this statement in conjunction with a FORMAT statement are given in Table 7-2.

The PUNCH Statement. An alternate FORTRAN statement for obtaining punched cards for output is the PUNCH statement. The general form of it is

$$\text{PUNCH } f, \text{ var}_1, \text{ var}_2, \ldots, \text{ var}_n$$

where f refers to a FORMAT statement number and var_1, var_2, $\ldots$, var_n are a list of variables to be punched.

TABLE 7-2.   *Examples of PRINT Statements.*

Statement	Explanation
PRINT 1000, A, B, C, I, J, K 1000 FORMAT(3F20.3, I4, I5, I6)	*The values of 6 variables A, B, C, I, J, K are printed out; A, B, C take 20 spaces each; I, J, K take 4, 5, 6 spaces each, respectively.*
PRINT 7, X, Y 7 FORMAT(1H1, 20X, 3HX =, 1F6.2, 10X, 3HY =, F6.2)	*First, the printer skips to a new page, 20 columns are skipped, the characters X = are printed, then the value of X is printed. Then 10 columns are skipped and the characters Y = are printed. Next, the value of Y is printed.*

For example,

```
    PUNCH 101, LIST, ARRAY
101   FORMAT(I3, F10.2)
```

will result in the values of the two variables LIST and ARRAY being punched on a card according to the form as specified in Statement 101.

■ A Exercises

1. Examples are given below of input-output statements. If the statement is valid, mark a V next to it; if not, make a suitable correction to make it valid.

    (a)   READ(1, 2) JUMP, OVER
          2 FORMAT(10X, I6, 2X, F10.8)

    (b)   WRITE(2, 90) THE, ANSWER
         90 FORMAT(25X, ////, 5X, 2F11.3)

    (c)   WRITE(2, 80)
         80 FORMAT(1H1, 20X, 14H THE ANSWER IS)

    (d)   READ(1, 1) I, (X(J), J = 1, I)
          1 FORMAT(I8/ (8F10.2))

    (e)   WRITE(2, 30) ALPHA, BETA, GO
         30 FORMAT(4F10.8)

1.—continued

(f)   READ(1, 10) X, Y, ZZ
     10 FORMAT(2F10.0)

(g)   DIMENSION X(10, 100)
           WRITE(2, 800) ((X(I, J), I = 1, 4), J = 1, 60)
   800 FORMAT(10X, 4F30.8)

(h)   N = 4
           DIMENSION X(N)
           READ(1, 11) (X(I), I = 1, 2)
    11 FORMAT(10F4.2)

(i)   DIMENSION X(20), Y(20)
     7 FORMAT(F8.2)
           DO 12 J = 1, 20, 2
    12 READ(1, 7) X(J)
           DO 5 J = 1, 20
     5 Y(J) = X(J)*X(J)

2. Below are a few examples of the READ statement. Determine how many data cards are actually used for each case.

(a)   READ(1, 2) A, C, B, D
     2 FORMAT(3F10.4)

(b)   READ(1, 30) I, J, X, Y, Z
    30 FORMAT(I3, I4/2F10.2/F20.8)

(c)   DO 10 I = 1, 4
           DO 10 J = 1, 4
    10 READ(1, 11) X(I, J)
    11 FORMAT(2F10.6)

(d)   READ(1, 100) (X(I), I = 1, 19)
   100 FORMAT(6F10.3)

(e)   READ(1, 99) (Y(I), I = 1, 20)
    99 FORMAT(4F8.2/3F8.1/2F10.2/(3F10.3))

(f)   READ(1, 10) ((ARRAY (I, J), I = 1, 10), J = 1, 9)
    10 FORMAT(7F10.4)

3. Write the FORTRAN statements to correspond to the flowchart in Fig. 1-13.

4. Write the FORTRAN statements to correspond to the accompanying flowchart.

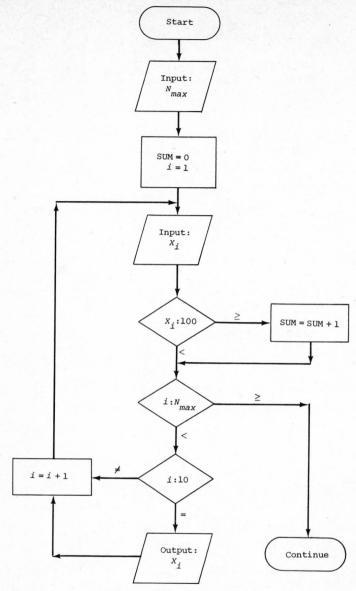

Flowchart for Exercise 4

5. Write the FORTRAN statements that will result in the following inputs or outputs:

(a) Skip to a new page, skip 10 lines, output the values of X and Y in a field F20.8.

(b) Skip 5 lines, skip 20 spaces, print the heading X-VALUE, skip 10 spaces, print the heading Y-VALUE, skip a line,

5. (b)—continued

> then print the values of X and Y under the headings according to a field of F20.4.

(c) Assume a 132 column printer. The 20 values of the two arrays X and Y are to be printed with headings X-ARRAY and Y-ARRAY. The arrays are to be centered on the page.

(d) Read in 800 values of Z into an array. The data are punched 8 to a card, each value is 10 columns long.

(e) The variable array Z is to be read in from punched cards, with 1 value per card. Each card is punched according to a field E20.4. The last card has -.999E+3 in this field. This is *not* a data card, but will be used to control the input statement. There are fewer than 1,000 values of Z. Write the FORTRAN to input the array and let *N* be the number of cards read in.

(f) Output on a printer according to format F30.4 the values just read into the computer in part e. Make appropriate headings and include the subscript along with the variable.

6. Write the FORTRAN statements to read in 30 values of X and Y; find their sum, SUMXY; their difference, DIFXY; and their products, PRDXY. The output is to be both in tabled form and punched cards.

7. Write the FORTRAN statements to input three numbers, N, A1, and D. Then calculate

$$SN = \frac{N}{2}\left[2\,(A1) \;+\; (N \,-\, 1)\,D\right]$$

and output the results. This is to be repeated until a value of N is input that is either 0 or negative.

■ B Exercises

1. A hallway 6 feet wide meets another that is 4 feet wide at a right angle. What is the longest length of a perfectly straight ladder that can be carried around the corner? It can be shown that the length *L* is given in terms of *x* as

$$L = x + \frac{6x}{\sqrt{x^2 - 16}}$$

Find *L* correct to the nearest 0.1 foot be setting *x* = 4.1 and incrementing it until the maximum *L* is found. Have your output include a sketch of the problem to be solved as shown in the accompanying mock printout.

1.—continued

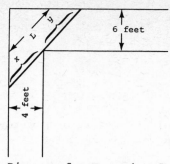

Diagram for Exercise 1

LADDER PROBLEM FIND LONGEST LENGTH TO FIT AROUND CORNER

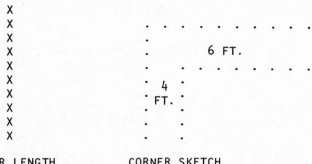

LADDER LENGTH   CORNER SKETCH

Possible Printout for Exercise 1

2. A company keeps its monthly billing statements on computer cards. On each card, the following data is punched:

Columns	1-20	Person's name	(To be ignored in input-output for now)
Columns	21-25	NUMB	5-digit account number
Columns	26-31	AMTOLD	Amount of money owed
Columns	32-37	AMTPD	Amount paid this month

To figure out a new balance for each person, the following equation is used:

$$BAL = AMTOLD(1.015) - AMTPD$$

Write a program to read in any number of cards and print a statement for each card read. This statement will read (for a typical case)

2.—continued

ACCT. NO.   OLD BALANCE   AMT. PAID   NEW BALANCE

05213 $126.00 $50.00 $77.89

THANK YOU FOR YOUR PROMPT PAYMENT.   NEXT PAYMENT IS DUE
BY THE FIRST OF THE MONTH.

If no amount was paid, the new balance is still figured, but a
message is printed warning what happens to people who do not
pay their bills.   If the old balance was 0, nothing is output.

3. Generalize Exercise 1 for any two hallways *a* and *b* feet wide.

4. The Pythagorean theorem states that the sum of the squares of
the sides of a right-angled triangle is equal to the square of
the hypotenuse.   The most common such triangle is the one whose
sides are 3, 4, and 5.   Other such triangles are 5, 12, 13;
7, 24, 25; and 8, 15, 17.   There are, of course, an infinite
number of such triangles.   To generate these, the following formulas can be used:

$$\text{One side:} \quad X = m^2 - n^2$$
$$\text{Other side:} \quad Y = 2mn$$
$$\text{Hypotenuse:} \quad Z = m^2 + n^2$$

where *n* is any positive integer and *m* is any integer larger
than *n*.   You can readily verify that, using the above, one
does obtain a triangle that satisfies the Pythagorean theorem.

Write a program to construct a table of 100 such triangles.
Since *m* and *n* are arbitrary, take *n* = 1, let *m* start with
m = 2 and increment it by 1.   Your output should include an
appropriate table heading as well as a listing of *m*, *n*, *X*,
Y, and *Z*.

5. The results of an English examination are punched on cards as
follows:

Columns 1-20   Name (not used in this problem)
Columns 21-22   Score on test—a 2-digit integer from
                        0 to 99 inclusive

Write a program to draw a bar graph like the accompanying
mock printout (page 158), giving the number of students whose
grades fell in the categories shown.

6. To launch a spaceship from the earth that will reach the moon,
the ship's velocity must be sufficient to escape the earth's
gravitaional field.   This minimum velocity is called the
escape velocity, V_o, and one expression for it is

. . . .
.
.
.
0-50 . 1 1 1 1
.
.
.
51-60 . 1 1 1 1 1 1 1 1 1 1
.
.
.
61-70 . 1 1 1 1 1 1 1 1 1 1 1 1
.
.
.
71-80 . 1 1 1 1
.
.
.
81-90 . 1 1 1 1 1 1
.
.
.
91-99 . 1 1 1
.
.
.

Printout for Exercise 5

6.—continued

$$V_o{}^2 = 2gR_e - \frac{200gR_e{}^2}{81(a + R_m + R_e)} + \frac{2gR_e{}^2}{81(a + R_m)}$$

where

       R_e = radius of earth (earth is assumed a sphere)
       R_m = radius of moon
        a = distance between earth and moon
        g = acceleration due to gravity on earth

Write a program to evaluate the above for the following values:

        a = 240,000 miles
       R_e = 4,000 miles
        g = 32 feet per second per second
      R_m = $R_e/4$

If there were no moon (or any other heavenly body attracting the spaceship), the escape velocity would be given by

$$V_o{}^2 = 2gR_e$$

6.—continued

By how much do the two values differ?

If the rocket is fired from the earth with velocity equal to the escape velocity, its velocity, V, at any distance r is given by

$$V^2 = \frac{2gR_e^2}{r + R_e}$$

(again neglecting all heavenly bodies). Tabulate V for r going from 0 to 240,000 miles in increments of 10,000 miles.

PART TWO

Additional FORTRAN

Chapter

Subprograms

It is often necessary in a program to perform a procedure
several times. Such a procedure may be regarded as a subprogram.
In general, a subprogram is any part of a program that we want to
consider separately. There are several statements in FORTRAN that
we can use to create subprograms and relate them to a main program.
In this chapter, we shall see how they are used.

In Chapter 2 we learned that to take the absolute value of a
number all that was needed was to use the function ABS. Suppose,
however, that we want to write an actual program to do this. A
flowchart to read in a number and print out its absolute value is
shown in Fig. 8-1. The procedure used to calculate Y in this flowchart may be regarded as a subprogram. We can flowchart this subprogram separately, as shown in Fig. 8-2. Here we have given the

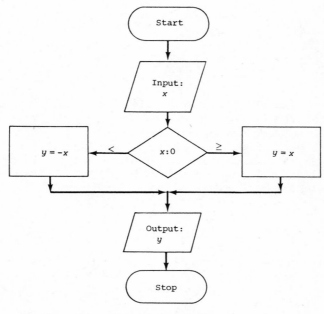

FIGURE 8-1

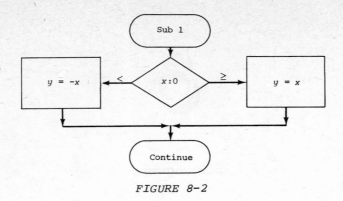

FIGURE 8-2

name Sub 1 to the entire procedure represented by the flowchart in Fig. 8-2. Now, any time we want to set Y equal to the absolute value of X in a flowchart, we can use the flowchart box shown below:

This box represents the whole procedure defined by Fig. 8-2. Using this method, we can rewrite Fig. 8-1 as shown in Fig. 8-3.

FIGURE 8-3

While this example may seem trivial, we shall see examples later where the use of subprograms is extremely useful. Once we have defined a subprogram, we can use it again and again without writing it out each time. In FORTRAN, there are four basic types of subprograms: statement functions; intrinsic functions; external functions; and external subroutines. We shall consider each of these in this chapter.

■ Statement Functions

A statement function is used to evaluate an arithmetic expression. Suppose that in a program we are going to want to evaluate the expression X**2 + X + 1.0 several times for different values of X. We can set up a statement function Y(X) by putting the following statement at the beginning of the program:

```
Y(X) = X**2 + X + 1.0
```

This statement is not an assignment statement. The equals sign
here does not have its usual meaning to evaluate the right-hand
side and assign the value to the left-hand side. Instead, it
serves to define a function Y. Actually, the statement tells three
things:

1. that Y is a function;

2. that the function Y involves one variable, X;

3. how Y is to be evaluated.

What we are actually doing is defining the *expression* Y(X) to be
equivalent to the *expression* X**2 + X + 1.0. In the rest of the
program, every time we write the expression Y(X), it will be the
same as though we had written the expression X**2 + X + 1.0. For
example, consider the program

```
Y(X) = X**2 + X + 1.0
X = 3.0
Z = Y(X)
```

The first statement serves to define the function Y, the second statement sets X = 3.0, and the third statement evaluates the
function Y for this value of X. That is, the statement Z = Y(X)
assigns Z the value 13.0, just as though we had put Z = 3.0**2 +
3.0 + 1.0.

The expression Y(X) must not be confused with a subscripted
variable. Although it looks like one, it is entirely different.
A subscripted variable is always defined by a DIMENSION statement,
while a statement function is always defined in a statement like
the one above.

A statement function involves one or more variables in its
definition. The function Y(X) defined above is a function of the
variable X. These variables are the so-called *dummy arguments* of
the function. When we evaluate a function, we replace each dummy
argument with an expression called an *actual argument*. For example,
suppose we define a function F(X) by the statement

```
F(X) = X + 3.0
```

Then, later in the program, we could have the statements

```
A = F(1.0)
B = F(2.0)
C = F(3.0)
```

The statement A = F(1.0) will replace the dummy argument X in the
definition of F with the actual argument 1.0 and evaluate
A = 1.0 + 3.0 = 4.0.

Similarly, B will be set equal to 5.0, and C will be set equal to 6.0. The value of whatever expression appears in the parentheses of the function will replace the variable in the definition of the function. If we had the statements

```
X = 2.0
A = F(X**2)
```

then A would be evaluated as A = F(X**2) = X**2 + 3.0 = 7.0.

In general, to define a statement function in a program, we use a statement of the form

$$f(x_1, x_2, \ldots, x_n) = e$$

where

f is any FORTRAN variable that will serve as the name of the function;

$x_1, x_2, \ldots, x_n$ are FORTRAN variables that are the dummy arguments, telling what variables the function involves;

e is any arithmetic expression involving the variables $x_1, x_2, \ldots, x_n$.

This type of statement must come at the beginning of the program, before the first instruction. If a DIMENSION statement is used in the program, the function definition would come after the DIMENSION statement.[1]

Now, what this statement does is to define the expression $f(x_1, x_2, \ldots, x_n)$ to be equivalent to the expression e in the definition. Once a function has been defined in this way, we can *evaluate* it by writing the expression $f(y_1, y_2, \ldots, y_n)$. This expression has a value obtained by replacing each x_i with y_i in the defining expression e. The following rules must be observed:

Rule 1:   Each actual argument may be any arithmetic expression.

Rule 2:   Each actual argument must be the same type as the corresponding dummy argument; if x_1 is a fixed-point variable, y_1 must be a fixed-point expression. Also, there must be the same number of actual arguments as dummy arguments.

Rule 3:   The mode of the function is determined by the first letter of its name, the same as for a variable.

---

[1]All statement function definitions come before the first instruction (executable statement) in the program and after all the declarations, such as DIMENSION, COMMON, and LOGICAL.

As an example of these rules, suppose that the statement function

        POW(X, N) = X**N

is used to define a function of two variables. Later in the program we could evaluate this function, replacing the variables with constants. The statement

        Y = POW(3.0, 2)

would set Y equal to POW(3.0, 2) = 3.0**2 = 9. By Rule 1, the quantities in parentheses may be any arithmetic expressions. For instance, the statements

        X = 3.0
        N = 2
        Y = POW(X + 1.0, N**2)

would set Y = (X + 1.0)**(N**2) = 4.0**4 = 256. Evaluating the function in this manner simply substitutes the expressions in parentheses for the items in the definition of the function. By Rule 2, it would be incorrect to have the statement

        Y = POW(X)

since the definition of the function POW requires that it is a function of two variables. Also, by Rule 2, it would be incorrect to have the statement

        Y = POW(4, 3.0)

The first variable in the definition of the function is the floating-point variable X, so the first item in parentheses when we are evaluating the function must also be a floating-point quantity.

Rule 3 means that since POW is a floating-point name, the value of the function POW(X, N) will be a floating-point number. If we define a function by the statement

        NSUM(M, N) = M + N

then the value of this function will be an integer; NSUM(1, 2) would have the integer value 3. The function HAT(Y) = Y - 6.0 would be a floating-point function since HAT is a floating-point variable name.

Once a function has been defined, we can use it as a part of any arithmetic expression. If we define the function SUM by

        SUM(X, Y, Z) = X + Y + Z

then later in the program we could have the statement

        Y = 2.0*SUM(P, Q, 1.0)**2 + 10.0

This would mean the same thing as the statement

$$Y = 2.0*(P + Q + 1.0)**2 + 10.0$$

Table 8-1 gives more examples of statement functions.

TABLE 8-1. *Examples of statement functions.*

Definition	Example	Value
DIF(X, Y) = X - Y	DIF(1.0, (A**2))	1.0 - A**2
CUBE(X) = X**3	CUBE(X + 1.0)	(X + 1.0)**3
MPROD(I, J, K) = I*J*K	MPROD(2, M, 1/N)	2*M*1/N
CU(X) = X**(1./3.)	CU(27.)	3.0
APB(I, J) = A(I) + B(J)	APB(1, 2)	A(1) + B(2)
DEG(THETA) = 180.0*THETA/3.1416	DEG(2.0*3.1416)	360.0

Example 1

Let us see how statement functions may be used to solve a quadratic equation in a program. Recall that the equation $Ax^2 + Bx + C = 0$ has solutions

$$X_1 = \frac{-B + \sqrt{B^2 - 4AC}}{2A} \qquad X_2 = \frac{-B - \sqrt{B^2 - 4AC}}{2A}$$

The quantity $B^2 - 4AC$ is called the *discriminant* of the equation. If it is negative, the solutions will be complex numbers. For this example, we shall stop in this case after printing out the message COMPLEX SOLUTIONS. The program will read numbers A, B, and C, and print out the values for X1 and X2. Four statement functions are used in the program, which is given below:[2]

```
        DISC(A, B, C) = B**2 - 4.0*A*C
        D(A, B, C) = SQRT(DISC(A, B, C))
        X1(A, B, C) = (-B + D(A, B, C))/(2.0*A)
        X2(A, B, C) = (-B - D(A, B, C))/(2.0*A)
        READ(1, 5) A, B, C
     5  FORMAT(3F10.1)
        IF(DISC(A, B, C).GE.0.) GO TO 20
        WRITE(2, 15)
    15  FORMAT(' COMPLEX SOLUTIONS')
        STOP
    20  X = X1(A, B, C)
        Y = X2(A, B, C)
        WRITE(2, 25) X, Y
    25  FORMAT(2F10.3)
        STOP
        END
```

[2]Quote marks are used in FORMAT specifications in this and succeeding chapters since they eliminate counting every character in the field.

Note that the function D uses the function DISC in its definition. This is alright, since DISC(A, B, C) just represents an
arithmetic expression. Reasonable care must be exercised in defining function statements. Consider the statements

```
A(X) = B(X) + 1.0
B(X) = A(X) - 1.0
```

These define the function B in terms of the function A, and
the function A in terms of the function B. Obviously, nothing is
defined at all in this way, and the statements would be illegal in
FORTRAN as function definitions.

To output the solutions in the program, note that we must use
the variables X and Y to store the values computed for X1 and X2.
We could not use the statement

```
WRITE(2, 25) X1(A, B, C), X2(A, B, C)
```

since the list of the WRITE statement can only be composed of variable names, and X1(A, B, C) and X2(A, B, C) are function references,
which are expressions, and so would be illegal in this context.

Example 2

We already know how to declare a doubly subscripted array by
using a DIMENSION statement. We shall see now how we can treat a
singly subscripted array as though it were doubly subscripted by
using a statement function. Consider the function NSUB, defined as

```
NSUB(I, J) = I + 3*(J - 1)
```

If I and J are both between 1 and 3, then each pair of numbers I, J
will determine a unique number between 1 and 9:

```
NSUB(1, 1) = 1    NSUB(1, 2) = 4    NSUB(1, 3) = 7
NSUB(2, 1) = 2    NSUB(2, 2) = 5    NSUB(2, 3) = 8
NSUB(3, 1) = 3    NSUB(3, 2) = 6    NSUB(3, 3) = 9
```

Now, suppose that A and B are arrays defined by the statement

```
DIMENSION  A(9), B(3, 3)
```

We can use the function NSUB to treat A as a doubly subscripted
array. For example, to set each element of A equal to a corresponding element of B, we could use the statements

```
      DO 10 I = 1, 3
      DO 10 J = 1, 3
      N = NSUB(I, J)
   10 A(N) = B(I, J)
```

As a matter of fact, all doubly subscripted arrays are set up in a
similar way in the computer. FORTRAN does this same procedure automatically every time a doubly subscripted array is used in a program.

In the above case, it would undoubtedly be simpler just to declare A as a doubly subscripted array. Suppose, however, that we
wanted to use a quadruply subscripted array. This is not always
permissible in FORTRAN, but we can accomplish the same thing by
defining a function of four variables in a way similar to the above.
If we wanted to set up an array B of dimension 3 X 3 X 3 X 3, we
would make B an array of 81 elements and use the function NSUB defined by

$$NSUB(I, J, K, L) = I + 3*(J - 1) + 9*(K - 1) + 27*(L - 1)$$

Then the statements

```
N = NSUM(I, J, K, L)
B(N) = X
```

would, in effect, set B(I, J, K, L) = X.

■ FORTRAN-Supplied Functions

Statement functions are just one type of function subprogram.
In the next section, we shall learn how to define more complicated
functions that may involve many statements in their definitions.
We were introduced to a few of the more common FORTRAN-supplied
functions in Chapter 2. The Appendix lists the functions supplied
by a typical large computer system, but even more may be available
on certain computers. Many of the FORTRAN-supplied functions are
not used too often, but when a particular one is needed, it can
prove very useful. For this reason, you would probably find it
beneficial to examine the Appendix for future reference. What the
functions do can readily be ascertained by considering their definitions.

Some FORTRAN-supplied functions, like ABS, are "intrinsically"
defined by the compiler itself. Others, like SIN, are called
external functions. When they are used in a program, they are
called in from a library of function subprograms. This distinction
does not usually concern us, however, since all FORTRAN-supplied
functions are used in the same way in a program. If f is the name
of any FORTRAN-supplied function, we can reference this function at
any point in a program by writing the expression

$$f(y_1, y_2, \ldots, y_n)$$

Here, $y_1, y_2, \ldots, y_n$ are expressions which are actual arguments of
the function f. This usage must conform to the same rules as for
statement functions.

Rule 1:   Each actual argument may be a constant, a variable
name, an array element name, or an arithmetic
expression.

Rule 2: The actual arguments must agree in number and type with the dummy arguments in the definition of the function.

Rule 3: The value of the function is a fixed- or floating-point number, depending on the first letter of the name.

For example, ABS finds the absolute value of a single floating-point expression. Thus, by Rule 2, it would be incorrect to write ABS(N), since N is a fixed-point variable. Similarly, it would be incorrect to write ABS(A, B), since the function ABS is defined for one variable only. Rule 3 means that since SIN is a floating-point variable name, the value of the expression SIN(X) is a floating-point number.

Now, consider the FORTRAN-supplied functions MOD and AMOD, which are used for determining remainders. MOD(N, M) is the remainder when N is divided by M. The exact definition can be given in terms of fixed-point arithmetic as

$$MOD(N, M) = N - (N/M)*M$$

For example, MOD(10, 4) has the value 2, and MOD(N, 3) = 0 if and only if N is divisible by 3. The function AMOD is defined similarly for floating-point numbers. The exact definition is

$$AMOD(X, Y) = X - FLOAT(INT(X/Y))*Y$$

For example,

$$
\begin{aligned}
AMOD(9.1, 3.0) &= 9.1 - FLOAT(INT(9.1/3.0))*3.0 \\
&= 9.1 - 3.0*3.0 \\
&= 0.1
\end{aligned}
$$

which is the decimal fraction remainder obtained by dividing 9.1 by 3.0. As with MOD, AMOD(X, Y) = 0 if and only if X is an integral multiple of Y. Notice that the second argument must not be zero.

Recall that the trigonometric functions SIN and COS assume the argument is given in radians. Thus, SIN(3.14159/2.0) = 1.0. Similarly, the function ATAN will return the value of the arctangent in radians, so ATAN(1.0) would have the value $\pi/2$. [The value of ATAN(X) will be between $-\pi/2$ and $\pi/2$. For other angles, ATAN2 must be used.]

A commonly available group of functions is used to find maximum and minimum values of a list of arguments. For example, the function MIN0 will find the minimum value of any number of fixed-point arguments. MIN0(1, 2, 3) has the value 1. MIN0(1, 2, 3, 4, -5) has the value -5. These functions are unusual because they can take any number of arguments.

TABLE 8-2

Function	Type of Arguments	Type of Function
AMAX0	Fixed-point	Floating-point
AMAX1	Floating-point	Floating-point
MAX0	Fixed-point	Fixed-point
MAX1	Floating-point	Fixed-point
AMIN0	Fixed-point	Floating-point
AMIN1	Floating-point	Floating-point
MIN0	Fixed-point	Fixed-point
MIN1	Floating-point	Fixed-point

Some related functions are given in Table 8-2. Each of these functions can take any number of arguments greater than or equal to two. To find the maximum value of five floating-point variables A, B, C, D, and E and set this equal to a floating-point number, we use the expression AMAX1(A, B, C, D, E). The expression MAX1(A, B, C, D, E) would do the same thing, except that the value of the function would be a fixed-point number, since MAX1 is a fixed-point variable name. The expression MIN0(I, J, K) would have the fixed-point value equal to the minimum value of I, J, and K.

■ Function Subprograms

Often we want to use a function that is either not supplied by FORTRAN or else too complicated to write as a single statement used in defining a statement function. We can define functions by using a function subprogram.

A function subprogram is a self-contained program segment. It has an END statement of its own, and it is independent of the main program. To use a function subprogram with a program, we arrange the program input deck with all the cards of the main program first. After the last card of the main program (the END card), we put the first card of the function subprogram. This card will contain the (declaration) statement

FUNCTION $f(x_1, x_2, \ldots, x_n)$

Then the statements that evaluate this function follow. Finally, the function subprogram has an END card of its own. When the input cards are arranged in this way, the main program can evaluate the function f at any point by using the expression $f(y_1, y_2, \ldots, y_n)$. The card deck arrangement is shown in Fig. 8-4.

Each function subprogram must include four things: a FUNCTION statement (declaration); an assignment statement; a RETURN statement; and an END line. The FUNCTION statement is always the first statement in the function subprogram, as we mentioned earlier. In the statement

FUNCTION $f(x_1, x_2, \ldots, x_n)$

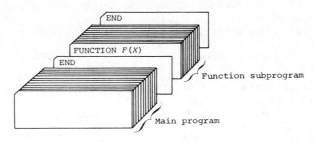

FIGURE 8-4
Relative positions of main program and
function subprogram in card deck

f is the name of the function. It has the same form as a FORTRAN variable name. The dummy arguments x_1, x_2, ..., x_n are FORTRAN variables that tell what the function involves.

The function name should not be the same as any variable name in the main program in which it is used. We could not, for instance, use an array AA and a function AA in the same program, because then the expression AA(I) would be ambiguous.

A function subprogram is referenced in the main program in the usual way by writing $f(y_1, y_2, ..., y_n)$ as part of an expression. When this expression is evaluated, it will cause the whole function subprogram to be executed with the actual argument values y_1, y_2, ..., y_n. Once this has been done, we want to branch back into the main program. To accomplish this, we use a RETURN statement in the function subprogram. This statement has the form

RETURN

When this statement is encountered in the function subprogram, it tells the computer that the evaluation of the function is complete, and control returns to the main program.

The function name must also appear as a variable somewhere in the function subprogram. There must be an assignment statement of the form

$$f = e$$

where *f* is a variable identical to the function name and *e* is some arithmetic expression. There may be more than one such statement in a function subprogram, and any such statement may be executed more than once. Whatever value is assigned to *f* on the last execution of this statement will be the value of the function that is returned to the main program.

Example 3

We know that the absolute value of an expression can be found by using the FORTRAN-supplied function ABS, but for this example,

let us write a function subprogram of our own to do this. We shall
call the function AB. It will be a function of one floating-point
variable, X, and the first statement in the subprogram will be

        FUNCTION AB(X)

Next, we shall want an IF statement to determine whether X is negative or positive. If X is negative, we shall set AB = -X; otherwise, we shall set AB = X. In either case, after we assign a value
to AB, we shall write a RETURN statement to branch back to the main
program. The complete subprogram would be

```
        FUNCTION AB(X)
        IF(X.GE.0.0) GO TO 10
        AB = -X
        RETURN
   10   AB = X
        RETURN
        END
```

A flowchart for this function is shown in Fig. 8-5.

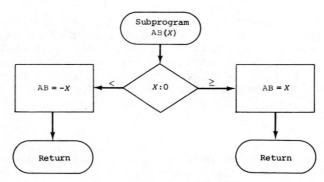

FIGURE 8-5
Flowchart for Example 3

To see how this function can be used, let us write a program
to read five values into an array A and write out the absolute
value of each. A flowchart for this program is shown in Fig. 8-6.
Here we have used a 6-sided box to represent the function AB defined in Fig. 8-5. This tells us to replace the 6-sided box with
the entire function subprogram. To do this in FORTRAN, we write
the main program first, followed by the function subprogram. Each
time the expression AB(Y) occurs in the main program, it will be
evaluated by branching to the subprogram for AB and executing the
subprogram, replacing the dummy argument in the definition of AB
with the actual argument in the main program. This may be any
expression. In this case, the actual argument will be the name
of an array element. When a RETURN statement is executed in the
subprogram, the main program will continue from where it left off.
The complete program is

```
      DIMENSION A(5)
      READ(1, 2) (A(I), I = 1, 5)
   2  FORMAT(5F10.3)
      DO 10 I = 1, 5
  10  A(I) = AB(A(I))
      WRITE(2, 2) (A(I), I = 1, 5)
      STOP
      END
      FUNCTION AB(X)
      IF(X.GE.0.0) GO TO 10
      AB = -X
      RETURN
  10  AB = X
      RETURN
      END
```

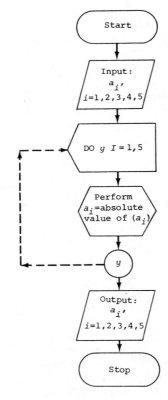

FIGURE 8-6

Notice that Statement 10 is utilized both in the main program
and in the function subprogram. This is perfectly acceptable,
since they are separate programs. We can use the same statement
or variable names in the function subprogram as we use in the main
program, and they will not mean the same thing. For example, we
could have used an array X instead of the array A in the main
program. This would not have been confused with the variable X in

the function AB. The only way that the main program communicates
with the function AB is by means of the arguments. Other than this,
they are like two entirely different programs. Declarations such as
the DIMENSION statement are local to main programs or subprograms
and may have to be repeated.

A program may use more than one function subprogram. In fact,
a function subprogram may itself use one or more function subprograms. When this is done, the program deck is arranged with the
main program first, then all the function subprograms used (either
by the main program, or by the other function subprograms). The
order of the functions does not matter, as long as all functions
referenced are included. This is illustrated in our next example.

Example 4

First, we define a function NPROD of two integer variables:

$$NPROD(N, M) = (N + 1)*(N + 2)* \cdots *(M - 1)*M$$

If N and M are equal, we define NPROD to be 1. If N > M, we set
NPROD = 0 and return. Otherwise, we continue with the calculations.
The FORTRAN function program is

```
          FUNCTION NPROD(N, M)
          IF(M - N) 10, 20, 30
      10  NPROD = 0
          RETURN
      20  NPROD = 1
          RETURN
      30  L = N + 1
          NPROD = 1
          DO 40 I = L, M
      40  NPROD = NPROD*I
          RETURN
          END
```

The flowchart for this program is shown in Fig. 8-7.

If M < N, the subprogram assigns the value 0 to NPROD and then
returns. If M = N, the subprogram assigns the value 1 to NPROD and
returns. If N < M, the DO loop is performed. Statement 40 illustrates the fact that the function name may be used in the function
subprogram just like any other variable name. This statement is
executed M - N times, assigning a different value to NPROD each
time. As far as the main program is concerned, it is only the last
time Statement 40 is executed that is important; this last value of
NPROD is the value the function assumes in the main program.

We can use the function NPROD to define two other functions.
NFAC(N) will compute factorial N, or, as it is written $N!$. It is
defined in the function subprogram:

```
FUNCTION NFAC(N)
NFAC = NPROD(1, N)
RETURN
END
```

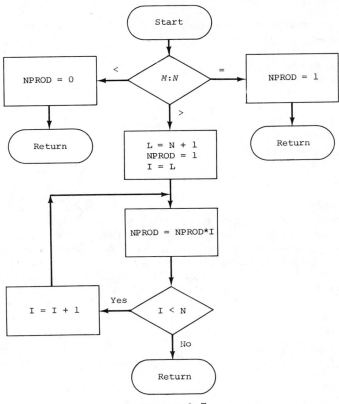

FIGURE 8-7
Flowchart for Example 4

The function C(N, M) will give the binomial coefficient

$$^nC_m \equiv C_m^n \equiv \frac{n!}{m!\,(n-m)!} = \frac{n(n-1)(n-2)\ \cdot\ \cdots\ \cdot\ (n-m+1)}{m!}$$

This function may be defined by the statements

```
FUNCTION C(N, M)
C = NPROD(M, N)/NFAC(N - M)
RETURN
END
```

Note that C is a floating-point function, although it has fixed-point parameters.

Now, suppose we want to write a simple program to read in three numbers N, X, and Y, and compute P = (X + Y)**N, using the binomial formula

$$(x + y)^n = \sum_{i=0}^{n} C_i^n x^i y^{n-i}$$

This could be done using the functions defined above with the following program:

```
      READ(1, 5) N, X, Y
    5 FORMAT(I5, 2F10.0)
      P = Y**N
      DO 10 I = 1, N
   10 P = P + C(N, I)*X**I*Y**(N - I)
      WRITE(2, 15) P
   15 FORMAT(F12.4)
      STOP
      END
```

Since this program uses the function C, when we execute the program we must furnish the subprogram for C as well. Since the function C uses the functions NPROD and NFAC for its definition, we must also include these subprograms. The three subprograms may appear in any order as long as they follow the main program, and as long as they are all there. Thus, the input deck of cards for the computer would be set up as follows:

```
      READ(1, 5) N, X, Y
      ...

      (main program)
      ...

      END
      FUNCTION C(N, M)
      ...

      END
      FUNCTION NPROD(N, M)
      ...

      END
      FUNCTION NFAC(N)
      ...

      END
      [(data card) to be read by main program]
```

Example 5[3]

Function subprograms are often used to compute functions which are defined in terms of power series. This is how the exponential

---

[3]This example may be omitted by those not familiar with hyperbolic functions.

function EXP is computed. Of course, this function is supplied by FORTRAN. Suppose that we want to compute the hyperbolic sine of a number, and that there is no FORTRAN-supplied function available to do this. We shall write a function subprogram SINH to compute this function. The hyperbolic sine, sinh x is defined as

$$\sinh x \equiv x + \frac{x^3}{3!} + \frac{x^5}{5!} + \cdots$$

This is the sum of an infinite number of terms, and so it cannot be computed exactly. A common procedure is to agree to compute enough terms so that the absolute value of the last term $x^n/n!$ is less than some small number, say 10^{-8}. Also, in case x is very large, we should agree to compute no more than, say, 15 terms at most.

The computational procedure we shall use makes use of the fact that

$$\frac{x^{n-2}}{(n-2)!} \cdot \frac{x^2}{(n-1) \cdot n} = \frac{x^n}{n!}$$

and, if TERM = $x^3/3!$, then the next term may be computed by

TERM = TERM*X**2/(5.*(5. - 1.))

In the program, we shall set XSQ = X*X, and we shall define a statement function D(N) = FLOAT(N*N - N). Then if TERM is the value of the N - 2nd term in the series, the Nth term may be computed by TERM = TERM*XSQ/D(N).

After computing each term, we add it to SINH. Then we test to see if the absolute value of TERM is less than 1.0E-8. If so, we branch to a RETURN statement; otherwise, we see if we have computed more than the allowable number of terms. For our particular problem, we arbitrarily test N with 15. If N $\geq$ 15, we branch to a RETURN statement. A flowchart for this program is shown in Fig. 8-8. The FORTRAN subprogram is given below:

```
      FUNCTION SINH(X)
      D(N) = FLOAT(N*N - N)
      SINH = X
      XSQ = X*X
      TERM = X
      DO 25 N = 3, 15, 2
      TERM = TERM*XSQ/D(N)
      SINH = SINH + TERM
      IF(ABS(TERM).LT.1.0E-8) GO TO 50
   25 CONTINUE
   50 RETURN
      END
```

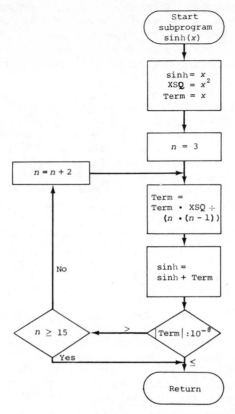

FIGURE 8-8
Flowchart for Example 5

■ Subroutines

The function subprograms we have been discussing give us a way of linking up two programs. On one hand, we have the main program; and on the other, we have the function subprogram. These are separate and constitute two independent programs except for the fact that the main program can execute the function subprogram to evaluate the function, communicating only by means of the arguments.

A subroutine subprogram in FORTRAN is, in a sense, a more general form of a function subprogram. Like a function, a subroutine is separate from the main program, and is almost a program in itself. Also, like a function, a subroutine can be executed under the control of a main program. The difference is that while a function has the specific job of finding a value for some expression, a subroutine does not have this restriction.

Subroutines can be useful in many ways. Instead of writing one long program to do a job, we can break it down into several shorter subroutines. The job could then be done by a short main program that executes the various subroutines. Another advantage is that when it is necessary to perform the same procedure in several programs, the procedure could be written as a subroutine. Instead of having to write out the whole procedure in each of the programs, we could make a copy of the subroutine and just include a statement in each program.

In FORTRAN, there are certain statements that are used to define and reference subroutines. The procedure is similar to using function subprograms.

A subroutine is defined with a SUBROUTINE declaration statement. This statement has the form

$$\text{SUBROUTINE name}(x_1, x_2, \ldots, x_n)$$

where name is any FORTRAN variable name and $x_1, x_2, \ldots, x_n$ are FORTRAN variables that are dummy arguments.

The first statement in any subroutine subprogram must always be a SUBROUTINE statement of this form. After this statement, we can write any instructions to tell what the subroutine is to do. These statements will be followed by an END statement.

To execute a subroutine, we use a CALL statement in the main program. This statement has the form

$$\text{CALL name}(y_1, y_2, \ldots, y_n)$$

where name is the name of a subroutine, as defined in a SUBROUTINE statement, and $y_1, y_2, \ldots, y_n$ are any FORTRAN expressions.

This statement transfers control from the main program to the first executable statement in the subroutine "name." The expressions $y_1, y_2, \ldots, y_n$ correspond to the dummy variable names $x_1, x_2, \ldots, x_n$ in much the same way as for function subprograms. The subroutine will be executed with each y_i taking the place of the corresponding x_i in the definition of the subroutine. As with functions, the y's must agree in number and type with the x's. The computer continues to execute the subroutine until a RETURN statement in the subroutine is executed. When this happens, control returns to the first statement after the CALL statement that called the subroutine.

To illustrate, we shall write a simple subroutine called ADD. This subroutine will involve three variables. The purpose of the subroutine will be to add the first two variables and store the result in the third variable. This subroutine can be defined with the statements

```
SUBROUTINE ADD(A, B, C)
C = A + B
RETURN
END
```

Now, say we want to write a program which uses two arrays X and Y. For each I, we want to set Y(I) = X(I) + 2.0. This could be done using the subroutine ADD in the following manner:

```
        DIMENSION  X(10), Y(10)
        DO 5 I = 1, 10
        CALL ADD(X(I), 2.0, Y(I))
    5   CONTINUE
        STOP
        END
```

When this program is read into the computer, the cards for the subroutine ADD would follow the cards for the main program. The CALL statement in the program calls this subroutine and causes the entire subroutine ADD to be performed. Every time A, B, and C appear in the subroutine, they are replaced by X(I), 2.0, and Y(I), respectively. Thus, the subroutine would set Y(I) = X(I) + 2.0. The RETURN statement in the subroutine causes control to return to the main program.

The variables that appear in the SUBROUTINE statement are dummy variables, or arguments, which do not correspond to any actual variables in the main program. The actual arguments are the expressions that appear in the CALL statement. As with function subprograms, the actual parameters of a subroutine may be any expressions, and not just simple variable names. The only restriction is that the actual arguments in the CALL statement must correspond exactly to the dummy arguments in the SUBROUTINE statement that defines the subroutine. Each argument in the CALL statement must be of the same mode as the corresponding argument in the SUBROUTINE statement. Thus, in the above example, we could not use the statement

```
        CALL ADD(N, A, B)
```

since N is a fixed-point mode.

A dummy argument in a SUBROUTINE statement may also be an array name. When this is done, the subroutine must contain a DIMENSION statement for the array. For instance, the following subroutine will set SUM equal to the sum of the first N elements of the array X and also set SUMSQ equal to the sum of the squares of the first N elements of X:

```
        SUBROUTINE SIGMA(X, N, SUM, SUMSQ)
        DIMENSION  X(100)
        SUM = 0.0
        SUMSQ = 0.0
        DO 10 I = 1, N
        SUM = SUM + X(I)
    10  SUMSQ = SUMSQ + X(I)**2
        RETURN
        END
```

In a main program, if A is an array with 100 elements, then the statement

        CALL SIGMA(A, 25, X, Y)

will set

        X = A(1) + A(2) + ··· + A(25)

and

        Y = A(1)**2 + A(2)**2 + ··· + A(25)**2

This subroutine has the drawback that the size of the dummy array X is fixed. A very useful feature of subroutines is that we can use arrays with *variable dimensions*. If L, M, and N are any fixed-point variables, we can use the statement

        DIMENSION X(L, M, N)

in a subroutine. The variables L, M, and N, as well as the array name, X, *must* appear in the parameter list of the SUBROUTINE statement, and their values may not be changed within the subroutine. Since the array name X is also a dummy argument in the SUBROUTINE statement, the subroutine can be called using any array as the actual argument. When this is done, the actual arguments corresponding to L, M, and N should be set equal to the actual dimensions of the array when executing the CALL statement. For example, we could rewrite the subroutine SIGMA shown above to make X an array of variable dimension. This is done by changing the DIMENSION statement to

        DIMENSION X(N)

The subroutine can then be used with an array of any size.

Example 6

For this example, we shall write a subroutine which will multiply two matrices to give the resulting product matrix. If *X* is an array having *L* rows and *M* columns, and *Y* is an array having *M* rows and *N* columns, then the product *Z* = *XY* is an array having *L* rows and *N* columns with elements defined by

$$Z_{ij} = \sum_{k=1}^{m} X_{ik} Y_{kj} \qquad \begin{array}{l} i = 1, \cdots, L \\ \\ j = 1, \cdots, N \end{array}$$

We can calculate *Z* easily using a subroutine with a variable DIMENSION statement. The subroutine will be called

        MULT(X, Y, Z, L, M, N)

We first set all the elements of Z equal to 0, and then calculate Z(I, J) from the above formula. This is done using three nested DO loops. The complete subroutine is as follows:

```
        SUBROUTINE MULT(X, Y, Z, L, M, N)
C       X IS AN L X M ARRAY
C       Y IS AN M X N ARRAY
C       Z IS THE L X N PRODUCT ARRAY
        DIMENSION  X(L,M), Y(M,N), Z(L,N)
        DO 20 I = 1, L
        DO 20 J = 1, N
        Z(I, J) = 0.0
        DO 20 K = 1, M
   20   Z(I, J) = Z(I, J) + X(I, K)*Y(K, J)
        RETURN
        END
```

Example 7

Let us write a subroutine to evaluate a polynomial, $p(x)$:

$$p(x) = a_1 + a_2 x + a_3 x^2 + \cdots + a_n x^{n-1}$$

For our program, it is convenient to write the above as

$$p(x) = a_1 + \{[(a_n x + a_{n-1})x + a_{n-2}]x + \cdots + a_2\}x$$

This looks strange, but will greatly assist in the programming. To illustrate the above, suppose we have a cubic equation given by

$$p(x) = a_1 + a_2 x + a_3 x^2 + a_4 x^3$$

We evaluate it by the above scheme as follows: Define polynomials p_1, p_2, p_3, and p_4. Then

$$
\begin{aligned}
p_1(x) &= a_4 \\
p_2(x) &= p_1(x) \cdot x + a_3 &= a_4 x + a_3 \\
p_3(x) &= p_2(x) \cdot x + a_2 &= a_4 x^2 + a_3 x + a_2 \\
p_4(x) &= p_3(x) \cdot x + a_1 &= a_4 x^3 + a_3 x^2 + a_2 x + a_1
\end{aligned}
$$

Clearly,

$$p(x) = p_4(x)$$

The FORTRAN subroutine will find the value of $p(x)$ for any given x, knowing the coefficients a_1, a_2, ..., a_n. Let A be the array giving these. A flowchart for the evaluation procedure is shown in Fig. 8-9.

The FORTRAN subroutine will be called PVALU(A, N, X, Y). Here, N is the number of coefficients in the array A, X is the variable, and Y is the result. The complete subroutine is:

```
        SUBROUTINE PVALU(A, N, X, Y)
        DIMENSION  A(N)
        IF(N.GT.1) GO TO 20
        Y = A(1)
        RETURN
  20    NN = N - 1
        Y = A(N)
        DO 30 I = 1, NN
        K = N - I
  30    Y = Y*X + A(K)
        RETURN
        END
```

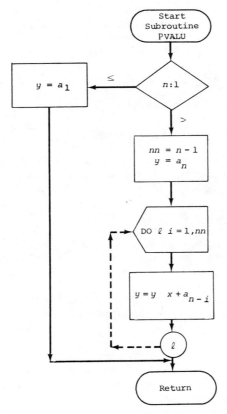

FIGURE 8-9
Flowchart for Example 7

■ The COMMON Statement

As we have seen, a subroutine is compiled as a separate program from the main program, and also from any other subprograms it uses. This means that we can use a variable name in both the main program and a subprogram and it will refer to two different variables. For instance, in Example 7, we used the variable name NN.

In a main program, which calls the subroutine PVALU, we can also use variable NN, and it will be a different variable from that in the subroutine.

Sometimes it is desirable to use the same storage locations for some of the variables in a subroutine as the variables in the main program or another subroutine. This can be done by using the COMMON statement. This statement has the form

COMMON A, B, ..., N

where A, B, ..., N are variable, or array, names. When this statement is used, it must be among the first group of statements in the program. In a function or subroutine subprogram, it should be the first statement after the FUNCTION or SUBROUTINE statement. This statement allows a main program and a subprogram to share storage in the following manner: If the main program contains the statement

COMMON A1, A2, A3

and a subprogram contains the statement

COMMON B1, B2, B3

then the variable B1 is assigned the same location in storage as the variable A1, B2 is assigned the same location as A2, and B3 is assigned the same location as A3. If another subroutine contains the statement

COMMON C1, C2

then C1, B1, and A1 all share the same location in storage as do C2, B2, and A2.

The items in the list of the COMMON statement may be arrays. We can give dimension information in the COMMON statement when this is done. For instance, the statement

COMMON X(10)

would specify an array, X, of ten elements in common storage. If a subroutine then contained the statement

COMMON Y(10)

the array Y would be stored in the same location as the array X.

In general, what the COMMON statement does is to specify the arrangement of computer memory called common storage. The first variable in the list of the COMMON statement is stored in the first memory location in common storage, the second variable is stored in the second location, and so on. When another subprogram uses a COMMON statement, the first variable in the list is also stored in the first location in common storage, and so on, so that the

corresponding variables in the lists of the two COMMON statements
share the same storage locations in common storage.

If a main program contains the statement

COMMON X(3), Y, Z

and a subroutine contains the statement

COMMON A, B, C, D, E

then the variable A and the variable X(1) are both stored in the
first location in common storage. The variables B and X(2) are
both stored in the second location in common storage, and the variables C and X(3) are both stored in the third location in common
storage. Then D corresponds to Y and E to Z.

Example 8

If A is a 3 X 3 array, the determinant D of A is defined by

$$D = a_{11}(a_{22}a_{33} - a_{23}a_{32}) - a_{21}(a_{12}a_{33} - a_{13}a_{32}) + a_{31}(a_{12}a_{23} - a_{13}a_{22})$$

The following subroutine DET(D, A) will compute the determinant of
a 3 X 3 array A and store it in D:

```
SUBROUTINE DET(D, A)
DIMENSION  A(3,3)
D1 = A(2, 2)*A(3, 3) - A(2, 3)*A(3, 2)
D2 = A(1, 2)*A(3, 3) - A(1, 3)*A(3, 2)
D3 = A(1, 2)*A(2, 3) - A(1, 3)*A(2, 2)
D = A(1, 1)*D1 - A(2, 1)*D2 + A(3, 1)*D3
RETURN
END
```

Now, let us see how we can use the subroutine DET to write a
subroutine SOLV which we can use to solve a system of three linear
equations in three unknowns. The equations are

$$a_{11}x_1 + a_{12}x_2 + a_{13}x_3 = b_1$$
$$a_{21}x_1 + a_{22}x_2 + a_{23}x_3 = b_2$$
$$a_{31}x_1 + a_{32}x_2 + a_{33}x_3 = b_3$$

These equations can be solved by Cramer's rule, which says that
x_1, x_2, and x_3 are given by

$$x_1 = \frac{1}{D}\begin{vmatrix} b_1 & a_{12} & a_{13} \\ b_2 & a_{22} & a_{23} \\ b_3 & a_{32} & a_{33} \end{vmatrix} \qquad x_2 = \frac{1}{D}\begin{vmatrix} a_{11} & b_1 & a_{13} \\ a_{21} & b_2 & a_{23} \\ a_{31} & b_3 & a_{33} \end{vmatrix} \qquad x_3 = \frac{1}{D}\begin{vmatrix} a_{11} & a_{12} & b_1 \\ a_{21} & a_{22} & b_2 \\ a_{31} & a_{32} & b_3 \end{vmatrix}$$

where

$$D = \begin{vmatrix} a_{11} & a_{12} & a_{13} \\ a_{21} & a_{22} & a_{23} \\ a_{31} & a_{32} & a_{33} \end{vmatrix}$$

Each of the determinants D_i is just the determinant of the matrix obtained by replacing the ith column of the matrix A with the elements b_1, b_2, and b_3. If the determinant $D = 0$, then the equations do not have a unique solution.

The FORTRAN subroutine SOLV will first compute the determinant D. If $D = 0$, the subroutine will print a message to this effect and then stop, since there are no solutions for x_1, x_2, and x_3. If $D \neq 0$, then each x_i is found by setting an array C equal to the array A, and then replacing the ith column of C by b_1, b_2, and b_3. We first call DET(X(I), C) and then set X(I) = X(I)/D. This procedure is shown in the flowchart of Fig. 8-10.

In the FORTRAN subroutine, we could make the arrays A, B, and X parameters of the subroutine with the statement

    SUBROUTINE SOLV(A, B, X)

However, we shall be using these same arrays in a main program. But it does take time to establish the correspondence whenever the subroutine is called. A more efficient method is to place the arrays A, B, and X in common storage. The subroutine would then contain the statement

    COMMON A(3, 3), B(3), X(3)

The main program would contain an identical statement, and the same storage areas would be used for the arrays in the subroutine as for the arrays in the main program. Since by using this method, the subroutine does not need any variables, the variable list can be omitted, and the subroutine can be declared with the statement

    SUBROUTINE SOLV

The complete subroutine is shown on page 190.

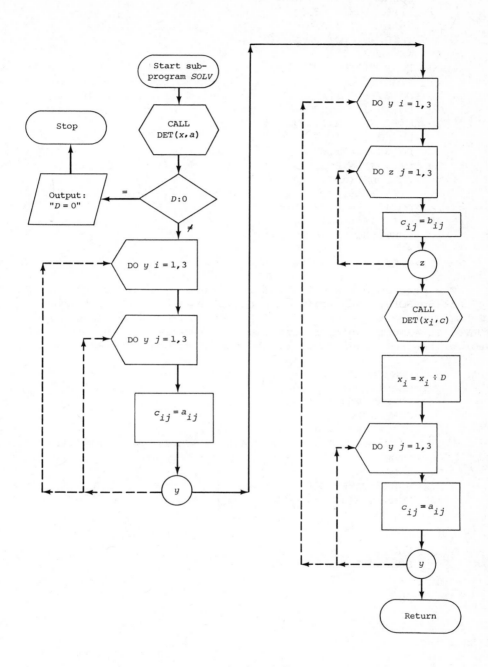

FIGURE 8-10
Flowchart for Example 8

```
        SUBROUTINE SOLV
        COMMON A(3, 3), B(3), X(3)
        DIMENSION  C(3,3)
        CALL DET(D, A)
        IF(D.NE.0.0) GO TO 20
        WRITE(2, 15)
    15  FORMAT(' D = 0')
        STOP
    20  DO 25 I = 1, 3
        DO 25 J = 1, 3
    25  C(I, J) = A(I, J)
        DO 50 I = 1, 3
        DO 30 J = 1, 3
    30  C(I, J) = B(J)
        CALL DET(X(I), C)
        X(I) = X(I)/D
        DO 40 J = 1, 3
    40  C(I, J) = A(I, J)
    50  CONTINUE
        RETURN
        END
```

The program below will read in values for A and B, compute X by calling SOLV, then write out the values for X. Notice that the COMMON statement is identical to the one used in the subroutine SOLV. To execute this program, we must remember to include the subroutines SOLV and DET after the end of the program as shown:

```
        COMMON A(3, 3), B(3), X(3)
        READ(1, 5) A, B
     5  FORMAT(4(3F10.0/))
        CALL SOLV
        WRITE(2, 10) X
    10  FORMAT(1X, 'X1 =', E13.4, 'X2 =', E13.4, 'X3 =', E13.4)
        STOP
        END
        SUBROUTINE SOLV
        COMMON A(3, 3), B(3), X(3)
        ...
        ...

        END
        SUBROUTINE DET(D, C)
        ...

        END
```

■ A Exercises

1. Examples of function subprograms are given below. If the statements are valid, mark a V next to them; otherwise, make suitable corrections to make them valid.

1.—continued

(a)
```
F(A, B, C) = A + B - C
X = Z - F(Y(1), 2.0)
```

(b)
```
ZERO(A, C, D, 4) = A - C*D/4.0
X = ZERO(1.0, 2.0, 3.0, 4.0)
```

(c)
```
PRINC(A, R, N) = A*(1. - R**N)
AMT = SUM - PRINC(100., .06, 30)
```

(d)
```
FUNCTION ANS(A, B, C)
SUM = A + B + C
PROD = A*B*C
D1 = A - B
ANS = SUM + PROD - D1
RETURN
END
```

(e)
```
FUNCTION DIST(A, B, THETA)
C = A**2 + B**2
D = -2.*A*B*COS(THETA)
IF(C.LT.D) GO TO 5
DIST = SQRT(C - D)
RETURN
5    DIST = 0.0
RETURN
END
```

(f)
```
SUBROUTINE BIG(X, N, XMAX)
DIMENSION X(N)
XMAX = X(1)
DO 10 I = 2, N
IF(X(I).LT.XMAX) GO TO 10
XMAX = X(I)
10   CONTINUE
RETURN
END
```

(g)
```
N = 6
PAY(AMT, XINT) = AMT*(XINT*(1. + XINT)**N)
Y = PAY(100.0, .05)
```

(h)
```
FUNCTION FLOW(AREA, RADIUS, SLOPE, COEF)
Q = 1.49*AREA*(RADIUS**(2./3.))*SQRT(SLOPE)
FLOW = Q/COEF
RETURN
END
```

1.—continued

(i)
```
        SUBROUTINE LIST(X, Y, N)
        DIMENSION X(N), Y(N)
        DO 100 I = 1, N
  100   WRITE(2, 101) X(I), Y(I)
  101   FORMAT(1H1, 20X, N(2F20.4))
        RETURN
        END
```

2. The equation

$$M = \frac{Ai(1 + i)^n}{(1 + i)^n - 1}$$

gives the monthly payment to repay an amount of money, where

M = monthly payment,
A = principal amount,
n = number of monthly payments,
i = annual interest rate.

Write the formula for the above as a

(a) statement function;
(b) FUNCTION subprogram;
(c) SUBROUTINE.

3. Write a FUNCTION subprogram to determine the average of N numbers.

4. The formula for the length C of a triangle, given two sides A and B and the included angle c, is

$$C^2 = A^2 + B^2 - 2AB \cos c$$

(a) Write a FUNCTION subprogram to calculate the equation.
(b) Write a SUBROUTINE to calculate the equation.

5. Write a subroutine to draw a large number, either a 1, a 2, or a 3, in the center of the printout page. The number printed is to be determined through the CALL statement. Have the number surrounded by a rectangular border of asterisks.

6. Suppose an object falls vertically from a building 1,000 feet above the cab of a truck. Its distance, s, above the ground is given by $s = 1,000 - 16t^2$, where t is in seconds. The same time that it starts to fall, a truck located 200 feet away from the building drives to intercept it before it hits the ground. This truck moves with constant velocity v_0 until it reaches the building and then instantaneously stops and waits for the object to fall on top of it. Its distance is

6.—continued

given by $s = v_0 t$. Write a program to output the following
table (the first line of output is filled in):

Time (Seconds)	D1—Object from Ground in Feet	D2—Truck from Intercept in Feet	D3—Truck from Object in Feet
0	1000.000	200.000	1019.804
.	.	.	.
.	.	.	.
.	.	.	.

Use FUNCTION subprograms as much as possible. Input an arbitrary velocity so that the truck will not necessarily make it to the intercept point every time. In these cases, have a message printed out as follows:

YOU DROVE TOO SLOWLY - THE OBJECT HIT THE GROUND ALREADY

■ B Exercises

1. For the two functions $f_1(x) = x^2 + 3x - 2$ and $f_2(x) = x^4 - x$, we wish to evaluate their sum $F = f_1 + f_2$ for values of $x = 0, 0.5, 1, \ldots, 20$. Write a FORTRAN program to do this, using function statements.

2. Do Exercise 1 using a FUNCTION subprogram.

3. Write a subroutine STAT which computes the mean and standard deviation of an array of N numbers ($N \geq 1$). (See Exercise A5, Chapter 6.)

4. Write a FUNCTION subprogram to evaluate

$$f(d, m, s) = \sin(d, m, s)$$

where d, m, and s represent an angle in degrees, minutes, and seconds.

5. A subfactorial is defined as follows:

$$!N = N \cdot !(N - 1) + (-1)^N$$

with $!0 = 1$ (for example, $!1 = 0$, $!2 = 1$, $!3 = 2$). Write a FUNCTION subprogram to calculate subfactorials.

6. Write a program to calculate the first 20 subfactorials using the subprogram for Exercise 5.

7. For an $n \times n$ array, A, write a subroutine to calculate the new matrix:

   (a) B, where each element of B is x times the value of each element of A;

   (b) C, where each element of C, c_{ij}, is related to A in the following manner:

$$a_{ij} = c_{ji}$$

   (c) D, where each element of D, d_{ij}, is obtained by

$$d_{ij} = \sum_{k=1}^{n} a_{ik} a_{kj}$$

8. A particle moves in a plane along the circumference of a circle in a counterclockwise manner. The circle is of radius 4 and is centered at (0, 10). At time $t = 0$, the particle is at (0, 14), and it takes 5 minutes to make a complete revolution. Also, at time $t = 0$, another particle is at the origin. It moves in a straight line with constant velocity to the point (10, 10) in 10 minutes. Write a program using a subroutine to give the distances between the two particles for any time t. When are they closest together? (See the accompanying figure.)

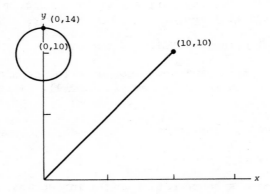

Diagram for Exercise 8

Chapter

Logical Expressions and Conditional Statements

■ Logical Constants and Variables

In Chapter 3 we introduced logical expressions and the logical IF statement. We shall now continue this treatment with the additional study of logical constants and variables. In addition to the fixed- and floating-point constants we have been using, there is a type of constant in FORTRAN called a *logical constant*. These constants are not numeric; that is, they do not have values that are numbers. In fact, there are only two values for a logical constant: .TRUE. and .FALSE. (it was pointed out in Chapter 3 that a period always precedes and follows these constants).

We may also use *logical variables* in a program. The only value a logical variable can assume is one of the two logical values, .TRUE. and .FALSE. . Such variables are not used in arithmetic statements like fixed- or floating-point variables; that is, we would not add or multiply two logical variables. Instead, they are used in logical expressions such as P .OR. (Q .AND. R), which consist of logical variables and constants connected by logical operators in a manner analogous to the connections of fixed- and floating-point variables and constants by arithmetic operators to form arithmetic expressions. In this chapter, we shall see how such expressions are developed and used to form statements.

In order to specify that a certain variable is going to be used as a logical variable, we must use a LOGICAL (declaration) statement at the beginning of the program. This statement has the form

LOGICAL name$_1$, name$_2$, ..., name$_n$

where name$_1$, name$_2$, ..., name$_n$ are variable names. This statement must come before the first executable statement in the program. It will cause the variables which appear in the list to be treated as logical variables throughout the program.

Logical variables must conform to the usual rules for naming variables in FORTRAN.

1. The name must consist of no more than six characters.[1]

2. The name must contain only letters and numbers (no punctuation marks).

3. The name must begin with a letter.

However, it makes no difference whether the names have the form of floating- or fixed-point variables, since they will not be used as either one; *the LOGICAL declaration overrides the usual rule for determining the variable type, and all variables in the list of the LOGICAL statement will be used only as logical variables.* For example, the variables

        Il, LOGO, MA3

would normally be of fixed-point mode, and A, B, C would be variables of floating-point mode. But if the statement declaration

        LOGICAL Il, LOGO, MA3, A, B, C

appeared at the beginning of a program, then all these variables would be treated as logical variables throughout the program, and each of them would be allowed to assume only one of the two values .TRUE. and .FALSE. .   Thus, we could have the statements

        Il = .TRUE.
        C = .FALSE.
        LOGO = B

but it would be incorrect to have the statements

        Il = 6

or

        B = 3.1

since a logical variable cannot assume a numeric value.

■ Logical Operators

   Logical variables can be combined to form more complicated logical expressions. This is done by using logical operators. An example is the expression

        P .AND. *Q*

where *P* and *Q* are logical variables. The characters .AND. (with periods preceding and following AND) comprise the logical operator

------

[1]See footnote on page 29.

which connects the two variables. Depending on the values of *P* and *Q*, the expression *P* .AND. *Q* will have either the value .TRUE. or the value .FALSE. . In this case, if *P* and *Q* both have the value .TRUE., then the expression *P* .AND. *Q* will have the value .TRUE. . If *R* is another logical variable, the statements

```
P = .TRUE.
Q = .TRUE.
R = P .AND. Q
```

will assign the value .TRUE. to *R*.

The use of logical operators in logical expressions is analogous to the use of arithmetic operators in arithmetic expressions. Just as

$$I + J$$

is an integer arithmetic expression which takes on integer values, depending on the values of the integer variables *I* and *J*,

$$P \text{ .AND. } Q$$

is a logical expression which takes on logical values, depending on the values of the logical variables *P* and *Q*.

Three logical operators are used in FORTRAN. They are .NOT., .AND., and .OR. . We shall see how each of these is used.

The operator .NOT. changes the value of the expression following it to the complement value of the expression; that is, it changes .TRUE. to .FALSE., and vice versa. Thus, the expression .NOT. X has the value .FALSE. if X is .TRUE., and .TRUE. if X is .FALSE.

If the statements

```
LOGICAL M, N, A, B
A = .TRUE.
B = .FALSE.
M = .NOT. A
N = .NOT. B
```

were encountered in a program, then M would be assigned the value .FALSE., and N would be assigned the value .TRUE. .

The operator .NOT. can be used in this way by placing it in front of any logical expression (that is, a logical constant, variable, or more complex combination of these). If E is any logical expression, then the value of .NOT. E is given by Table 9-1. Whatever the expression E may be, its value will be either .TRUE. or .FALSE., and placing the operator .NOT. in front of the expression will change the value to the opposite value.

TABLE 9-1

E	.NOT. E
.TRUE.	.FALSE.
.FALSE.	.TRUE.

The logical operator .AND. takes two logical expressions and connects them to form a logical expression whose value is determined as shown in Table 9-2. In the table, P and Q may be any logical constants, variables, or other expressions. So, the logical expression P .AND. Q has the value .TRUE. if and only if both P and Q have the value .TRUE. . If P has the value .FALSE. and Q has the value .TRUE. (as in the third line of the table), then the expression P .AND. Q has the value .FALSE. . The expressions .FALSE. .AND. .TRUE., .TRUE. .AND. .FALSE., and .FALSE. .AND. .FALSE. will all have the value .FALSE.

TABLE 9-2

P	Q	P .AND. Q
.TRUE.	.TRUE.	.TRUE.
.TRUE.	.FALSE.	.FALSE.
.FALSE.	.TRUE.	.FALSE.
.FALSE.	.FALSE.	.FALSE.

The operator .OR., like .AND., connects two expressions to form a logical expression whose value is determined as shown in Table 9-3. We see from this table that if at least one of the expressions P or Q has the value .TRUE., then P .OR. Q will have the value .TRUE. . The only case in which P .OR. Q is .FALSE. is when both P and Q have the value .FALSE. . The statements

```
LOGICAL P, Q, R, S
P = .TRUE.
Q = .FALSE.
R = P .OR. .TRUE.
S = Q .OR. R
```

would assign the value .TRUE. to R and S.

TABLE 9-3

P	Q	P .OR. Q
.TRUE.	.TRUE.	.TRUE.
.TRUE.	.FALSE.	.TRUE.
.FALSE.	.TRUE.	.TRUE.
.FALSE.	.FALSE.	.FALSE.

■ Evaluation of Expressions

The operators .NOT., .AND., and .OR. can be used in the same logical expression to form more complicated constructions. For example,

(.NOT. P) .AND. Q

contains the two operators .NOT. and .AND. . To evaluate such an expression, we proceed a step at a time. Suppose P is .TRUE. and Q is .FALSE., then the values of the above expression would be found as follows:

(.NOT. P) .AND. Q
(.NOT. .TRUE.) .AND. .FALSE.
.FALSE. .AND. .FALSE.
.FALSE.

The order in which the operations are grouped is important. The expression .NOT. (P .AND. Q) is *not* the same as (.NOT. P) .AND. Q. Note that if P is .TRUE. and Q is .FALSE.,

.NOT. (P .AND. Q)

has the value

.NOT. (.TRUE. .AND. .FALSE.)
.NOT. .FALSE.
.TRUE.

For the same values of P and Q, the expression (.NOT. P) .AND. Q has the value .FALSE. . The order in which the operations in any expression are evaluated may be determined by the following rules.

Rule 1: Any part of the expression enclosed in parentheses is evaluated completely before proceeding to evaluate any part of the expression outside the parentheses. This rule applies to each set of parentheses. For example, in evaluating the expression

((P .AND. Q) .OR. R) .AND. S

(P .AND. Q) would be evaluated first, then ((P .AND. Q) .OR. R), and finally the whole expression.

Rule 2: Unless otherwise grouped by parentheses, occurrences of the operator .NOT. are evaluated before evaluating the operators .AND. or .OR. . In the expression

.NOT. P .OR. Q

the .NOT. P would be evaluated first. Thus, this

expression is assumed to mean (.NOT. P) .OR. Q, rather than .NOT. (P .OR. Q).

Rule 3: Unless otherwise grouped by parentheses, the operator .AND. is evaluated before the operator .OR. . This means that P .OR. Q .AND. R would be interpreted as P .OR. (Q .AND. R) rather than as (P .OR. Q) .AND. R.

Rule 4: The expression is evaluated from left to right, unless otherwise specified by the above three rules.

As an illustration of these rules, consider the expression

.NOT. P .AND. Q .OR. R .AND. S

In evaluating this expression, the .NOT. P is evaluated first, then the .AND. operator in (.NOT. P) .AND. Q, next the .AND. operator in R .AND. S, and finally the .OR. operator connecting these parts.

So the whole expression is evaluated as though it were written

((.NOT. P) .AND. Q) .OR. (R .AND. S)

Of course, there is nothing wrong with using parentheses. Just as with arithmetic statements such as $A/B - C$, the rules remove the ambiguity which might otherwise result from omitting parentheses.

■ Truth Tables

Given a fairly complicated expression such as

.NOT. (P .AND. .NOT. Q)

the question sometimes arises, "For what values of P and Q will the expression have the value .TRUE.?" This question can best be answered by setting up what is known as a *truth table*. This is a convenient way of evaluating an expression for all possible values of the variable involved. The above expression involves two variables, P and Q. Each of these may have either of the values .TRUE. or .FALSE., so there are four combinations to consider:

P =	.TRUE.	and	Q =	.TRUE.
P =	.TRUE.	and	Q =	.FALSE.
P =	.FALSE.	and	Q =	.TRUE.
P =	.FALSE.	and	Q =	.FALSE.

To set up a truth table, first we list in a column the possible values of the variables involved. (For the purpose of setting up a truth table, it will be convenient to use the letter T for the value .TRUE., and F for .FALSE. .) Then, using the rules of the preceding section, we find the first operation performed in evaluating the expression and write this part of the expression at the top of the column in the table. Then we find the next operation to be evaluated, and write the first operation plus this part of the expression at the top of the next column. We continue this until finally we have the whole expression to be evaluated at the top of the last column of the table.

For example, the first operation to be evaluated in the expression

.NOT. (P .AND. .NOT. Q)

would be the occurrence of .NOT. within the parentheses. So we would write .NOT. Q at the top of a column. The next operation performed would be the evaluation of the operator .AND.; and finally, the .NOT. outside the parentheses would be evaluated. The resulting truth table looks like Table 9-4.

TABLE 9-4

P	Q	.NOT. Q	P .AND. .NOT. Q	.NOT. (P .AND. .NOT. Q)
T	T			
T	F			
F	T			
F	F			

Now that the expression is broken down into parts, it is easy to fill in the values in the three blank columns. In the first row, P and Q are both .TRUE., so .NOT. Q is .FALSE. . We can write an F in column 3. Then to evaluate P .AND. .NOT. Q, we substitute .TRUE. for P and .FALSE. for .NOT. Q, and we see that this part of the expression is .FALSE. . We write an F in column 4. In the last column of the first row, .NOT. (P .AND. .NOT. Q) is just .NOT. operating on the value in column 4, so we have a T in the last column. Continuing in this manner for the other three rows, we arrive at Table 9-5. Since we have included each intermediate step in the

TABLE 9-5

P	Q	.NOT. Q	P .AND. .NOT. Q	.NOT. (P .AND. .NOT. Q)
T	T	F	F	T
T	F	T	T	F
F	T	F	F	T
F	F	T	F	T

calculation, it is necessary to evaluate only one operator at a time as we proceed from column to column.

Now, if we want to know what the value of the expression .NOT. (P .AND. .NOT. Q) is for P = .TRUE. and Q = .FALSE., we look in the second row of the table and find from the last column that the expression is .FALSE.. We can also see that this is the only case in which the expression will be .FALSE..

This method of constructing a truth table will work for any expression. The intermediate steps can be omitted, but it is easier to put them in. In case the expression contains more than two variables, additional rows will be needed. For three variables, there are eight combinations of values. An illustration of this is given in Table 9-6 for the expression (P .OR. Q) .AND. R.

TABLE 9-6

P	Q	R	P .OR. Q	(P .OR. Q) .AND. R
T	T	T	T	T
T	T	F	T	F
T	F	T	T	T
T	F	F	T	F
F	T	T	T	T
F	T	F	T	F
F	F	T	F	F
F	F	F	F	F

■ Relational Expressions and Logical Variables

In Chapter 3 we were introduced to the six relational operators which may be used in FORTRAN. For convenience, they are repeated here in Table 9-7:

TABLE 9-7. Relational operators.

Operator	Meaning	Operator	Meaning
.EQ.	Equal to (=)	.LT.	Less than (<)
.NE.	Not equal to (≠)	.GE.	Greater than or equal to (≥)
.GT.	Greater than (>)	.LE.	Less than or equal to (≤)

The general form of a relational expression was given as

$$A.R.B$$

where .R. was one of the six relational operators above, and A and B were arithmetic expressions.

It is possible for A and B to be logical variables as well as arithmetic expressions. Consider, for instance, the statements

```
LOGICAL Z
I = 10
Z = I.LT.5
```

When the relational expression is evaluated, I has the value 10, so I does not satisfy the relation I.LT.5 (meaning "$I < 5$"), and the expression takes the value .FALSE.. So, Z is .FALSE.. Similarly, the statements

```
LOGICAL Z
G = 4.1
H = 5.3
Z = H - 1.0.GE.G
```

would assign the value .TRUE. to the logical variable Z, since H - 1.0 is, in fact, greater than or equal to G.

Using the logical operators .AND. and .OR., we may connect relational expressions with other logical expressions. For instance, suppose that *P* is a logical variable, and we want to assign the value .TRUE. to *P* if $0 \leq X < 1.0$, and .FALSE. otherwise. Since $0 \leq X < 1.0$ is really a shorthand way of writing the two statements $0 \leq X$ and $X < 1.0$, we must use two relational operators. This may be done with the single statement

```
P = (0.0.LE.X) .AND. (X.LT.1.0)
```

When compound statements such as this are evaluated, the relational operators are evaluated before the logical operators. If $X = 2.0$, the above expression would be evaluated thus:

0.0.LE.X	is assigned the value .TRUE.
X.LT.1.0	is assigned the value .FALSE.
.TRUE. .AND. .FALSE.	is assigned the value .FALSE.
P	is assigned the value .FALSE.

In general, expressions are evaluated in the following order:

1. arithmetic expressions;
2. relational operators;
3. logical operators.

Thus, if we write

```
3.0*A - 1.0.LT.B .AND. B.LT.3.0*A + 1.0
```

it would be interpreted as

```
((3.0*A - 1.0).LT.B) .AND. (B.LT.(3.0*A + 1.0))
```

which is the FORTRAN equivalent of the statement $(3A - 1) < B < (3A + 1)$.

■ The Logical IF Statement

The logical IF statement was given in Chapter 3 as having the general form

        IF(*E*)*S*

where *E* is any logical expression, and *S* is any executable FORTRAN
statement except a DO statement or another IF statement. Logical
operators are incorporated into logical IF statements. For example,
the flowchart of Fig. 3-12 (which is repeated here for convenience
as Fig. 9-1) can be programmed as

        IF(X.GT.1.0) GO TO 20
        IF(X.GT.0.0) X = 0.0
    20 Y = X

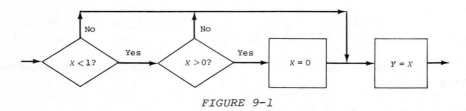

FIGURE 9-1

The same thing can be accomplished with the statements

        IF(0.0.LT.X .AND. X.LT.1.0) X = 0.0
        Y = X

Similarly, Fig. 9-2 shows a procedure that will set X = 0 if either
X > 1 or X < 0. This would also require two arithmetic IF statements, but it can be done with one logical IF statement:

        IF(X.GT.1.0 .OR. X.LT.0.) X = 0.0
        Y = X

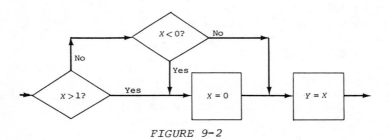

FIGURE 9-2

    The examples below will demonstrate the use of logical vari-
ables and the logical IF statement in complete programs.

Example 1

A teacher uses the following system in grading tests:

Test Score	Grade
91-100	4
81-89	3
71-79	2
61-69	1
59 & below	0

For borderline cases with scores of 60, 70, 80, or 90, homework is taken into consideration in deciding the grade. If a student has turned in all three homework assignments, the higher grade would be assigned; otherwise, the student would get the lower grade.

Suppose there are *N* students and that the test score for student I is stored in an array element NSCOR(I). The number of homework assignments turned in by student I is stored in NHMWK(I). The problem is to write a program to compute each student's grade NGRAD(I).

A solution to this problem is shown in the flowchart in Fig. 9-3. Just for comparison, consider how this flowchart could be programmed using the arithmetic IF statement. The first part would look something like this:

```
        DO 100 I = 1, N
        IF(NSCOR(I) - 91) 10, 4, 4
   10   IF(NSCOR(I) - 90) 20, 15, 20
   15   IF(NHMWK(I) - 3) 3, 4, 3
    4   NGRAD(I) = 4
        GO TO 100
   20   IF(NSCOR(I) - 81) 25, 3, 3
          .          .
          .          .
          .          .
```

The first three IF statements correspond to one phase of the testing. We shall see that these three arithmetic IF statements can be replaced by a single logical IF statement. There are several advantages to doing so. First, since the four IF statements above are interconnected, they must have statement numbers. Using the logical operator .OR., we are able to avoid so many statement numbers, and the program will be easier to construct. Second, it is more difficult to follow a program with multiple IF statements like the above. It is hard to look at the program and tell what it is supposed to do. With the use of logical IF statements, the operation of the program will be clearer. The program corresponding to the flowchart in Fig. 9-3 is given on page 207.

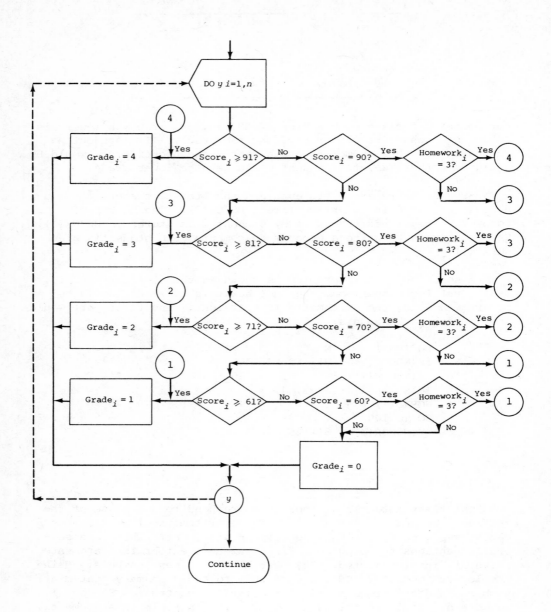

FIGURE 9-3
Flowchart for Example 1

```
LOGICAL H
DIMENSION NSCOR(100), NGRAD(100), NHMWK(100)
    .
    .
    .
DO 100 I = 1, N
H = NHMWK(I).EQ.3
M = NSCOR(I)
IF(M.GE.91 .OR. M.EQ.90 .AND. H) GO TO 4
IF(M.GE.81 .OR. M.EQ.80 .AND. H) GO TO 3
IF(M.GE.71 .OR. M.EQ.70 .AND. H) GO TO 2
IF(M.GE.61 .OR. M.EQ.60 .AND. H) GO TO 1
NGRAD(I) = 0
GO TO 100
1   NGRAD(I) = 1
GO TO 100
2   NGRAD(I) = 2
GO TO 100
3   NGRAD(I) = 3
GO TO 100
4   NGRAD(I) = 4
100 CONTINUE
STOP
END
```

Here we have set the logical variable H equal to the condition NHMWK(I).EQ.3, and we have set M = NSCOR(I). This was done to make the writing shorter in the IF statements. Each IF statement corresponds to three of the arithmetic IF statements used before. Notice that the logical expressions within the IF statements have been written without parentheses. Because of the precedence of the operator .AND. over .OR., they will be interpreted as though they had been written:

$$(M.GE.91) .OR. ((M.EQ.90) .AND. H), \text{ etc.}$$

which is the same as

$$(NSCOR(I).GE.91) .OR. ((NSCOR(I).EQ.90) .AND. (NHMWK(I).EQ.3))$$

The student can easily verify that this is exactly the condition under which the NGRAD(I) is set equal to 4 in the flowchart.

Example 2

Table 9-8 shows a hypothetical schedule for figuring the income tax for a married person. For an unmarried person, the tax is 2% greater than this (that is, 1.02 times whatever tax a married person with the same income pays). Suppose that the data for each person is punched on cards in the following format:

Column   1   1 if person is unmarried; 2 if married
Columns   2-10   Social security number
Columns 11-19   Income (with 2 assumed decimal places)

TABLE 9-8

If Income Is at Least	But Less Than	Tax Is
$ 0.00	$1,000.00	5% of income
1,000.00	2,000.00	$ 50.00 plus 15% of excess over $1,000.00
2,000.00	3,000.00	$200.00 plus 20% of excess over $2,000.00
3,000.00	4,500.00	$400.00 plus 30% of excess over $3,000.00
More than $4,500.00		$850.00 plus 40% of excess over $4,500.00

After the last card in the data set, there is a card with a 0 punched in column 1. Write a program to read each card, compute the tax, and output the social security number and the tax for each person.

This problem can easily be solved using the method shown in the flowchart in Fig. 9-4. First, the marital status, MS; social security number, NSS; and income, X, are read in. If MS = 0, then we have already read the last data card, so we stop. Otherwise, we compute the tax as though the person were married, and then multiply the tax by 1.02 if the person is single. Finally, we output the results and begin anew with another card.

The following program shows a simple way to write this procedure in FORTRAN, using the logical IF statement:

```
 1   READ(1, 5) MS, NSS, X
 5   FORMAT(I1, I9, F9.2)
     IF(MS.EQ.0) STOP
     TAX = 850.0 + .40*(X - 4500.0)
     IF(X.LT.4500.0) TAX = 400.0 + .30*(X - 3000.0)
     IF(X.LT.3000.0) TAX = 200.0 + .20*(X - 2000.0)
     IF(X.LT.2000.0) TAX = 50.0 + .15*(X - 1000.0)
     IF(X.LT.1000.0) TAX = .05*X
     IF(MS.EQ.1) TAX = 1.02*TAX
     WRITE(2, 10) NSS, TAX
10   FORMAT(I10, F8.2)
     GO TO 1
     END
```

Note, however, that this program does not exactly correspond to the flowchart shown in Fig. 9-4. According to the flowchart, if X < 1,000, the tax will be computed by the formula TAX = .05*X, and then the next statement executed will be the comparison of MS to 1 by the decision box at the bottom of the flowchart. In the program above, if X < 1,000, then after computing the tax, the next

statement performed will be the comparison of X to 2,000 by the
statement

$$IF(X.LT.2000.0) \; TAX = 50.0 + .15*(X - 1000.0)$$

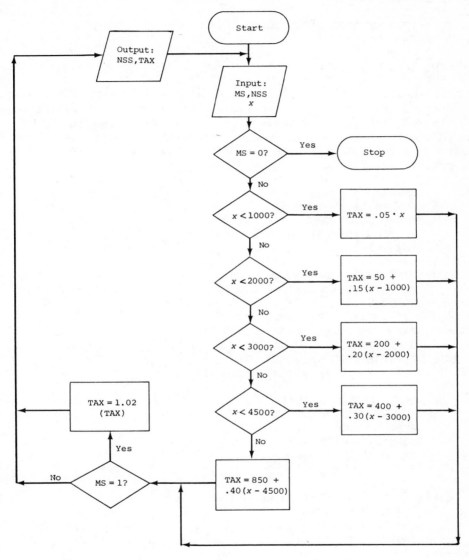

FIGURE 9-4
Flowchart for Example 2

In fact, all the IF statements in the above program will be performed no matter what X is. This is really unnecessary. The
problem is that only one executable statement can follow the
logical expression in a logical IF statement. In the flowchart, we
actually want to execute two statements if X < 1,000: one statement

to compute the tax and a GO TO statement to jump to the last decision box.

In order to do this using a logical IF statement, we would
need statements such as

```
        IF(X.GE.1000.0) GO TO 20
        TAX = .05*X
        GO TO 75
    20  IF(X.GE.2000.0) GO TO 30
```

Here the condition in the first IF statement is X.GE.1000.0.
If this is .TRUE., then $X \geq 1,000$, so we jump to the next IF statement. If X.GE.1000.0 is .FALSE., then $X < 1,000$, so the tax is
computed and then the program jumps to Statement 75, which will
correspond to the last decision box of the flowchart. The complete program written this way would be:

```
     1  READ(1, 5) MS, NSS, X
     5  FORMAT(I1, I9, F9.2)
        IF(MS.EQ.0) STOP
        IF(X.GE.1000.0) GO TO 20
        TAX = .05*X
        GO TO 75
    20  IF(X.GE.2000.0) GO TO 30
        TAX = 50.0 + .15*(X - 1000.0)
        GO TO 75
    30  IF(X.GE.3000.0) GO TO 40
        TAX = 200.0 + .20*(X - 2000.0)
        GO TO 75
    40  IF(X.GE.4500.0) GO TO 50
        TAX = 400.0 + .30*(X - 3000.0)
        GO TO 75
    50  TAX = 850.0 + .40*(X - 4500.0)
    75  IF(MS.EQ.1) TAX = 1.02*TAX
        WRITE(2, 80) NSS, TAX
    80  FORMAT(I10, F8.2)
        GO TO 1
        END
```

This is longer to write but faster to execute.

This example illustrates a fact which should be kept in mind.
When using logical IF statements in a program instead of using the
statements

$$IF(E)S_1$$
$$S_2$$

where E is a logical expression and S_1 and S_2 are statements, it
may be more convenient to use the form

$$IF(.NOT. \ E)S_2$$
$$S_1$$

which will accomplish the same thing in a slightly different manner.

Example 3

The mess sergeant at a military base is faced with the problem of ordering food for the month. He generally serves either potatoes or macaroni with the meals, and he wants to buy some of each, but there are certain restrictions that he must observe.

The first restriction is that there is enough money in the mess fund to buy at most 160 sacks of potatoes or 80 boxes of macaroni. If he buys some of each, then the total number of sacks of potatoes plus 2 times the number of boxes of macaroni must be less than 160. Letting P be the number of sacks of potatoes and M be the number of boxes of macaroni, this condition can be expressed as $P + 2M \leq 160$.

The second restriction is that in order to be able to provide enough meals for the month, he must buy at least 70 boxes of macaroni or 70 sacks of potatoes. If he buys some of each, this restriction is $P + M \geq 70$.

The third restriction is that since macaroni is less expensive than potatoes, he wants to buy more macaroni than potatoes, so $M > P$.

Finally, he always serves potatoes on weekends, so he needs at least 20 sacks of potatoes; thus, $P \geq 20$.

The problem is to find some possible quantities of potatoes and macaroni that meet the requirements. That is, we want to find numbers P and M that satisfy all four of the inequalities:

$$P + 2M \leq 160$$
$$P + M \geq 70$$
$$M > P$$
$$P \geq 20$$

This problem can be solved graphically. To do this, we set up axes for P and M, and graph the equations

(a) $P + 2M = 160$;
(b) $P + M = 70$;
(c) $M = P$;
(d) $P = 20$.

Each of these graphs is a straight line and is plotted in Fig. 9-5. Line a is the graph of the equation $P + 2M = 160$. We are interested in points for which $P + 2M \leq 160$, and this corresponds to the region on or below line a; if P and M are the coordinates of any point on or below line a, then $P + 2M \leq 160$.

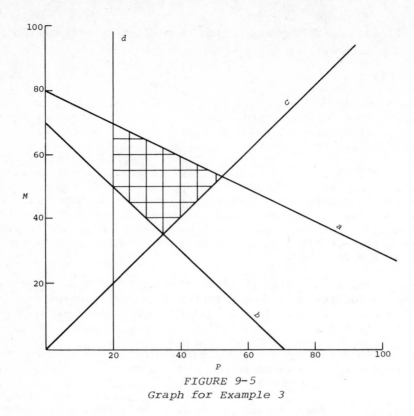

FIGURE 9-5
Graph for Example 3

Similarly, line b is the graph of the equation $P + M = 70$, and any points on or above this line will satisfy $P + M \geq 70$. Thus, any point with coordinates P and M which lies on or above line b *and* on or below line a will satisfy both conditions $P + 2M \leq 160$ and $P + M \geq 70$.

Continuing this reasoning for the other two conditions, we arrive at the conclusion that the coordinates of any point which lies on or below line a, *and* on or above line b, *and* to the left of line c, *and* on or to the right of line d will satisfy all four given conditions. This set of points consists of the cross-hatched region in Fig. 9-5. For instance, $P = 30$ and $M = 60$ is a possible solution.

This method of solution is easy to visualize, but we are more interested in programming the problem for a computer solution. While we are at it, we might as well find several solutions. Suppose that the sergeant wants to buy 5 sacks of potatoes or 5 boxes of macaroni at a time. This means that we shall want to find all the pairs of integers P and M that satisfy the conditions and are also divisible by 5.

A simple way to do this is to try out various combinations such as $P = 5$ and $M = 5$, $P = 5$ and $M = 10$, etc., and to write out any combinations that satisfy the conditions. This can easily be done by using nested DO loops. We note that the first condition implies that *P* will be no greater than 160 and *M* will be no greater than 80. So, we can try out all combinations with the nested DO statements

```
        DO 500 NP = 5, 160, 5
        DO 500 M = 5, 80, 5
```

Here we have used NP instead of P since we want a fixed-point variable. These statements will provide all combinations of NP and M in the range $5 \le NP \le 160$ and $5 \le M \le 80$, incrementing by 5 each time on each variable.

In order to test each combination, it will be convenient to have four logical variables in the program. We shall call them A, B, C, and D. We first set A equal to the value of the relational expression corresponding to the first condition:

```
        A = NP + 2*M.LE.160
```

If A is .FALSE., NP and M do not satisfy the first condition, and there is no need to continue. So we shall branch to the end of the DO loops and start again with a different set of values for NP and M. This can be done with the logical IF statement

```
        IF(.NOT. A) GO TO 500
```

If the first condition is satisfied, then A is .TRUE., and .NOT. A is .FALSE.; this IF statement will not cause the program to branch to Statement 500. Next, we set the logical variable B equal to the second condition,

```
        B = NP + M.GE.70
```

Once again, if B is .FALSE., we branch to the end of the DO loops by using the statement IF(.NOT. B) GO TO 500.

This same procedure is carried out for the other two conditions. If NP and M satisfy all four conditions, we output their values before continuing with the DO loops. The complete program is

```
            LOGICAL A, B, C, D
            DO 500 NP = 5, 160, 5
            D = NP.GE.20
            IF(.NOT. D) GO TO 500
            DO 400 M = 5, 80, 5
            A = NP + 2*M.LE.160
            IF(.NOT. A) GO TO 400
            B = NP + M.GE.70
            IF(.NOT. B) GO TO 400
            C = M.GT.NP
            IF(.NOT. C) GO TO 400
            WRITE(2, 10) NP, M
    10      FORMAT(5X, 'P = ', I4, 3X, 'M = ', I4)
   400      CONTINUE
   500      CONTINUE
            STOP
            END
```

While this example was rather simple, this sort of problem arises frequently, and it can be of immense practical importance. One aspect, which is quite common, is this: Suppose that potatoes cost $2.00 per sack and macaroni costs $1.15 per box. Find the solution that satisfies the given conditions and that costs the least. This is an example of what is called the *general linear programming problem*. Much work has been done on the subject to develop efficient algorithms for finding such solutions, and the subject is too complex to go into here. Imagine, however, what it would be like if our mess sergeant were trying to find the least expensive way to buy 100 different items, subject to, say, 200 conditions about the minimum quantity of each needed, maximum funds available for each item, maximum amount of each item that could be kept on hand, etc. Such problems can become very complicated, and a computer is definitely needed to find a solution. However, we could add a few statements to find an approximate best solution among the points covered during the search. (See Exercise 47 at the end of this chapter.)

■ Logical Arrays

We can form logical arrays in much the same way that we formed fixed- or floating-point arrays. The difference is that each variable associated with a logical array is a logical variable.

Recall that the statement DIMENSION A(10) sets up an array of ten elements A(1), A(2), ..., A(10), and that each of these is a floating-point variable. If we write the statements

        LOGICAL A
        DIMENSION A(10)

then A will be set up as a logical array consisting of ten elements, each of which is a logical variable. So the value of A(1) will be either .TRUE. or .FALSE. . The LOGICAL statement specifies that A is of logical type and the DIMENSION statement specifies that A is an array.

There is a shorter way of writing the above two statements, which is often more convenient to use. We can combine the DIMENSION statement with the LOGICAL statement and write

        LOGICAL A(10)

This means the same thing as the above two statements: that A is a logical array of ten elements. In the general statement

        LOGICAL var_1, var_2, ..., var_n

each of the variable names may be either a simple variable or a subscripted variable with the dimensions given. For example, the statement

```
LOGICAL A, B, P(10), Q(3)
```

would specify that A and B are logical variables and P and Q are logical arrays of size 10 and 3, respectively. So P(1), P(2), ..., P(10), Q(1), Q(2), Q(3) are all logical variables.

We can also use two- and three-dimensional logical arrays. The statement

```
LOGICAL XL(2, 5)
```

would establish XL as a logical array with the ten elements

```
XL(1, 1), XL(1, 2), XL(1, 3), XL(1, 4), XL(1, 5)
XL(2, 1), XL(2, 2), XL(2, 3), XL(2, 4), XL(2, 5)
```

Logical arrays can be useful when repeated tests must be made and the results stored. For instance, suppose that A and B are floating-point arrays and that L is a logical array. We might want to set L(I) = .TRUE. if A(I) > B(I). This can be done as follows:

```
      DIMENSION A(50), B(50)
      LOGICAL L(50)
      DO 5 K = 1, 50
    5 L(K) = A(K).GT.B(K)
```

Sometimes iterative procedures involving logical variables are required. This is another case where logical arrays can be useful. Suppose that L is a logical array of size 50; then we want to assign values to the logical variables P and Q by

```
P = L(1) .OR. L(2) .OR. L(3) .OR. ... .OR. L(50)
Q = L(1) .AND. L(2) .AND. L(3) .AND. ... .AND. L(50)
```

Rather than write out the whole expressions, we can use an iterative procedure. One way would be to use the statements

```
      P = .FALSE.
      Q = .TRUE.
      DO 9 K = 1, 50
      P = P .OR. L(K)
    9 Q = Q .AND. L(K)
```

Since P is .FALSE. to start with, P .OR. L(1) will have the same value as L(1). On the next time through the DO loop, P .OR. L(2) will have the same value as L(1) .OR. L(2), etc.

In the same way, since Q is .TRUE. to start with, Q .AND. L(1) will have the same value as L(1). On the second time through the DO loop, Q .AND. L(2) will have the same value as L(1) .AND. L(2). At the completion of the DO loop, P and Q will have the desired values.

We have seen that when complicated tests must be made in a program, logical variables and the logical IF statement can be of great help in programming. When many similar tests involving logical variables are required, logical arrays can be useful. We shall see an application of logical arrays in the next example.

Example 4

In a certain city all the streets downtown are one-way. The city planners were thoughtful enough so that even with this system one could travel from any one place to any other. The trouble is that some of the streets pass under low bridges, and so cannot be used by large trucks. Figure 9-6 shows the six major intersections in the city (identified by the numbers 1-6), and the lines in the figure show the roads between the intersections that can be used by trucks with the directions of travel indicated by arrows.

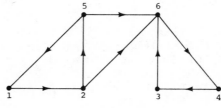

FIGURE 9-6

A trucking firm wants to know from which points to which a truck can travel. For instance, a truck can get from 1 to 3 by going from 1 to 2, 2 to 6, 6 to 4, and 4 to 3. But a truck could not get back from 6 to 1 by any route.

Before trying to program a solution to this problem, let us consider the method to be used. For our method, we shall construct a tree diagram for each starting point, which will show what points can be reached from the starting point.

We begin with point 1. The only point that can be reached from point 1 by a direct route (that is, along a straight line) is point 2. We write this diagrammatically as shown in Fig. 9-7.

1——2

FIGURE 9-7

Now from point 2, there are two direct routes which can be taken: one leading to 5 and the other leading to 6. This we write as shown in Fig. 9-8. From each of these points, we show in Fig. 9-9 the points that can be reached by a direct route. On the bottom branch, we note that the only point that can be reached from 5

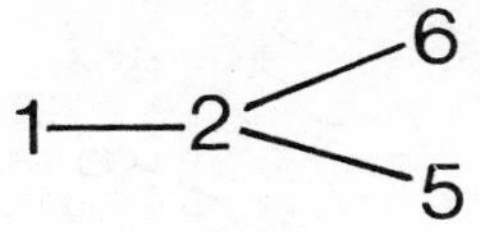

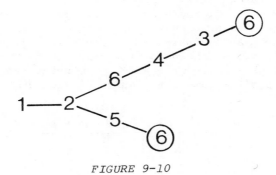

FIGURE 9-8

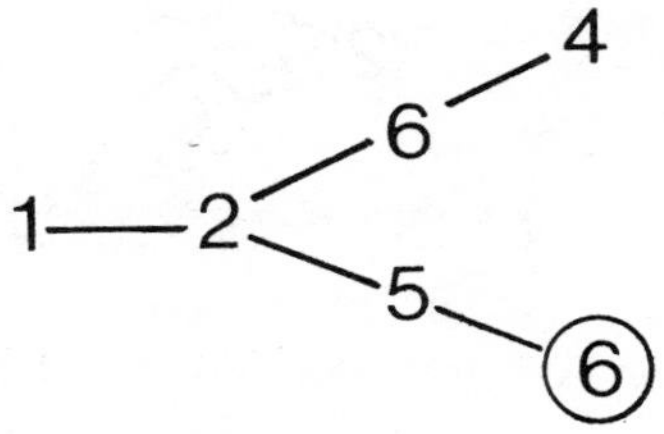

FIGURE 9-9

(besides the starting point, 1) is 6. But we have already succeeded in reaching 6 at an earlier step (on the top branch). So, by continuing the bottom branch, we can reach no points which have not already been reached. To indicate that we are at the end of a limb on this branch, we circle the 6. We continue the top branch until we arrive at a point which is already in the diagram.

When all branches have been terminated in this way, the diagram is complete. This is shown in Fig. 9-10. Any point that appears in Fig. 9-10 can be reached from point 1 (the starting point), and all points that can be reached from point 1 appear in this diagram.

FIGURE 9-10

Starting now from point 5, we obtain the diagram shown in Fig. 9-11. As before, this diagram contains all the points 1, 2, 3, 4, 5, and 6. This means that starting from point 5, any other point may be reached.

Starting from point 3, we obtain the diagram shown in Fig. 9-12. This diagram shows that points 6 and 4 may be reached from

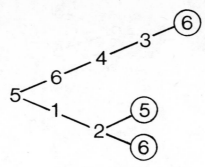

FIGURE 9-11

point 3, but 1, 2, and 5 may not be reached by any route starting at point 3.

$$3 — 6 — 4 — ③$$

FIGURE 9-12

We have made diagrams for the cases of starting at points 1, 3, and 5. If we also make diagrams starting with points 2, 4, and 6, we will have a complete solution to the problem. To determine whether a truck can travel from point I to point J, we look at the diagram starting with I and see if J is in I.

To program this in FORTRAN, we will use several logical arrays. The first array we will call RT (short for route). It will be a 6 X 6 logical array which will represent Fig. 9-6. We will define RT(I, J) to be .TRUE. if there is a direct route from point I to point J. If there is no such route, RT(I, J) = .FALSE. . By a direct route, we mean a straight-line route in Fig. 9-6. Thus, RT will have the values shown in Fig. 9-13, where T stands for .TRUE. and a blank stands for .FALSE. . Convince yourself that this array conveys the same information as Fig. 9-6:

	1	2	3	4	5	6
1	T	T				
2		T			T	T
3			T			T
4			T	T		T
5	T				T	T
6				T		T

FIGURE 9-13
Values of the array RT

(We would probably want to read in these values from the cards, but we will ignore this for the moment since input and output of logical variables is taken up in the next section.)

What we want to find in this problem is whether or not there is any path (not necessarily a direct route) from point I to point J. We shall set up a 6 X 6 logical matrix PATH, and the program will have to set PATH(I, J) = .TRUE. if there is a path from I to J, and .FALSE. if there is no path.

Now, we shall need some way to represent the process of making the diagrams we use to solve the problem. To represent this process in a FORTRAN program, it will be convenient to use three logical arrays, which we will call POINT, PRES, and NEXT. These will be one-dimensional logical arrays.

At each step of constructing a tree, PRES tells which points are under consideration in the present step. For example, in the third step of making the diagram starting with 5, the diagram looks like Fig. 9-14. The points under consideration in this step are 2 and 4. To indicate this, we shall set PRES(2) and PRES(4) equal to .TRUE.; PRES(1), PRES(3), PRES(5), and PRES(6) will be .FALSE. .

FIGURE 9-14

The array POINT tells which points are already in the diagram. In the third step of making the diagram beginning with 5 (see Fig. 9-14), the points 1, 2, 4, 5, and 6 have already been reached in the diagram, so POINT(1), POINT(2), POINT(4), POINT(5), and POINT(6) will be .TRUE., and POINT(3) will be .FALSE. at this step.

To go from the present step to the next step, we shall set NEXT(I) = .TRUE. if point I can be reached by a direct route from any of the points under consideration in the present step. To do this, we can use the statements

```
      DO 26 I = 1, 6
      IF(.NOT. PRES(I)) GO TO 26
      DO 25 J = 1, 6
      IF(RT(I, J)) NEXT(J) = .TRUE.
   25 CONTINUE
   26 CONTINUE
```

The first DO loop will examine each of the points to see if it is in the present step. If not, the second DO loop is not performed for the value of I. If point I is in the current step [that is, if PRES(I) = .TRUE.], the second DO loop determines which points

can be reached from I by a direct route, and sets NEXT(J) = .TRUE.
for these points. In the step corresponding to Fig. 9-14, PRES(2)
and PRES(4) are the only elements of PRES which are .TRUE., so we
examine

$$RT(2, 1), RT(2, 2), \ldots, RT(2, 6)$$
$$RT(4, 1), RT(4, 2), \ldots, RT(4, 6)$$

Of these, only RT(4, 3) and RT(2, 5) and RT(2, 6) are .TRUE., so
we set NEXT(3), NEXT(5), and NEXT(6) equal to .TRUE. to show that
the points 3, 5, and 6 are in the next step. This corresponds to
drawing the next branches in the diagram, as shown in Fig. 9-15.

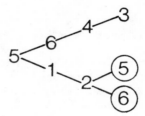

FIGURE 9-15

Of the new points 3, 5, and 6, we want to see which ones have already been reached in the diagram. To do this, we compare NEXT(I)
with POINT(I). If they both are .TRUE., this means that point I
is in the present step or some previous step, as well as in the
next step. We shall set NEXT(I) = .FALSE., since there is no need
to consider point I again. This corresponds to circling the 5 and
6 in Fig. 9-15 to show that they are already in the diagram. This
process can be carried out by the statements

```
        DO 30 I = 1, 6
        IF(NEXT(I) .AND. POINT(I)) NEXT(I) = .FALSE.
    30  CONTINUE
```

   Next, we test to see if we are finished with the diagram.
To do this in the program, we test to see if there are any points
in the next step which were not already reached. Since we have
already set NEXT(I) = .FALSE. if point I has been reached, we set
L = NEXT(1) .OR. NEXT(2) .OR. ... .OR. NEXT(6) and then if L is
.TRUE., we are not finished, so we reinitialize the arrays
involved and repeat the above process.

   If L is .FALSE., we are finished with the diagram, so we fill
in a row of the array PATH by setting PATH(N, J) = .TRUE. if
POINT(J) is .TRUE. . After this is done, we reinitialize the
various arrays and begin again with a different starting point N.
The complete program is as follows:

```
        LOGICAL RT(6, 6), PATH(6, 6), POINT(6), PRES(6), NEXT(6), L
C       INITIALIZE PATH
        DO 1 I = 1, 6
        DO 1 J = 1, 6
   1    PATH(I, J) = .FALSE.
C       BEGIN TREE STARTING WITH POINT N
        DO 100 N = 1, 6
        DO 5 I = 1, 6
        POINT(I) = .FALSE.
   5    PRES(I) = .FALSE.
        POINT(N) = .TRUE.
        PRES(N) = .TRUE.
  10    DO 15 I = 1, 6
  15    NEXT(I) = .FALSE.
C       FOR EACH POINT IN THE PRESENT STEP, SET
C       NEXT(J) = .TRUE. IF J CAN BE REACHED
C       BY A DIRECT ROUTE FROM I
        DO 26 I = 1, 6
        IF(.NOT. PRES(I)) GO TO 26
        DO 25 J = 1, 6
        IF(RT(I, J)) NEXT(J) = .TRUE.
  25    CONTINUE
  26    CONTINUE
C       SET NEXT(I) = .FALSE. IF I HAS
C       ALREADY BEEN REACHED ON A PREVIOUS
C       STEP
        DO 30 I = 1, 6
        IF(NEXT(I) .AND. POINT(I)) NEXT(I) = .FALSE.
  30    CONTINUE
C       IF NO NEW POINTS HAVE BEEN REACHED,
C       THE DIAGRAM BEGINNING WITH N IS
C       COMPLETE
        L = .FALSE.
        DO 35 I = 1, 6
  35    L = L .OR. NEXT(I)
        IF(.NOT. L) GO TO 50
C       SET POINT (I) = .TRUE. IF I HAS BEEN
C       REACHED ON THIS STEP.  NEXT STEP BECOMES
C       CURRENT STEP
        DO 40 I = 1, 6
        IF(NEXT(I)) POINT(I) = .TRUE.
  40    PRES(I) = NEXT(I)
        GO TO 10
C       THE DIAGRAM BEGINNING WITH N IS
C       COMPLETE.  FILL IN THE NTH ROW
C       OF PATH AND BEGIN A NEW DIAGRAM
  50    DO 60 J = 1, 6
        IF(POINT(J)) PATH(N, J) = .TRUE.
  60    CONTINUE
 100    CONTINUE
        STOP
        END
```

At the completion of this program, the array PATH will have the values shown in Fig. 9-16, where T stands for .TRUE. and blank stands for .FALSE. From Fig. 9-16, we see that there is a path from point 1 to any other point, and from point 5 to any other point, but that starting at point 3 only points 3, 4, and 6 can be reached—the same results as those we found using tree diagrams.

	1	2	3	4	5	6
1	T	T	T	T	T	T
2	T	T	T	T	T	T
3			T	T		T
4			T	T		T
5	T	T	T	T	T	T
6			T	T		T

FIGURE 9-16

■ Input and Output of Logical Variables

Values for logical variables can be read or written in FORTRAN just as numeric data are. To do this, the L field descriptor is used. The L field descriptor is used in a FORMAT statement just like the other field descriptors discussed in Chapter 6. The general form is

$$L n$$

where n is an unsigned integer constant giving the length of the field.

When the value of a logical variable is written under an Ln specification, $n - 1$ blanks will be printed, followed by the character T or F according to whether the value is .TRUE. or .FALSE. . For example, if P, Q, and R are logical variables with values .TRUE., .FALSE., and .TRUE., respectively, then the statements

```
      WRITE(2, 11) P, Q, R
   11 FORMAT(L3, L2, L1)
```

would print out the data bbTbFT. The L3 field for P prints two leading blanks before the T, the L2 field for Q prints one leading blank, and the L1 field for R does not print any leading blanks.

When it is used for input, the Ln field causes n characters to be read. Blank spaces may precede the data if desired. Only the first nonblank character in the field is interpreted. It must be either T or F, and the variable will be assigned a value .TRUE. or .FALSE. accordingly. If the statements

```
      READ(1, 5) P
    5 FORMAT(L6)
```

were used to read the characters bbTbbb from a card, then the variable P would receive the value .TRUE. since the first nonblank character in the input field is T. The data Tbbbbb or bbbbbT would
also be read as .TRUE. . If the input field contained the characters bbTRUE, this again would cause a value of .TRUE. to be read,
since the first nonblank character is T, and it is only the first
nonblank character in the field that is used to determine the value
of the data. Actually, bbTOMb or bbFRED would also work but, in
practice, the L1 field is usually used for input of logical variables.

Example 5

In this example, we shall write a program to grade a true-
false test. The test consists of 20 questions and each question
is worth 5 points. The input data consists of one card for each
student. The student's matriculation number is punched in columns 1-6, and columns 7-26 contain answers (each answer being a T
or an F) to the questions. The first card read will have zeros in
columns 1-6 and the correct answers to the questions in columns
7-26. The last card read will have 9's in columns 1-6. For each
student, the program must print out the matriculation number,
answers, and a score.

To solve this problem, we shall first read the correct answers
into a logical array, CA, of correct answers. This will be a one-
dimensional array of size 20 with CA(I) equal to the correct answer for question I. This read operation is accomplished with the
statements

```
        READ(1, 5) MAT, (CA(I), I = 1, 20)
     5  FORMAT(I6, 20L1)
```

The implied DO loop in the READ statement reads in all 20 answers,
each under an L1 format. We have also read in the value of the
matriculation number MAT, which should be 0 on the first card.
Just to make sure that it is, we can test as follows:

```
        IF(MAT.NE.0) STOP
```

Then if the correct answer card is accidentally left out of the
data set, the program would stop rather than give everyone the
wrong scores. To read in the first student's answers, we use
the statement

```
        READ(1, 5) MAT, (SA(I), I = 1, 20)
```

where SA is another logical array in which the student's answers
are stored.

The next thing to be done in the program is to see if MAT is
999999; if it is, we are finished. For any other value of MAT,
we compute the student's score by comparing each SA(I) to each

CA(I). If they are the same, we shall add 5 points to the score NSC. This is done using a logical IF statement. Note that SA(I) and CA(I) are the same if they are either both .TRUE. or both .FALSE., so the expression

    CA(I) .AND. SA(I) .OR. .NOT. CA(I) .AND. .NOT. SA(I)

will be .TRUE. if and only if CA(I) and SA(I) have the same value.

To output the results, we use the statements

```
      WRITE(2, 60) MAT, (SA(I), I = 1, 20), NSC
   60 FORMAT(1H0, I6, 20L2, ' SCORE =', I4)
```

The L2 output fields will skip a space between each consecutive answer. A sample line of output would be

    142200 T F F T ... T SCORE = 50

The flowchart for this program is shown in Fig. 9-17. The complete program is:

```
      LOGICAL SA(20), CA(20)
      READ(1, 5) MAT, (CA(I), I = 1, 20)
    5 FORMAT(I6, 20L1)
      IF(MAT.NE.0) STOP
   10 READ(1, 5) MAT, (SA(I), I = 1, 20)
      IF(MAT.EQ.999999) STOP
      NSC = 0
      DO 50 I = 1, 20
      IF(CA(I) .AND. SA(I) .OR. .NOT. CA(I) .AND. .NOT. SA(I))
     1NSC = NSC + 5
   50 CONTINUE
      WRITE(2, 60) MAT, (SA(I), I = 1, 20), NSC
   60 FORMAT(1H0, I6, 20L2, ' SCORE =', I4)
      GO TO 10
      END
```

We conclude this chapter with a final example showing again the power of logical variables and the logical IF statement in dealing with multiple tests in a fairly involved program.

Example 6[2]

We want to program the machine to play the game tic-tac-toe. The game is played on a 3 X 3 board like the one shown in Fig. 9-18. The machine moves first by printing one of the numbers on the board to indicate its move. The player then selects a number

---

[2]This problem is best done where on-line devices such as teletypes or typewriter consoles are available so that one or more students can use it in a conversational mode.

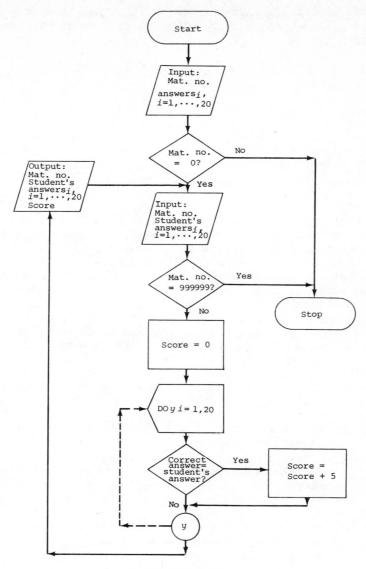

FIGURE 9-17
Flowchart for Example 5

to indicate a move and this number is read into the machine. The
machine then prints out its second move, and so forth until one
player wins or the game is a draw. A player wins if three moves
form a row, either horizontally, vertically, or diagonally. If
all the cells have been taken and neither player has three in a
row, the game is a draw.

A little experimentation will show that when properly played
the game will always result in a draw. What we want to do is to

program the machine so that the game will result in a draw unless the second player makes a mistake, in which case the machine should win if possible.

11	12	13
21	22	23
31	32	33

FIGURE 9-18

Although this game is very simple in nature, it turns out to be rather complicated to program the machine to play it because there are so many possibilities to be considered. The first thing we have to do is to decide on a strategy for the machine to follow. That is, we need a set of rules so that when the machine knows what moves have been made, it will be able to determine what its next move will be.

There are several possible strategies which could be used. We shall use the following rules for determining the machine's moves.

Rule 1: The machine's first move will be in the center (cell 22).

Rule 2: If the machine can get three in a row on its move, it should do so.

Rule 3: If the machine cannot get three in a row, but the second player has two in a row, the machine should block by moving to the vacant cell in that row.

Rule 4: If the machine cannot win on its move, and it is not necessary to block as in Rule 3, then the machine should move to get two moves in the same row.

Rule 5: If this can be done by moving in a corner, the machine should do so.

Rule 6: If none of the above rules apply, the machine should move in any vacant cell.

To illustrate these rules, consider an example. Rule 1 says that the first move is in the center. Suppose the second player's first move is in cell 11 (see Fig. 9-19). There is no way the machine can get three in a row, so Rule 2 does not apply, and we go on to consider Rule 3. The second player does not have two in a row, so Rule 3 does not apply either. Rule 4 does apply, since

the machine can get two in a row by moving at any one of the cells
12, 21, 32, 23, 13, or 31. (Moving to 33 would not count as getting
two in a row, since the second player already has a move in that
diagonal.) In order to choose among these possible moves, we must
consider Rule 5, which says that a corner should be tried first.

11	12	13
O		
21	22	23
	X	
31	32	33

X = Machine's move
O = Second player's move

FIGURE 9-19

Thus, the machine should move in either 31 or 13. It does not
matter which of these is selected as long as the machine has some
way of choosing one or the other. Suppose it takes 13. The second
player would then be forced to move in 31 as shown in Fig. 9-20.

11	12	13
O		X
21	22	23
	X	
31	32	33
O		

FIGURE 9-20

Now, the decision process starts again for the machine's next
move. Rule 2 does not apply, because the machine cannot get three
in a row, but Rule 3 applies, since the second player has two in a
row in the first column. So, the machine should move in 21. If
the second player now moves in cell 23, the game will result in a
draw. Otherwise, the machine will win on its next move. In either
case, the machine should print out a message announcing that the
game is over.

The complete strategy for the machine is represented in the
flowchart of Fig. 9-21. Of course, this is just a general strategy.
In order to program the solution in FORTRAN, we shall need a more
specific procedure.

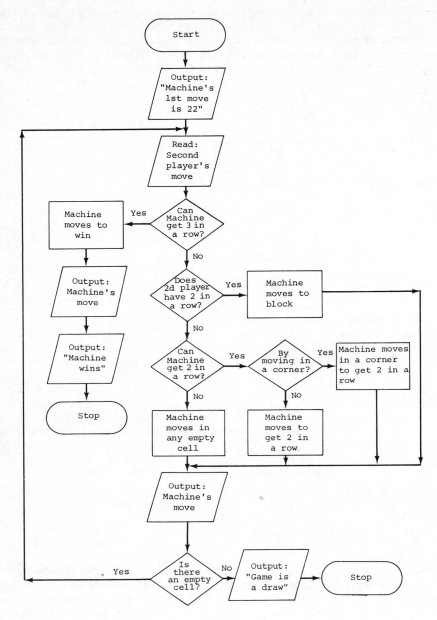

FIGURE 9-21
General flowchart for Example 6

The first thing we need is some way of representing the board and moves. To do this, we shall use a 3 X 3 fixed-point array called M. We shall set

$$M(I, J) = 0 \quad \text{if no move has been made in cell IJ}$$
$$M(I, J) = 1 \quad \text{if the machine has moved in cell IJ}$$
$$M(I, J) = -1 \quad \text{if the second player has moved in cell IJ}$$

The first step in the program will be to initialize the array M. Then the machine will make its first move, and the second player's first move will be read. First, to make sure the second player is not cheating, we shall test to see if the move is in an empty cell. If it is not, we shall ask for another move. When a valid move is made, it will be recorded by assigning -1 to the proper element of the array M.

Now, we shall be using three arrays besides M in the program. These arrays will give the sums of the rows, columns, and diagonals of the array M. NROW gives the sum of the rows, so

$$NROW(1) = M(1, 1) + M(1, 2) + M(1, 3)$$
$$NROW(2) = M(2, 1) + M(2, 2) + M(2, 3)$$
$$NROW(3) = M(3, 1) + M(3, 2) + M(3, 3)$$

Likewise, NCOL gives the sums of the columns, so

$$NCOL(1) = M(1, 1) + M(2, 1) + M(3, 1)$$
$$NCOL(2) = M(1, 2) + M(2, 2) + M(3, 2)$$
$$NCOL(3) = M(1, 3) + M(2, 3) + M(3, 3)$$

NDIAG gives the sums of the diagonals, so

$$NDIAG(1) = M(1, 1) + M(2, 2) + M(3, 3)$$
$$NDIAG(2) = M(1, 3) + M(2, 2) + M(3, 1)$$

These arrays will be used in determining the machine's move. For instance, if NROW(1) = 2, we shall know that the machine can win by playing in row 1, since the machine must already have two moves in row 1. But we shall come to that in a moment. What concerns us now is that after each move by the second player, we have to recompute the values of these arrays.

The flowchart corresponding to this first part of the program is shown in Fig. 9-22. The FORTRAN statements are as follows:

```
       DIMENSION M(3,3), NROW(3), NCOL(3), NDIAG(3)
       LOGICAL Z
       COMMON N, I, J, ND
       DO 10 I = 1, 3
       DO 10 J = 1, 3
  10   M(I, J) = 0
       I = 2
       J = 2
       NMOVE = 1
  20   M(I, J) = 1
       WRITE(2, 25) I, J
  25   FORMAT(' MACHINE MOVES AT' , 1X, 2I1)
  30   WRITE(2, 35)
  35   FORMAT(' ENTER YOUR MOVE')
       READ(1, 40) I, J
  40   FORMAT(2I1)
```

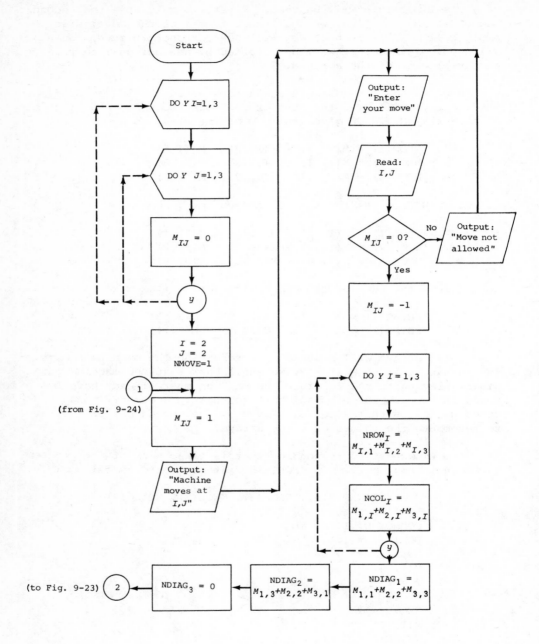

FIGURE 9-22

```
       IF(M(I, J).EQ.0) GO TO 50
       WRITE(2, 45)
   45  FORMAT(' MOVE NOT ALLOWED')
       GO TO 30
   50  M(I, J) = -1
       DO 55 I = 1, 3
       NROW(I) = M(I, 1) + M(I, 2) + M(I, 3)
   55  NCOL(I) = M(1, I) + M(2, I) + M(3, I)
       NDIAG(1) = M(1, 1) + M(2, 2) + M(3, 3)
       NDIAG(2) = M(1, 3) + M(2, 2) + M(3, 1)
       NDIAG(3) = 0
```

The LOGICAL and COMMON are for use with later parts of the program. The variable NMOVE will also be used later. The statement

```
       NDIAG(3) = 0
```

needs a little explanation. Actually, of course, there is no "third" diagonal on the board. It will turn out, however, that it is convenient to have a dummy element for the array NDIAG in order to make the testing sections shorter. We shall see shortly how this works.

Now, the first part of our strategy is to see if the machine can win. This is possible if the machine has two moves in a row. This will be the case if and only if some element NROW(I), NCOL(I), or NDIAG(I) is equal to 2. In order to test for this, we shall consider each cell IJ on the board, and we test to see if the cell is empty, (M(I, J) = 0), and to see if the row, column, or diagonal containing that cell has a sum of 2. If this is the case, we shall move in the cell; otherwise, we shall go on to the next part of the strategy.

In order to carry out the testing involved, we shall have to repeatedly generate the pairs of subscripts for the array M. It will be convenient to have a subroutine to do this. The subroutine will be called CELL. It will share four variables in common with the main program:

N is an integer from 1 to 8; it will be used as an index of a DO loop in the main program.

I and J are integers from 1 to 3 which will be used as subscripts for the array M; I and J depend on N.

ND is a number from 1 to 3 which depends on N; it tells which diagonal the cell M(I, J) is in.

```
       ND = 1 if cell IJ is in the diagonal from 11 to 33.
       ND = 2 if cell IJ is in the diagonal from 13 to 31.
       ND = 3 if cell IJ is in no diagonal.
```

Given a number N, the values of I, J, and ND may be determined from the following table:

N	I	J	ND
1	1	1	1
2	1	3	2
3	3	3	1
4	3	1	2
5	1	2	3
6	2	3	3
7	3	2	3
8	2	1	3

The subroutine to generate these values is very straightforward:

```
      SUBROUTINE CELL
      COMMON N, I, J, ND
      IF(N.NE.1) GO TO 2
      I = 1
      J = 1
      ND = 1
      RETURN
    2 IF(N.NE.2) GO TO 3
      I = 1
      J = 3
      ND = 2
      RETURN
    3 IF(N.NE.3) GO TO 4
      I = 3
      J = 3
      ND = 1
      RETURN
    4 IF(N.NE.4) GO TO 5
      I = 3
      J = 1
      ND = 2
      RETURN
    5 IF(N.NE.5) GO TO 6
      I = 1
      J = 2
      ND = 3
      RETURN
    6 IF(N.NE.6) GO TO 7
      I = 2
      J = 3
      ND = 3
      RETURN
```

```
   7  IF(N.NE.7) GO TO 8
      I = 3
      J = 2
      ND = 3
      RETURN
   8  IF(N.NE.8) STOP
      I = 2
      J = 1
      ND = 3
      RETURN
      END
```

Now, getting back to the main program, consider the corner cells 11, 13, 33, and 31. The machine can win by playing in one of these cells if

1. the cell is empty (M(I, J) = 0);

2. either the row, column, or diagonal containing the cell has a sum of 2.

For the cell 11, this condition can be expressed as

```
      ((NROW(1).EQ.2) .OR. (NCOL(1).EQ.2) .OR. (NDIAG(1).EQ.2))
         .AND. (M(1, 1).EQ.0)
```

Using the logical variable Z, we can break this into four parts:

```
      Z = NROW(1).EQ.2
      Z = Z .OR. NCOL(1).EQ.2
      Z = Z .OR. NDIAG(1).EQ.2
      Z = Z .AND. M(1, 1).EQ.0
```

Then Z will be .TRUE. if and only if the machine can win by playing cell 11.

For the other three corner cells, the procedure is similar. Now, the coordinates of the four corner cells are returned by the subroutine CELL for the first four values of N, and we can perform the same test for all four corner cells by using the following DO loop.

```
      DO 75 N = 1, 4
      CALL CELL
      Z = NROW(I).EQ.2
      Z = Z .OR. NCOL(J).EQ.2
      Z = Z .OR. NDIAG(ND).EQ.2
      Z = Z .AND. M(I, J).EQ.0
      IF(Z) GO TO 100
   75 CONTINUE
```

At Statement 100 the machine will indicate that it has won. If the program "falls through" the DO loop, then we want to test to see if the machine can win by moving at one of the cells 12, 23, 32, or 21.

The procedure for this is like the one above. The only difference is that these cells are not in any diagonal, so that part of the test is unnecessary. The coordinates of these cells are returned for the second four values of N by the subroutine CELL, and again we can use a DO loop:

```
      DO 80 N = 5, 8
      CALL CELL
      Z = NROW(I).EQ.2
      Z = Z .OR. NCOL(J).EQ.2
      Z = Z .AND. M(I, J).EQ.0
      IF(Z) GO TO 100
   80 CONTINUE
```

Actually, this DO loop can be combined with the previous loop to make the program a little shorter. This is done by using the dummy element NDIAG(3) which was set equal to 0 earlier in the program. When ND = 3, the statement Z = Z .OR. NDIAG(ND).EQ.2 will leave the value of Z unchanged. In other words, we can let N run from 1 to 8 in the first DO loop and just omit the second DO loop.

If the machine cannot get three in a row, the program will fall through this DO loop and branch to Statement 105, where we begin the next part of the strategy. If the machine can get three in a row, the program will branch to Statement 100, where the machine will indicate its move and stop. The flowchart for this part of the program is given in Fig. 9-23. The FORTRAN statements are as follows:

```
      DO 75 N = 1, 8
      CALL CELL
      Z = NROW(I).EQ.2
      Z = Z .OR. NCOL(J).EQ.2
      Z = Z .OR. NDIAG(ND).EQ.2
      Z = Z .AND. M(I, J).EQ. 0
      IF(Z) GO TO 100
   75 CONTINUE
      GO TO 105
  100 WRITE(2, 25) I, J
      WRITE(2, 101)
  101 FORMAT(' MACHINE WINS')
      STOP
```

The next part of the strategy is to block the second player if he has two in a row. This will be the case if the sum of a row, column, or diagonal is -2. To test for this condition, we use a procedure much like the one used to test for a machine win. For each cell, we test to see if the cell is empty and if the sum of the row, column, or diagonal containing the cell is -2. If so, the machine will move in the cell. Referring to Fig. 9-21, however, we see that we must remember to test to see if the game is a draw. An easy way to do this is to observe that since there are nine cells on the board, the game will be a draw if the machine has not won on

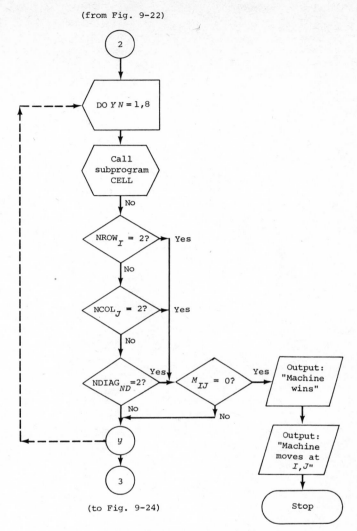

(from Fig. 9-22)

FIGURE 9-23
Machine wins if possible

its fifth move. We can test easily for this by initializing a
variable NMOVE to 1 after the machine's first move, and then adding
1 to NMOVE each time the machine moves. If NMOVE = 5 and the
machine has not won, the game is a draw.

The flowchart for this part of the program is given in Fig.
9-24. The FORTRAN statements are listed on page 237.

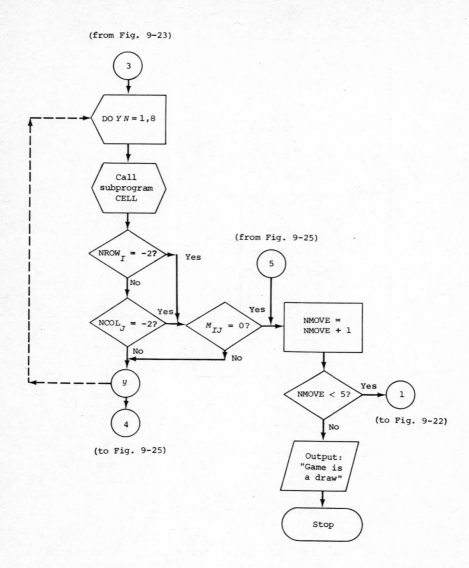

FIGURE 9-24
Machine moves to block if necessary

```
105   DO 110 N = 1, 8
      CALL CELL
      Z = NROW(I).EQ.-2
      Z = Z .OR. NCOL(J).EQ.-2
      Z = Z .AND. M(I, J).EQ.0
      IF(Z) GO TO 200
110   CONTINUE
      .
      .
      .

200   NMOVE = NMOVE + 1
      IF(NMOVE.LT.5) GO TO 20
      WRITE(2, 25) I, J
      WRITE(2, 205)
205   FORMAT(' GAME IS A DRAW')
      STOP
```

Notice that it is not necessary to check whether or not the second player has two in a row diagonally, since the machine has a move in the center.

If the second player does not have two in a row, the machine will try to get two in a row. Thus, the machine will move in a row, column, or diagonal whose sum is 1, and where there is an empty cell. This, again, is done by considering each cell in turn, calling the subroutine CELL, and determining whether or not the machine should move there. Recall that Rule 5 says that the machine should first try to move at a corner. Since CELL returns the coordinates of the corner cells for the first four values of N, we can just use a DO loop to do this.

Finally, if it is not possible to get two in a row, the machine should move in any vacant cell.

The flowchart for this last part of the program is shown in Fig. 9-25. The complete tic-tac-toe program is:

```
C     PROGRAM TO PLAY TIC-TAC-TOE
C     USES SUBROUTINE CELL
      DIMENSION M(3,3), NROW(3), NCOL(3), NDIAG(3)
      LOGICAL Z
      COMMON N, I, J, ND
      DO 10 I = 1, 3
      DO 10 J = 1, 3
10    M(I, J) = 0
      I = 2
      J = 2
      NMOVE = 1
20    M(I, J) = 1
      WRITE(2, 25) I, J
25    FORMAT(' MACHINE MOVES AT' ,1X, 2I1)
30    WRITE(2, 35)
35    FORMAT(' ENTER YOUR MOVE')
```

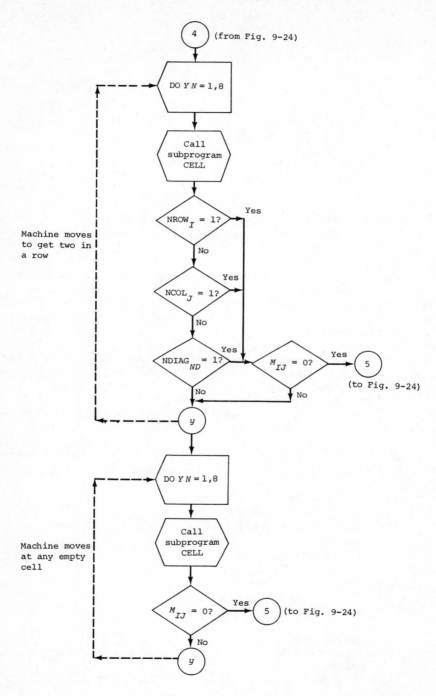

FIGURE 9-25

```
         READ(1, 40) I, J
   40    FORMAT(2I1)
         IF(M(I, J).EQ.0) GO TO 50
         WRITE(2, 45)
   45    FORMAT(' MOVE NOT ALLOWED')
         GO TO 30
   50    M(I, J) = -1
         DO 55 I = 1, 3
         NROW(I) = M(I, 1) + M(I, 2) + M(I, 3)
   55    NCOL(I) = M(1, I) + M(2, I) + M(3, I)
         NDIAG(1) = M(1, 1) + M(2, 2) + M(3, 3)
         NDIAG(2) + M(1, 3) + M(2, 2) + M(3, 1)
         NDIAG(3) = 0
C        MACHINE MOVES TO GET THREE
C        IN A FOW IF POSSIBLE
         DO 75 N = 1, 8
         CALL CELL
         Z = NROW(I).EQ.2
         Z = Z .OR. NCOL(J).EQ.2
         Z = Z .OR. NDIAG(ND).EQ.2
         Z = Z .AND. M(I, J).EQ.0
         IF(Z) GO TO 100
   75    CONTINUE
         GO TO 105
  100    WRITE(2, 25) I, J
         WRITE(2, 101)
  101    FORMAT(' MACHINE WINS')
         STOP
C        IF SECOND PLAYER HAS TWO IN A ROW, BLOCK
  105    DO 110 N = 1, 8
         CALL CELL
         Z = NROW(I).EQ.-2
         Z = Z .OR. NCOL(J).EQ.-2
         Z = Z .AND. M(I, J).EQ.0
         IF(Z) GO TO 200
  110    CONTINUE
C        MACHINE MOVES TO GET TWO IN A ROW IF POSSIBLE
         DO 120 N = 1, 8
         CALL CELL
         Z = NROW(I).EQ.1
         Z = Z .OR. NCOL(J).EQ.1
         Z = Z .OR. NDIAG(ND).EQ.1
         Z = Z .AND. M(I, J).EQ.0
         IF(Z) GO TO 200
  120    CONTINUE
C        MACHINE MOVES IN ANY VACANT CELL
         DO 130 N = 1, 8
         CALL CELL
         Z = M(I, J).EQ.0
         IF(Z) GO TO 200
  130    CONTINUE
         STOP
C        TEST TO SEE IF GAME IS A DRAW
```

```
    200   NMOVE = NMOVE + 1
          IF(NMOVE.LT.5) GO TO 20
          WRITE(2, 25) I, J
          WRITE(2, 205)
    205   FORMAT(' GAME IS A DRAW')
          STOP
          END
```

■ Exercises

What is the value of each logical expression?

1. .TRUE. .AND. .TRUE.
2. .FALSE. .AND. .FALSE.
3. .FALSE. .AND. .TRUE.
4. .FALSE. .OR. .TRUE.
5. .FALSE. .OR. .FALSE.
6. (.TRUE. .AND. .FALSE.) .OR. .FALSE.
7. .TRUE. .AND. (.FALSE. .OR. .FALSE.)
8. (.NOT. .FALSE.) .AND. .TRUE.
9. (.NOT. .FALSE.) .OR. .FALSE.
10. .NOT. (.FALSE. .OR. .FALSE.)

When the value of P is .TRUE., Q is .FALSE., and R is .TRUE., what is the value of the logical variable S in each of the following?

11. S = P .OR. .NOT. Q
12. S = P .AND. R
13. S = .NOT. (P .OR. R)

14. S = .NOT. P .OR. .NOT. Q
15. S = .NOT. (P .AND. Q)

Construct truth tables for each expression.

16. P .AND. .NOT. Q
17. .NOT. (P .OR. Q)
18. .NOT. P .AND. .NOT. Q

19. P .OR. Q .AND. R
20. P .OR. .NOT. (Q .AND. R)

For what values of the variables is each logical expression .TRUE.?

21. P .OR. .NOT. Q
22. .NOT. (P .AND. Q)
23. .NOT. (.NOT. P .OR. .NOT. Q)

24. P .AND. Q .AND. .NOT. R
25. .NOT. .NOT. P

What is the value of each relational expression?

26. 1.GE.0
27. 5.LT.10
28. 2.1.GE.2.1

29. 1.NE.2
30. 6.0.EQ.7.0
31. 10.2.GT.10.2

Find values of A, B, and C for which each expression is .TRUE. .

32. A.GT.B .OR. B.GT.C
33. A.LE.B .OR. B.LE.C

34. A.GE.B .AND. B.LT.C
35. .NOT. (A.LT.B .AND. B.LT.C)
36. A.EQ.B .OR. A.EQ.C .OR. B.EQ.C

Write a single logical IF statement for each decision flowchart.

37.

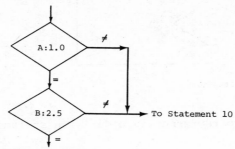

38.

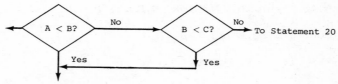

39.

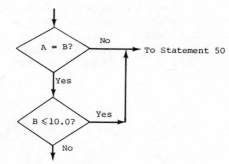

40.

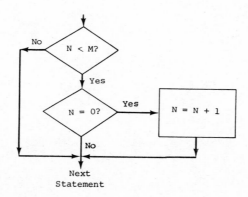

41.

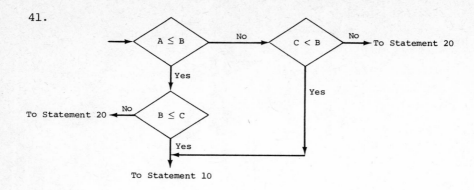

Write flowcharts to represent each decision statement in Exercises 42-26.

42. IF(A.LT.9.0 .AND. A.GT.0.0) B = 2.0*A

43. IF(N.EQ.1 .OR. N.EQ.3 .OR. N.EQ.5) M = N

44. IF(MOLL/J*J.EQ.MOLL) LAB = 0

45. IF(P.EQ.1.0 .OR. Q.EQ.P) GO TO 10

46. IF(R.LE.0.0 .OR. G.GT.100.0) R = 50.0

47. Modify Example 3 of this chapter (the macaroni and potatoes example) to find the minimum cost during the search. Before the outside loop, set CMIN = a large value, NPBEST = 0, and MBEST = 0. Near the WRITE statement, set C = 2.00*FLOAT(NP) + 1.15*FLOAT(M). Then if C < CMIN, set CMIN = C, NPBEST = NP, and MBEST = M.

Chapter

Alphameric Data and the DATA Statement

■ The A Specification

In the preceding chapters, we have been careful to use only numbers for all our FORTRAN arithmetic as well as input data. Output headings were made by using the Hollerith specification. Often our input will not be only in the form of numbers. For example, we might have the results of a mathematics examination punched on cards with the student's name in columns 1-20, identification number in columns 21-26, and score in columns 27-30. All that we need for any manipulations are the ID number and the score. However, in this example, we would also like to read in the name of the student and be able to list it in the output. FORTRAN provides a method for doing this with the A specification.

Characters used in this specification are known as *alphameric*, which comes from a combination of the words "alphabetic" and "numeric." However, any FORTRAN character, such as +, -, /, or *, can be input and output under the A format. The general form of this format is

   *m*A*n*

where *n* is the field length and *m* is a repeat factor. This *n* varies with the computer and may be as much as ten characters in word length. However, in all of our examples, we shall assume that an alphameric variable can have a maximum of only six characters.

Suppose we want to read a card that has the characters JOHN DOE in columns 1-8. To do so, we can consider it as two words, JOHN and DOE. We assign variable names just as we did in using numerical variables. Thus, the statement

```
      READ(1, 100) M, N
  100 FORMAT(A4, A4)
```

would read in JOHN for M and DOE for N. Also,

```
      WRITE(2, 101) M, N
  101 FORMAT(10X, A4, A4)
```

would print out the same characters, after skipping ten spaces.

Several alternate forms of input that accomplish the same
steps are:

```
        READ(1, 10) A, B, C, D, E, F, G, H
   10   FORMAT(8A1)
        READ(1, 11) H, I, J
   11   FORMAT(A3, A3, A2)
        READ(1, 12) A, B, C, D
   12   FORMAT(A2, A2, A2, A2)
        READ(1, 13) A, B
   13   FORMAT(A6, A2)
```

If a great deal of data is to be input under alphameric form, one
can use alphameric arrays. For example, suppose a data card is
punched as follows:

```
        Columns  1-5    ID number of a student
        Columns  6-8    Score on English final exam
        Columns  9-11   Score on Mathematics final exam
        Columns 12-14   Score on Chemistry final exam
        Column  15      Letter grade in English
        Column  16      Letter grade in Mathematics
        Column  17      Letter grade in Chemistry
        Columns 18-77   Student's name and address
        Columns 78-80   Blank; can be used to stop input data
```

A typical card might be

```
   12345092085087ABBJOHN DOE     123 MAIN ST     CHICAGO IL     60105
```

The following FORTRAN statements can be used to input the data:

```
        DIMENSION NAME(15)
        READ(1, 2) ID, IENG, IMATH, ICHEM, IE, IM, IC,
       1(NAME(I), I = 1, 15), LAST
     2  FORMAT(I5, 3I3, 3A1, 15A4, I3)
```

There is no special type of declaration statement associated with
alphameric data to indicate that the variables are different from
numerical ones.

Example 1

A deck of data cards contains the following information:

```
        Columns  1-24   Name of an individual
        Columns 25-48   Address
        Columns 49-72   City and state
        Columns 73-74   Blank
        Columns 75-79   Zip code
        Column  80      Blank
```

The cards are to be read into the computer and address labels printed. This can be done by manually setting up the printer with special paper. The blank labels can contain up to six lines of printing and are ten lines apart vertically. Also, they are positioned on the left side of the printer and each line can contain 30 characters. To stop the program, a card is inserted at the end of the data deck with a 1 punched in column 80. The program to do this is given below for any number of data cards.

```
        DIMENSION NAME(6), ADDRS(6), TOWN(6)
    1   READ(1, 100) (NAME(I), I = 1, 6), (ADDRS(I), I = 1, 6),
        1(TOWN(I), I = 1, 6), IZIP, ITEST
  100   FORMAT(18A4, 2X, I5, I1)
        IF(ITEST.EQ.1) GO TO 200
        WRITE(2, 101) (NAME(I), I = 1, 6), (ADDRS(I), I = 1, 6),
        1(TOWN(I), I = 1, 6), IZIP
  101   FORMAT(4X////4X,6A4/4X,6A4/4X,6A4,2X,I5,12(/))
        GO TO 1
  200   STOP
        END
```

For most applications, we use the same format for both input and output as was done in the above example, except that carriage control must precede descriptors on output.

The rules below must be followed for the more general cases of input and output using the A format. As sample input data, let us assume that each data card read in has the alphabet punched in the first 26 columns.

Rule 1: If the READ statement has a format specification of A1, A2, ..., or A5, the variable is read and stored left-justified, with blanks to the right.

```
        READ(1, 100) NAME1
  100   FORMAT(A1)
        READ(1, 101) NAME2
  101   FORMAT(A2)
        READ(1, 102) NAME3
  102   FORMAT(A4)
        READ(1, 103) NAME4
  103   FORMAT(A6)
```

These statements will result in NAME1 being stored as Abbbbb, NAME2 as ABbbbb, NAME3 as ABCDbb, and NAME4 as ABCDEF.

Rule 2: If the READ statement has a format specification of A7 or larger, the computer ignores the first columns and takes the last six characters for the variable.

Using the same data as above,

```
        READ(1, 50)A
   50   FORMAT(A8)
```

results in the variable A being stored as CDEFGH.

> *Rule 3:* If the WRITE statement has a format specification
> A1, A2, ..., or A5, the computer outputs the first
> 1, 2, ..., or 5 characters.

When compared to Rule 1, this is what we would expect: the
statements

```
        READ(1, 20) N
    20  FORMAT(A6)
        WRITE(2, 21) N
    21  FORMAT(1X, A5)
```

will output ABCDE. The statements

```
        READ(1, 22) M
    22  FORMAT(A2)
        WRITE(2, 23) M
    23  FORMAT(1X, A4)
```

will output ABbb.

> *Rule 4:* If the WRITE statement has a format specification of
> A7 or larger, the left column(s) is(are) blank and
> six characters are printed.

The statements

```
        READ(1, 40) INAME
    40  FORMAT(5X, A2)
        WRITE(2, 30) INAME
    30  FORMAT(A10)
```

will output INAME as bbbbFGbbbb.

■ The R Specification

Another way of defining alphameric data is with the R specification. The general form of this format is

mRn

where *n* is the field length and *m* is a repeat factor. This is nearly identical to the A specification, except that now the input data
is stored with blanks on the left.[1]

The rules for the A format can be rewritten to give the rules
for using the R format as follows. Again, assume the sample data

---

[1]Some computers use R*n* to right-justify with *zero* fill on the
left.

is a deck of cards with the alphabet punched in the first 26 columns.

> *Rule 1:* If the READ statement has a format specification of R1, R2, ..., or R5, the variable is read and stored right-justified, blanks to the left.

The statements

        READ(1, 200) NAME
    200 FORMAT(R1)

result in NAME being stored as bbbbbA.

> *Rule 2:* If the READ statement has a format specification of R7 or larger, the computer ignores the first column and takes the next six characters. Notice that this is identical to Rule 2 for the A format.

The statements

        READ(1, 201) X
    201 FORMAT(R7)

result in X being stored as BCDEFG.

> *Rule 3:* If the WRITE statement has a format specification of R1, R2, ..., or R5, the computer outputs the last 1, 2, ..., or 5 characters.

The statements

        READ(1, 202) Y
    202 FORMAT(R4)
        WRITE(2, 203) Y
    203 FORMAT(1X, R2)

results in the output bCD. The statements

        READ(1, 204) W
    204 FORMAT(R1)
        WRITE(2, 205) W
    205 FORMAT(R4)

will output bbbA.

> *Rule 4:* If the WRITE statement has a format specification of R7 or larger, the left column(s) is(are) blank and the word is output in the next six spaces, according to Rule 3.

The statements

```
        READ(1, 204) B
   204  FORMAT(5X, R2)
        WRITE(2, 205) B
   205  FORMAT(R10)
```

result in the output bbbbbbbbFG.

It is possible to use alphameric variables in IF statements. For example, if A and B are both alphameric, the statement

```
        IF(A.EQ.B) GO TO 100
```

will transfer control to Statement 100 if A and B are identical. There are some restrictions in using statements such as the one above.   These are as follows:

Restriction 1: The modes of the variables should not be mixed. Thus, for A and I both alphameric,

```
IF(A.EQ.I) GO TO 100
```

is not acceptable and may result in an error message or, even worse, may be executed but give an erroneous answer.

Restriction 2: Alphameric variables can be compared only with other alphameric variables. Thus, for A an alphameric variable and B a floating-point variable, the statements

```
IF(A.EQ.9) GO TO 10
IF(A.LE.B) STOP
```

are incorrect.

Example 2

A data card contains alphameric data punched in columns 1-80. This data consists of only the 26 letters of the alphabet and blanks between words. Let us write a program to count the number of times the letter E occurs and then the corresponding percentage of occurrence. To compute this percentage, we shall need to count every character except blanks.

To solve this, we can read in the 80 possible characters as an array having 80 elements. Since we are going to compare each of these variables with the letter E, it is necessary to specify E as an alphameric variable. One way to do this is to use another READ statement. (Alternate ways are given in the next sections of this chapter.) This variable is called TEST. In addition, we must define a variable to be equal to a blank space. The flowchart shown in Fig. 10-1 illustrates the logic used in the solution.

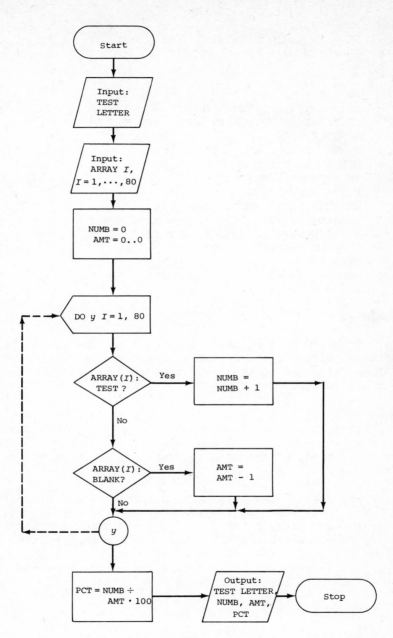

FIGURE 10-1
Flowchart for Example 2

The program corresponding to this flowchart is:

```
        DIMENSION ARRAY(80)
        READ(1, 100) TEST, BLANK
  100   FORMAT(2A1)
        READ(1, 101) (ARRAY(I), I = 1, 80)
  101   FORMAT(80A1)
        AMT = 80.0
        NUMB = 0
        DO 1 I = 1, 80
        IF(ARRAY(I).EQ.TEST) GO TO 2
        IF(ARRAY(I).EQ.BLANK) AMT = AMT - 1.0
        GO TO 1
    2   NUMB = NUMB + 1
    1   CONTINUE
        XN = FLOAT(NUMB)
        PCT = XN/AMT*100.0
        WRITE(2, 103) TEST, NUMB, PCT
  103   FORMAT(1H1 //// 20X, ' TEST LETTER WAS ',
       1A1, ' NUMBER OF THIS LETTER IS ', I2,
       2' PERCENTAGE IS ', F5.2
        STOP
        END
```

Example 3

It is possible to generalize Example 1 and determine the number of times each letter of the alphabet occurs for any number of data cards. From this, one can determine the relative frequency of occurrence of each letter.

To solve this, let us assume that only the 26 letters of the alphabet, blanks, periods, and commas make up the data. The data is punched in columns 1-72 and a card with a 1 punched in column 73 is placed at the end of the data to assist in terminating execution of the program.

The characters on the data cards are read in and stored in the array ARRAY. The letters of the alphabet are also read in as the single-dimensioned array ALPHA. Each letter is counted and stored in an array COUNT, where COUNT(1) tabulates the number of times the letter A appears, COUNT(2) the number of times the letter B appears, etc. Twenty-six frequencies are determined by dividing the total number of times each letter appears by the total of all letters.

The DIMENSION statement is written

```
        DIMENSION ARRAY(72), ALPHA(26), COUNT(26), FREQ(26)
```

We first read in a data card and use an IF statement below it to determine if a 1 was punched in column 73. If not, we increment the counter for the total amount of characters by 72. Later, each time a character is encountered that is not a letter, but a blank, comma, or period, this counter is decreased by 1.

   The actual counting of the letters is done by using two DO
loops. The outer loop is done 72 times, conce for each character
on the data card. The inner loop, corresponding to the actual
search, is done a maximum of 26 times. As soon as the search is
successful,, either the counter corresponding to the letter is
incremented or the total number of characters is decreased by 1.
Then control transfers from the inner loop to the outer loop.
This transfer of control must be done using another logical IF
statement.

   A portion of the DO loop to illustrate this point can be
written:

```
        DO 20 I = 1, 72
        DO 21 J = 1, 26
        IF(ARRAY(I).NE.BLANK) GO TO 20
        AMT = AMT - 1.0
          .
          .
          .
        IF(ARRAY(I).EQ.ALPHA(J)) GO TO 20
   21   CONTINUE
   20   CONTINUE
```

   Suppose the first character on the data card is a blank. Then
the first two IF statements decrease the number of characters by 1
and transfer control out of the inner loop. The complete program is
now given. The first six IF statements have been combined to make
two statements.

```
        DIMENSION ARRAY(72), ALPHA(26), COUNT(26), FREQ(26)
        READ(1, 1) BLANK, DOT, COMMA
   1    FORMAT(3A1)
        READ(1, 2) (ALPHA(I), I = 1, 26)
   2    FORMAT(26A1)
        AMT = 0.0
        DO 10 I = 1, 26
   10   COUNT(I) = 0.0
   70   READ(1, 3) (ARRAY(I), I = 1, 72), ITEST
   3    FORMAT(72A1, I1)
        IF(ITEST.EQ.1) GO TO 50
        AMT = AMT + 72.0
        DO 45 I = 1, 72
        IF(ARRAY(I).EQ.BLANK .OR. ARRAY(I).EQ.DOT .OR. ARRAY(I)
       1.EQ.COMMA) GO TO 30
        DO 21 J = 1, 26
        IF(ARRAY(I).EQ.ALPHA(J)) GO TO 40
   21   CONTINUE
        GO TO 45
   30   AMT = AMT - 1.0
        GO TO 45
   40   COUNT(J) = COUNT(J) + 1.0
   45   CONTINUE
```

```
        GO TO 70
 50     DO 60 I = 1, 26
 60     FREQ(I) = COUNT(I)/AMT
        WRITE(2, 100) AMT
100     FORMAT(1H1, ////, 10X, 'THE TOTAL NUMBER OF LETTERS IS',
        1F5.0, //, 10X, 'BELOW ARE THE FREQUENCIES OF EACH LETTER',/)
        WRITE(2, 101) (ALPHA(I), COUNT(I), FREQ(I), I = 1, 26)
101     FORMAT(///, 12X, 'LETTER', 11X, 'FREQ.',
        18X, 'REL. FREQ.',/,
        2(15X, A1, 5X, F10.0, 5X, F10.4))
        STOP
        END
```

The program can easily be generalized to handle characters such as numbers or parentheses that might be part of the data. This is done by adding appropriate IF statements in the DO loop and defining proper alphameric variables for each character.

■ The DATA Statement

There is another way to assign alphameric values to variables which does not involve the READ statement. This is by using the DATA declaration statement. One general form is

$$\text{DATA } var_1, var_2, \ldots, var_n/a_1, a_2, \ldots, a_n/, var_m,$$

$$var_{m+1}, \ldots, var_r/b_1, b_2, \ldots, b_r, \ldots/$$

When this statement occurs in the program, the variable var_1 is initially given the value a_1, variable var_2 is a_2, and so on. Thus,

```
        DATA A, B, C/1.0, 3.0, 5.0/
```

sets A = 1.0, B = 3.0, and C = 5.0. The variables may be subscripted, but standard FORTRAN allows only fixed-point constants for subscripts. Many systems allow the implied DO loop, as in the list of an input or output statement. To use a DATA statement to initialize variables as alphameric values, we use a Hollerith specification. Again, let us assume that the size of the alphameric variable is limited to a maximum of six characters. Then

```
        DATA A, B, I, J/3HABC, 2HAB, 6HXYZWST, 1Hb/
```

will set

```
        A = ABCbbb      B = ABbbbb      I = XYZWST      J = bbbbbb
```

For subscripted variables, either of the following two forms may be used:

```
DIMENSION A(6)
DATA A(1), A(2), A(3), A(4), A(5), A(6)/1H+, 1H-, 1H=, 1H*, 1H$, 1H./
```

or

```
        DATA A/1H+, 1H-, 1H=, 1H*, 1H$, 1H./
```

Both will define an array A consisting of six variables such that

```
    A(1) is a +,   A(2) is a -,   A(3) is an =,   A(4) is an *,
        A(5) is a $,   and A(6) is a .
```

The DATA statement is nonexecutable and must appear before any executable statement. It is placed after declaration statements, such as the DIMENSION statement.

It is important to remember that the DATA statement, being non-executable, initializes values once and only once. If the variable is used in the program and its value is changed by an executable statement, it takes on this new value. Thus, the statements

```
        DATA X/0.0/
        WRITE(2, 1)X
    1   FORMAT(1X, F3.1)
        X = X + 1.0
        WRITE(2, 1)X
```

will result in two different values of X being printed, namely, 0.0 and 1.0. This should not cause the programmer any problem since the equals sign in the arithmetic statement acts to define a new value for a variable. Where one must be careful is when the DATA statement is used in a subprogram. There its value is *not* initialized every time the subprogram is called. Each time the subroutine TEST, as given below, is called, the value of N is the previous value (N + 1) and not 0.

```
        SUBROUTINE TEST
        DATA N/0/
        .
        .
        .
        N = N + 1
        RETURN
        END
```

A useful feature of the DATA statement is that it may include repetition factors. A repetition factor in a DATA statement is a fixed-point constant followed by an asterisk. This will cause the following constants to be repeated. For example,

```
        3*1.0
```

would mean three factors of 1.0. Thus, the statement

```
        DATA A, B, C/3*1.0/
```

would set A, B, and C to an initial value of 1.0, just like the statement

       DATA A, B, C/1.0, 1.0, 1.0/

As another example, suppose we want to initialize A, B, and C to equal 0.0, and we also want to initialize I, J, K, and L to equal 1. This can be done with the statement

       DATA A, B, C/3*0.0/, I, J, K, L/4*1/

   The variables in the DATA statement may be array names. When this is the case, it is the same as writing out all the elements in the array. For example, the statements

       DIMENSION X(10)
       DATA X/10*0.0/

would set each of the variables X(1), X(2), ..., X(10) initially equal to 0.0. The X in the DATA statement specifies the whole array X, that is, all ten variables. The repetition factor 10 denotes ten factors of the constant 0.0.

   As another example, suppose MAT is declared as a fixed-point array by the statement

       DIMENSION MAT(3,2)

Then, the statement

       DATA MAT/6*5/

would give all six of the elements of the array MAT an initial value of 5.

   The implied DO loop form used in a READ or WRITE statement may also be used in a DATA statement. For example, the statement

       DATA(X(1, I), I = 2, 7)/6*0.0/

would set each of the variables X(1, 2), X(1, 3), X(1, 4), ..., X(1, 7) equal to 0.0 at the start of the program.

   The statement

       DATA(X(I), I = 1, 21, 2)/11*1.0/

would initialize X(1), X(3), X(5), ..., X(21) to equal 1.0.

   A final feature of the DATA statement is that the constants may be grouped by parentheses, each preceded by a repetition factor. Thus, 2*(1.0, 2.0) would mean the same thing in a DATA statement as 1.0, 2.0, 1.0, 2.0. The whole group is repeated. This is similar to repeated groups in a FORMAT statement. The statement

```
        DATA(X(I), I = 1, 10)/5*(0.0, 1.0)/
```

would initialize the elements X(1), X(3), ..., X(9) equal to 0.0, while initializing X(2), X(4), ..., X(10) equal to 1.0.

Any type of constant can be used in a DATA statement. The constants must be of the correct type for the corresponding type of associated variable. The statements

```
        DIMENSION X(2), NAME(3)
        LOGICAL L, M
        DATA L, M/.TRUE., .FALSE./,
        1X/1.0, 2.0/,
        2NAME/4HPROB, 4HLEMb, 1H2/
```

would serve to initialize the logical constants L and M as well as the arrays X and NAME.

Example 4

Alphameric characters can be used in printing out contoured plots. Often this is a very convenient and illuminating way of presenting data. For example, the array might represent barometric pressure values, pollen counts, or temperature values. Suppose the data is stored in a 50 X 50 array called ARRAY. While it may be desired to also have the 2,500 elements listed, the array will be much easier to view if presented as a plot. Let us assume that the values of the data are known to be between 0.0 and 50.0.

Let us now write a program to draw the contours. A contour interval of 10.0 is chosen. Thus, we shall have five different characters plotted. We can now examine every value of ARRAY and define a new array, called PLOT, such that each element of PLOT is equal to one of the five characters. However, the characters will be easier to view if we print a few blanks between each of them. These blanks will then actually be the contours. Our contour scheme is:

$$
\text{Plotted character is} \begin{cases} \text{A} & \text{for} & 0.0 \le \text{array value} \le 07.0 \\ \text{.} & \text{for} & 10.0 \le \text{array value} \le 17.0 \\ \text{B} & \text{for} & 20.0 \le \text{array value} \le 27.0 \\ \text{/} & \text{for} & 30.0 \le \text{array value} \le 37.0 \\ \text{D} & \text{for} & 40.0 \le \text{array value} \le 47.0 \\ & & \text{blank otherwise} \end{cases}
$$

The necessary FORTRAN statements are:

```
        DIMENSION ARRAY(50, 50), PLOT(50, 50), CHAR(6)
C       THE DIMENSION STATEMENT IS TO BE PLACED AT THE START
C       OF THE PROGRAM.  LIKEWISE, THE DATA STATEMENT
        DATA CHAR/1HA, 1H., 1HB, 1H/, 1HD, 1H/
          .
          .
          .
        DO 500 I = 1, 50
```

```
      DO 500 J = 1, 50
      IF(ARRAY(I, J).LE.7.0) GO TO 510
      IF(ARRAY(I, J).LE.17.0 .AND. ARRAY(I, J).GE.10.0) GO TO 520
      IF(ARRAY(I, J).LE.27.0 .AND. ARRAY(I, J).GE.20.0) GO TO 530
      IF(ARRAY(I, J).LE.37.0 .AND. ARRAY(I, J).GE.30.0) GO TO 540
      IF(ARRAY(I, J).LE.47.0 .AND. ARRAY(I, J).GE.40.0) GO TO 550
      PLOT(I, J) = CHAR(6)
      GO TO 500
  510 PLOT(I, J) = CHAR(1)
      GO TO 500
  520 PLOT(I, J) = CHAR(2)
      GO TO 500
  530 PLOT(I, J) = CHAR(3)
      GO TO 500
  540 PLOT(I, J) = CHAR(4)
      GO TO 500
  550 PLOT(I, J) = CHAR(5)
  500 CONTINUE
      WRITE(2, 501) ((PLOT(I, J), J = 1, 50), I = 1, 50)
  501 FORMAT(1H1, 10(/), (40X, 50A1))
      STOP
      END
```

The logic used in this program can be compared with the program on page 210.

Alternate to the DATA Statement[2]

Another method to specify alphameric values is to use the Hollerith specification in an arithmetic expression. This is done as follows:

```
      A = 4HABCD
      BLANK = 1Hb
```

The alphameric variabla A is now stored as ABCD and the variable BLANK is stored as a blank. For systems that allow this statement, one can also use the Hollerith specification in IF statements. To illustrate this, suppose we have an array ARRAY consisting of 1,000 alphameric variables. We wish to determine how many of these are the character 9. FORTRAN statements that will do this are

```
      NUMBER = 0
      DO 1 I = 1, 1000
      IF(ARRAY(I).EQ.1H9) NUMBER = NUMBER + 1
    1 CONTINUE
```

---

[2]This method will not work on all systems.

■ Exercises

1. A deck of data cards contains names and addresses punched as follows:

        Columns 1-25   Name
        Columns 26-50   Street
        Columns 51-75   Town and state
        Columns 76-80   Zip code

   Write the FORTRAN statements that will read in the cards and then output the people with zip codes starting with the digit 6.   To stop the program, have a card with 99999 punched in the last five columns.   The output should be in standard address form.

2. For the data in Exercise 1, output all the names and addresses according to the numerical order of the zip codes. For this, assume a maximum of 1,000 data cards.

3. The results of a 25 question true-false history examination are punched on cards as follows:

        Columns 1-25   Student's name
        Columns 26-50   Either a 2, 1, or 0 in each column:
                        2 for "true" answer; 1 for "false"
                        answer; 0 for no answer

   The first data card contains the answer code punched in the first 25 columns. The grading system is given by

        SCORE = number of correct answers X 4 - number of
                incorrect answers X 5

   Thus, it is theoretically possible for a student to obtain a negative score. Rather than have this happen, the lowest score possible will be 0. Write a program to input the cards, calculate a score for each student, and output name and score.

4. Letter grades for the exam in Exercise 3 are

        100-85   A
         84-70   B
         69-55   C
         54-40   D
         39-0   F

   Add the necessary statements to the program to

   (a) calculate a letter grade for each student;
   (b) output the grades in descending order.

5. Suppose state license plates for cars are given by six characters, the first three being letters and the last three numbers.

5.—continued

These are punched on cards in the first six columns. In column 80 a 1 is punched if the license belongs to a stolen car; otherwise, it is blank. Write a program to input the deck and list every stolen license plate number. To stop the program, use a card with a 9 punched in column 80 at the end of the data deck.

6. Using the same data deck as in Exercise 1, write a program to list only those names and addresses of people from the city of New York.

7. (a) Write a program that will read a 2-digit number and print out the number in words. For example, the number 23 would be output as

   TWENTY THREE

   (b) When some companies print their payroll checks, the amount is written out together with the dollar amount. Write a program that first reads the following data from a card:

   Columns 1-29   Name of employee
   Column 30   Dollar sign
   Columns 31-37 Employee's wage (assume between $10
                        and $100)

   Then, have the computer print out the message:

   PAY TO THE ORDER OF: (employee's name)
   (amount, written out) $ (wage)

8. The international Morse code for the alphabet is

A •—	H ••••	O ———	V •••—
B —•••	I ••	P •——•	W •——
C —•—•	J •———	Q ——•—	X —••—
D —••	K —•—	R •—•	Y —•——
E •	L •—••	S •••	Z ——••
F ••—•	M ——	T —	
G ——•	N —•	U ••—	

The dots and dashes can be punched on data cards as periods and minus signs. Write a program to read a number of cards on which are punched a message in Morse code and determine what the message is. Each code letter is punched in a field length of four spaces. The letter A is .-bb, E is .bbb, and so on. Thus, each data card can contain a maximum of 20 letters. Whenever four blanks are encountered in a data field, this is to be interpreted as a blank between words.

This problem can be solved by writing a long series of logical IF statements. For example, if the 80 characters are read

8.—continued

into a one-dimensional array ARRAY, an IF statement for the letter A might be

```
IF(ARRAY(I).EQ.DOT .AND. ARRAY(I + 1).EQ.DASH .AND.
   ARRAY(I + 2).EQ.BLANK) CODE(J) = ALPHA(1)
```

where DOT is a period, DASH is a minus sign, CODE is an array that will be filled with letters, and ALPHA is an array that contains the alphabet.

Rather than do this search by using the alphabet in proper order from A to Z, a more efficient way would be to search using the letters arranged in order of their expected relative frequencies of occurrence. This is

ETOANIRSHDLCFUMPYWGBVKXJQZ

9. Most computers list the actual time (usually in seconds) a program took to run as part of the output. In addition, there generally is a special subroutine such as CALL SECOND(t), CALL TIME, etc., so that the actual time to run a particular portion of the program can be found. If this option is available on your computer, run the program given for Example 4 both as is and with IF statements of the form

```
IF(ARRAY(I, J).LE.7.0) PLOT(I, J) = CHAR(1)
IF(ARRAY(I, J).LE.7.0) GO TO 500
```

Determine which program runs faster.

11

Double-Precision and Complex Variables

There are still two types of variables used in FORTRAN that we have not yet covered, double-precision and complex variables. These types are not used as frequently as regular floating- or fixed-point variables, but they can be useful for certain specific applications.

■ Double-Precision Numbers

Remember that in a computer we must represent all numbers with a finite number of digits. A number like $\sqrt{2}$ (1.41421...) requires an infinite number of decimal digits for its exact representation, and so it cannot be represented on a computer; we have to approximate it with a finite number of decimal digits. If the computer can handle five significant digits, then $\sqrt{2}$ would be represented as 1.4142. Thus, in all floating-point computer arithmetic there is an inherent error caused by the limited number of digits a computer word can store. Much of the time this error can be ignored. In some instances, however, more accuracy is needed than is available in floating-point arithmetic. For such cases, we can use double-precision arithmetic.

A double-precision constant or variable is stored in two storage locations. This has the effect of doubling the number of significant digits, as compared to a regular floating-point number. If the computer used can store eight decimal digits for a floating-point variable, it will be able to store sixteen decimal digits for a double-precision variable.

A double-precision constant has a form that is very similar to the form of a floating-point number written in exponential form. An example of a double-precision constant is 6.2D+4. This means 6.2×10^4. That is, it represents the same number as the FORTRAN floating-point constant 6.2E+4. The difference is that the double-precision constant 6.2D+4 would be stored in two storage locations, and so it would be represented in the computer by twice as many digits as 6.2E+4. The rules for forming a double-precision constant are given below.

$$6.2 \quad D \quad + \quad 04$$

a   b   c   d

Rule a: The first part of the number is a regular fixed- or floating-point constant. It can be written with or without the decimal point, but we can include more digits.

Rule b: Next, we put the letter D.

Rule c: Here we place a plus or minus sign. If no sign appears, the computer assumes that it is a plus sign. Thus, 6.2D4 is the same as 6.2D+4.

Rule d: The last part is the exponent. Just as for the E-form, this number is an integer that gives the power of ten to which the decimal part of the number is to be raised. Thus, 6.2D4 represents $6.2 \times 10^4 = 62,000.0$; 6.2D-4 represents $6.2 \times 10^{-4} = 0.00062$.

Some examples of double-precision constants are given in Table 11-1.

TABLE 11-1

Double-Precision Constant	Meaning
.07D-1	0.007
7D+2	700.0
7.00D2	700.0
8D-3	0.008
-55D0	-55.0
-55D	-55.0
3.14159265358979300	Value of π to 16 digits

Variables in FORTRAN can also be declared as double-precision. A double-precision variable is like a regular floating-point variable except that it is stored by the computer in two storage locations (just as is a double-precision constant). In order to tell the computer that a variable is to be used as a double-precision variable, a special declaration statement must be used. This statement has the form

DOUBLE PRECISION $name_1$, $name_2$, ..., $name_n$

where each of the names is a FORTRAN variable name. This statement is similar to the LOGICAL statement we used in Chapter 9. Each of the variables named in the list will be treated as a double-precision variable throughout the program. The DOUBLE PRECISION statement should come at the beginning of the program. For example, if we want to use the variables I, MINE, X, and R as double-precision variables, then the program should include the statement

        DOUBLE PRECISION I, MINE, X, R

Although I and MINE would normally be fixed-point variables, they would be treated as double-precision because the DOUBLE PRECISION declaration statement overrides the usual rules for naming variables. This statement applies to the whole main program. We could not use the variable I as a regular fixed-point variable later in the program, since it has already been declared as double-precision.

    The DOUBLE PRECISION statement can also be used to give dimension information about the variables named. For example, suppose we want an array Z with 100 elements to be a double-precision array [that is, each Z(I) is a double-precision variable]. We could specify this with the two statements

        DOUBLE PRECISION Z
        DIMENSION Z(100)

But it is easier to combine them into the single statement

        DOUBLE PRECISION Z(100)

This statement does the same thing. In general, any variable name in the list of the DOUBLE PRECISION statement may be dimensioned.

■ Double-Precision Arithmetic

    Arithmetic using double-precision numbers is performed differently by the computer than floating-point arithmetic. Each number is stored in two storage locations to give twice the accuracy provided by regular floating-point arithmetic. The only difference in FORTRAN, however, is that double-precision constants and variables are used. If X is a double-precision variable, then

        2.0D0*(X - 1.0D0)/X

is a double-precision arithmetic expression.

    Double-precision constants and variables may be combined in arithmetic expressions with regular floating-point constants and variables. In this case, the result is a double-precision number. For example, suppose X is a double-precision variable. Then the expression

        2.0D0*X + 1.0D0

is a double-precision expression. Both the constants and variables are double-precision in this case. Suppose now that we had the expression

```
     2.0*X + 1.0
```

In this case, X is a double-precision variable, and 2.0 and 1.0 are regular floating-point constants. This sort of expression is allowed in FORTRAN. When the expression is evaluated, the constant 2.0 is automatically converted to the double-precision constant 2.0D0, and this is multiplied by X to give the double-precision result. The constant 1.0 is then converted to the double-precision constant 1.0D0, and this is added to the previous result to give another double-precision number. In general, if X is a double-precision expression and Y is a regular floating-point expression, then

```
     X + Y     Y + X
     X - Y     Y - X
     X * Y     Y * X
     X / Y     Y / X
     X ** Y    Y ** X
```

are all valid double-precision expressions. In each case, the floating-point portion of the expression is converted to double-precision and then the indicated operation is performed, giving a double-precision result. The following are some examples of valid double-precision expressions (X is assumed to be a double-precision variable):

```
     X + 1.9D-2
     X + 1.9E-2
     X + .019
     2.0D0*X
     2.0*X
     X**2 + 1.0
     X/2.0 + .999999999D2
```

The assignment statement has the same form for use with double-precision expressions as it ordinarily does. If X is a double-precision variable and E is any double-precision expression, then the statement

```
     X = E
```

will simply take the double-precision value of E and store it in the double-precision variable X. We may ask what happens if only one of the parts of this statement is double-precision. The answer is given by the following rules.

Rule 1: If X is a double-precision variable and E is a regular floating- or fixed-point expression, then the statement X = E will evaluate E as usual, convert the final result to double-precision form, and store it in X.

Rule 2: If X is a regular floating-point variable and E is a double-precision expression, then E is evaluated in double-precision form and the result is truncated and stored in X. If X is a fixed-point variable, only the integer part of E is stored.

As an example of the first rule, suppose that our computer can store eight decimal digits for a single-precision variable. If X is a double-precision variable, it can then store sixteen digits. Then the statement

        X = .99999999

would convert the constant .99999999 to double-precision and store it in X as .9999999900000000. As an example of the second rule, the statement

        X = .999999999999999999D0

would convert the double-precision constant to single-precision and store it in X as .99999999.

    The exact degree of accuracy will depend on the computer used. But just for an example, suppose we have a computer that uses eight decimal digits in a single-precision variable. Let us perform the calculation

        X = 4.0 - 4.0*.99999999

When we multiply 4.0 by .99999999, the exact answer is 3.99999996. This number has nine digits, however, so the last digit would be truncated, not rounded, and the number would be stored as .39999999 X 10. When we subtract this from 4.0, the result is $0.0000001 = 0.1 \times 10^{-6}$. Now, if we perform the same calculation using double-precision numbers, the last place is not truncated, and we have 4.0 - 3.99999996, which is 0.4×10^{-7}. Thus, we see that the statement

        X = 4.0 - 4.0*.99999999

will assign to X the value 0.1×10^{-6}, while the statement

        X = 4.0D0 - 4.0D0*.99999999D0

will assign to X the value 0.4×10^{-7}. While these results are very close in absolute value, the first result is more than twice as large as the second. In some computations, such a difference can be very important, and this is where double-precision arithmetic is useful in FORTRAN.[1]

---

[1] See G. E. Forsyth, "Pitfalls in Computation, or Why a Math Book Isn't Enough," *Amer. Math. Mon.*, Vol. 77, No. 9 (1970), 931-959, for a study of how roundoff error affects computation.

■ Input and Output of Double-Precision Numbers

When we want to input or output the value of a double-precision variable, we must use a special format field description. This field descriptor has the form

D*n*.*m*

where *n* and *m* are unsigned fixed-point constants. The number *n* gives the size of the field and *m* tells how many decimal places are to be used. The D field is used exactly like the E field for regular floating-point numbers. The only difference is that the D field must be used with double-precision variables.

As an example of how the D field is used for input, suppose we read the following data from a card:

111D-122.22D233333

using the statements

```
      DOUBLE PRECISION X, Y, Z
      READ(1, 7) X, Y, Z
    7 FORMAT(D6.1, D7.1, D5.4)
```

The first field is the D6.1. Since the field width is 6, the characters read for X are 111D-1. The 1 in D6.1 means that there is one assumed decimal place in the input data, so the number is stored in X as 11.1D-1. The second field is 22.22D2. Since it is written with a decimal point, the 1 in D7.1 has no effect, and the number is stored in Y as 22.22D2. The last field is 33333, read with a D5.4 description. The 4 in D5.4 means to assume four decimal places, so Z receives the value 3.3333D0.

When it is used for output, the D*n*.*m* field is just like the E*n*.*m* field except that the number written must be double-precision. Specifically, a field written with a D*n*.*m* format will contain the following characters:

1. (*n* - *m* - 6) blank spaces
2. a minus sign or another blank space
3. a decimal point
4. *m* decimal digits
5. the letter D
6. a plus or minus sign for the exponent
7. a 2-digit exponent

For example, if X = -77.66 is a double-precision number, then the statements

```
      WRITE(2, 1) X
    1 FORMAT(D13.5)
```

will print the characters

        b-0.77660D+02

(where the b stands for a blank space).

    Note that *n* must always be greater than or eaual to *m* + 6 to
allow room to print the decimal point, minus sign, and exponent.

■ Double-Precision Functions

    When using a function subprogram in FORTRAN, the parameters
and the function itself must be of a certain type. For instance,
the function ABS(X) will give the absolute value of a number X,
but X must be a floating-point number. If we want to find the
absolute value of a fixed-point variable, we must use the function
IABS(N). It is incorrect to use the function ABS(X) to find the
absolute value of a fixed-point variable because ABS assumes that
the argument of the function is a floating-point number. Similarly,
we must use double-precision functions when we want the result or
the parameters to be double-precision numbers. Table 11-2 gives a
partial list of double-precision functions supplied by FORTRAN. In
each case, the variables are assumed to be double-precision, and
the value of the function itself will be double-precision.

        TABLE 11-2.   Some double-precision functions.

Function	Definition
DABS(X)	*Absolute value of x*
DMAX1(X1, ..., XN)	*Maximum value of x_1, ..., x_n*
DMIN1(X1, ..., XN)	*Minimum value of x_1, ..., x_n*
DEXP(X)	*Exponential function, e^x*
DLOG(X)	*Natural logarithm, $\log_e x$*
DLOG10(X)	*Common logarithm, $\log_{10} x$*
DSIN(X)	*Trigonometric sine, $\sin x$*
DCOS(X)	*Trigonometric cosine, $\cos x$*
DSQRT(X)	*Square root of x*
DATAN(X)	*Arctangent of x*

Each of these functions is used just like its counterpart for single-
precision numbers. The only difference is that both the variable
and the values of the function are double-precision. For example, if
X and Y are double-precision variables, we can set Y equal to the
sine of X with the statement

        Y = DSIN(X)

    If we wanted to define a double-precision function of our own,
we could do so by using the statement

        DOUBLE PRECISION FUNCTION name(x_1, x_2, ..., x_n)

This statement works in the same way as the ordinary FUNCTION statement. The difference is that the final value of the function named
will be a double-precision number. For example, we could use the
following statements to define a double-precision function ZZZ to
find the absolute value of a fixed-point variable:

```
        DOUBLE PRECISION FUNCTION ZZZ(N)
        IF(N.LT.0) GO TO 20
        ZZZ = N
        RETURN
   20   ZZZ = -N
        RETURN
        END
```

or, more simply,

```
        DOUBLE PRECISION FUNCTION ZZZ(N)
        ZZZ = IABS(N)
        RETURN
        END
```

When we use this function in an expression, ZZZ is treated just
like a double-precision variable. Therefore, *we should declare
it as double-precision in the main program.* Note that N itself is
a fixed-point variable. The DOUBLE PRECISION FUNCTION *statement
means that the function is double-precision*; the arguments may be
any type. If the dummy argument is to be double-precision, then
it must be declared so in the subprogram, and the actual argument
must be double-precision in the main program.

Example 1

As was pointed out earlier, we can use the FORTRAN-supplied
function DLOG(X) to find the double-precision natural logarithm
of the double-precision number X. For this example, however, we
shall write a double-precision function subprogram of our own to
do this.

The formula we shall use is

$$\log_e x = 2 \left[\frac{x-1}{x+1} + \frac{1}{3} \left(\frac{x-1}{x+1} \right)^3 + \frac{1}{5} \left(\frac{x-1}{x+1} \right)^5 + \cdots \right]$$

where $e = 2.71828 \cdots$. This formula holds for all positive values
of x. The difficulty is that for large values of x, the series
converges very slowly, so we have to use a large number of terms to
approximate the true logarithm of x with any degree of accuracy.
This difficulty is easily overcome, however, if we recall the
formula

$$\log_e (ye^n) = \log_e y + \log_e e^n = \log_e y + n$$

If $x > 1$, we divide x by some power of e so that $x = ye^n$ with $1/e < y < 1$. For y in this range, $(y - 1)/(y + 1)$ will lie between -0.426 and 0. The formula converges quite rapidly in this range. Furthermore, since $(y - 1)/(y + 1)$ is negative, if we compute m terms of the series, the error will be less than the absolute value of the $(m + 1)$st term. Having found $\log_e y$ by the formula, we can compute $\log_e x = \log_e y + n$. Similarly, if $x < 1/e$, we multiply x by some power of e so that $x = y/e^n$ with $1/e < y < 1$. Then $\log_e x = \log_e y - n$.

The first step in our subprogram, which we shall call BLOG, is to find the correct power of e to multiply or divide x by. This procedure is shown in the flowchart of Fig. 11-1. Notice that if x is an exact multiple of e, $y = 1$, so $\log_e x = \log_e 1 + n = 0 + n = n$, and there is no need to carry out the rest of the calculation.

The procedure used in computing the formula for $\log_e y$ is shown in Fig. 11-2. Setting $y = (x - 1)/(x + 1)$ and BLOG $= y$, we compute the next term TERM $= y^3/3$, and add TERM to BLOG. If TERM $< 0.5 \times 10^{-10}$ in absolute value, then BLOG will be accurate to ten decimal places and we compute BLOG $= 2.0*$BLOG $+$ AN. Otherwise, we compute another term and repeat the process.

The FORTRAN program for this job uses double-precision for the variables X, Y, E, TERM, YSQ, and EINV, as well as for BLOG itself. The complete program follows:

```
        DOUBLE PRECISION FUNCTION BLOG(X)
C       BLOG(X) = NATURAL LOGARITHM OF X WHERE X IS DOUBLE
C       PRECISION.  BLOG HAS 10 PLACE ACCURACY.
        DOUBLE PRECISION X, Y, E, TERM, YSQ, EINV
        E = 2.718281828459045D0
        EINV = 1.0/E
        IF(X.GT.0.0) GO TO 10
        WRITE(2, 5)
    5   FORMAT(' NEGATIVE ARGUMENT')
        BLOG = 0.0
        RETURN
   10   AN = 0.0
        IF(X - 1.0) 30, 15, 20
   15   BLOG = AN
        RETURN
C       X IS GREATER THAN 1.  DIVIDE BY E UNTIL X IS
C       LESS THAN 1
   20   X = X/E
        AN = AN + 1.0
        IF(X.GT.1.0) GO TO 20
        GO TO 50
C       X IS LESS THAN 1.  MULTIPLY BY E UNTIL X IS
C       GREATER THAN 1/E.
   30   IF(X.GT.EINV) GO TO 50
        X = E*X
        AN = AN - 1.0
        GO TO 30
```

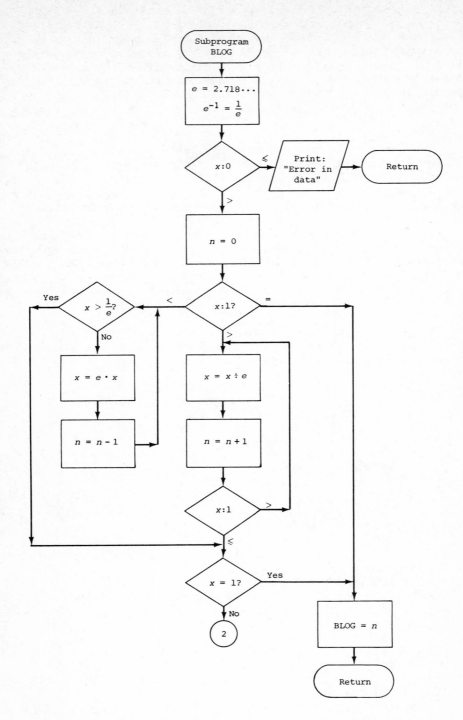

FIGURE 11-1

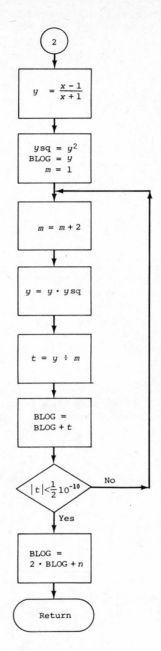

FIGURE 11-2

```
     50   IF(X.EQ.1.0) GO TO 15
  C       X IS BETWEEN 1/E AND 1. BLOG = LOG X + AN.
  C       LET Y = (X - 1)/(X + 1)
  C       THEN Y IS BETWEEN -.426 AND 0.0.
  C       LOG X = 2(Y + Y**3/3 + Y**5/5 + ···)
          Y = (X - 1.0)/(X + 1.0)
          YSQ = Y*Y
          BLOG = Y
          AM = 1.0
     60   AM = AM + 2.0
          Y = Y*YSQ
          TERM = Y/AM
          BLOG = BLOG + TERM
          IF(DABS(TERM).GE.0.5D-10) GO TO 60
          BLOG = 2.0*BLOG + AN
          RETURN
          END
```

■ Complex Numbers

A complex number in algebra is a number of the form $a + bi$, where a and b are real[2] numbers and $i = \sqrt{-1}$ is the base of the imaginary numbers. Complex constants and variables can be used in FORTRAN too, and they have a special arithmetic of their own.

A complex constant in FORTRAN has the form

(a, b)

where a and b are FORTRAN floating-point constants. This number is interpreted as meaning the same thing as $a + bi$. Some examples of valid FORTRAN complex constants are given in Table 11-3.

TABLE 11-3

FORTRAN Constant	Meaning	FORTRAN Constant	Meaning
(1.0, 1.0)	*1 + i*	*(0.0, 0.0)*	*0.0*
(0.0, 1.0)	*0 + i = i*	*(6.2, .2E2)*	*6.2 + 20.0i*
(5.0, 0.0)	*5.0*		

We may form arithmetic expressions using complex constants and the operators +, -, *, and /. For complex numbers, these operators have special meanings which are defined below:

---

[2]The word "real" as used here and in the rest of this chapter has the mathematical meaning in referring to complex numbers. In computer terminology a *real* constant (or variable) is the same as a *floating-point* constant (or variable).

$$(a,\ b) + (c,\ d) = (a + c,\ b + d)$$
$$(a,\ b) - (c,\ d) = (a - c,\ b - d)$$
$$(a,\ b) * (c,\ d) = (ac - bd,\ ad + bc)$$
$$(a,\ b) / (c,\ d) = ((ac + bd)/(c^2 + d^2),\ (-ad + bc)/(c^2 + d^2))$$

As examples of complex multiplication in FORTRAN, we see that

$$(0.0,\ 1.0) * (0.0,\ 1.0) = (-1.0,\ 0.0)$$

by the above definitions. This just expresses the fact that $i^2 = -1$. As another case, for any real constants a, c, and d,

$$(a,\ 0.0) * (c,\ d) = (ac,\ ad)$$

which expresses the algebraic fact that $a(b + ci) = ab + aci$. Using the above definition of complex division, we find that for any real constants c and d,

$$(1.0,\ 0.0)/(c,\ d) = (c/(c^2 + d^2),\ -d/(c^2 + d^2))$$

and when we use the above rule for multiplication, we find that

$$(c,\ d) * (c/(c^2 + d^2),\ -d/(c^2 + d^2)) = (1.0,\ 0.0)$$

as it should.

The exponential operator ** is not generally defined for complex numbers except in the case where the exponent is an integer. Thus,

$$(a,\ b)**4$$

would mean the same thing as

$$(a,\ b) * (a,\ b) * (a,\ b) * (a,\ b)$$

It is not permissible to raise a complex number to a floating-point or a complex exponent using the ** operator. However, we can use the complex exponential function to raise a complex number to a power which is a rational number with reasonably small denominator, as we shall explain later.

Variables may also be defined as complex variables in FORTRAN using the COMPLEX statement. This is a declaration statement similar to the DOUBLE PRECISION statement. The form is

$$\text{COMPLEX name}_1,\ \text{name}_2,\ \cdots,\ \text{name}_N$$

where name_1, name_2, ..., name_N are FORTRAN variable names. This statement will cause the variables named to be treated as complex variables throughout the program and the values will use two storage locations. When a variable is defined as complex, it may assume complex values and be used in arithmetic expressions involving complex arithmetic. For example, the statements

```
COMPLEX Z
Z = (1.0, 1.0)
Z = Z*Z
```

would first assign the complex variable Z the value (1.0, 1.0), and then multiply this value by itself to give Z the value (1.0, 1.0)*(1.0, 1.0) = (0.0, 2.0). Any of the variables names in the COMPLEX statement may be dimensioned. The statement

```
COMPLEX WXY(5)
```

would set up an array of five elements, each occupying two storage locations. Each WXY(I) would then be treated as a complex variable. Like the LOGICAL and DOUBLE PRECISION statements, the COMPLEX statement should come at the beginning of the program, before the first executable statement, and before DATA and statement functions.

When the assignment statement Z = E is used with complex numbers, both the variable Z and the expression E *must* be complex. Thus, it would be incorrect to have the statement

```
Z = (1.0, 0.0)
```

unless Z were defined as complex in a statement COMPLEX Z. Also, if Z is a complex variable, it is incorrect to have the statement

```
Z = 1.0
```

since 1.0 is not a complex expression. We would have to rewrite this as

```
Z = (1.0, 0.0)
```

It is permissible to use floating-point constants and variables in a complex expression. For instance, if Z is a complex variable, then the expression

```
(2.0, 0.0)*Z  +  (1.0, 0.0)
```

could be written as

```
2.0*Z + 1.0
```

since (2.0, 0.0) and (1.0, 0.0) mean the same thing, algebraically, as 2.0 and 1.0. In general, if X is a floating-point variable or constant and Y is a complex variable or constant, then all the following are valid FORTRAN expressions:

```
X + Y     Y + X
X - Y     Y - X
X * Y     Y * X
X / Y     Y / X
```

In each case, X is first converted to complex form, and then the

operation is performed. The result is a complex number. All the
above expressions would be invalid in FORTRAN, however, if X were
a fixed-point constant or variable. For example, it is incorrect
to have the expression

        2*Z + 1

where Z is a complex variable. The following are some examples of
valid complex arithmetic expressions:

        COMPLEX X, Z
        X*Z + (1.0, 0.0)
        X*Z + 1.0
        X**2
        X/(Z + 2.0)
        (0.0, 1.0)*(X + Z)/2.0

■ Mixed-Mode Arithmetic

    Some FORTRAN compilers allow a completely general mixed-mode
arithmetic. That is, any combination of variables may be used
together in an expression, no matter what their types. This means
we could add a complex variable to a double-precision variable. In
this case, the result would be a complex number. This calculation
would be carried out in three steps:

    1. First, the double-precision number is converted to
        single-precision by truncation.

    2. Next, the result of Step 1 is converted to a complex
        number by adding an imaginary part of 0.

    3. Finally, the two complex numbers are added.

    Thus, the FORTRAN statements

        COMPLEX Z
        Z = (1.0, 2.0) + 3.0D-1

would assign the value (1.3, 2.0) to Z.

    The same procedure is used when multiplying a complex number
by a double-precision number, except, of course, in Step 3, the
two complex numbers are multiplied instead of added. The statements

        COMPLEX Z
        Z = (0.0, 1.0)*2.0D

would assign the value (0.0, 2.0) to Z.

    Statements involving complex and floating-point numbers or
complex and fixed-point numbers are handled in a similar manner.
For instance, if a complex number is added to a fixed-point number,

the fixed-point number will be converted to floating-point, given an imaginary part of 0, and then added to the complex number. Thus, the value of (0.0, 1.0) + 2 is (2.0, 1.0).

The mode of any mixed-mode operation can be determined from Table 11-4. This table gives the type of the result of any arithmetic operation +, -, *, /, **. As an example, suppose that C is complex, D is double-precision, R is floating-point, and I is fixed-point. Suppose they have the following values:

$$C = (1.0, 2.0) \qquad D = 3.1D0 \qquad R = 2.0 \qquad I = 4$$

Then the expression (C + D)*I/R would be evaluated as follows:

```
((1.0, 2.0) + 3.1)*4/2.0
((1.0, 2.0) + (3.1, 0.0)*4/2.0
(4.1, 2.0)*(4.0, 0.0)/2.0
(16.4, 8.0)/(2.0, 0.0)
(8.2, 4.0)
```

TABLE 11-4

	Complex	Double-Precision	Floating-Point	Fixed-Point
Complex	Complex	Complex	Complex	Complex
Double-Precision	Complex	Double-Precision	Double-Precision	Double-Precision
Floating-Point	Complex	Double-Precision	Floating-Point	Floating-Point
Fixed-Point	Complex	Double-Precision	Floating-Point	Fixed-Point

■ Input and Output of Complex Numbers

A complex number corresponds to a pair of real numbers. The FORTRAN representation of the complex number $1 + 2i$ is (1.0, 2.0), which is a pair of FORTRAN floating-point numbers. There is no separate field description in FORTRAN to use for printing complex numbers. Instead, we use two F- or E-type field descriptors, one for each part of the complex number. For example, suppose Z is a complex variable. To print its value, we could use the statements

```
      WRITE(2, 11) Z
   11 FORMAT(2F12.4)
```

The field description in the FORMAT statement consists of two F12.4 fields. The first of these would be used to print the real

part of Z, and the second would be used to print the imaginary part.
If Z = (32.4, -5.0), the resulting output would be
bbbbb32.4000bbbbb-5.0000. If we used the FORMAT statement

    11 FORMAT(F6.1, E8.1)

then the real part of Z would be printed with an F6.1 format, while
the imaginary part of Z would be printed with an E8.1 format. The
output in this case would be bb32.4b-.5E+01.

To read the value of a complex number, we simply put an F or
an E field for each part of the number. When a complex variable
name appears in the list of a READ statement, the next two fields
of the FORMAT statement will be used to read it. The first field
will be used to read the real part, and the second field will be
used to read the imaginary part of the number. For example, if a
program contained the statements

        COMPLEX X, Y
        READ(1, 9) X, Y
    9   FORMAT(F5.1, F4.1, F5.1, F4.1)

then the real part of X would be read with the F5.1 field, and the
imaginary part of X would be read with the F4.1 field. If an input
card contained the data

    000100020 23.1 0.0

then the resulting values for X and Y would be

        X = (1.0, 2.0)
        Y = (23.1, 0.0)

■ Complex Functions

Several function subprograms are provided by FORTRAN, which are
often useful for programs involving complex variables. For instance,
it is frequently necessary to find the square root of a complex number. This *cannot* be done, however, by using the function SQRT; that
function is only for finding the square root of a real variable.
When we write Y = SQRT(X), FORTRAN expects that X is a real variable,
and if X were a complex variable, the results would be unpredictable.
For complex numbers, we have the special function CSQRT. This
function takes a complex argument and returns a complex value. If
Y is a complex variable in FORTRAN, then the statement

        Y = CSQRT((-1.0, 0.0))

would assign to Y the complex value (0.0, 1.0).

The trigonometric and exponential functions also have their
counterparts for complex variables. These are given in Table 11-5.

The argument of each function must be of complex type, and the value returned will also be complex.

TABLE 11-5. *Some complex-valued functions.*

Function	Definition
CSQRT(X)	*Square root of x*
CEXP(X)	*Exponential function, e^x*
CLOG(X)	*Natural logarithm, $\log_e x$*
CSIN(X)	*Trigonometric sine, $\sin x$*
CCOS(X)	*Trigonometric cosine, $\cos x$*
CONJG(X)	*Conjugate of x; the conjugate of (a, b) is (a, -b)*

Some other useful FORTRAN functions take complex variables and return real function values. These are given in Table 11-6.

TABLE 11-6

Function	Definition
REAL(X)	*Real part of complex number:* REAL((A, B)) = A
AIMAG(X)	*Imaginary part of complex number:* AIMAG((A, B)) = B
CABS(X)	*Modulus of complex number:* CABS((A, B)) $= \sqrt{A^2 + B^2}$

One final function takes two real arguments and returns a complex number; this is defined in Table 11-7.

TABLE 11-7

Function	Definition
CMPLX(X, Y)	*Expresses the two real numbers X and Y as the complex number X + Yi*

Some examples of the functions listed in Tables 11-6 and 11-7 are given in Table 11-8.

TABLE 11-8

Example	Value	Example	Value
REAL((3.1, 4.0))	3.1	CABS((3.0, 4.0))	5.0
AIMAG((3.1, 4.0))	4.0	CMPLX(3.0, 4.0)	(3.0, 4.0)

To define a complex-valued function of our own, we use the statement

COMPLEX FUNCTION name$(x_1, x_2, \ldots, x_n)$

This statement works just like the DOUBLE PRECISION FUNCTION statement, except that the value of the function named will be complex. For example, the following is a function subroutine to compute the reciprocal of a complex number:

```
COMPLEX FUNCTION REC(Z)
COMPLEX Z
REC = (1.0, 0.0)/Z
RETURN
END
```

The COMPLEX statement specifies that the variable Z is a complex variable. The COMPLEX FUNCTION statement specifies that the function itself will take a complex value. The statements

```
COMPLEX X, Y, REC
X = (0.0, 1.0)
Y = REC(X)
```

would then set Y = (0.0, -1.0), which is 1.0/(0.0, 1.0).

Example 2

For positive real numbers, we can find the positive nth root using the exponential operator **. For instance, to find the fifth root of X, we can use the statement

```
Y = X**(1.0/5.0)
```

For complex numbers, the situation is more complicated. In general, there are n nth roots of a complex number. If $z = a + bi$ is a complex number, and n is any positive integer, the n nth roots of z are the complex numbers $w_1, w_2, \ldots, w_n$ given by

$$w_k = |z|^{1/n} \left[\cos\left(\frac{\theta + 2\pi k}{n}\right) + i \sin\left(\frac{\theta + 2\pi k}{n}\right) \right]$$

where

$$k = 1, 2, \ldots, n$$
$$\theta = \text{Tan}^{-1}(b/a)$$
$$|z| = \sqrt{a^2 + b^2}$$

In this example, we want to write a subroutine ROOT(N, Z, W), where N is a positive integer, Z is a complex variable, and W is a complex array of N elements, which will set W(K) equal to the Kth Nth root of Z as defined by the above formula.

The subroutine will use several of the functions discussed in the previous section. The first thing we must do is to find θ. To do this, we shall use the function ATAN2, which gives the arctangent of a number expressed in radians (the angle lies between 0 and 2π). We use the statements

```
X = REAL(Z)
Y = AIMAG(Z)
THETA = ATAN2(Y, X)
```

and $|Z|$ can be computed with the function CABS as

```
AA = CABS(Z)**(1.0/AN)
```

where AN = N in floating-point form. When we have computed the quantities

$$X = \cos\left(\frac{\theta + 2\pi k}{n}\right) \quad \text{and} \quad Y = \sin\left(\frac{\theta + 2\pi k}{n}\right)$$

we can use the function CMPLX to express these as a complex number $x + ny_i$. We can then compute W(K) with the statement

```
W(K) = CMPLX(AA*X, AA*Y)
```

The complete FORTRAN subroutine is:

```
      SUBROUTINE ROOT(N, Z, W)
C     THIS SUBROUTINE STORES THE N NTH ROOTS OF THE
C     COMPLEX NUMBER Z IN THE COMPLEX ARRAY W.
      COMPLEX Z, W(N)
      AN = N
      PI = 3.14159
      X = REAL(Z)
      Y = AIMAG(Z)
      THETA = PI/2.0
      IF(X.NE.0.0)THETA = ATAN2(Y, X)
      AA = CABS(Z)**(1.0/AN)
      THETA = THETA/AN
      PHI = 2.0*PI/AN
```

```
        DO 10 K = 1, N
        THETA = THETA + PHI
        X = COS(THETA)
        Y = SIN(THETA)
   10   W(K) = CMPLX(AA*X, AA*Y)
        RETURN
        END
```

■ Exercises

1. Which of the following are valid FORTRAN double-precision constants?

   (a) .99   (f) 100.0
   (b) 9.5D3   (g) .01D4
   (c) 7.2E1   (h) .9999999
   (d) 6.0D   (i) 0D
   (e) 7D0   (j) 0.0D

2. A certain computer stores five digits in a memory location and truncates any digits beyond this. What is the result of the following computation?

       12345*67890

   What is the exact value? How could using double-precision variables make the result more accurate?

3. Write a double-precision function ROOT to find the square root of a double-precision variable. Do this two ways, one using the exponential operator ** and one without it.

4. Which of the following are valid FORTRAN complex constants?

   (a) (1.0, 1.0)   (f) (0, 0)
   (b) (0.0, 0.0)   (g) (12.0E2, 0.0)
   (c) (0.0)   (h) (1.4E-2, -1.4E2)
   (d) (5, 2)   (i) (7.0, 1.1)
   (e) (5.0, 2.0)   (j) (X, 1.0)

5. Perform the indicated operations, using complex arithmetic.

   (a) (1.0, 2.0) + (3.0, 4.0)   (d) (0.0, -1.0)**2
   (b) (1.0, 1.0)/(0.0,1.0)   (e) (10.0, 0.0)/(0.0, 10.0)
   (c) (0.0, 2.0)*(0.0,2.0)

6. Evaluate the following functions:

   (a) REAL((4.0, 2.0))   (d) CMPLX(1.0, 0.0)
   (b) AIMAG((1.0, 0.0))   (e) CONJG((1.0, 5.0))
   (c) CABS((5.0, 12.0))

7. If $Y = A(1) + A(2)*Z + A(3)*Z**2 + \cdots + A(N)*Z**(N - 1)$, where $A(I)$ and Z are complex, write a complex function POLY(N, A, Z) to compute this expression.

8. If Z and W are complex numbers, write a function subprogram NSIGN, which will set

$$\text{NSIGN} = \begin{cases} 1 \text{ if } Z = W \\ -1 \text{ if } Z = \text{CONJG}(W) \\ 0 \text{ otherwise} \end{cases}$$

9. A complex number (x, y) can be expressed in polar coordinates as (r, A), where $r^2 = x^2 + y^2$ and $A = \text{Tan}^{-1}(y/x)$. Write a complex function POLE(Z) which will express the complex number Z as a complex number in polar coordinate form.

10. If W1 and W2 are complex numbers in polar coordinate form (r_1, A_1) and (r_2, A_2), then W1*W2 in polar coordinate form is $(r_1 r_2, A_1 + A_2)$. Write a complex function subroutine PROD(W1, W2) which will set PROD equal to the polar coordinate form of the product of W1 and W2, where W1 and W2 are in polar coordinate form.

Chapter

12

Magnetic Tape and Disk Storage

■ Tape and Disk Storage

Until now in our discussion of input and output operations, we have assumed the input always comes from a card reader and the output is always printed on a printer. Actually, there are several other devices that are more commonly used to store large volumes of information. The most common are magnetic tape and disk units. In this chapter, we shall see how to use these in a FORTRAN program.

A magnetic tape can be used by a computer to store data in much the same way that the magnetic tape used by a tape recorder stores sound signals. The surface of the tape is coated with a substance which can be magnetized. In the case of the audio tape recorder, sound signals are transformed into variations in a magnetic field, and these variations are recorded on the tape as it moves past the recording head. Once magnetized, the tape can be played back, and the variations in magnetism can be transformed into sound waves to produce the original sound. The tape drives used by a computer are bigger and more complicated than the average tape recorder, but they use the same principle.

Instead of storing sound waves, however, a computer tape stores numeric and alphabetic data. Any information that can be printed on a printer could just as well be written on a tape. We would not be able to read it directly, of course, but the tape could be saved, and then at some future time the information could be read back into the computer to be used by another program.

Data is stored on tape by using magnetized pulses. These pulses represent either one of two digits, a zero (0) or a one (1), and are known as *bits*. These bits correspond to the columns on a punch card. Instead of punching holes in the columns as on a card, the tape unit magnetizes the bits on the tape. A tape unit typically writes (or reads) 800 columns of such bits in a single inch of tape. So, a reel containing 100 feet of tape can store a very large amount of information very compactly.

In addition to being considerably more compact, information on a tape can be processed much faster than information punched on

cards. Also, tapes are reusable. After we are through with the
data on a tape, we can write new data on the same tape; we may even
want to do this many times in a single program. As we go along, we
shall see how these properties can make tape storage very advanta-
geous for some applications.

A reel of tape is mounted on a tape drive by an operator
before the beginning of a program. The tape is positioned at the
load point, which is a mark on the tape to indicate where the information on the tape begins. A FORTRAN program can then either read
information which has already been written on the tape, or write
new information on the tape. Each READ or WRITE operation will
advance the position of the tape. We rarely have to worry about
coming to the end of a tape, since a reel can store so much data.
At the conclusion of a program, the tape is rewound (either by the
program or the operator) and it is then dismounted by the operator
to be saved for later use.

The data on a tape cannot be seen as can the data on a punch
card. The method of recording the data is different, but the
FORTRAN programming is virtually the same. The complicated process
of decoding the magnetic tape into numeric data for use by a program is taken care of automatically, just as it is for reading cards.
A programmer only has to know *how* the data is written on the tape,
so it can be read into a program.

A disk unit operates on the same principle as a tape unit,
except that the data is recorded on a magnetic disk. This disk is
something like a phonograph record covered with magnetic material.
The disk revolves at high speed, and data is read or written by
movable arms which are free to move over the surface of the disk.
Some systems use a drum instead of a disk, but the idea is the
same.

There is no "beginning" to a disk as there is to a tape. When
we write information on a disk, the computer will pick out some
location on the disk (which it keeps track of automatically), and
then start writing information at that point on the disk surface.
The next time we write on the disk, the recording arm may move to
another area before it starts to write. On a third WRITE operation, still another area may be used. Obviously, it is a complicated process to keep track of all the areas on the disk where
information has been written. Fortunately for us, however, this is
done automatically by the computer, and we do not have to worry
about it at all in FORTRAN. After we have finished writing information on a disk, we can reposition the reading arm at its original
point, and begin to read the information just as it was written.
As an example, suppose that unit number 7 is a disk unit. In a
FORTRAN program, we might want to write the values of three variables A, B, and C on this unit, using the statements

```
WRITE(7, 99) A
WRITE(7, 99) B
WRITE(7, 99) C
```

where 99 is some FORMAT statement. We have no idea where these
numbers are actually written on the disk. The computer knows, but
we do not. However, as we shall see, we can reposition the read
arm of the disk at the starting point, wherever that may be, by
using the FORTRAN statement

        REWIND 7

We can then read the data back into the computer by using the
statements

        READ(7, 99) A
        READ(7, 99) B
        READ(7, 99) C

As with tape storage, the complicated process of reading and writing the data is done automatically by the computer. In FORTRAN,
we only need to know how the data is written on the disk, so we
can always read it back in by using the same FORMAT statement.

   Thus, in FORTRAN, we can think of a disk unit as functioning
just like a tape unit. Actually, we can think of a disk unit as
functioning just like several tape units. In the above example, we
assumed that the number 7 corresponded to a disk unit. In the same
program, we might use the numbers 8 and 9 to correspond to the same
disk unit. However, since different numbers are used, the computer
would keep track of the information separately, just as though
three different disk units were being used.

   The question of what type of device is most suitable for a job
depends on the nature of the information to be stored. Cards may
be easily prepared on a keypunch, but reading cards is slower than
reading tapes. Also, tape storage is much more compact than card
storage. When dealing with large amounts of data, where it would
be impractical to save all the information on cards, a common practice is to punch the data on cards, and then have a program transfer
the data to tape. Since a disk unit can take the place of many tape
units, disk storage is well-suited to many applications where it is
necessary to store large amounts of information only for the dura-
tion of a program. Later in this chapter, we shall see examples
of how each type of unit may be used in a specific application.

■ Files and Records

   FORTRAN does not explicitly distinguish among the different
input-output devices. Data is thought of as being organized into
files, and it makes little difference as far as FORTRAN is concerned, whether the file is a tape, disk, or card or print file.

   A file is an area used by a program as input or output. An
example of an input file is a deck of cards to be read. Printed
output from a program is an example of an output file. A tape on
a tape drive may be used either as an input or an output file. As

mentioned before, a disk unit can accommodate many files. This emphasizes the difference between files and input-output devices. Even though the same device is used for many files, each file may be thought of as a separate body of data, just as though each one were written on a different device. The unit number in the READ or WRITE statements is different for each file.

Files are made up of records. A record is the smallest element of a file which can be read or written by a single operation in FORTRAN. For a card reader, each card is a record. As we know, each READ statement in FORTRAN will start reading at the beginning of a new card. For a printer, a record consists of one print line, since each WRITE statement will start at the beginning of a new line.

On a tape, the information is written sequentially, so while we do not talk about reading the next card or writing the next line, we can think about it that way. A record on a tape or disk file is just a group of characters that is read or written together. When we talk about reading the next record from a tape, this is just like reading the next card. While for cards we are limited by the fact that each card has 80 columns, on a tape or disk file we can make records any size we want. If we write out 500 characters using a single WRITE statement, this will result in a record 500 characters long. When reading such a record, we would have to read it with a single READ statement, since the next READ statement would automatically start reading at the beginning of the next record (just as for reading cards).

We shall now describe examples of programs that use several types of input and output files.

Consider the problem of ordering items for a large store. First, we need to know what items are carried by the store. This information might be kept in a tape file. Each record in the file would contain an identification number for some item, the name of the item, the amount to be stocked, the price per unit, and so forth. Next, we need to know how much of each item is actually on hand. This is determined by taking inventory and then punching a card for each item, giving the item number and the amount on hand. Both of these files are used as input to the program, which then computes the amount of each item to be ordered and the price. This information might be written on a tape to be used in other programs. The program might also make a printed copy of the output. Thus, in this program, we have two input files and two output files.

It is sometimes convenient to be able to diagram the files used by a program. We can use flowchart symbols for this. The symbol for each type of file is shown in Fig. 12-1. Using a rectangular box to represent the program, we can make a diagram of the files used by a program which looks something like a flowchart. A diagram for the example above regarding the store inventory would be like the one shown in Fig. 12-2.

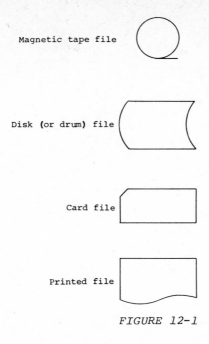

FIGURE 12-1

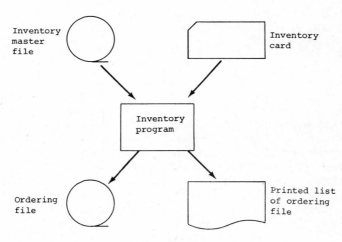

FIGURE 12-2

This type of diagram can be especially useful in keeping track of files which are used in several programs. For instance, the inventory master file shown in Fig. 12-2 might have come from another program which created it by making changes in an old master file to tell what new products were to be carried or what old products were to be discontinued. The whole process could be represented as shown in Fig. 12-3.

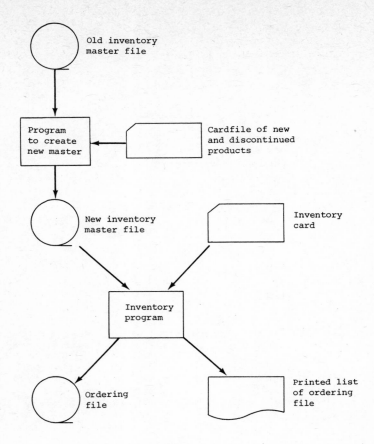

FIGURE 12-3

■ The READ and WRITE Statements for Tape and Disk Files

The READ and WRITE statements in FORTRAN are the same for tape or disk files as they are for card and print files. The form of the WRITE statement is

WRITE(*u*, *f*) list

where

> *u* is a fixed-point constant or a simple fixed-point variable which denotes the unit number designating the file;

> *f* is the number of a FORMAT statement;

list is the list of variables to be written.

What *u* actually is will depend on the particular computer used. On some systems, the programmer can assign any number to any device by using control cards in front of the FORTRAN program. For now, we shall assume that the computer in question has two tape drives and a disk unit, and that the numbers are as follows:

3   designates a tape file;

4   designates another tape file;

5, 6, 7, and any higher numbers   correspond to disk files on the disk unit.

The form of the READ statement is

READ(*u*, *f*) list

where *u*, *f*, and list are as above for the WRITE statement.

Each WRITE statement will begin writing a new record, and each READ statement will begin reading at the beginning of a new record. Suppose that A, B, C, D, E, and F are variables having the values 1.0, 2.0, 3.0, 4.0, 5.0, and 6.0. If we write on a tape, using the statements

```
        WRITE(3, 50) A
    50  FORMAT(F4.2)
        WRITE(3, 51) B, C, D
    51  FORMAT(3F4.2)
        WRITE(3, 52) E, F
    52  FORMAT(2F4.2)
```

then the resulting output may be thought of as looking like Fig. 12-4. Each block in this figure represents one record on the tape.

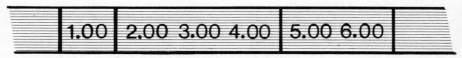

FIGURE 12-4

Of course, the tape does not really look like this. The numbers are represented by magnetized bits, and the end-of-record marks would also be special magnetized patterns on the tape. But we can think of it in this way. Now, suppose the tape is rewound, and suppose we read it with the statements

```
        READ(3, 50) X
        READ(3, 50) Y
        READ(3, 50) Z
    50  FORMAT(F4.2)
```

The value read for X will be 1.0. The value read for Y will be 2.0.
But the value read for Z will be 5.0, not 3.0. The reason for this
is that the second READ statement reads all of the second record,
but the second record consists of 12 characters, and only the first
4 are assigned to a variable, so the last part is lost. The third
READ statement starts reading at the beginning of the third record,
which begins with the characters 5.00.

We can process more than one record at a time with a single
READ or WRITE statement by using the slash (/) in a FORMAT statement. For instance, the statements

```
        WRITE(3, 99) (A(I), I = 1, 15)
    99  FORMAT(5(3F10.0/))
```

would create the next five records on a tape, and each record would
consist of three F10.0 fields. The slash means to begin a new record on the tape just like beginning a new print line, as we did in
Chapter 7. In a READ statement, the slash means to start reading
at the beginning of the next record. Thus, to read the tape segment shown in Fig. 12-4, we could use the statements

```
        READ(3, 100) A, B, C, D, E, F
    100 FORMAT(F4.2 / 3F4.2 / 2F4.2)
```

and this would read all three records.

For reading or writing on a disk file, the statements are the
same as for reading or writing on a tape. As we have seen, there
is really no difference between these statements and those used
for reading cards or writing on the printer. The only difference
is that the records are groups of characters on the tape or disk,
rather than individual cards or print lines, and they may be longer.

■ Tape-Handling Statements

Every file has a beginning: for a card file, it is the first
card in the deck; for a printed file, it is the first line printed;
for a tape file, there will be a mark on the tape before the first
record. We can reposition a file at its beginning by using the
REWIND statement. This statement has the form

```
        REWIND n
```

where n is a fixed-point constant or a simple fixed-point variable
giving the number of the unit containing the file. This statement
simply repositions file n at its starting point. If n is a tape
file, the tape will be physically rewound on the tape drive to the
beginning of the first record. For a disk file, this statement
will position the read arms at the initial point of the file. If
file n is already at the beginning, or if the statement is not
applicable (as for a card file), the REWIND statement will do
nothing. It is a good idea to rewind all tape and disk files at

the beginning of a program to make sure they are positioned at the beginning before they are used the first time.

As an example of this statement, suppose that A is an array, and we have written 100 records on a tape or disk file with the statements

```
      WRITE(JOE, 57) (A(I), I = 1, 100)
   57 FORMAT(100(F12.3/))
```

Then the statement

```
      REWIND JOE
```

will position this file at its beginning, and we can then read the values and store them in an array B with the statement

```
      READ(JOE, 57) (B(I), I = 1, 100)
```

To indicate that the end of a file has been reached, we can create a special mark on the file called an *end-of-file-mark*. This is done with the ENDFILE statement, which has the form

```
      ENDFILE n
```

where *n* is again the file number. This statement will simply write a mark on the file which the computer will recognize as an indication that there is nothing more to be read on the file. When an end-of-file mark is encountered on a read operation, the computer will take note of the fact, and any further attempt to read the file will either result in an execution error or serve to terminate the program, depending on the computer.

We can test for an end-of-file mark by using a special logical function which has the form[1]

```
      EOF(n)
```

where *n* is the file number. This function will return a value of .TRUE. if an end-of-file mark was encountered on file *n* on the last read operation, and a value of .FALSE. otherwise. Since EOF is a logical function, the variable EOF must be declared in a LOGICAL statement. Usually, each time we read a tape or disk file, we follow the READ statement with an IF statement such as

```
      IF(EOF(K)) GO TO 99
```

This will cause the program to go to Statement 99 if an end-of-file mark was read on file K. If no such mark was read, the next statement will be performed. Suppose we have written 100 records on a

---

[1]The form of this function may vary somewhat on different computer systems.

tape, using the statements

```
      WRITE(3, 77) (A(I), I = 1, 100)
   77 FORMAT(100(F10.3/))
      ENDFILE 3
```

The ENDFILE statement will write an end-of-file mark after the last record written. Now, we could go back and add up all these values written by using the statements

```
      SUM = 0.0
      REWIND 3
   10 READ(3, 78) X
   78 FORMAT(F10.3)
      IF(EOF(3)) GO TO 79
      SUM = SUM + X
      GO TO 10
   79 REWIND 3
      STOP
```

Each READ statement will read one record. For the first 100 times the READ statement is performed, the function EOF(3) will be .FALSE., so the number read will be added to the sum. On the 101st time, however, the READ statement will read an end-of-file mark. In this case, the FORMAT statement will have no meaning, and X will have an undefined value. But the function EOF(3) will be .TRUE., so the program will branch to Statement 79, where the input tape is rewound.

Example 1

A certain company keeps a tape file of employees. Each record on the tape consists of 44 characters giving the following data:

```
      Characters  1-5    Employee number
      Characters  6-30   Name
      Characters 31-35   Pay rate—a five-digit number with an
                            assumed decimal point before the
                            last two digits
      Characters 36-44   Social security number
```

There is an end-of-file mark after the last record. Now, every employee is to get a 5 percent pay raise. The problem is to read the old tape and to create a new tape with the new pay rates.

The files used in this program are shown in Fig. 12-5. The numbers 3 and 4 indicate the numbers we shall call the files by in the FORTRAN program.

The solution to this problem is quite simple. We just read a record from the old file, compute the new pay rate, and write a record on the new file. We continue this procedure until an end-of-file mark is encountered on the old file, at which time we write an end-of-file on the new file, rewind both files, and stop.

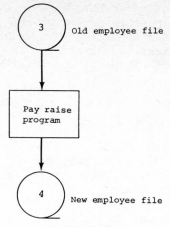

FIGURE 12-5

The flowchart for this program is shown in Fig. 12-6. Notice that we rewind both files at the beginning of the program. This is always a good idea, as it ensures that the files are positioned at their starting points. If the files are already at their starting points (as they should be), the REWIND statements cause no action.

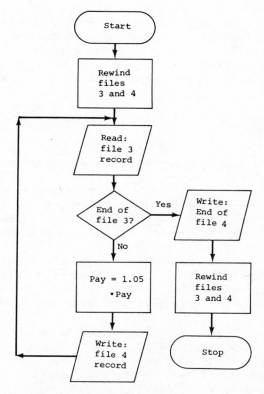

FIGURE 12-6
Flowchart for Example 1

In the FORTRAN program for this job, we use an array NAME to hold the name. We shall assume here that the computer can store 10 characters in a word. So, the array NAME will have three elements that will contain the first 10 characters, the second 10 characters, and the last 5 characters of the 25 character name on the employee record. The program is:

```
      LOGICAL EOF
      DIMENSION NAME(3)
      REWIND 3
      REWIND 4
   5  READ(3, 10) NUM, NAME, PAY, NSS
  10  FORMAT(I5, 2A10, A5, F5.0, I9)
      IF(EOF(3)) GO TO 99
      PAY = 1.05*PAY
      WRITE(4, 10) NUM, NAME, PAY, NSS
      GO TO 5
  99  ENDFILE 4
      REWIND 3
      REWIND 4
      STOP
      END
```

In FORMAT Statement 10, we have specified that the pay is read with an F5.0 format. The reason for this is that when we write the pay again we shall not write a decimal point, since we do not want one to appear explicitly. For instance, if the pay is written 02500, this means 25.00. But we are going to read it as 2500.0. The new pay rate will be computed as 2625.0, but when we write it with the F5.0 format, it will be written as b2625, as we want it to be.

Example 2

In the above example, we assumed that everyone received the same raise. Now let's consider the general problem of how to update the employee file. There are three things we might want to do to an employee's record on the tape. First, we might want to change some of the information, as we did above. In addition, some employees will leave the company for various reasons, so we will want to be able to delete certain records from the tape. Finally, we shall need to be able to add records to the tape for new employees. In order to tell what changes are to be made to the tape file, we shall use a card file. Each card will correspond to one record on the tape, and will have the following format:

Columns	1–5	Employee number
Columns	6–30	Name
Columns	31–35	Pay rate
Columns	36–44	Social security number
Columns	45–79	Blank
Column	80	Operation code—either "1" or blank

The operation code in column 80 tells what is to be done with the record. If column 80 contains a 1, the card is a deletion, so the record on the tape with the same employee number as the card will not be written on the new tape file. If column 80 is blank, the card is an insertion or a correction card. If there is a record on the tape with the same employee number as on the card, then the information on this tape record will be replaced with the information on the card record on the new tape file. If there is no record on the tape with the same employee number as the card, a record will be created on the new tape from the information on the card. The three files used in the program are shown in Fig. 12-7.

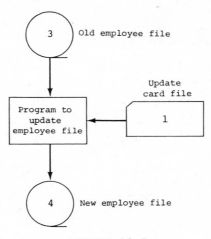

FIGURE 12-7

To program this problem, we must assume that the input files are sorted according to the employee number. In other words, we assume that the cards and the tape records are sorted so that each record read will have a greater employee number than the previous record. With this assumption, the main idea of the program will be to compare the employee number on the card to the employee number of the tape and determine the appropriate action to be taken based on this comparison. Suppose, then, that we have read in a tape record and a card record. There are four possible situations:

1. The employee number on the card is greater than the employee number on the tape. In this case, we are not ready to do anything with the card. The record on the tape will go onto the new tape just as it is, so we write a new tape record, then read another old tape record, and again compare the employee numbers.

2. The employee number on the tape is greater than the employee number on the card. Since the tape is sorted, and we have suddenly come to a number higher than the one on the card, the record on the card must be an

addition to the tape. So we write a new tape record
from the information on the card, then we read another
card, and go back to the comparison.

3. The card and tape numbers are equal, and column 80 on
   the card contains a 1. In this case, the record on the
   tape is to be deleted from the new tape. To do this,
   we simply read another card and tape record, and go
   back to the comparison.

4. The card and tape numbers are equal, and column 80 of
   the card does not contain a 1. In this case, the card
   is a correction for the tape record, so we write a
   record on the new tape using the information on the
   card, then we read another card and tape record, and go
   back to the comparison.

This procedure is shown in the flowchart in Fig. 12-8. In
this flowchart, NUM1 and NUM3 are the employee numbers for files 1
and 3, and NOP is the operation code (column 80) on the card. The
statements such as "Record 4 = Record 1" are a shorthand way of
saying that the information to be written on the file 4 record comes
from the information read from file 1. In the FORTRAN program, we
will read information from file 1 into variables NUM1, NAME1, PAY1,
and NSS1. The variables NUM3, NAME3, PAY3, and NSS3 are the corresponding items read from file 3. To write a record on file 4 from
the information on file 1, we would use the statement

    WRITE(4, 11) NUM1, NAME1, PAY1, NSS1

This sort of procedure occurs frequently in programs dealing with
several files which have to be matched. In order to visualize
the method, suppose that the numbers on the input files are as
given in Table 12-1:

TABLE 12-1

NUM1 (Card File)	Operation Code (Column 80)	NUM3 (Tape File)
3		1
5		2
6	1	4
10	1	5
11		6
		8
		9
		10
		11

On the first comparison, the tape number is lower, so a new tape
record is written from the old tape record, and another old tape
record is read. The same thing happens on the second comparison.

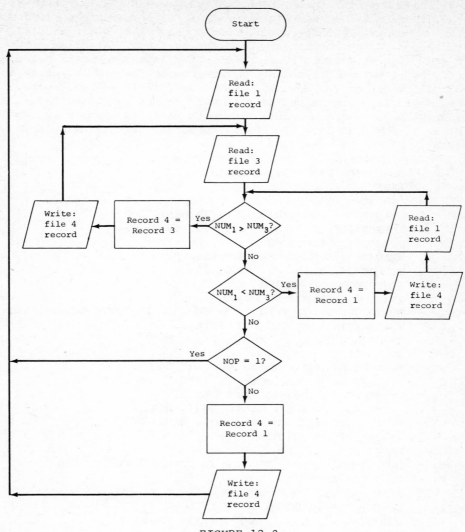

FIGURE 12-8
Flowchart for Example 2

On the third comparison, however, the card number is lower, so the card is an addition to the tape. A new tape record is written from the card, and another card is read before the next comparison. Convince yourself that the new tape would have the records numbered

1, 2, 3, 4, 5, 8, 9, 11

Records 6 and 10 are deleted from the tape. Records 5 and 11 are corrected on the new tape.

We have omitted one thing from the flowchart shown in Fig. 12-8. We have not considered the action to be taken after the end is

reached on one of the input files. After we read the last tape
record, there still might be some cards left to indicate additions
to the new tape. In this case, we would read each remaining card
and create a corresponding record on the new tape. Also, we might
have tape records left to be read after the last card is processed.
In this case, we would read each remaining tape record and write an
identical record on the new tape. When the end is reached on both
files, we shall write an end-of-file mark on the new tape, then
rewind the tapes. The complete flowchart for this example is shown
in Figs. 12-9 and 12-10. The FORTRAN program for this example is as
follows:

```
        LOGICAL EOF
        DIMENSION NAME1(3), NAME3(3)
        REWIND 3
        REWIND 4
     5  READ(1, 6) NUM1, NAME1, PAY1, NSS1, NOP
     6  FORMAT(I5, 2A10, A5, F5.0, I9, 35X, I1)
        IF(EOF(1)) GO TO 99
    10  READ(3, 11) NUM3, NAME3, PAY3, NSS3
    11  FORMAT(I5, 2A10, A5, F5.0, I9)
        IF(EOF(3)) GO TO 100
    15  IF(NUM1.LE.NUM3) GO TO 20
C       NUM1 IS GREATER THAN NUM3, SO CARD IS NOT PROCESSED YET.
C       WRITE FILE 4 RECORD FROM FILE 3.
        WRITE(4, 11) NUM3, NAME3, PAY3, NSS3
        GO TO 10
    20  IF(NUM1.GE.NUM3) GO TO 25
C       NUM1 IS LESS THAN NUM3, SO CARD IS AN ADDITION.
C       WRITE FILE 4 RECORD FROM FILE 1.
        WRITE(4, 11) NUM1, NAME1, PAY1, NSS1
        READ(1, 6) NUM1, NAME1, PAY1, NSS1, NOP
        IF(EOF(1)) GO TO 99
        GO TO 15
C       NUM1 EQUALS NUM3, SO CARD IS EITHER A CORRECTION
C       OR REPLACEMENT.
    25  IF(NOP.EQ.1) GO TO 5
C       IF NOP IS 1, RECORD IS DELETED
        WRITE(4, 11) NUM1, NAME1, PAY1, NSS1
        GO TO 5
C       END OF FILE 1 REACHED
    99  IF(EOF(3)) GO TO 200
        WRITE(4, 11) NUM3, NAME3, PAY3, NSS3
        READ(3, 11) NUM3, NAME3, PAY3, NSS3
        GO TO 99
C       END OF FILE 3 REACHED
   100  IF(EOF(1)) GO TO 200
        WRITE(4, 11) NUM1, NAME1, PAY1, NSS1
        READ(1, 6) NUM1, NAME1, PAY1, NSS1, NOP
        GO TO 100
C       END OF BOTH INPUT FILES REACHED
   200  ENDFILE 4
        REWIND 3
        REWIND 4
        STOP
        END
```

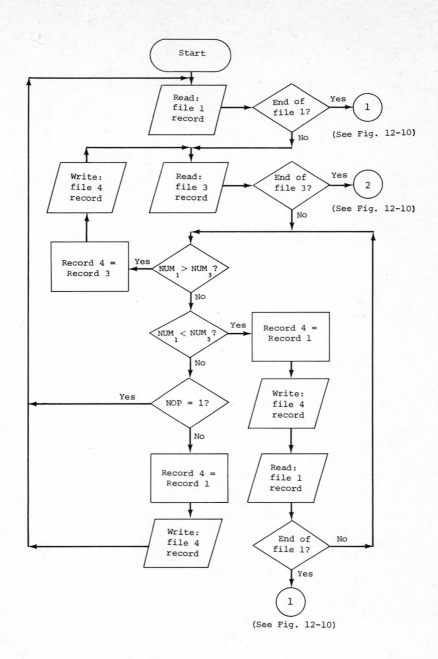

FIGURE 12-9

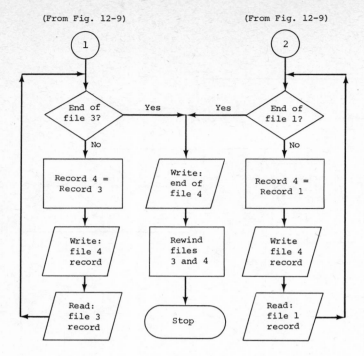

FIGURE 12-10

Example 3

Let us now consider one aspect of record-keeping in a library —mailing overdue book notices. We shall assume that we have two input files. The first of these is the name and address file. For each patron of the library, this file will give a library card number, name, and address. The other file will be a file of books checked out. For each book checked out, this file gives the library card number of the person the book is loaned to, the author and title of the book, and the date due. The program will also read a card which gives today's date. The object of the program will then be to match the information on the two input files and to print a notice to each patron who has overdue books, listing the books that are overdue and asking for their return. The files used in the program are shown in Fig. 12-11. The format of these files is given in Fig. 12-12.

Both of the tape files must be sorted according to the library card number. Note that the file of books checked out may have several records for one library card number (as would be the case if one person has several books checked out), but if these records are arranged by library card number, the records for all the books checked out will fall together. Thus, the order of some records in the books checked out file might be 1, 3, 3, 3, 6, 7, 7, 8, ... In the name and address file, some numbers might not be used as library card numbers, but each patron will have a single number. So, the records in this file might be numbered 1, 2, 4, 7, 8, 11, ...

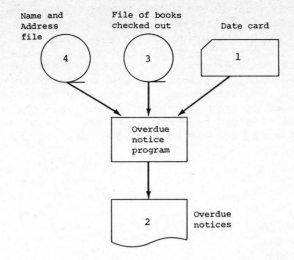

FIGURE 12-11

FILE OF BOOKS CHECKED OUT (File 3)	
Characters	*Data*
1-5	*Library card number of person to whom loaned*
6-15	*Call number of book*
16-25	*Author's last name (or first 10 characters if name is too long)*
26-45	*Title of book (or first 20 characters if title is too long)*
46-51	*Date due (written in form MMDDYY—i.e., 022375 would mean February 23, 1975)*
NAME AND ADDRESS FILE (File 4)	
Characters	*Data*
1-5	*Library card number of patron*
6-25	*Patron's name*
26-45	*First line of address*
46-65	*Second line of address*
66-85	*Third line of address*
DATE CARD (File 1)	
Columns	*Data*
1-6	*Today's date (written in form MMDDYY)*
7-80	*Blank*

FIGURE 12-12

Since the object of the program is to print overdue notices, it will be useful to decide how we want these notices to look before trying to write the program. In some situations, the simplest thing to do would be to use special paper for the output. Instead of the standard computer paper, a set of specially printed forms could be loaded onto the printer, and we could write the output right on these. We will assume, however, that we are using standard paper, so our program will have to print all the headings. The output will have one page for every patron who has overdue books, so that each page can be mailed separately. A sample page is shown in Fig. 12-13.

```
                                              7/ 9/77

        JOHN DOE
        411 OAK ST
        TUCSON, AZ
        85710

        DEAR SIR,
        THE FOLLOWING BOOKS ARE NOW OVERDUE.

        AUTHOR      TITLE               DATE DUE
        YOLK        THE PRICE OF EGGS    7/ 7/77
        YOLK        EGGS AND THEIR PRICE 7/ 7/77
        YOLK        EGG PRICE ANALYSIS   7/ 7/77
        YOLK        COLLECTED WORKS      7/ 7/77

        PLEASE RETURN THESE PROMPTLY.
        A FINE OF FIVE CENTS PER DAY IS CHARGED.
                                THANK YOU
```

FIGURE 12-13
Sample output from library program

The basic logic of the program is shown in the flowchart in Fig. 12-14. We begin by reading a record from each file. We shall call the library card numbers of files 3 and 4 NUM3 and NUM4. If NUM4 is less than NUM3, then the person with number NUM4 has not checked out any books, so we go back and read another file 4 record. NUM4 should never be greater than NUM3, since this would mean that a book was checked out to someone not on the name and address file. In this case, we would stop after printing an error message. If NUM4 equals NUM3, we check to see if the book represented by the file 3 record is overdue. This is the case when the date due (which we shall call NDATD) is less than the current date (which we shall call NDATE). If the book is overdue, we print the book title, author, and date due on an overdue notice. If not, we go back to read another file 3 record.

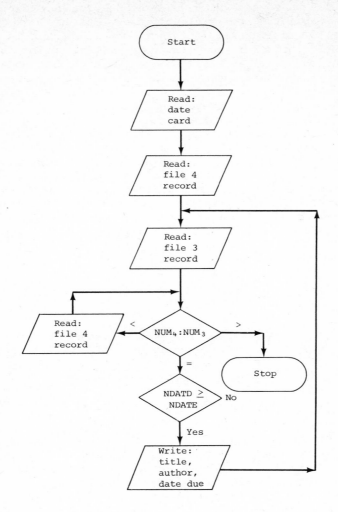

FIGURE 12-14

While Fig. 12-14 gives the basic idea of the program, there
are a few problems still to be worked out. First, we must remember
to test for an end-of-file on the input file, and if one is read,
we rewind the input tapes and stop. A more difficult problem is
the job of separating the output into pages with heading and
closing messages on each page. To do this, we must know when we
change from one person to the next. This can be done by using a
logical variable which we shall call FIRST. Every time we read a
record from file 4, we shall set FIRST = .TRUE., and every time
we print an overdue book title, we shall set FIRST = .FALSE. .
This will give the variable FIRST the value .TRUE. when we have

just changed from one person to the next on the name and address
tape, and enables us to determine when the heading should be
printed. Before printing the title of an overdue book, we see if
the value of FIRST is .TRUE.. If it is, then the title is the
first one to be printed for the person, so we first print the heading, giving the address, date, and so on. To determine when the
closing message is to be printed, we can also use the variable
FIRST. Each time a new record from file 4 is read, we are changing
to a new person. Now, if an overdue notice was printed for the previous person, the variable FIRST would have the value .FALSE., so
we would print the closing message at this time. If FIRST has the
value .TRUE., then the previous person did not get an overdue
notice, so we would not print the closing message before reading
the next file 4 record. The complete flowchart for this example is
shown in Fig. 12-15. Notice from the flowchart that when the end
of file 3 is reached, we must write the closing on the last overdue
notice before stopping. The student should try going through this
flowchart to see what would happen if the input were as given in
Table 12-2.

TABLE 12-2

NUM4	NUM3
1	2 (book not overdue)
2	2 (book overdue)
3	4 (book overdue)
4	4 (book not overdue)
5	4 (book overdue)

The only difficulty encountered in writing the FORTRAN program
from the flowchart is in the input and output statements. We shall
consider these individually. First, we assume that the computer
used can store ten characters of alphabetic data in a word. Now,
to read a record from the name and address file, we shall use an
array NAME of two elements to store the name, and an array ADDR of
six elements to store the address. The name is read with a 2A10
format, so the first ten characters of the name go in NAME(1), and
the last ten characters go in NAME(2). The same format is used to
read each line of the address, so the first line of the address is
in ADDR(1) and ADDR(2), the second line is in ADDR(3) and ADDR(4),
and the third line is in ADDR(5) and ADDR(6). The READ statement
for file 4 would then be

```
        READ(4, 10) NUM4, NAME, ADDR
   10   FORMAT(I5, 8A10)
```

To read a record from the file of books checked out, we shall
use the array TITLE to store the title. The date due for each
book could be read as a six-digit number. However, on the overdue
notice, we are going to want to print it in the form MM/DD/YY,
rather than just as MMDDYY. To facilitate this, we can read the

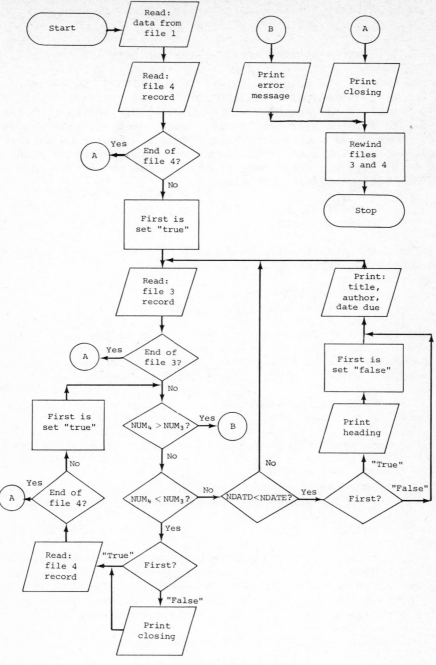

FIGURE 12-15
Flowchart for Example 3

date due into an array MDATD. MDATD(1) will be a two-digit number
giving the month, MDATD(2) will give the day, and MDATD(3) will

give the year. For the purpose of comparing the date due with the current date, we can convert the values in this array back into a single number with the formula

$$NDATD = 10000*MDATD(3) + 100*MDATD(1) + MDATD(2)$$

For example, if the date due is written as 113375, we would read it and store it as MDATD(1) = 11, MDATD(2) = 33, MDATD(3) = 75. The above formula would set NDATD equal to 751133. Notice that the two digits for the year come first. When dates are written like this, we can tell whether or not one date is later than another by simply subtracting them. This same procedure is used in reading the date card, so the current date can be printed on each overdue notice. The READ statement for file 3 is

```
      READ(3, 20) NUM3, AUTH, TITLE, MDATD
  20  FORMAT(I5, 10X, 3A10, 3I2)
```

The first item for the heading of the overdue notice is the date. This is written with the statements

```
      WRITE (2, 50) MDATE
  50  FORMAT(1H1, 32X,  I2, 1H/, I2, 1H/, I2)
```

The 1H1 field will cause the printer to skip to the top of the next page. The 1H/ fields will insert the slashes between the values of the array MDATE, so the date will be written as MM/DD/YY. The name and address are written with the statements

```
      WRITE(2, 55) NAME, ADDR
  55  FORMAT(1H0, 2A10)
```

The last part of the heading is printed with an H field to print

```
      DEAR SIR,
      THE FOLLOWING BOOKS ARE NOW OVERDUE.

      AUTHOR     TITLE                DATE DUE
```

The only problem here is to get everything in the right column. The word "AUTHOR" starts in column 2 (remember that column 1 is only for carriage control), "TITLE" starts in column 13, and "DATE DUE" starts in column 34. This is so we can print the author, title, and date due with one space between the columns.

The output statement for each overdue book is

```
      WRITE(2, 80) AUTH, TITLE, MDATD
  80  FORMAT(1X, A10, 1X, 2A10, 1X, I2, 1H/, I2, 1H/, I2)
```

This leaves a space for carriage control and a space between each field. The date will be written MM/DD/YY, with the slashes provided by the 1H fields. The closing message is written with H fields, just as the heading was.

With the READ and WRITE statements done, the rest of the program is easily written from the flowchart. The complete program is as follows:

```
      C       PROGRAM TO PRINT OVERDUE BOOK NOTICES
              DIMENSION NAME(2), ADDR(6), TITLE(2), MDATE(3), MDATD(3)
              LOGICAL FIRST, EOF
              READ(1, 5) MDATE
          5   FORMAT(3I2)
      C       CONVERT DATE TO COMPUTATIONAL VALUE
              NDATE = 10000*MDATE(3) + 100*MDATE(1) + MDATE(2)
              REWIND 3
              REWIND 4
      C       READ NAME/ADDRESS RECORD
              READ(4, 10) NUM4, NAME, ADDR
         10   FORMAT(I5, 8A10)
              IF(EOF(4)) GO TO 99
              FIRST = .TRUE.
      C       READ BOOK FILE RECORD
         15   READ(3, 20) NUM3, AUTH, TITLE, MDATD
         20   FORMAT(I5, 10X, 3A10, 3I2)
              IF(EOF(3)) GO TO 99
      C       CONVERT DATE TO COMPUTATIONAL VALUE
              NDATD = 10000*MDATD(3) + 100*MDATD(1) + MDATD(2)
      C       IF NUM4 IS GREATER THAN NUM3, FILE 3 RECORD HAS NO MATCH
      C       ON FILE 4
         25   IF(NUM4 - NUM3) 35, 30, 26
         26   WRITE(2, 27)
         27   FORMAT(' UNMATCHED RECORD')
              GO TO 100
      C       IF NUM4 IS LESS THAN NUM3, READ ANOTHER NAME/ADDRESS RECORD
      C       IF THEY ARE EQUAL, SEE IF BOOK IS OVERDUE
         30   IF(NDATD.LT.NDATE) GO TO 45
      C       PRINT CLOSING IF FIRST IS .FALSE.
         35   IF(.NOT. FIRST) WRITE(2, 40)
         40   FORMAT(' PLEASE RETURN THESE PROMPTLY.'/
             1' A FINE OF FIVE CENTS PER DAY IS CHARGED.'/
             231X, 'THANK YOU')
      C       READ NAME/ADDRESS RECORD.  SET FIRST = .TRUE.
              READ(4, 10) NUM4, NAME, ADDR
              IF(EOF(4)) GO TO 99
              FIRST = .TRUE.
              GO TO 25
      C       IF BOOK IS OVERDUE, PRINT RECORD ON OVERDUE NOTICE
      C       IF FIRST IS .TRUE., PRINT HEADING
         45   IF(.NOT. FIRST) GO TO 75
              WRITE(2, 50) MDATE
         50   FORMAT(1H1, 32X, I2, 1H/, I2, 1H/, I2)
              WRITE(2, 55) NAME, ADDR
         55   FORMAT(1H0, 2A10)
```

```
        WRITE(2, 60)
  60    FORMAT(' DEAR SIR',/ ' THE FOLLOWING BOOKS ARE NOW OVERDUE.')
        WRITE(2, 65)
  65    FORMAT('0AUTHOR', 5X, 'TITLE', 16X, 'DATE DUE')
  75    WRITE(2, 80) AUTH, TITLE, MDATD
  80    FORMAT(1X, A10, 1X, 2A10, 1X, I2, 1H/, I2, 1H/, I2)
        GO TO 15
  C     AT END OF INPUT, WRITE CLOSING AND REWIND FILES
  99    WRITE(2, 40)
 100    REWIND 3
        REWIND 4
        STOP
        END
```

■ The Unformatted READ and WRITE Statements

When we read a card, what we are actually reading is a string of
characters. It is the FORMAT statement which tells the computer how
these characters are to be interpreted. The computer then stores
the information read as the value of some variable. Thus, when we
read the characters 12.76 into the variable X, the computer converts
the characters 12.76 into the value 12.76, and stores the value in
the variable X. All this is done electronically, of course. As
far as the computer is concerned, the value of the variable X is
just some electronic configuration of the computer memory. To find
out what the value of X is, we must convert the value back to a
string of characters and print it out.

Suppose we write the value of a variable X on a tape with the
statements

```
        WRITE(3, 3)X
  3     FORMAT(F12.4)
```

This causes the value of X to be converted into a string of 12
characters and written on the tape. When we reread the tape, the
12 characters will be converted back to a value and assigned to a
variable. There is a way, in FORTRAN, of eliminating this intermediate step of changing values into character strings and vice
versa. This is done with the unformatted READ and WRITE statements.

The form of the unformatted WRITE statement is

```
        WRITE(n) list
```

where *n* is a fixed-point constant or variable that denotes the
file, and list is the variable list. In other words, the unformatted WRITE statement has the same form as the WRITE statement we
have been using, except that there is no FORMAT statement number.

This statement takes each variable in the list and writes its
value on file *n*. The values are written in the internal code of
the machine, just as they are stored. We would not use this type

of WRITE statement to write data on the printer, because the data
is output in internal machine code and we would not be able to read
it. We must have data that is written this way read back using an
unformatted READ statement.

The unformatted READ statement has the form

READ(n) list

where n and list are as above. This statement is the reverse of
the unformatted WRITE statement. Values from file n are read and
assigned to the variables in the list. The values read must have
been written with an unformatted WRITE statement and the list in
READ must agree with the list in WRITE. It is not possible to
write information with a formatted WRITE statement and read it
with an unformatted READ statement.

Each execution of the unformatted WRITE statement will create
exactly one record in the file. The length of the record is the
number of variables written. For instance, the statement

WRITE(3) A, B, C, N, M

would write the values of the variables A, B, C, N, and M in file 3
to create a record five values long. Note that it does not make
sense in this case to ask how many characters are in the record,
since we are writing values instead of characters.

The unformatted READ statement will read exactly one record
of file n. There should be the same number of variables in the
list as there were in the list of the unformatted WRITE statement
which created the record. If the record created by the above
unformatted WRITE statement were read with the statement

READ(3) D, E, F, I, J

this would result in these variables receiving the values of the
variables written, just as though we had put

D = A
E = B
F = C
I = N
J = M

A file created by unformatted WRITE statements is called an
unformatted file. The records in such a file consist of values
written in the machine's internal code, so we could not print such
a file or read it in any format other than the machine's code.
The only thing we would normally do with an unformatted file would
be to rewind and read it again using unformatted READ statements.

Remember that when the data in an unformatted file is read,
it will be stored in the computer exactly as it was before it was

written. Thus, the statements

```
        REWIND 7
        WRITE(7) X
        REWIND 7
        READ(7) Y
```

will have the same effect as the statement

```
        Y = X
```

The advantage of using an unformatted file for some applications is that since no conversion of values is needed to change the internal representation in the machine into character strings, the input and output are faster. It is also sometimes more convenient if we do not care how the data "looks" on a tape or disk file, but only that it is stored there. We shall see this in Example 4.

Example 4

We have a tape file on which each record is a single decimal number written in an F12.4 format. This file is sorted in descending order. We want to write a program to create an identical file, but with the numbers written in ascending order.

If the input file contained only a few numbers, the solution to this problem would be simple. We could just read the entire file and write it out in reverse order. Suppose, however, that the input file is very large, containing thousands of numbers, and there is not enough storage available in the computer to read them all in at the same time. In this case, we would have to use intermediate files to store the numbers. We will call the input file, file 3. The output file will be called file 4. In addition to these, we will use two files for intermediate storage. Each of these files will be used both as an input and an output file; we shall call these file 5 and file 6. Since these files are used only for intermediate storage, and not saved at the end of the program, we shall assume that they are disk files. The files used by the program are shown in Fig. 12-16.

The basic procedure we shall use in this program can be understood by considering a specific example. Suppose the input tape contains the following values:

        File 3: 12, 11, 10, 9, 8, 7, 6, 5, 4, 3, 2, 1

Now, we are assuming that we cannot read in the whole file at once, so we start by reading the first four values. We then write these in reverse order on file 6. Now, we read in four more values from file 3, and we write them in reverse order on file 5. We then rewind file 6 and copy it onto file 5. Altogether, we have written eight numbers on file 5:

File 5:   5, 6, 7, 8, 9, 10, 11, 12

The next step is to read the last four numbers on file 3 and write
them in reverse order on file 5.   Now, we rewind files 5 and 6.
Then the numbers from file 5 are read and copied onto file 6.
File 6 now contains twelve values.   The first four were just read
from file 3, and the last eight were copied from file 5:

File 6:   1, 2, 3, 4, 5, 6, 7, 8, 9, 10, 11, 12

Since we have finished reading file 3, we are through.   All that
remains to be done is to copy file 6 onto the output tape, file 4.

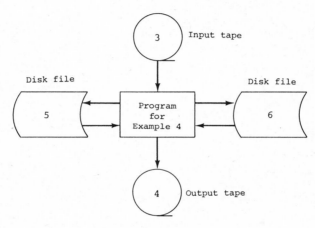

FIGURE 12-16

If there were more numbers to be read on file 3, we would read
another group, write it in reverse order on file 5, then copy file
6 onto file 5.   We see that files 5 and 6 keep interchanging roles
in the program.   First, file 5 is used as input and file 6 is used
as output, then file 6 becomes the input file, with file 5 as the
output file.   It will be helpful to use fixed-point variables to refer
to these two files.   Start with M = 5 and N = 6.   The procedure
just described can then be expressed as follows:

Step 1:   Read a group of numbers from the input tape (file 3).
Step 2:   Write them in reverse order on file N.
Step 3:   Copy file M onto file N.
Step 4:   Rewind files M and N.
Step 5:   Interchange the values of M and N and go back to
          Step 1.

These steps are repeated until we have read all the numbers on the
input tape.   In the FORTRAN program, we shall read groups of 100
numbers from the input tape and store them in an array called A.
The procedure is illustrated in the flowchart in Fig. 12-17.

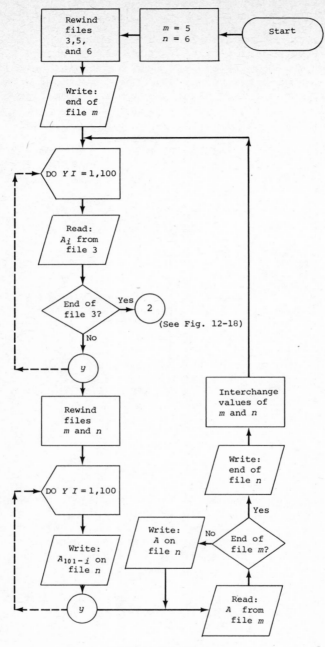

FIGURE 12-17
Flowchart for Example 4

Notice from the flowchart that we write an end-of-file mark on
file M at the very beginning of the program. Thus, on the first
time through, the first read operation on file M will encounter an
end-of-file mark, and nothing will be copied from file M to file N.

Notice also that we must remember to write an end-of-file mark on file N after each step.

The disk files used in this program will not be saved after the end of the program, and so we are free to choose whatever format we like for these files. The easiest (and probably the most efficient) thing to do is to make them unformatted files, using unformatted READ and WRITE statements. Now, the input tape file is given to be a formatted file. To read this file, we shall use the statements

```
        READ(3, 15) A(I)
   15   FORMAT(F12.4)
```

However, when we write the values of the array A, we can use the statement

```
        WRITE(N) (A(101 - I), I = 1, 100)
```

Since this is an unformatted WRITE statement, it will create a record on file N consisting of a string of values. The variable list in this case is an implied DO loop that causes the values of the array A to be written in reverse order. Thus, the first value written (corresponding to I = 1) is A(100), and the last value written (corresponding to I = 100) is A(1). This method has a drawback, however, in that the expression A(101 - I) is an illegal subscripted variable in standard FORTRAN, since 101 - I is not one of the allowable forms of a subscript. While many systems would permit this, some would not. A simple way around this difficulty is to copy the array A to an array B in reverse order with the statements

```
        DO 25 I = 1, 100
        K = 101 - I
   25   B(K) = A(I)
```

Then the array B is written with the statement

```
        WRITE(N) B
```

When we copy file M onto file N, we will also use unformatted READ and WRITE statements. These would be

```
        READ(M) A
        WRITE(N) A
```

Remember that A is an array of dimension 100, so each of these statements deals with 100 variables, just as though they were written

```
        READ(M) (A(I), I = 1, 100)
        WRITE(N) (A(I), I = 1, 100)
```

One problem we have not yet considered is what happens when we reach the end of the input tape. There may be fewer than 100 values to read on the last time through the program. This is handled easily, however. When we read an end-of-file mark on file 3, we branch out of the DO loop used to read the variables. The last value read from file 3 is then written on the output tape, file 4. Then the next-to-last value read from file 3 is written on the output tape, and so on for all the leftover values. After this, we copy the values on file M onto the output tape. This has to be done for 100 values at a time, since each record on file M consists of 100 values. The statements used are

```
        READ(M) A
        WRITE(4, 135) A
  135   FORMAT(F12.4)
```

After reaching the end of file M, we are finished, so we rewind the tape files and stop. The whole procedure to be followed after reaching the end of the input tape is given by the flowchart in Fig. 12-18. The complete FORTRAN program is the following:

```
        LOGICAL EOF
        DIMENSION A(100), B(100)
C       M IS THE INPUT INTERMEDIATE FILE
C       N IS THE OUTPUT INTERMEDIATE FILE
        M = 5
        N = 6
        DO 5 I = 3, 6
   5    REWIND I
        ENDFILE M
  10    DO 20 I = 1, 100
        READ(3, 15) A(I)
  15    FORMAT(F12.4)
        IF(EOF(3)) GO TO 100
  20    CONTINUE
C       IF ALL 100 VALUES HAVE BEEN READ, WRITE THEM
C       IN REVERSE ORDER ON FILE N
        DO 25 I = 1, 100
        K = 101 - I
  25    B(K) = A(I)
        REWIND N
        WRITE(N) B
C       COPY FILE M ONTO FILE N
        REWIND M
  30    READ(M) A
        IF(EOF(M)) GO TO 40
        WRITE(N) A
        GO TO 30
C       WRITE END OF FILE ON N
C       INTERCHANGE VALUES OF M AND N
  40    ENDFILE N
        L = N
        N = M
```

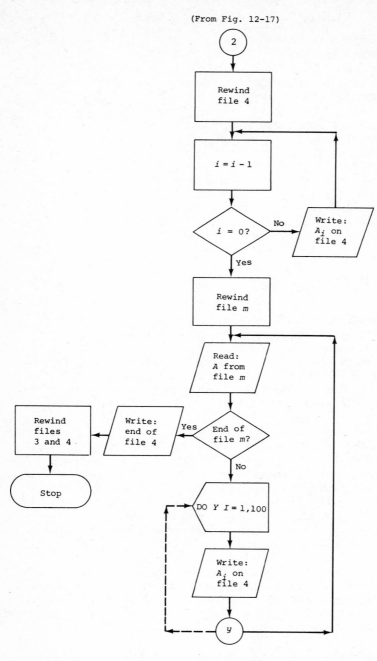

FIGURE 12-18

```
        M = L
        GO TO 10
C       WRITE LEFTOVER VALUES ON FILE 4 IN REVERSE ORDER
100     REWIND 4
110     I = I - 1
        IF(I.EQ.0) GO TO 120
        WRITE(4, 15) A(I)
        GO TO 110
C       COPY FILE M ONTO FILE 4
120     REWIND M
130     READ(M) A
        IF(EOF(M)) GO TO 200
        WRITE(4, 135) A
135     FORMAT(F12.4)
        GO TO 130
C       AT END OF FILE M, REWIND FILES AND STOP
200     ENDFILE 4
        REWIND 4
        REWIND 3
        STOP
        END
```

Example 5

During registration at a certain school, three cards are prepared for each student: a name card, an address card, and a degree card. The format of each of these cards is given in Fig. 12-19. Each of these sets of cards is sorted according to the matric number. We want to write a program that will create a master tape file for students by reading all three sets of cards and merging the information onto a tape file in the format shown in Fig. 12-20.

The basic idea of the program is to merge the three cards for each student. However, the input cards are in three different sets, so in order to merge them, we first have to read them in and create three separate files. These will be disk files 5, 6, and 7. In order to separate the three sets of cards, we shall put a blank card after each set of cards, then we shall arrange the sets as shown in Fig. 12-21, with the name cards first, then the address cards, and then the degree cards.

The first part of the program will be concerned merely with copying the three decks of cards onto the three disk files. After this is done, the program will rewind the disk files and read them in again to merge them into the master file. The files used by the program are shown in Fig. 12-22.

While in the process of creating the disk files, we shall check the input cards to make sure they are in the right order. We can perform two checks on the cards. The first is to see that column 80 contains an N, A, or D. When reading the name cards, we

NAME CARDS	
Columns	Item
1-5	Matric number
6-25	Last name
26-40	First name
41	Middle initial
42-79	Blank
80	"N"

ADDRESS CARDS	
Columns	Item
1-5	Matric number
6-25	First line of address
26-45	Second line of address
46-65	Third line of address
66-79	Blank
80	"A"

DEGREE CARDS	
Columns	Item
1-5	Matric number
6-10	Student's department
11-15	Degree sought
16-19	Graduation date
20-79	Blank
80	"D"

FIGURE 12-19

TAPE FILE	
Characters	Item
1-5	Matric number
6-25	Last name
26-40	First name
41	Middle initial
42-61	First line of address
62-81	Second line of address
82-101	Third line of address
102-106	Student's department
107-111	Degree sought
112-115	Graduation date

FIGURE 12-20

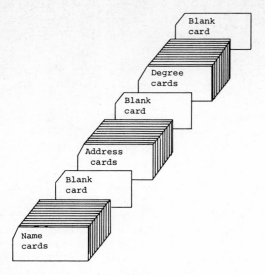

FIGURE 12-21

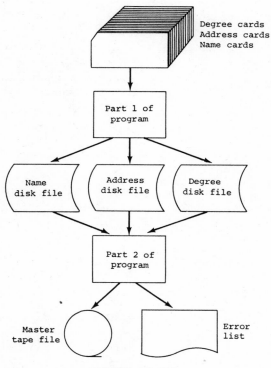

FIGURE 12-22

shall read column 80 into a variable called N80. This is read
with an A1 format. If we set NN = 1HN, then the statement

IF(N80.EQ.NN) GO TO 25

will cause the program to go to 25 only if column 80 contains an N. If not, we shall print a message saying INPUT ERROR ON N CARDS, then stop, since there is no use continuing if the input data is wrong. We can also check to see if the cards are sorted properly. To do this, we use a variable called MPREV to represent the previous matric number read. If the matric number MAT is not greater than the previous matric number MPREV, the name cards are out of order, so we print a message saying N CARDS OUT OF SEQUENCE, and stop. Similar procedures are used when reading the address and degree cards. The flowchart for this part of the program is shown in Fig. 12-23.

After the disk files 5, 6, and 7 are created, they are rewound for use in the second part of the program. The basic idea of this part of the program is to read one record from each disk file, and merge the three records into one record on the output tape. We must consider, however, the possibility that a student might be missing one or more cards. There might, for instance, be a name card, but no address or degree card. To account for this possibility, we shall test the matric numbers read to see if they are all the same. If one of them is less than the others, we shall print a message to indicate there is no match for the card with the lowest number, and then we shall read another record from that file. No record will be written on the output tape unless we have all three cards for the student. The output from the program will consist of two files: the tape file, for students whose records are complete; and a printed file, telling which students are missing cards.

To program this part of the job, we shall read the matric numbers from disk files 5, 6, and 7 into variables M5, M6, and M7, respectively. After each read operation, we shall set a variable called MAX equal to the maximum value of M5, M6, and M7. This can be done using the standard function MAX0 (see Chapter 8). If M5 is less than MAX, we shall know that either an address or a degree card is missing for the student with matric number M5. We print a message to this effect, and then read another record from file 5. Similar tests are made to see if M6 or M7 is less than MAX. The flowchart for this part of the program is shown in Fig. 12-24.

When an end is reached on one of the disk files, the other disk files should also be at the end. Suppose, however, that the last record on the name file has no matching address or degree record. We still want to print out the message saying that the name record is unmatched. So, when the end of any file is reached, we test each of the other files to see if there are any records left on them, and if there are, we print an error message for each record left to indicate that it was unmatched. After this, we can write an end-of-file mark on the output tape and rewind it. This last part of the program is illustrated in the flowchart of Fig. 12-25.

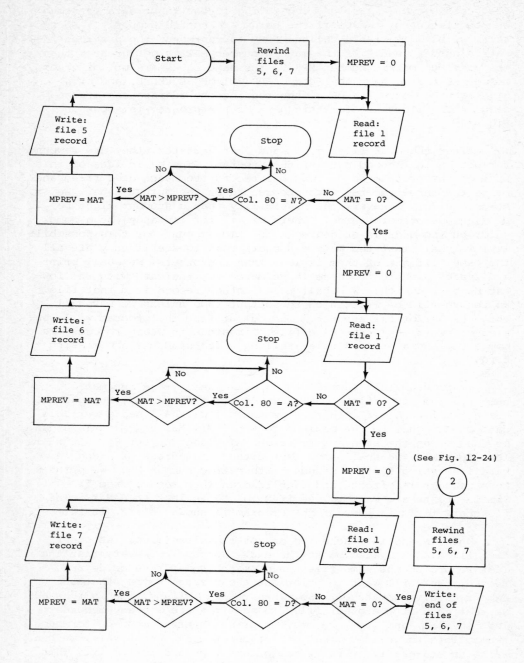

FIGURE 12-23

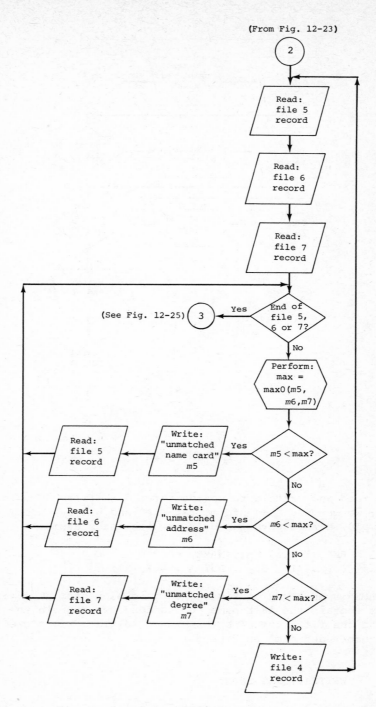

FIGURE 12-24

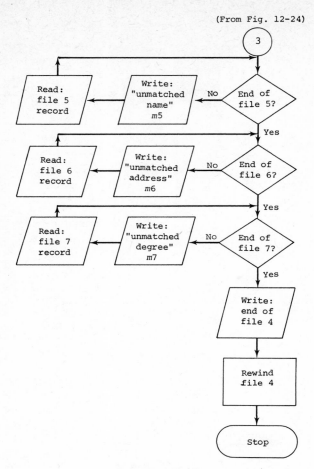

FIGURE 12-25

To read and write data on the three disk files used in the program, we can use the unformatted READ and WRITE statements. For example, a name card can be read with the statements

```
      READ(1, 15) MAT, NAME, N80
   15 FORMAT(I5, 3A10, A5, A1, 38X, A1)
```

where NAME is an array consisting of five elements. The first two elements contain the last name, the second two contain the first name, and the fifth contains the middle initial. To store the matric number and name on disk file 5, we can use the statement

```
      WRITE(5) MAT, NAME
```

This will write a record consisting of a string of six values: one for MAT and five for the array NAME. These values will be reread in the second part of the program with the statement

```
          READ(5) M5, NAME
```

which will read the matric number into the variable M5, and the
name back into the array NAME. The complete FORTRAN program for
this example is:

```
     C      PROGRAM TO CREATE STUDENT MASTER TAPE
            DIMENSION NAME(5), ADDR(6), DEG(3)
            LOGICAL EOF
            DATA NA, NN, ND / 1HA, 1HN, 1HD /
     C      REWIND DISK FILES
            REWIND 5
            REWIND 6
            REWIND 7
            MPREV = 0
     C      COPY NAME CARDS ONTO DISK FILE 5
       10   READ(1, 15) MAT, NAME, N80
       15   FORMAT(I5, 3A10, A5, A1, 38X, A1)
            IF(MAT.EQ.0) GO TO 40
     C      CHECK SEQUENCE AND COLUMN 80
            IF(N80.EQ.NN) GO TO 25
            WRITE(2, 20)
       20   FORMAT(' INPUT ERROR ON N CARDS')
            STOP
       25   IF(MAT.GT.MPREV) GO TO 35
            WRITE(2, 30)
       30   FORMAT(' N CARDS OUT OF SEQUENCE')
            STOP
       35   WRITE(5) MAT, NAME
            GO TO 10
     C      COPY ADDRESS CARDS TO DISK FILE 6
       40   MPREV = 0
       45   READ(1, 50) MAT, ADDR, N80
       50   FORMAT(I5, 6A10, 14X, A1)
            IF(MAT.EQ.0) GO TO 75
     C      CHECK SEQUENCE AND COLUMN 80
            IF(N80.EQ.NA) GO TO 60
            WRITE(2, 55)
       55   FORMAT(' INPUT ERROR ON A CARDS')
            STOP
       60   IF(MAT.GT.MPREV) GO TO 70
            WRITE(2, 65)
       65   FORMAT(' A CARDS OUT OF SEQUENCE')
            STOP
       70   WRITE(6) MAT, ADDR
            GO TO 45
     C      COPY D CARDS TO DISK FILE 7
       75   MPREV = 0
       80   READ(1, 85) MAT, DEG, N80
       85   FORMAT(I5, 2A5, A4, 60X, A1)
            IF(MAT.EQ.0) GO TO 110
     C      CHECK SEQUENCE AND COLUMN 80
            IF(N80.EQ.ND) GO TO 95
            WRITE(2, 90)
```

```
     90   FORMAT(' INPUT ERROR ON D CARDS')
          STOP
     95   IF(MAT.GT.MPREV) GO TO 105
          WRITE(2, 100)
    100   FORMAT(' D CARDS OUT OF SEQUENCE')
          STOP
    105   WRITE(7) MAT, DEG
          GO TO 80
    110   ENDFILE 5
          ENDFILE 6
          ENDFILE 7
          REWIND 5
          REWIND 6
          REWIND 7
C         READ NAME, ADDRESS, AND DEGREE RECORD
    120   READ(5) M5, NAME
          READ(6) M6, ADDR
          READ(7) M7, DEG
    125   IF(EOF(5) .OR. EOF(6) .OR. EOF(7)) GO TO 900
          MAX = MAX0(M5, M6, M7)
C         IF M5 IS LESS THAN MAX, THERE IS A NAME CARD WITH
C         NO ADDRESS OR DEGREE CARD
          IF(M5.EQ.MAX) GO TO 135
          WRITE(2, 130) M5
    130   FORMAT(' UNMATCHED N CARD', I6)
          READ(5) M5, NAME
C         IF M6 IS LESS THAN MAX, THERE IS AN ADDRESS CARD
C         WITH NO NAME OR NO DEGREE CARD
    135   IF(M6.EQ.MAX) GO TO 145
          WRITE(2, 140) M6
    140   FORMAT(' UNMATCHED A CARD', I6)
          READ(6) M6, ADDR
C         IF M7 IS LESS THAN MAX, THERE IS A DEGREE CARD
C         WITH NO NAME OR NO ADDRESS CARD
    145   IF(M7.EQ.MAX) GO TO 155
          WRITE(2, 150) M7
    150   FORMAT(' UNMATCHED D CARD', I6)
          READ(7) M7, DEG
          GO TO 125
C         WRITE OUTPUT TAPE RECORD
    155   WRITE(2, 160) M5, NAME, ADDR, DEG
    160   FORMAT(I5, 3A10, A5, A1, 6A10, 2A5, A4)
          GO TO 120
C         AT END OF ANY INPUT FILE, ALL RECORDS LEFT
C         ON THE OTHER FILES ARE UNMATCHED
    900   IF(EOF(5)) GO TO 905
          WRITE(2, 130) M5
          READ(5) M5, NAME
          GO TO 900
    905   IF(EOF(6)) GO TO 910
          WRITE(2, 140) M6
          READ(6) M6, ADDR
          GO TO 905
    910   IF(EOF(7)) GO TO 915
          WRITE(2, 150) M7
```

```
      READ(7) M7, DEG
      GO TO 910
C     END OF JOB
915   ENDFILE 4
      REWIND 4
      STOP
      END
```

■ Exercises

1. In Example 2, what would happen if we had a deletion card for which there was no corresponding tape record? Include statements to detect this possibility and print an error message when it occurs.

2. In Example 2, what might happen if the correction cards were not in order? What might happen if the master tape were not sorted in the proper order? Include statements to detect these possibilities and print error messages if they occur.

3. In Example 2, it is necessary to punch a whole new card to change any part of an employee's tape record. It would be easier for the computer if we wrote the program so that any item that is blank on the correction card will be replaced by the corresponding item from the old master tape. This way, only the information that changes need be punched on the correction card; the other information is supplied automatically from the old tape. Write a flowchart and a program to do this.

4. Write a program to update the file of books checked out used in Example 3. Two kinds of input cards will be used: one for books being checked out and one for books being returned. An input card for a book being checked out will have the following format:

        Columns   1-5   Library card number of person to whom loaned
        Columns   6-15 Call number of book
        Columns 16-25 Author's last name
        Columns 26-45 Title of book
        Columns 46-51 Date due
        Columns 52-80 Blank

An input card for a book being returned will have the following format:

        Columns   1-5   Library card number of person to whom loaned
        Columns   6-15 Call number of book
        Columns 16-45 Blank
        Columns 46-51 Date returned
        Columns 52-79 Blank
        Column   80   "R"

Assume the tape file of books checked out and the input cards

4.—continued

are sorted according to the library card number and the call
number of the book.

5. Include statements in the program of Exercise 4 to compute
the total fines collected for books being returned. A fine
of five cents per day is charged on each overdue book.

6. Files 1 and 2 are unformatted files giving weather observa-
tions on different days. Each record consists of the following values:

         Item 1   Date
         Item 2   Temperature
         Item 3   Barometric pressure
         Item 4   Wind velocity

The files are sorted according to the date. Write a program
to merge these two files into an output tape called file 3,
which is also sorted according to the date.

7. Write a subroutine to compare two unformatted files, M and
N, to make sure they are identical. Assume that the records
consist of L values. The values of L, M, and N will be
parameters in the subroutine list. If the files are identical, print a message to that effect. If a record on one file
is different from the corresponding record on the other file,
print an error message and stop.

Chapter

13

Additional FORTRAN Statements

In this chapter, we shall cover some additional FORTRAN
statements. Some versions of FORTRAN do not admit all these
statements; beginning students will probably not find too many
occasions to use them. When they are available, however, they
can be quite useful.

■ INTEGER and REAL Statements

We have seen how the LOGICAL, COMPLEX, and DOUBLE PRECISION
statements can be used to declare variable types. In the absence
of such statements, a variable is assumed to be either integer
(fixed-point) or real (floating-point). FORTRAN determines
whether a variable is integer or real by the first letter of the
variable name. If we wish to depart from the usual naming conven-
tion for these types, we can use the INTEGER and REAL statements.
The first of these has the form

$$\text{INTEGER } name_1, name_2, \ldots, name_n$$

All the variables named in the list will be treated as integer
variables throughout the program. For instance, if a program contains the statement

$$\text{INTEGER A, B, C}$$

then the variables A, B, and C will be used as integer variables
in the program, although they would normally be real variables.
Similarly, the statement

$$\text{REAL } name_1, name_2, \ldots, name_n$$

would cause the variables named to be treated as real variables
throughout the program, regardless of the usual naming conventions.

As with other type declaration statements, these, if used,
must come at the beginning of the program. They may also give
dimension information. For instance, the statement

```
        REAL I(10, 5)
```

would cause I to be set up as a 10 X 5 real array in the program.

■ The IMPLICIT Statement

Some systems allow an IMPLICIT statement which can be used to implicitly define the types of variables. Instead of explicitly naming the variables which are to be of a certain type, the IMPLICIT statement declares that all variables beginning with a certain letter be of a certain type. For example, the declaration

```
        IMPLICIT INTEGER(A), LOGICAL(P-S)
```

means that all variable names which begin with the letter A will be integer variables, and all variable names which begin with letters P through S (P, Q, R, and S) will be logical variables.

In general, the IMPLICIT statement has the form

$$\text{IMPLICIT type}_1(a_1), \text{ type}_2(a_2), \ldots$$

where "type_i" is INTEGER, REAL, DOUBLE PRECISION, COMPLEX, or LOGICAL, and "a_i" is either a simple letter or two letters separated by a hyphen (minus sign) to indicate a range of letters. This statement should come at the beginning of a program before any other declarative statements. The effect of the IMPLICIT statement may be overridden by explicit declaration. For example, if the following two statements appear in the beginning of a program, then all variables will be integer variables, except for the variable MASS and any variables beginning with the letter A, which are real variables:

```
        IMPLICIT INTEGER(B-Z), REAL(A)
        REAL MASS
```


■ The EQUIVALENCE Statement

The EQUIVALENCE statement permits us to use two different names for the same memory location in a program. This statement has the form

$$\text{EQUIVALENCE}(\text{name}_1, \text{ name}_2, \ldots, \text{name}_n), (\ldots), (\ldots)$$

where each set of parentheses encloses a list of variable names. All the names enclosed in each set of parentheses will refer to a single memory location in the program.

For example, the statement

```
        EQUIVALENCE(A, B), (I, J)
```

would cause the names A and B to refer to the same memory location; and I would refer to the same memory location as J.

Array names cannot be equivalenced by this statement, but array elements can. If X is an array, the statement

    EQUIVALENCE(X(1), FIRST)

would allow us to use the names X(1) and FIRST interchangeably in a program.

■ The Labeled COMMON Statement

This statement is simply an extension of the regular COMMON statement. Instead of having just one block of common storage, we can have several such blocks by using this form:

    COMMON/x_1/a_1/x_2/a_2/ ... /x_n/a_n

Here each x is the name of a common block, while each a is the list of variables to be placed in the common block. For example, suppose a main program uses two subroutines ALPHA and BETA. We want the variables I, J, and K to be shared between the main program and the subroutine ALPHA, and we want the variable X to be shared between the main program and the subroutine BETA. To do this, we place I, J, and K in a common block called BLK1, and we place X in a common block called BLK2. The labeled COMMON statement in the main program would be

    COMMON/BLK1/I, J, K/BLK2/X

Then, in subroutine ALPHA, we would use the statement

    COMMON/BLK1/I, J, K

For subroutine BETA, we would use the statement

    COMMON/BLK2/X

This way, the two subroutines do not share any storage in common with each other, but each shares common storage with the main program.

The following example illustrates the use of the labeled COMMON statement.

Example 1

Write a subroutine POLAR(X, Y, R, THETA) which will convert X and Y to polar coordinates and store the result in R and THETA. THETA should be in degrees. The value of π (PI) is computed from the formula

π = 4.0 X arctangent 1

This value is computed by the subroutine SETUP and stored in the
labeled common block POLCAT. The main program calls SETUP only
once—sometime before the first call to POLAR. It does not need
any COMMON statement, but SETUP and POLAR will have identical
COMMON statements. Since they are labeled COMMON statements, the
main program and any other subroutines used could have blank COMMON
or labeled COMMON declarations without interfering with the labeled
common storage POLCAT. One of the chief advantages of labeled common blocks is that they allow subroutines to be written to share
common storage without interfering with the common storage of other
subprograms. The program would be:

```
      CALL SETUP
      CALL POLAR(1.0, 2.0, R, THETA)
      WRITE(6, 501) R, THETA
      CALL POLAR(2., -3., R, THETA)
      WRITE(6, 501) R, THETA
501   FORMAT(2F15.6)
      STOP
      END

      SUBROUTINE POLAR(X, Y, R, THETA)
      COMMON/POLCAT/PI
      R = SQRT(X**2 + Y**2)
      THETA = 180./PI*ATAN2(Y, X)
      RETURN
      END

      SUBROUTINE SETUP
      COMMON/POLCAT/PI
      PI = 4.0*ATAN(1.0)
      RETURN
      END
```

■ BLOCK DATA Subprograms

A DATA statement may not be used to initialize variables in
common storage. However, variables in labeled common storage may
be initialized by DATA statements. (This is one important difference between blank common and labeled common storage.) In standard FORTRAN, a special type of subprogram, the BLOCK DATA subprogram,
must be used to initialize labeled common with DATA statements.

The BLOCK DATA subprogram contains no executable statements—
only type statements (INTEGER, REAL, etc.), COMMON statements,
DIMENSION statements, EQUIVALENCE statements, and DATA statements
may appear. The subprogram begins with the statement

```
      BLOCK DATA
```

and continues through the next END statement. For example, the subroutine SETUP could be eliminated from the previous example, and the common block POLCAT could be initialized by a DATA statement using the following statements:

```
BLOCK DATA
COMMON/POLCAT/PI
DATA PI/3.141592654
END
```

■ The Computed GO TO Statement

The computed GO TO statement can be used to replace a series of IF statements. The form of the statement is

$$GO\ TO\ (k_1,\ k_2,\ \ldots,\ k_n),\ I$$

where k_1, k_2, $\ldots$, k_n are statement numbers and I is any fixed-point variable name. When this statement is executed, if $I = 1$, the program will go to Statement k_1. If $I = 2$, the program will go to Statement k_2, and so on.

If I is less than 1 or greater than n, the result is undefined; on some systems, an error results, while on other systems if I is less than 1, control transfers to k_1 and if I is greater than n, control transfers to k_n. On some computer systems, the comma following the parenthesis is optional. As an example, Fig. 13-1 shows a flowchart for the statement

```
GO TO(5, 10, 5, 20), I
```

The statement

```
GO TO(10, 11, 12, 25, 50), NOD
```

will make the program go to Statement 11 if NOD = 2. If NOD = 4, it will act like the statement GO TO 25. For NOD = 7, the statement does the same as for NOD = 5; it will act like GO TO 50.

The following statements will write out one, two, three, or four values, depending on whether N is 1, 2, 3, or 4:

```
      GO TO(5, 10, 15, 20), N
  5   WRITE(2, 105) X
      GO TO 100
 10   WRITE(2, 110) X, Y
      GO TO 100
 15   WRITE(2, 115) X, Y, Z
      GO TO 100
 20   WRITE(2, 120) X, Y, Z, W
100   CONTINUE
```

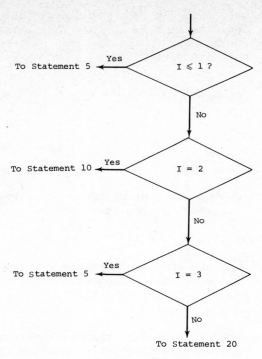

FIGURE 13-1

■ The Assigned GO TO Statement

The assigned GO TO is a GO TO statement with a variable
statement number. The form of the statement is

GO TO i, $(k_1, k_2, \ldots, k_n)$

where i is a fixed-point variable, and k_1, k_2, $\ldots$, k_n are state-
ment numbers. Before executing this statement, we must use an
ASSIGN statement to assign a statement number to the variable i.
The ASSIGN statement has the form

ASSIGN k TO i

where k is the statement number and i is the fixed-point variable.
The statement number which is assigned to i must be one of the
statement numbers k_1, k_2, $\ldots$, k in the list of the assigned GO TO.
The statement GO TO i, $(k_1, k_2, \ldots, k_n)$ will then cause the program
to branch to the statement number.

For example, the statements

ASSIGN 100 to IVY
GO TO IVY, (10, 15, 100)

would cause the assigned GO TO statement to act just like the statement GO TO 100. The other numbers 10 and 15 which appear in the list are the other possible statement numbers we might want to branch to. Whenever we execute the statement

        GO TO IVY, (10, 15, 100)

we must first execute one of the statements

        ASSIGN 10 TO IVY
        ASSIGN 15 TO IVY
        ASSIGN 100 TO IVY

■ The STOP *n* and PAUSE *n* Statements

     An alternate form of the STOP statement is the statement

        STOP *n*

where *n* is an octal number of four or fewer digits. An octal number is a number in base 8. For the purpose of this statement, it is just a number that does not contain the digits 8 or 9. So, 1125 is correct but 93 is not, since it contains the digit 9.

     The STOP *n* statement does exactly the same thing as a STOP statement. The only difference is that the number *n* will be displayed on the program listing when the STOP *n* statement is executed. If the program uses several STOP *n* statements with different values of *n*, this allows the programmer to determine where the program stopped. For instance, suppose we are dividing Y by X to give A. The value of X should never be zero, but just in case, we might include the statement

        IF(X.EQ.0.0) STOP 3

If X were, in fact, equal to zero, the number 3 would be displayed in the output and we would be able to go back and find the trouble in the program.

     The PAUSE and PAUSE *n* statements do almost the same thing as the STOP and STOP *n* statements. The difference is that the computer operator can restart the program manually. Suppose that in some program we want the computer operator to mount a magnetic tape on unit 3. We then want to read this tape. The program might include the statements

        WRITE(2, 25)
    25 FORMAT(' MOUNT TAPE 3')
        PAUSE
        READ(3, 30) X

When the PAUSE statement is executed, the program will pause and wait for the operator to take some manual action. When the operator restarts the program, the next statement (the READ statement in this case) is performed.

Reading into an H Field

Normally, an H field in FORTRAN is used only for output. The statements

```
      WRITE(2, 5)
    5 FORMAT(8H HEADING)
```

would print the eight characters bHEADING. We may also read into an existing H field. When the field *n*H is used with a READ statement, the next *n* characters are read into the H field. For example, the statement

```
    5 FORMAT(20H                    )
```

sets up an H field consisting of 20 blanks. The statement

```
      READ(1, 5)
```

would read the next 20 characters from unit 1 into the existing H field in the FORMAT statement. Those characters would replace the blanks. For instance, if the program contains the statements

```
       READ(1, 10)
    10 FORMAT(1X, 5H12345)
       WRITE(2, 10)
```

then if their input card contains the characters ABCDE, these characters would replece the H field 12345. The WRITE statement would then write out the characters ABCDE, just as though the FORMAT statement had been written as FORMAT (5HABCDE).

The EXTERNAL Statement

In Chapter 8, we saw that the dummy argument of a function or subroutine may be a variable name or an array name. It may also be the name of a subroutine or a function subprogram. For example, the following subroutine prints out the values of the function F from A to B in steps of DX:

```
      SUBROUTINE TABLE(F, A, B, DX)
      X = A
    1 Y = F(X)
      WRITE(2, 5) X, Y
    5 FORMAT(1X, 2F20.5)
      X = X + DX
      IF(X.LE.B) GO TO 1
      RETURN
      END
```

When the subroutine is called, the function F may be replaced by
any external function name. There is one important rule which must
be followed.

> *Rule:* When the actual argument is the name of a subprogram,
> the calling program must declare this name in an
> EXTERNAL statement.

The EXTERNAL statement has the form

> EXTERNAL name$_1$, name$_2$, ...

where name$_1$, name$_2$, ... are names of the subprograms to be used as
arguments. The EXTERNAL statement is a declaration, and should come
before any executable statement in the program or subprogram.

The following program uses the subroutine TABLE defined above
to print a table of values of sin x + cos x between 0 and $\pi/2$:

```
EXTERNAL FCN
CALL TABLE(FCN, 0.0, 3.1416/2.0, 0.01)
STOP
END
FUNCTION FCN(X)
FCN = SIN(X) + COS(X)
RETURN
END
```

Notice that the EXTERNAL declaration goes in the main program,
not in the function or in the subroutine.

■ The ENTRY Statement

When a subprogram is called by either the main program or
another subprogram, the first statement executed is the first
executable one encountered. The ENTRY statement allows us to call
a function or subroutine subprogram and begin execution at any
desired entry point. This entry point is given a variable name,
and the associated statement has the form

> ENTRY name

where name specifies the entry point. It does not have an associated statement number and may appear anywhere within the subprogram.

For use with a subroutine subprogram, it has an associated
CALL statement. For example,

```
        Main Program              Subprogram
                                  SUBROUTINE ADD
              .                        .
              .                        .
              .                        .
        CALL ADD                  ENTRY HERE
              .                        .
              .                        .
        CALL HERE                 RETURN
              .                   END
              .

        END
```

The first time the subroutine ADD is called by CALL ADD, execution begins with the first executable statement after the SUBROUTINE ADD, but the next time it is entered by CALL HERE. This time execution begins with the statement following the ENTRY HERE statement.

The ENTRY statement can be used with dummy arguments. The CALL statement and the corresponding ENTRY statement must have the same number, order, and mode of these dummy arguments. An example of this would be:

```
        Main Program              Subprogram
                                  SUBROUTINE TEST(X, Z, J)
              .                        .
              .                        .
              .                        .
        CALL ENTER1(SUM, DIFF, MAX)
              .                   ENTRY ENTER1(X, Z, J)
              .                        .
        END                            .

                                  RETURN
                                  END
```

The subroutine TEST is entered at ENTRY ENTER1(X, Z, J).

■ G Field Descriptor Input-Output

Another field descriptor that can be used for inputting or outputting floating-point numbers is the G field descriptor. This is actually not a separate field but acts to convert the number to either the F or E field. This can be very useful when the programmer is not certain of the magnitude of the numbers which will be printed.

When it is used for input, the form is

$$G n.m$$

and acts in a manner similar to the Fn.m field specification. Data is input, and stored exactly the same way as if the F field had been used. The rules covered in Chapter 4 hold and will not be repeated here.

When it is used to output data, however, the G field descriptor acts in a different manner. The form for the output is also

> Gn.m

When used in a format statement, the data to be output will be converted to either F field or E field. First, the conversion to the F field is attempted. The conversion to F field is subject to certain rules that apply to both the specification numbers n and m. The first is that the data is to be output with four blanks in the field, right-justified. This has the effect of always reducing the actual field width as given by n in Gn.m to $n - 4$. For example, the 7 in G7.1 is converted to a 3 as in F3.1. The specification number m also is converted. This is done, depending on the magnitude of the number. If the magnitude, M, i $0.1 \leq M < 1$, the m in Gn.m converts directly to Fn.m; if the magnitude i $1 \leq M < 10$ the m converts to $m - 1$; for magnitudes $\leq M <$ the m converts to $m - 2$, and so on. A few examples of these conversions are given in Table 13-1:

TABLE 13-1

Magnitude M	Conversion to F Field	Example
$0.1 \leq M < 1$	F($n - 4$) $\cdot$ $m$bbbb	For: X = 0.12 under G10.3 outputs as b0.120bbbb
$1 \leq M < 10$	F($n - 4$) $\cdot$ ($m - 1$)bbbb	X = 1.2345 under G10.3 outputs as bb1.23bbbb
$10 \leq M < 100$	F($n - 4$) $\cdot$ ($m - 2$)bbbb	X = 12.345 under G10.3 outputs as bb12.3bbbb
$100 \leq M < 1000$	F($n - 4$) $\cdot$ ($m - 3$)bbbb	X = 123.455 under G10.3 outputs as bbb123bbbb
$\vdots$	$\vdots$	

If the conversion cannot be done for any reason such as the field being too small to contain the data (or, equivalently, if the data is to large for the field), the data is output under the E conversion. In this case, the data is output according to the rules given in Chapter 4. Thus, unlike conversion to the F field, four blanks are *not* inserted into the field.

Suppose, for example, TEST contains 12345.67. The statements

```
      WRITE(2, 50) TEST, TEST
   50 FORMAT(1X, G10.3/,1X, G10.4)
```

result in

```
        bbb1.235E+04
        b1.2346E+04
```

but

```
        WRITE(2, 50) TEST
   50   FORMAT(1X, G12.6)
```

result in

```
        bb12345.7bbbb
```

since conversion can occur.

■ The P Scale Factor

It is possible to have the D, E, and F fields as well as the G conversion field preceded by a scale factor. This scale factor, n, is a fixed-point constant. It can be written with or without a plus or minus sign, but it must be in the range $-8 \leq n \leq 8$. This scale factor appears in the format statement followed by the letter P, as nP, and then the appropriate D, E, F, or G specification. Samples of it as used in format statements are:

```
        FORMAT(6PF8.2)
        FORMAT(8PF20.4, 2PE10.3, 0PF10.2)
        FORMAT(-3PE20.2, 1PG8.3)
        FORMAT(-2PF6.1, E10.3, 0PF6.5)
```


Input—F or G Field. When a scale factor is used with the F field specification, it has a special definition. The scale factor acts as follows:

$$10^{-n} \cdot (\text{Actual external quantity}) = (\text{Actual quantity stored})$$

Example 2

Assume X is punched on a card as 1234.56 in columns 1-10. Then

```
        READ(1, 100) X
   100  FORMAT(1PF10.2)
```

stores X as 123.456 ($1234.56 \cdot 10^{-1}$), and

```
        READ(1, 101) X
   102  FORMAT(0PF10.1)
```

stores X as 1234.56, the same as if the FORMAT statement had been

```
        FORMAT(F10.1)
```

When we use a scale factor, either for input or output, the following is very important to remember: *Once a scale factor is encountered in a FORMAT statement, it holds for all subsequent F, E, G, or D field specifications.* Thus,

        FORMAT(F10.2, 1PF10.3, F12.6, I2)

is the same as

        FORMAT(F10.2, 1PF10.3, 1PF12.6, I2)

To write the above format and not have the F12.6 specification scaled, we must have

        FORMAT(F10.2, 1PF10.3, 0PF12.6, I2)

The scaling for the G conversion for input is the same as for the F scaling.

    E and D Fields—Input. Some computers will allow scale factors with D and E field specifications for input. In this case, they are ignored and the input data is stored under the E and D field specifications.

    F Fields—Output. When a scale factor is used with the F field specification for output, the scaling is done as follows:

        (Actual output quantity) = (Stored quantity) $\times$ 10^{+n}

    In the actual representation, the decimal point remains fixed and the number moves either right or left.

    Example 3

    For TEST stored as 1.2345, the statements

            WRITE(2, 20) X
            WRITE(2, 21) X
            WRITE(2, 22) X
            WRITE(2, 23) X
            WRITE(2, 24) X
        20 FORMAT(F10.2)
        21 FORMAT(1PF10.2)
        22 FORMAT(2PF10.2)
        23 FORMAT(3PF10.2)
        24 FORMAT(-1PF10.2)

result in the output

```
        1.23
       12.35
      123.45
     1234.50
         .12
```

E and D Fields—Output. In practice, scale factors are used mostly with the E field for output. This is because, unlike the F field, the number is not changed in value. As used with the E field, a positive scale factor has the effect of shifting the decimal in the output number to the right n places and reducing the exponent by n. A negative scale factor shifts the decimal to the left n places and raises the exponent by n. The actual representation of the output keeps the decimal point fixed and shifts the number to the left or right.

Example 4

For X stored as 123.45, the statements

```
        WRITE(2, 500) X
        WRITE(2, 501) X
        WRITE(2, 502) X
        WRITE(2, 503) X
    500 FORMAT(E10.2)
    501 FORMAT(1PE10.2)
    502 FORMAT(2PE10.2)
    503 FORMAT(-1PE10.2)
```

will result in X being output as

```
      1.23E+03
     12.35E+01
    123.45E+00
       .12E+03
```

When the scale factor is used with the D field, the effect is the same as with the E field.

G Field—Output. When used with the G field, the effect of a scale factor will depend on the particular computer. In some, the G output makes use of the scale factor only if E conversion is made.

■ The T Field

The T specification may be used in a FORMAT statement to indicate tabbing. The T field is not a standard FORTRAN feature, and it is not available on all systems. The form is

Tn

where n is an unsigned fixed-point constant. This means to "tab
to column n." In other words, it causes the next field descriptor
to begin in column n of the input or output record. For example,
consider the statements

```
        WRITE(2, 100) A, B
100     FORMAT(T20, F12.4, T50, F12.4)
```

The T20 field of the FORMAT statement causes the F12.4 field for
the variable A to begin in column 20. The T50 causes the F12.4
field for B to begin in column 50.

When the T field is used for input, the effect is similar.
The FORMAT statement below reads A, B, and C from the beginning
of a card, then tabs to column 80 to read the variable K.

```
        READ(1, 10) A, B, C, K
10      FORMAT(3F6.0, T80, I1)
```

The T field can be useful for aligning labels on output fields.
For example, the following FORMAT statement will print the words
QUANTITY, PRICE, and TOTAL starting in columns 20, 40, and 60,
respectively:

```
10    FORMAT(T20, 'QUANTITY', T40, 'PRICE', T60, 'TOTAL')
```

This eliminates the need to count spaces to align column headings.

■ Variable FORMAT Statements

Sometimes it is desirable to specify the FORMAT statement when
the program is run, rather than when the program is written. There
is a way to have a variable FORMAT statement. This is done by
reading the field descriptors, including the parentheses, into an
array using an A field. The name of the array can then be used in
place of a FORMAT statement number in an input or output statement.

Suppose we want to read a variable format from a card, reading
from columns 1 through 80. The variable format will be read into
the array X. This can be done with the following statements:

```
        DIMENSION X(20)
        READ(1, 10) X
10      FORMAT(20A4)
```

A sample data card to be read would be

```
        (1X, I4, 1X, F6.2)
```

Any other format description could be used instead, depending on
how we want to use the variable format. The input data can be

like any valid FORMAT statement, but without the statement number or the word FORMAT. As in all FORMAT statements, blanks are ignored except in H fields. Thus, the variable format above may be punched anywhere in the input card. The above statement defines the variable format X. To use the variable format X, an input or output statement will substitute the array name X for a FORMAT statement number. For example,

        WRITE(2, X) K, W

The X here means that the format to be used is the variable one read into the array X.

Example 5

A program is going to read a two-dimensional array A having M rows and N columns. The values of M and N are variables in the range $1 \le M \le 100$, $1 \le N \le 10$. The format used is also variable, subject to the restriction that the array is read in row order (A(1,1), A(1,2), A(1,3), ...) and each row begins on a new card. The first card gives the values of M and N, in a 2I3 format, followed by the variable format. The statements to read the array are as follows:

```
        DIMENSION A(100,10), FMT(19)
        READ(1, 5) M, N, FMT
     5  FORMAT(2I3, 18A4, A2)
        IF(M.GT.100 .OR. M.LT.1) STOP
        IF(N.GT.10 .OR. N.LT.1) STOP
        DO 10 I = 1, M
    10  READ(1, FMT) (A(I,J), J = 1, N)
```


■ The BACKSPACE Statement

The BACKSPACE statement is somewhat like a REWIND statement. It is used to position a magnetic tape or disk file. On some systems it may be used to position a card input file as well. Instead of moving the file back to the beginning, the BACKSPACE statement moves the file to the beginning of the previous record. The form is

        BACKSPACE unit

where unit is a constant or fixed-point variable giving the unit to be backspaced. For example,

        BACKSPACE K

The BACKSPACE statement may be used with either formatted or unformatted files. If the unit is already at the beginning, BACKSPACE has no effect.

Example 6

A payroll file has records in the format

        Columns   1-5   Employee number
        Columns   6-25   Name (5A4)
        Columns 26-35   Wage rate (F10.2)

Suppose the records are in order according to employee number.
Also, suppose the value of the variable NUMBER is a number which
may or may not match an employee number on the file. Write statements which read the file and print out the record for the employee
whose number equals NUMBER, if there is such a record. Otherwise,
write out the records of the two employees whose numbers are just
less than and just greater than the value of NUMBER. Assuming the
input is read from unit 5, the following statements will do this:

```
         DIMENSION NAME(5)
   10    READ(5, 20) ID, NAME, WAGE
   20    FORMAT(I5, 5A4, F10.2)
         IF(ID.LT.NUMBER) GO TO 10
         IF(ID.EQ.NUMBER) GO TO 30
         BACKSPACE 5
         READ(5, 20) ID, NAME, WAGE
         WRITE(2, 25) ID, NAME, WAGE
   25    FORMAT(10X, I5, 5X, 5A4, 5X, F10.2)
         READ(5, 20) ID, NAME, WAGE
   30    WRITE(2, 25) ID, NAME, WAGE
```

■ NAMELIST Input and Output

Some systems permit the use of a special form of input or output
called a NAMELIST. A NAMELIST is a list of variable (or array) names.
It is declared by a statement such as

        NAMELIST/GROUP1/RESIS, CAPAC, XINDUC

which declares the variables RESIS, CAPAC, and XINDUC to be in the
NAMELIST called GROUP1. A NAMELIST input statement using this
NAMELIST is

        READ(1, GROUP1)

Notice that the NAMELIST name is used in place of the FORMAT
statement number. Notice also that the input list is omitted from
this READ statement. The names of the variables to be read are
supplied by the NAMELIST. Data to be read by this statement must
be prepared in a special form. First, the system reads until finding a record with an ampersand (&) in column 2, followed by the
NAMELIST name, followed by a blank. The system then reads until
finding another ampersand (&). The intervening records contain
values for the variables in the NAMELIST. These are written in a
special form:

```
        Name = Value
```

just like an assignment statement in FORTRAN. Blanks are ignored
except within a variable name or within a constant value. The
individual assignments are separated by commas. For example, data
to be read by the above statement could be

```
        b&GROUP1    RESIS = 0.  ,     CAPAC = 3.0,    XINDUC = 1.0 , &
```

The variables can be in any order. They do not have to be all on
one line. The same data could, for example, be written as

```
        b&GROUP1
        bRESIS = 0.,
        bCAPAC = 3.0,
        bXINDUC = 1.0, &
```

The first column of each line is ignored, and so should not be used.

NAMELIST output produces output which is in a form suitable
for NAMELIST input. Each variable is output in the form

```
        Name = Value
```

The statement

```
        WRITE(2, GROUP1)
```

will produce the output

```
        b&GROUP1
        bRESIS = 0.00,
        bCAPAC = 3.00,
        bXINDUC = 1.00,
        b&END
```

(The exact form depends on the particular system used.)

In general, the NAMELIST statement has the form

```
        NAMELIST/name₁/list₁/name₂/list₂ ...
```

where $name_i$ is a NAMELIST name which has the same form as a variable
name, and $list_i$ is a list of variable or array names, separated from
each other by commas. This is a declarative statement, and should
come at the beginning of the program, before any executable statement. The general forms of the NAMELIST input and output statements
are

```
        READ(unit, name)
        WRITE(unit, name)
```

or

```
READ name
PRINT name
```

where unit is the unit number and name is the NAMELIST name.

The input data begins with an ampersand (&) in column 2, followed by the NAMELIST name, followed by one or more blanks. Then the variable names in the NAMELIST are assigned values. The input is terminated by another ampersand (&). Any remaining characters on the last record are ignored. Characters in column 1 of the input are also ignored.

The assignments are handled just like regular assignment statements in FORTRAN, with appropriate type conversions as necessary. For example,

```
LOGICAL P
COMPLEX Z
NAMELIST/VARS/A, K, P, Z
READ(1, VARS)
WRITE(2, VARS)
```

would read the input

```
        b&VARS    A = 2,    K = 1.,    P = .TRUE.,    Z = (1.0,0.0)&
```

and produce the output

```
        b&VARS
        bA = 2.00,
        bK = 1,
        bP = .TRUE.,
        bZ = (1.0,0.0),
        b&END
```

Arrays can be read or written as part of a NAMELIST. The input (or output) data consists of the array name followed by an equals sign followed by a list of values. For example, the statements

```
DIMENSION A(5)
NAMELIST/JOE/A
READ(1, JOE)
```

would read the record

```
        &JOE    A = 1.,   2.,   3.,   4.,   5.&
```

and assign $A(1) = 1.$, $A(2) = 2.$, ..., $A(5) = 5$. A two-dimensional array is read by columns (that is, $A(1,1)$, $A(2,1)$, $A(3,1)$, ...).

As in the DATA statement, a fixed-point constant followed by an asterisk may be used to indicate a repetition factor. The input record

        b&JOE   A = 5*2.6&

means the same as

        b&JOE   A = 2.6, 2.6, 2.6, 2.6, 2.6&

On NAMELIST input, any variable which is not specified will retain its previous value.

■ Exercises

1. Indicate which of the following are valid FORTRAN statements:

    (a) INTEGER I J K
    (b) REAL, X
    (c) REAL X
    (d) REAL X, I, K33
    (e) INTEGER/W/X, Y

2. Using a COMPUTED GO TO, write statements which will transfer to Statement 25, 50, 75, or 100 if K = 25, 50, 75, or 100, respectively. If K is none of these values, transfer to Statement 200.

3. Using a COMPUTED GO TO, write statements which will transfer to Statement 5, 10, 15, 20, or 25 if I = NN(1), NN(2), NN(3), NN(4), or NN(5), respectively. If I is equal to none of these, continue with the next statement.

4. Indicate which of the following is a valid statement:

    (a) COMMON W, X
    (b) COMMON/W/X
    (c) COMMON W/X/
    (d) COMMON/W/A, B, C

5. Write a subroutine SOLV(A, B, C) which solves the equation $Ax^2 + Bx + C = 0$ and prints out the solutions. Use an assigned GO TO to distinguish the three cases: one real solution, two real solutions, two complex solutions.

6. Write a program to list a deck of input cards. The first two cards in the deck give a heading which should be printed at the top of each page, followed by a blank line and up to 60 card images on each page.

7. Write a subroutine which evaluates the function $f(x)$ for $a \le x \le b$, incrementing x by dx each time. The call to the subroutine is CALL EVAL(F, A, B, DX). Here F may be any FORTRAN FUNCTION subprogram. Write a main program to test the subroutine.

8. Write a program to print a table of powers of 2, from 2^{-100} to 2^{100}. Output the results in 1PG12.4 format.

9. What is the effect of the following program?

```
      DIMENSION A(10), B(10)
      EQUIVALENCE(A(2), B(1))
      DO 10 I = 1, 10
   10 A(I) = I
      DO 20 I = 1, 10
   20 B(I) = A(I)
      WRITE(6, 25) B
   25 FORMAT(1X, 10F5.0)
      STOP
      END
```

10. Write a program which reads two complex numbers and prints them out along with their product, their polar coordinates, and the polar coordinates of their product. Use NAMELIST input and output.

APPENDIX

Standard FORTRAN Functions

■ Absolute Value

IABS(N)   Absolute value of N. That is, IABS(N) = N if $N \geq 0$; IABS(N) = -N if N < 0.
Example: IABS(-3) = 3

ABS(X)   Absolute value of X. Same as IABS for floating-point numbers.
Example: ABS(-3.2) = 3.2

■ Truncation

INT(X)   Sign of X times the largest integer less than or equal to ABS(X). This converts the floating-point expression X to fixed-point form.
Examples: INT(3.2) = 3; INT(-3.2) = -3

IFIX(X)   Same as INT(X).

AINT(X)   Sign of X times the largest integer less than or equal to ABS(X). Same as INT(X), but returns a floating-point number.
Examples: AINT(3.2) = 3.0; AINT(-3.2) = -3.0

■ Conversion from Fixed-Point to Floating-Point

FLOAT(N)   Converts N to floating-point form.
Example: FLOAT(2) = 2.0

■ Remaindering

MOD(N, K)

The remainder when N is divided by K (that is, N modulo K). The definition of this function is N - (N/K)*K
<u>Examples</u>: MOD(17, 5) = 2; MOD(8, 2) = 0;
                MOD(-5, 3) = -2

AMOD(X, A)

Similar to MOD, but for floating-point numbers. The definition is X - AINT(X/A)*A
<u>Examples</u>: AMOD(3.123, 1.0) = .123;
                AMOD(8.0, 2.0) = 0.0;
                AMOD(-7.5, 2.0) = -1.5

■ Maximum and Minimum

MAX0(L, M, N, ...)

Maximum of two or more fixed-point arguments.
<u>Examples</u>: MAX0(2, 5) = 5; MAX0(2, -5) = 2;
                MAX0(2, 3, 4) = 4

MAX1(A, B, C, ...)

Maximum of two or more floating-point arguments. Result is converted to fixed-point.
<u>Examples</u>: MAX1(2.1, 5.2) = 5;
                MAX1(-2.1, -5.2) = -2;
                MAX1(2.0, 3.0, 4.1) = 4

AMAX0(L, M, N, ...)

Maximum of two or more fixed-point arguments. Result is converted to floating-point.
<u>Example</u>: AMAX0(2, 3) = 3.0

AMAX1(A, B, C, ...)

Maximum of two or more floating-point arguments.
<u>Example</u>: AMAX1(2.0, 3.1) = 3.1

MIN0(L, M, N, ...)

Minimum of two or more fixed-point arguments.
<u>Examples</u>: MIN0(2, 5) = 2; MIN0(2, -5) = -5;
                MIN0(2, 3, 4) = 2

MIN1(A, B, C, ...)

Minimum of two or more floating-point arguments. Result is converted to fixed-point.
<u>Example</u>: MIN1(2.1, 5.2) = 2

AMIN0(L, M, N, ...)

Minimum of two or more fixed-point arguments. Result is converted to floating-point.
<u>Example</u>: AMIN0(2, 3) = 2.0

AMIN1(A, B, C, ...)

Minimum of two or more floating-point arguments.
<u>Example</u>: AMIN1(2.0, 3.1) = 2.0

■ Transfer of Sign

ISIGN(N, K)   Sign of K with the absolute value of N.
                               Examples: ISIGN(3, -1) = -3;
                                          ISIGN(-4, 2) = 4

SIGN(X, A)   Sign of A with the absolute value of X.
                               Examples: SIGN(2.1, -3.0) = -2.1;
                                          SIGN(-2.1, 3.0) = 2.1

■ Positive Difference

IDIM(N, K)   Equal to N - K if N $\geq$ K; otherwise, equal
                               to zero.
                               Examples: IDIM(5, 4) = 1; IDIM(4, 5) = 0

DIM(X, A)   Equal to X - A if X $\geq$ A; otherwise, equal
                               to zero.
                               Examples: DIM(4.0,0.0) = 4.0;
                                          DIM(-4.0,0.0) = 0.0

■ Square Root

SQRT(X)   Square root of X; X must be greater than
                               or equal to zero.
                               Example: SQRT(9.0) = 3.0

■ Exponential and Logarithmic

EXP(X)   Exponential function e^x.
                               Example: EXP(1.0) = 2.718282

ALOG(X)   Natural logarithm of x.
                               Example: ALOG(2.718282) = 1.0

ALOG10(X)   Common logarithm $\log_{10} x$.
                               Example: ALOG10(100.0) = 2.0

■ Trigonometric

SIN(X)   Sine of x, where x is in radians.
                               Example: SIN(3.14159) = 0.0

COS(X)   Cosine of x, where x is in radians.
                               Example: COS(3.14159) = -1.0

TAN(X)   Tangent of x, where x is in radians.
                               (*Note*: This function may not be available
                               on all systems.)
                               Example: TAN(3.14159/4.0) = 1.0

■ Inverse Trigonometric

ASIN(X)

Arcsine of x, where x is in radians. The value will be between $-\pi/2$ and $\pi/2$. (*Note*: This function may not be available on all systems.)
<u>Example</u>: ASIN(0.0) = 0.0

ACOS(X)

Arccosine of x, where x is in radians. The value will be between 0 and π. (*Note*: This function may not be available on all systems.)
<u>Example</u>: ACOS(0.0) = 1.57080 (= $\pi/2$)

ATAN(X)

Arctangent of x, where x is in radians. The value will be between $-\pi/2$ and $\pi/2$.
<u>Example</u>: ATAN(1.0) = 0.785398 (= $\pi/4$)

ATAN2(Y, X)

Arctangent of y/x, where x and y are in radians. The value will be between $-\pi$ and π. This will correctly handle the case where x is zero.
<u>Example</u>: ATAN2(1.0, 1.0) = 0.785398

ANSWERS

■ Exercises 1A (pages 19-20)

1. When I is 1, Y is 12, but if I is 2, there is an infinite loop. One way to guard against this is to test $Y \geq 12$.

3.

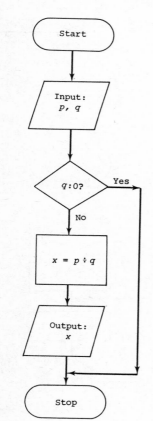

5.

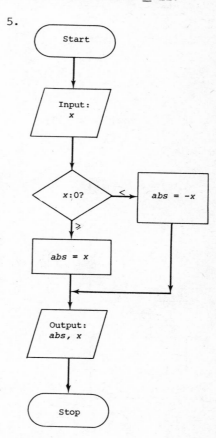

7.

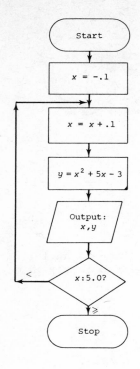

9.

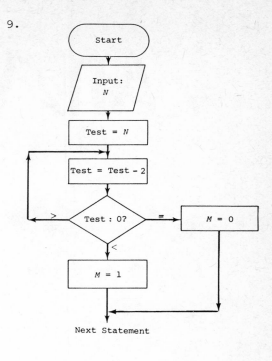

■ Exercises 1B (pages 20-23)

1.

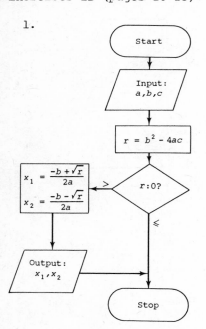

3.

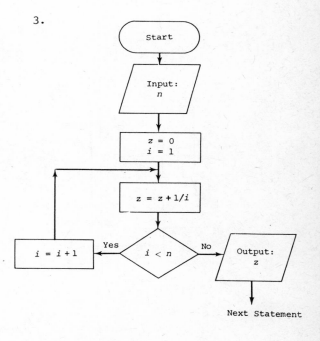

5.

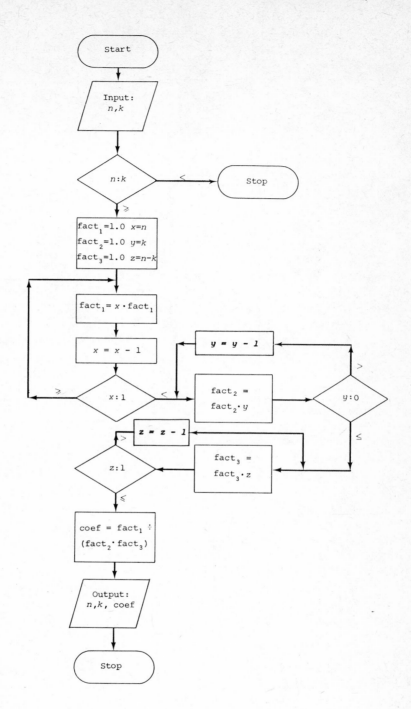

7.

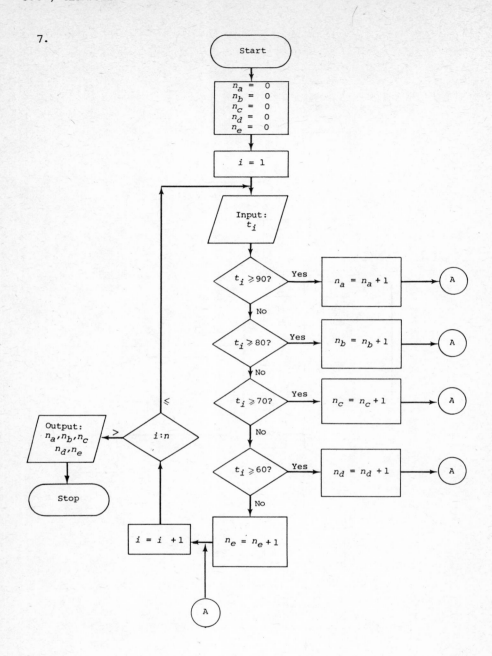

■ Exercises 2A (pages 45-47)

1. 6.2E00	3. 4.36E-05	5. 1.0E-10
7. 2.E02	9. 3.E08	11. .01
13. 1.0	15. 1010.0	17. .001

19. 1,000,000.   21. Valid fixed-point variable

23. Invalid: does not start with a letter

25. Invalid: too many characters

27. Valid floating-point variable
29. Invalid: has a character other than a letter or number
31. Invalid: has a character other than a letter or number
33. Valid floating-point variable
35. Valid fixed-point variable
37. Valid floating-point variable
39. Invalid: has a character other than a letter or number
41. $\dfrac{ab}{c}$ 43. $\dfrac{ab}{c}$ 45. $a + \dfrac{b}{c}$ 47. $a^b c$ 49. $\dfrac{2^{2x}}{x^2}$
51. A = R**2   53. R = 1./(1./R1 + 1./R2 + 1./R3)
55. V = SQRT(X**2 + Y**2)   57. AINP = X1*Y1 + X2*Y2 + X3*Y3
59. G = D/(B + C/(D + E/F))   61. Valid
63. Invalid: must have a variable on left side of equals sign
65. Valid   67. Valid
69. Invalid: variable name contains too many characters
71. Invalid: variable name contains a symbol
73. Invalid: mixed-mode division   75. Valid
77. Invalid: mixed-mode   79. Valid
81. -1.0   83. -7.0   85. .25   87. 20.0   89. 9.0
91. 0   93. 8   95. 0   97. 1   99. 6
101. N = N + 2   103. X = 4.0*(W3 - W4) - (W1 - W2)
105. K4B = K4B + 6
107. TOP = C1*D - B*C2   109. R = A + B + C
     BOT = C1*C4 - C2*C3   S = 1.0/A + 1.0/B + 1.0/C
     X = TOP/BOT   C = R/S
111. 2.0   113. 20.0

■ Exercises 2B (page 48)

1. $c = \dfrac{x}{\sqrt{x^2 + y^2 + z^2}}$ 3. $a = b + \dfrac{c}{d + e/f}$

5. $a = 4.7 \left(\dfrac{x_2 - x_1}{2}\right)^2 - 6\left(\dfrac{x_2 - x_1}{2}\right)$

7. S = -B + SQRT(B**2 - 4.0*A*C)**.5
   X = S/(2.0*A)

9. FIRST = 4./3.*((X - Y)/(Z - W))**E
   SECOND = ((A - B)/(C - D))**F
   THIRD = (P**2*(R - S))**(1./3.)
   G = FIRST*SECOND/THIRD

11. A = 2.0*3.1416*X/AL
    B = 2.0*3.1416*X/AM
    Z = SIN(A)*COS(B)/(SIN(B)*COS(A))

■ Exercises 3A (pages 69-72)

1. IF(X - Y) 10, 20, 20   3. IF(B**2 - 4.*A*C) 99, 50, 100
5. IF((4.*X+7.) -10.) 10, 20, 30

7. IF(X - (Y - 3.0)**3) 1, 4, 5
9. IF(R - P/Q) 999, 1, 999

11.

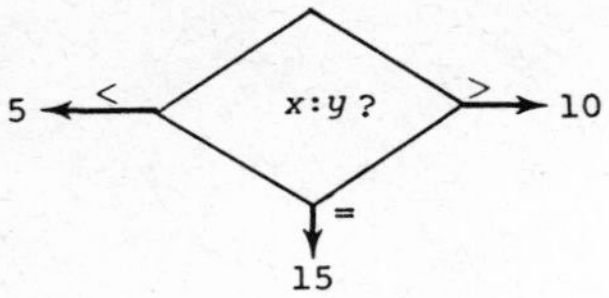

13.

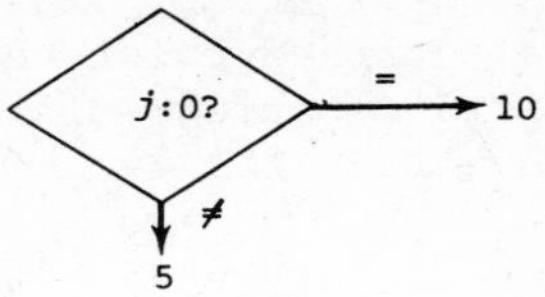

15.

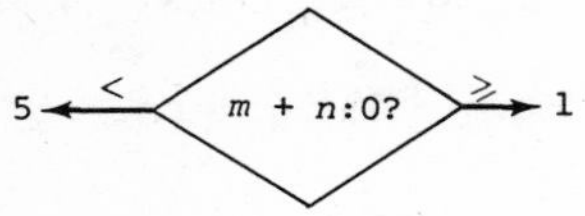

17.

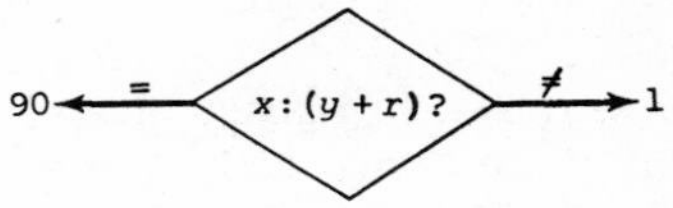

19.

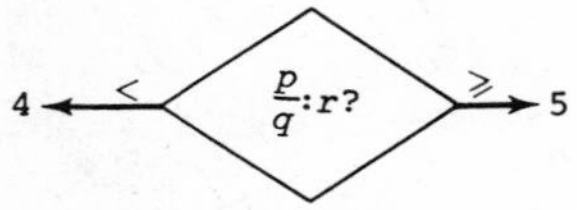

21. $x < 9$ transfer to 10; $x = 9$ transfer to 20; $x > 9$ transfer to 30
23. $x < -6$ transfer to 10; $x = -6$ transfer to 20; $x > -6$ transfer to 30
25. $x < 1$ transfer to 30; $x = 1$ transfer to 20; $x > 1$ transfer to 10
27. $x < 0$ transfer to 30; $x = 0$ transfer to 20; $0 < x < 2$ transfer to 10; $x = 2$ transfer to 20; $x > 2$ transfer to 30
29. $x = 0$ transfer to 20; transfer to 10 for any other value

31.
```
      IF(M - N) 5, 20, 20
    5 IF(M - 5) 30, 30, 40
```

33.
```
      IF(P/Q - (X + 1.0)) 1, 102, 2
    1 IF(P/Q - (X - 1.0)) 100, 100, 101
    2 IF(P/Q - Y) 102, 100, 100
```

35.

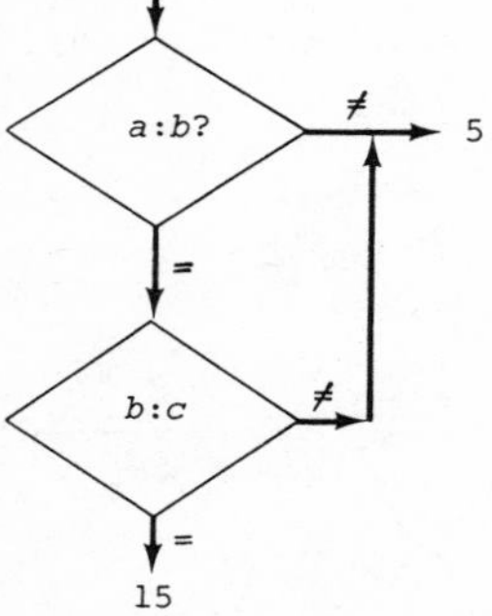

37.

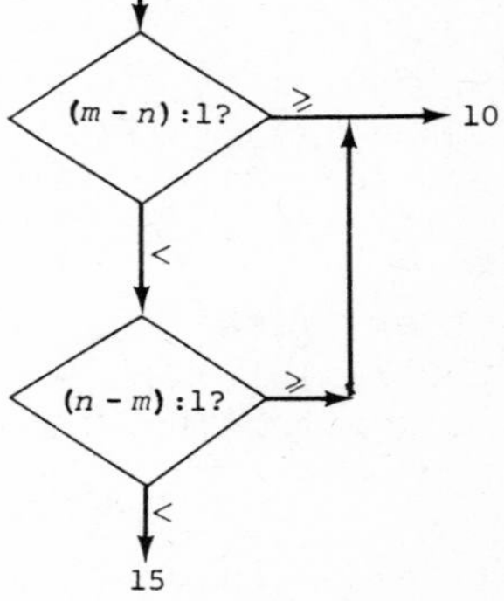

39.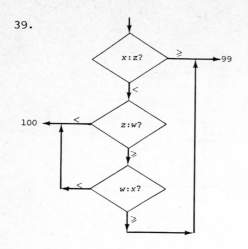

41.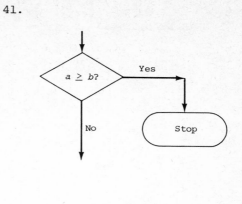

■ Exercises 3B (pages 72-75)

1.   M = I - I/2*2
        IF(M.EQ.0) GO TO 5
        J = 2
        GO TO 10
    5   J = 1
   10   Next Statement

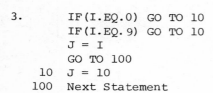

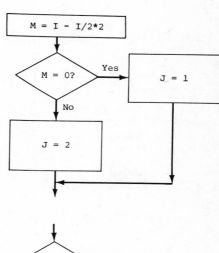

3.   IF(I.EQ.0) GO TO 10
        IF(I.EQ.9) GO TO 10
        J = I
        GO TO 100
   10   J = 10
  100   Next Statement

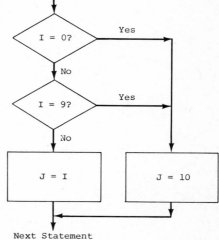

5. K = M - M/N*N
   IF(K.NE.0) K = 1

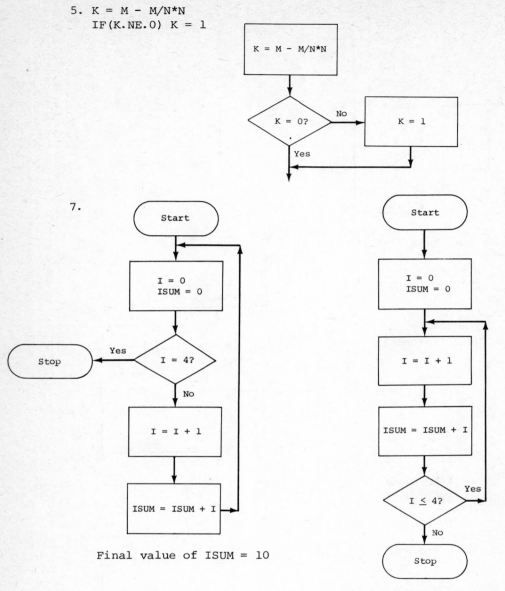

7.

Final value of ISUM = 10

Final value of ISUM = 15

9.

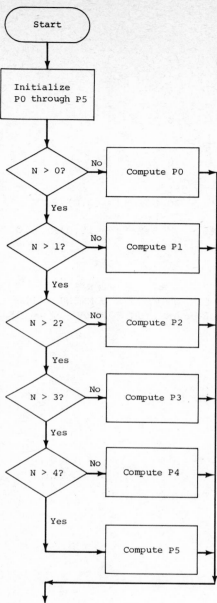

Next Statement

```
C      SET EACH POLYNOMIAL EQUAL TO ZERO
C      THEN LATER WE CAN OUTPUT EVERY ONE
       P0 = 0.
       P1 = 0.
       P2 = 0.
       P3 = 0.
       P4 = 0.
       P5 = 0.
       IF(N.GT.0) GO TO 1
       P0 = 1.
       GO TO 99
```

9.—continued

```
      1  IF(N.GT.1) GO TO 2
         P1 = X
         GO TO 99
      2  IF(N.GT.2) GO TO 3
         P2 = (3.0*X**2 - 1.0)/2.0
         GO TO 99
      3  IF(N.GT.3) GO TO 4
         P3 = (5.0*X**3 - 3.0*X)/2.0
         GO TO 99
      4  IF(N.GT.4) GO TO 5
         P4 = (35.0*X**4 - 30.0*X**2 + 3.0)/8.0
         GO TO 99
      5  P5 = (63.0*X**5 - 70.0*X**3 + 15.0*X)/8.0
     99  Next Statement
```

```
11. C     ASSUME N INPUT
    C     SEE FLOWCHART, PAGE 15, CHAPTER 1
    C     FOR INPUT AND OUTPUT WE USE COMMENT CARDS
    C     IN CHAPTER 4 WE LEARN THE FORTRAN TO DO THIS
          SUM = 0.
          I = 0
       1  I = I + 1
    C     INPUT X
          SUM = SUM + X
          IF(I.LT.N) GO TO 1
          XN = N
          AV = SUM/XN
    C     OUTPUT AV
          STOP
          END
```

```
13. C     INPUT N, THE NUMBER OF CHECKS
          XN = N
          IF(N.LE.5) GO TO 2
          IF(N.LE.10) GO TO 4
          IF(N.LE.15) GO TO 6
          GO TO 7
       2  TC = XN*.10
          GO TO 8
       4  TC = .50 + (XN - 5.)*.09
          GO TO 8
       6  TC = .95 + (XN - 10.)*.08
          GO TO 8
       7  TC = 1.35 + (XN - 15.)*.07
    C     STATEMENT 8 IS FOR OUTPUT OF TC AND N
          STOP
          END
```

13.—continued

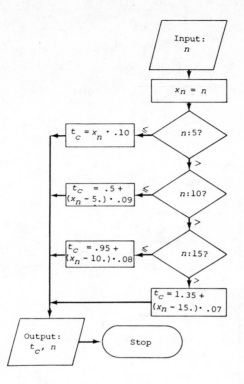

15.   X = -2.0
        Y = -2.0*X**2 + 4.0*X - 2.0
        YMAX = Y
        YMIN = Y
   10 X = X + .1
        Y = -2.0*X**2 + 4.0*X - 2.0
        IF(Y.GT.YMAX) YMAX = Y
        IF(Y.LT.YMIN) YMIN = Y
        IF(X.LT.2.0) GO TO 10
        Next Statement

15.—continued

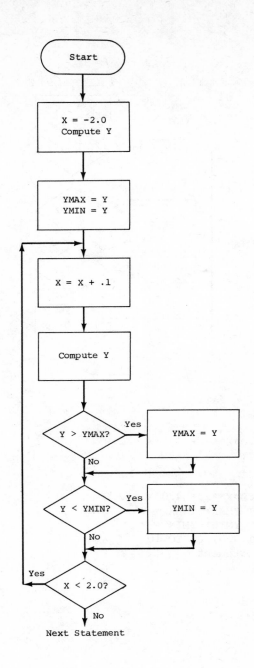

```
17. C       INPUT A, B, C, D
    C       LINES ARE SAME IF A = C AND B = D
    C       LINES ARE PARALLEL IF A = C AND B NOT EQUAL D
            IF(A.EQ.C) GO TO 10
    C       LINES ARE DIFFERENT
            X = (B - D)/(C - A)
            Y = A*X + B
            N = 1
            GO TO 99
    10      IF(B.EQ.D) GO TO 20
    C       LINES ARE PARALLEL
            N =- 1
            GO TO 80
    C       LINES ARE THE SAME
    20      N = 0
    80      X = 0.
            Y = 0.
    99      Next Statement
```

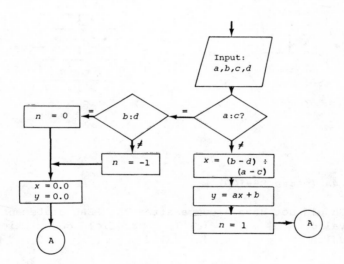

```
19.         X = 100.0
            N = 1
            M = 0
    4       XINT = .05*X
            X = X + XINT
            IF(X.GE.1000.) GO TO 2
    1       M = M + 1
            IF(M/4*4.NE.M) GO TO 4
            XINF = .03*X
            X = X - XINF
            N = N + 1
            GO TO 4
    C       STATEMENT 2 IS TO OUTPUT N
            STOP
```

19.—continued

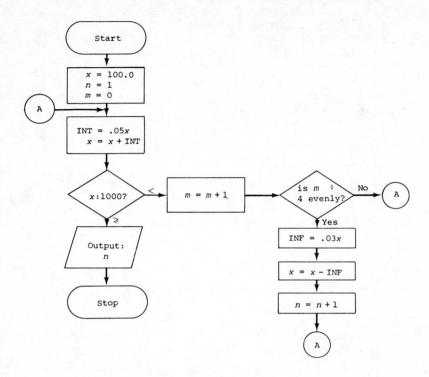

■ Exercises 4A (pages 99-100)

1. (a) Should not have a comma after the READ statement.
   (b) Valid   (c) Improper field description for ZZZ
   (d) Valid   (e) Valid

3.   READ(1, 1) N
    1   FORMAT(I10)
        I = 1
        KOUNT = 0
   10   READ(1, 12) GRADE
   12   FORMAT(F20.4)
        IF(GRADE.GE.90.0) KOUNT = KOUNT + 1
        I = I + 1
        IF(I.LE.N) GO TO 10
        WRITE(2, 14) KOUNT
   14   FORMAT(9H COUNT = , I6)

```
5.              READ(1, 3) A, B
       3  FORMAT(2F10.0)
                IF(A.EQ.1.) GO TO 10
                IF(B.EQ.1.) GO TO 20
                C = 3.
                GO TO 99
      10  IF(B.EQ.1) GO TO 30
      20  C = 2.
                GO TO 99
      30  C = 1.
      99  WRITE(2, 4) C
       4  FORMAT(5H C = , F10.0)
                STOP
                END


7.              WRITE(2, 1000)
    1000  FORMAT(6H TEST1, 6X, 6H TEST2, 6X, 6H TEST3, 6X, 11H FINAL AVG.)
                READ(1, 2000) T1, T2, T3
    2000  FORMAT(F4.0, F4.0, F4.0)
                AVG = .19*T1 + .37*T2 + .44*T3
                WRITE(2, 1001) T1, T2, T3, AVG
    1001  FORMAT(2X, F4.0, 8X, F4.0, 8X, F4.0, 8X, F4.0)
                STOP
                END
```

■ Exercises 4B (pages 101-102)

```
1.              WRITE(2, 200)
     200  FORMAT(7X, 1HX, 9X, 1HY, 9X, 1HR, 9X, 9H POSITION)
      14  READ(1, 300) X, Y, R
     300  FORMAT(F10.2, F10.2, F10.2)
   C            ON LAST DATA CARD TYPE A ZERO FOR R
                IF(R) 1, 99, 1
       1  IF((X**2 + Y**2) - R**2) 2, 3, 4
       2  M = 0
                GO TO 100
       3  M = 1
                GO TO 100
       4  M = 2
   C            M = 0 INSIDE, M = 1 ON, M = 2 OUTSIDE
     100  WRITE(2, 400) X, Y, R, M
     400  FORMAT(F10.2, F10.2, F10.2, I3)
                GO TO 14
      99  STOP
                END
```

```
3. C        ASSUME PRINTER HAS 120 CHARACTERS PER LINE
            WRITE(2, 1)
    1       FORMAT(36X, 4H30 X)
            WRITE(2, 2)
    2       FORMAT(39X, 1H.)
            WRITE(2, 2)
            WRITE(2, 2)
            WRITE(2, 2)
            WRITE(2, 4)
    4       FORMAT(33X, 7HY   20 X)
            WRITE(2, 5)
    5       FORMAT(31X, 9H VALUES .)
            WRITE(2, 2)
            WRITE(2, 2)
            WRITE(2, 2)
            WRITE(2, 6)
    6       FORMAT(36X, 4H10   X)
            WRITE(2, 2)
            WRITE(2, 2)
            WRITE(2, 2)
            WRITE(2, 2)
            WRITE(2, 7)
    7       FORMAT(39X, 39H. . . . X . . . . X . . . . X . . . . X)
            WRITE(2, 8)
    8       FORMAT(39X, 1H0, 7X, 2H10, 8X, 2H20, 8X, 2H30, 8X, 2H40)
            STOP
            END


5. C        ON LAST DATA CARD PUNCH A NEGATIVE
   C        NUMBER FOR THE TEST TO SEE IF DONE
            WRITE(2, 200)
  200       FORMAT(33X, 24HGPA FOR A MARKING PERIOD)
   10       READ(1, 100) NUM, M1, M2, M3, M4, M5
  100       FORMAT(I3, I1, I1, I1, I1, I1)
            IF(NUM.LT.0) GO TO 1
            READ(1, 101) N1, N2, N3, N4, N5
  101       FORMAT(I1, I1, I1, I1, I1)
            TOP = N1*M1 + N2*M2 + N3*M3 + N4*M4 + N5*M5
            BOT = N1 + N2 + N3 + N4 + N5
            GPA = TOP/BOT
            WRITE(2, 201) NUM, GPA
  201       FORMAT(20X, 13HSTUDENT ID = , I3, 7H GPA = , F7.2)
            GO TO 10
    1       STOP
            END
```

```
7.          I = 0
      10    I = I + 1
            IF(I.GT.100) STOP
            NDIG2 = I - I/10*10
            J = I/10
            NDIG1 = J - J/10*10
            NREM = I - I/3*3
C           NDIG1 IS THE TENS DIGIT OF THE NUMBER
C           NDIG2 IS THE ONES DIGIT OF THE NUMBER
C           NREM IS THE REMAINDER WHEN DIVIDED BY THREE
            IF(NDIG1.EQ.3) GO TO 20
            IF(NDIG2.EQ.3) GO TO 20
            IF(NREM.EQ.0) GO TO 20
            WRITE(2, 101) I
            GO TO 10
      20    WRITE(2, 102)
            GO TO 10
     101    FORMAT(10X, I3)
     102    FORMAT(12X, 1HX)
            END
```

■ Exercises 5A (pages 116-119)

1. (a) V   (b) V   (c) Y(5)   (d) V   (e) V
   (f) V   (g) V .   (h) V
   (i) DIMENSION X(10), ZZ(1000), Y(4)   (*Note:* The original
       statement is valid, but defines an array SX, not X.)
   (j) V   (k) BB(I + 5)
   (l) V   (m) V (GO TO 5 is a variable name.)
   (n) V   (o) B (IN, IOUT)   (p) V

```
3.          DIMENSION CBROOT(10)
            I = 1
            POWER = 1./3.
      1     XI = I
            CBROOT(I) = XI**POWER
            WRITE(2, 10) I, CBROOT(I)
      10    FORMAT(10X, I2, 2X, F20.8)
            I = I + 1
            IF(I.LE.10) GO TO 1
      2     STOP
            END
```

```
5.          DIMENSION SUM(5)
            READ(1, 100) N
     100    FORMAT(I3)
            I = 1
      1     SUM(I) = 0.
            I = I + 1
            IF(I.LE.5) GO TO 1
      2     J = 1
      3     X = J
            SUM(1) = SUM(1) + X
```

5.—continued

```
        SUM(2) = SUM(2) + 4.*X - 3.
        SUM(3) = SUM(3) + 2.*X - 1.
        SUM(4) = SUM(4) + X*X
        SUM(5) = SUM(5) + X**3
        J = J + 1
        IF(J.LE.N) GO TO 3

7.      DIMENSION MATH(1000), IENGL(1000), IDIFF(1000)
        I = 0
        ICOUNT = 0
        READ(1, 100) N
100     FORMAT(I4)
5       I = I + 1
        READ(1, 101) MATH(I), IENGL(I)
101     FORMAT(I3, I3)
        IDIFF(I) = IABS(MATH(I) - IENGL(I))
        IF(IDIFF(I).LT.20) GO TO 3
        ICOUNT = ICOUNT + 1
        IDIFF(I) = 1
        IF(I.LT.N) GO TO 5
3       IDIFF(I) = 0
        IF(I.LT.N) GO TO 5

9.      DIMENSION A(10,10), B(10,10), C(10,10)
        J = 1
3       I = 1
1       C(I,J) = A(I,J) + B(I,J)
        I = I + 1
        IF(I.LE.10) GO TO 1
2       J = J + 1
        IF(J.LE.10) GO TO 3

11.     DIMENSION SCORE(1000)
        A = 0.0
        I = 0
1       I = I + 1
        IF(SCORE(I).GE.90.) A = A + 1.
        IF(I.LT.1000) GO TO 1
```

■ Exercises 5B (pages 119-121)

```
1. (a) N = 0
        WTAVG = 0.0
        HTAVG = 0.0
        SCAVG = 0.0
C READ  IN DATA.   ON LAST CARD IS 00000 FOR ID TO STOP
3       N = N + 1
        READ(1, 100) ID, HT, WT, IAVAIL, SCORE, HAIR, SPORTS
```

1.(a)—continued

```
      1   FORMAT(I5, F2.0, F3.0, I1, F2.0, F1.0, F1.0)
          IF(ID.EQ.0) GO TO 99
          WTAVG = WTAVG + WT
          HTAVG = HTAVG + HT
          SCAVG = SCAVG + SCORE
          GO TO 3
     99   XN = FLOAT(N - 1)
          WTAVG = WTAVG/XN
          HTAVG = HTAVG/XN
          SCAVG = SCAVG/XN
          WRITE(2, 200) N, WTAVG, HTAVG, SCAVG
    200   FORMAT(10X, I4, F3.0, 1X, F3.0, 1X, F3.0)
          Next Statement
```

(b)
```
          N = 0
          NUMB = 0
     10   READ(1, 100) ID, HT, WT, IAVAIL, SCORE, HAIR, SPORTS
    100   FORMAT(I5, F2.0, F3.0, I1, F2.0, F1.0, F1.0)
          IF(ID.EQ.0) GO TO 99
          IF(HT.GE.69.0) GO TO 3
          IF(WT.LE.110.) GO TO 3
          IF(WT.GE.160.) GO TO 3
          IF(SCORE.LE.70.) GO TO 3
          IF(SPORTS.NE.1.) GO TO 3
          NUMB = NUMB + 1
      3   N = N + 1
          GO TO 10
     99   WRITE(2, 200) N, NUMB
    200   FORMAT(10X, 4HN = , I2, 5X, 7HNUMB = , I2)
          STOP
          END
```

3.
```
     50   FORMAT(F10.2, F10.2, F10.2)
     10   READ(1, 50) X, Y, Z
          IF(X.GE.9999.0) STOP
      1   P = .01*X*X + .0001*Y**3 + .05*Z*Z
          IF(P.GT.100.) P = 100.
          WRITE(2, 60) X, Y, Z, P
     60   FORMAT(10X, 4HX = , F10.2, 5X, 4HY = , F10.2, 5X,
          14HZ = , F10.2, 5X, 4HP = , F10.2)
          GO TO 10
          END
```

5.
```
          DIMENSION ITEAM(6), W(6), XL(6), PCT(6), GB(6)
          LIMIT = 6
    C     READ TEAM NO., WINS, LOSSES
    C     THEN COMPUTE PERCENTAGES
          I = 0
     10   I = I + 1
          READ(1, 101) ITEAM(I), W(I), XL(I)
          PCT(I) = W(I)/(W(I) + XL(I))
```

5.—continued

```
          IF(I.LT.LIMIT) GO TO 10
C         SORT TEAMS IN ORDER OF DECREASING PERCENTAGES
          I = 0
   20     I = I + 1
          J = I
   30     J = J + 1
          IF(PCT(I).GT.PCT(J)) GO TO 40
          TEMP = PCT(I)
          PCT(I) = PCT(J)
          PCT(J) = TEMP
          ITEMP = ITEAM(I)
          ITEAM(I) = ITEAM(J)
          ITEAM(J) = ITEMP
          TEMP = W(I)
          W(I) = W(J)
          W(J) = TEMP
          TEMP = XL(I)
          XL(I) = XL(J)
          XL(J) = TEMP
   40     IF(J.LT.LIMIT) GO TO 30
          IF(I.LT.LIMIT - 1) GO TO 20
C         COMPUTE GAMES BEHIND
          J = 0
   50     J = J + 1
          GB(J) = ((W(I) - XL(I)) - (W(J) - XL(J)))/2.0
          IF(J.LT.LIMIT) GO TO 50
C         OUTPUT TABLE
          WRITE(2, 200)
          I = 0
   60     I = I + 1
          WRITE(2, 201) ITEAM(I), W(I), XL(I), PCT(I), GB(I)
          IF(I.LT.LIMIT) GO TO 60
          STOP
  101     FORMAT(I1, F3.0, F3.0)
  200     FORMAT(10X, 4HTEAM, 5X, 4HWINS, 4X, 6HLOSSES,
         14X, 3HPCT, 4X, 12HGAMES BEHIND)
  201     FORMAT(12X, I1, 7X, F3.0, 6X, F3.0, 4X, F4.1)
          END
```

■ Exercises 6A (pages 135-138)

1. (a) V   (b) DO 3 K6 = I5, J, 2
   (c) DO 2 IX = J, N, M   (d) V
   (e) V (not a DO statement; DO I is a variable)   (f) V
   (g) V (not a DO statement)   (h) V
   (i) DO 3 MA = 1, N4A2, 2   (j) DO 17 IFEW = 1, N
   (k) V (statement executes only one time) (l) DO 10 IX2 = N, M
   (m) V (statement executes only one time)   (n) V

3. 9 (I = 5, J = 4)

```
5.          DIMENSION X(100)
                .
                .
                .
            XBAR = 0.0
            XSQ = 0.0
            DO 10 I = 1, N
            XBAR = XBAR + X(I)
     10     XSQ = XSQ + X(I)**2
            XBAR = XBAR/FLOAT(N)
            S = (XSQ - FLOAT(N)*XBAR)/FLOAT(N - 1)
            S = SQRT(S)


7.          IAMT = 0
            DO 2 I = 1, 1000
     C      ON LAST DATA CARD, ID = 0
            READ(1, 100) ID, ISEX, IHT, IWT, ICLASS, IATH
            IF(ID.LE.0) GO TO 1
     100    FORMAT(I5, I1, I2, I3, I1, I1)
            IF(ISEX.NE.1) GO TO 2
            IF(IHT.LE.60) GO TO 2
            IF(IWT.LE.180) GO TO 2
            IF(ICLASS.EQ.1) GO TO 2
            IF(IATH.LT.7) GO TO 2
            IAMT = IAMT + 1
            WRITE(2, 500) ID
     500    FORMAT(10X, I5)
       2    CONTINUE
       1    WRITE(2, 501) IAMT
     501    FORMAT(10X, 'NO. OF ATHLETES', I5)
            STOP
            END


9. C        ASSUME CHECKS ARE IN PROPER ORDER, I.E.
   C        THEY HAVE BEEN SORTED OUT FOR EACH PERSON
   C        READ IN DATA
       5    READ(1, 100) NUMDEP, NUMCHK, BAL
     100    FORMAT(I3, I3, F8.2)
            IF(NUMDEP.GE.999) GO TO 11
      10    DO 110 I = 1, NUMDEP
            READ(1, 101) NDEP, IDEP, DEP
     101    FORMAT(I3, I5, F8.2)
            IF(I.EQ.1) WRITE(2, 102) IDEP
     102    FORMAT(10X, 22H CHECKING ACCOUNT FOR, I5)
       2    BAL = BAL + DEP
     110    WRITE(2, 103) NDEP, DEP, BAL
     103    FORMAT(5X, 13H DEPOSIT NO. , I3, 6H AMT. , F8.2,
            111H BALANCE = , F8.2)
            DO 20 I = 1, NUMCHK
            READ(1, 104) IDEP, NCHK, AMT
     104    FORMAT(I5, I4, F8.2)
            BAL = BAL - AMT
      20    WRITE(2, 105) NCHK, AMT, BAL
```

9.—continued

```
    105   FORMAT(5X, 10HCHECK NO. , I4, 6H AMT. , F8.2,
          111H BALANCE = , F8.2)
          GO TO 5
     11   STOP
          END
```

■ Exercises 6B (pages 138-140)

```
1.          READ(1, 200) N
      200   FORMAT(I3)
            SUM1 = 0.
            SUM2 = 0.
            SUM3 = 0.
            DO 100 I = 1, N
            X = FLOAT(I)
            SUM1 = SUM1 + X
            SUM2 = SUM2 + X*X
      100   SUM3 = SUM3 + X**3
            WRITE(2, 300) SUM1, SUM2, SUM3
      300   FORMAT(10X, 6HSUM1 = , F10.2, 6HSUM2 = , F10.2,
            16HSUM3 = , F10.2)
            STOP
            END
```

3. (a)   (b)

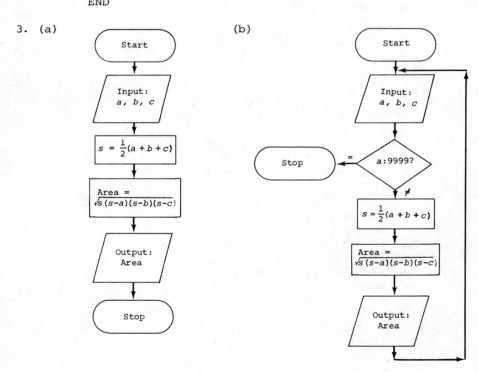

```
5.          READ(1, 50) M
      50    FORMAT(I2)
            A = 364.0
            P = 1.0
            DO 60 I = 2, M
      60    P = P*A/365.0
            P = 1.0 - P
            WRITE(2, 200) M, P
     200    FORMAT(10X, 5H FOR , I2, 15H PROBABILITY IS, F6.4)
            STOP
            END


7. C        SET UP ARRAY TO STORE DATA FOR SENIORS
            DIMENSION IDEN(1000), ICOLL(1000), GGPA(1000)
   C        ASSUME NO MORE THAN 1000 STUDENTS
   C        LAST DATA CARD HAS ZERO FOR IDEN
   C        ICOUNT COUNTS NUMBER OF SENIORS
            ICOUNT = 0
       3    READ(1, 100) JDEN, JCOLL, GPA, KLASS
     100    FORMAT(I5, I1, F5.2, I1)
            IF(JDEN.EQ.0) GO TO 2
            IF(KLASS.LT.4) GO TO 3
            ICOUNT = ICOUNT + 1
            IDEN(ICOUNT) = JDEN
            ICOLL(ICOUNT) = JCOLL
            GGPA(ICOUNT) = GPA
            GO TO 3
   C        THIS SECTION SORTS THE GPA S IN DESCENDING ORDER
   C        AND INTERCHANGES CORRESPONDING ID NUMBERS AND COLLEGES
       2    INDEX = ICOUNT - 1
            DO 10 I = 1, INDEX
            JJ = I + 1
            DO 11 J = JJ, ICOUNT
            IF(GGPA(I).GT.GGPA(J)) GO TO 11
            T = GGPA(I)
            GGPA(I) = GGPA(J)
            GGPA(J) = T
            IT = IDEN(I)
            IDEN(I) = IDEN(J)
            IDEN(J) = IT
            IT = ICOLL(I)
            ICOLL(I) = ICOLL(J)
            ICOLL(J) = IT
      11    CONTINUE
      10    CONTINUE
            WRITE(2, 150)
     150    FORMAT(1H1, 10X, 7HSTUDENT, 10X, 7HCOLLEGE, 10X, 3HGPA)
            DO 20 I = 1, ICOUNT
      20    WRITE(2, 200) IDEN(I), ICOLL(I), GGPA(I)
     200    FORMAT(12X, I5, 14X, I1, 10X, F5.2)
            STOP
            END
```

■ Exercises 7A (pages 152-155)

1. (a) V   (b) V   (c) V   (d) V
   (e) V   (f) V   (g) V

```
   (h)     DIMENSION X(4)
           N = 4
           READ(1, 11) (X(I), I = 1, 2)
       11  FORMAT(10F4.2)

   (i)     DIMENSION X(20), Y(20)
        7  FORMAT(F8.2)
           DO 12 J = 1, 20, 2
           READ(1, 7) X(J)
       12  Y(J) = X(J)**2
```

```
3.         DIMENSION X(1000)
           READ(1, 1) N
        1  FORMAT(I10)
           READ(1, 2) (X(I), I = 1, N)
        2  FORMAT(F10.2)
           INDEX = N - 1
           DO 3 I = 1, INDEX
           JJ = I + 1
           DO 4 J = JJ, N
           IF(X(I).LE.X(J)) GO TO 4
           TEMP = X(I)
           X(I) = X(J)
           X(J) = TEMP
        4  CONTINUE
        3  CONTINUE
           Next Statement
```

```
5. (a)     WRITE(2, 100) X, Y
      100  FORMAT(1H1, ///////////, 2F20.8)

   (b)     WRITE(2, 101) X, Y
      101  FORMAT(//////, 20X, 9HX - VALUE, 10X, 9HY - VALUE,
           1//, 10X, 2F20.4)

   (c)     WRITE(2, 100) (X(I), Y(I), I = 1, 20)
      100  FORMAT(1H1, 52X, 9HX - ARRAY, 9X, 9HY - ARRAY, /,
           1(44X, 2F18.4))

   (d)     READ(1, 99) (Z(I), I = 1, 800)
       99  FORMAT(8F10.3)

   (e)     DIMENSION Z(1000)
           N = 0
       10  N = N + 1
           READ(1, 20) Z(N)
       20  FORMAT(E20.4)
           IF(Z(N).NE.-999.) GO TO 10
           N = N - 1
```

5.—continued

```
   (f)      WRITE(2, 1)
       1    FORMAT(1H1, 19X, 1HI, 30X, 9HX - VALUE, /)
            DO 1000 INDEX = 1, N
    1000    WRITE(2, 2) INDEX, X(INDEX)
       2    FORMAT(19X, I3, 3X, F30.4)


7. C ASSUME NO MORE THAN 1000 DATA CARDS
            DO 600 I = 1, 1000
            READ(1, 3) N, A1, D
       3    FORMAT(I5, 2F10.4)
            IF(N.LE.0) GO TO 1001
       1    XN = FLOAT(N)
            SN = XN/2.*(2.*A1 + (XN - 1.)*D)
     600    WRITE(2, 4) N, A1, D, SN
       4    FORMAT(10X, I5, 3F10.4)
    1001    STOP
            END
```

■ Exercises 7B (pages 155-159)

```
1.          X = 4.1
            XL = X + 6.*X/SQRT(X**2 - 16.)
       3    X = X + .1
            XNEWXL = X + 6.*X/SQRT(X**2 - 16.)
            IF(XNEWXL.LE.XL) GO TO 2
            XL = XNEWXL
       2    IF(X.LE.6.0) GO TO 3
       4    WRITE(2, 100)
     100    FORMAT(1H1, 10X, 21H LADDER PROBLEM FIND,
            135HLONGEST LENGTH TO FIT AROUND CORNER,
            2//, 16X, 1HX, /, 16X, 1HX, 12X, 10(2H.), /,
            316X, 1HX, 12X, 1H., /, 16X, 1HX, 12X, 1H., 6X, 6H6 FEET,
            4/, 16X, 1HX, 12X, 1H.., 3X, 7(2H.), /, 16X, 1HX, 12X,
            51H., 1X, 1H4, 1X, 1H., /, 16X, 1HX, 12X, 5H. FT., /,
            616X, 1HX, 12X, 5H.  ., /, 16X, 1HX, 12X, 5H.   ., /,
            716X, 1HX, 12X, 5H.  ., /, 10X, 13HLADDER LENGTH,
            88X, 13CORNER SKETCH)
            WRITE(2, 101) XL
     101    FORMAT(//, 15X, 18H MAXIMUM LENGTH IS, F6.2)


3.          READ(1, 200) A, B
     200    FORMAT(2F10.4)
            AA = A + .1
            XL = AA + B*AA/SQRT(AA**2 - A**2)
            AA = AA + .1
            XLNEW = AA + B*AA/SQRT(AA**2 - A**2)
            Rest of statements similar to those in Exercise 1, above.
```

```
5.          DIMENSION NRANGE(7), NGRADE(7)
    C       NRANGE IS AN ARRAY WITH NRANGE(I) EQUAL
    C       TO THE LOWER LIMIT OF THE ITH RANGE
    C       OF GRADES.  THE LAST VALUE IS GREATER THAN
    C       THE HIGHEST POSSIBLE GRADE
            NRANGE(1) = 0
            NRANGE(2) = 51
            NRANGE(3) = 61
            NRANGE(4) = 71
            NRANGE(5) = 81
            NRANGE(6) = 91
            NRANGE(7) = 100
    C       NGRADE(I) = NO. OF GRADES IN RANGE(I) THROUGH RANGE(I + 1)
            DO 25 I = 1, 6
       25   NGRADE(I) = 0
    C       READ GRADES, COUNT NO. IN EACH RANGE
            DO 50 NTOTAL = 1, 1000
            READ(1, 501) IGR
    C       LAST CARD HAS NEGATIVE GRADE
            DO 50 I = 1, 6
            IF(IGR.LT.NRANGE(I)) GO TO 50
            IF(IGR.GE.NRANGE(I + 1)) GO TO 50
            NGRADE(I) = NGRADE(I) + 1
       50   CONTINUE
    C       PRINT THE GRAPH
      200   WRITE(2, 502)
            K1 = 1
            DO 250 I = 1, 6
            DO 225 J = 1, 3
      225   WRITE(2, 503)
            NUM = NGRADE(I)
            NL = NRANGE(I + 1) - 1
            WRITE(2, 504) NRANGE(I), NL, (K1, J = 1, NUM)
      250   CONTINUE
            DO 260 J = 1, 3
      260   WRITE(2, 503)
            WRITE(2, 502)
            STOP
      501   FORMAT(20X, I3)
      502   FORMAT(10X, 30(1H.))
      503   FORMAT(10X, 1H.)
      504   FORMAT(4X, I2, 1H-, I2, 1X, 1H., 30I1)
            END
```

■ Exercises 8A (pages 190-193)

1. (a) X = Z - F(1.0, Y(1), 2.0)   (b) ZERO(A, C, D, W) = A - C*D/W
   (c) V   (d) V   (e) V   (f) V
   (g) N = 6 must come in the function statement as one of the
       arguments
   (h) V   (i) 101 FORMAT(1H0, 20X, 2F20.4)

```
3.         FUNCTION AVG(X, N)
           DIMENSION X(1)
   C       NOTE.  THE ABOVE IS EQUIVALENT TO X(N)
           XN = FLOAT(N)
           SUM = 0.0
           DO 10 I = 1, N
     10    SUM = SUM + X(I)
           AVG = SUM/XN
           RETURN
           END


5.         SUBROUTINE NUMB(I)
   C       ASSUME 132 SPACES AVAILABLE ON PRINTER
           IF(I - 2) 2, 3, 4
      2    WRITE(2, 100)
    100    FORMAT(1H1, 27(/), 52X, 14(2H*),/, 52X, 1H*,
           125X, 1H*, /, 8(52X, 1H*, 11X, 2HXX, 12X, 1H*, /),
           252X, 1H*, 26X, 1H*, /, 52X, 14(2H* ))
           RETURN
      3    Similarly for I = 2
           .
           .
           .
      4    Similarly for I = 3
```

■ Exercises 8B (pages 193-194)

```
1.         DIMENSION F(41)
           F1(X) = X*X + 3.*X - 2.
           F2(X) = X**4 - X
           X = -.5
           DO 10 I = 1, 41
           X = X + .5
     10    F(I) = F1(X) + F2(X)
           .
           .
           .

3.         SUBROUTINE STAT(X, N, XBAR, SIGMA)
           DIMENSION X(N)
           XBAR = 0.
           XSQ = 0.
           DO 10 J = 1, N
           XBAR = XBAR + X(J)
     10    XSQ = XSQ + X(J)**2
           XBAR = XBAR/FLOAT(N)
           SIGMA = 0.
           IF(N.GT.1) SIGMA = SQRT((XSQ - FLOAT(N)*
           1XBAR**2)/FLOAT(N - 1))
           RETURN
           END
```

```
5.          FUNCTION ISUB(N)
            IF(N.GT.0) GO TO 2
            ISUB = 1
            RETURN
      2     ISUB1 = 1
            K = 1
      5     ISUB1 = K*ISUB1 + (-1)**K
            K = K + 1
            IF(K.LE.N) GO TO 5
      6     ISUB = ISUB1
            RETURN
            END


7. C ASSUME CALLING STATEMENT IS CALL ONE (A, B, N, X)
            SUBROUTINE ONE(A, B, M, Y)
            DIMENSION A(M,M), B(M,M)
            DO 1000 I = 1, M
            DO 1000 J = 1, M
   1000    B(I,J) = Y*A(I, J)
            RETURN
            END


   C ASSUME CALLING STATEMENT IS CALL TWO (A, C, N)
            SUBROUTINE TWO(A, C, M)
            DIMENSION A(M,M), C(M,M)
            DO 2000 I = 1, M
            DO 2000 J = 1, M
   2000    C(I,J) = A(J,I)
            RETURN
            END


   C ASSUME CALLING STATEMENT IS CALL THREE (A, D, N)
            SUBROUTINE THREE(A, D, M)
            DIMENSION A(M,M), D(M,M)
            DO 3000 I = 1, M
            DO 3000 J = 1, N
            D(I,J) = 0.0
            DO 4000 K = 1, M
   4000    D(I,J) = D(I,J) + A(I,K)*A(K,J)
   3000    CONTINUE
            RETURN
            END
```

■ Exercises 9 (pages 240-242)

1. .TRUE.   3. .FALSE.   5. .FALSE.   7. .FALSE.
9. .TRUE.   11. .TRUE.   13. .FALSE.   15. .TRUE.

17.

P	Q	P .OR. Q	.NOT. (P .OR. Q)
T	T	T	F
T	F	T	F
F	T	T	F
F	F	F	T

19.

P	Q	R	Q .AND. R	P .OR. Q .AND. R
T	T	T	T	T
T	T	F	F	T
T	F	T	F	T
T	F	F	F	T
F	T	T	T	T
F	T	F	F	F
F	F	T	F	F
F	F	F	F	F

21. For Q .FALSE., P either .FALSE. or .TRUE.
    For Q .TRUE., P .TRUE.

23. For P and Q .TRUE.   25. P .TRUE.   27. .TRUE.

29. .TRUE.   31. .FALSE.

33. A = B = C (one of many solutions)

35. A = 3, B = 2, C = 1 (one of many solutions)

37.   IF(A.NE.1.0 .OR. B.NE.2.5) GO TO 10
    20 Next Step

39.   IF(A.NE.B .OR. B.LE.10.0) GO TO 50
    60 Next Step

41.   IF(A.GT.B .AND. C.GE.B .OR. A.LE.B .AND. B.GT.C)
        1GO TO 20
    10 Next Statement

43.

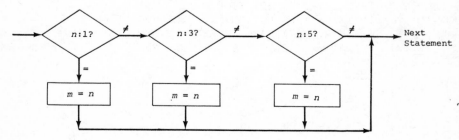

45.

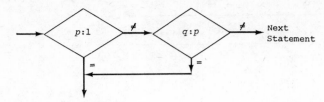

To Statement 10

```
47.        LOGICAL A, B, C, D
           CMIN = 100000.
           NPBEST = 0
           MBEST = 0
           DO 500 NP = 1, 160
           D = NP.GE.20
           IF(.NOT. D) GO TO 600
           DO 500 M = 1, 80
           A = NP + 2*M.LE.160
           IF(.NOT. A) GO TO 500
           B = NP + M.GE.70
           IF(.NOT. B) GO TO 500
           C = M.GT.NP
           IF(.NOT. C) GO TO 500
           COST = 2.*FLOAT(NP) + 1.15*FLOAT(M)
           IF(COST.GE.CMIN) GO TO 500
           CMIN = COST
           NPBEST = NP
           MBEST = M
     500   CONTINUE
     600   CONTINUE
           WRITE(2, 400) CMIN, NPBEST, MBEST
     400   FORMAT(1H1, 10(/), 20X, 'MINIMUM COST', F10.2, 3X,
          1'NO. POTATOES', I4, 'AMT. MACARONI', I4)
           STOP
           END
```

■ Exercises 10 (pages 257-259)

```
 1.        DIMENSION NAME(25), STREET(25), TWNST(25)
       1   READ(1, 100) NAME, STREET, TWNST, IZIP
     100   FORMAT(25A1, 25A1, 25A1, I5)
           IF(IZIP.EQ.99999) STOP
           IF(IZIP.LT.60000 .OR. IZIP.GE.70000) GO TO 1
           WRITE(2, 101) NAME, STREET, TWNST, IZIP
     101   FORMAT(//, 10X, 25A1, /, 10X, 25A1, /, 10X, 25A1, 2X, I5)
           GO TO 1
           END
```

```
3.          DIMENSION NAME(25), NANSW(25), NCODE(25)
            READ(1, 10) NCODE
     10     FORMAT(25I1)
      2     READ(1, 20) NAME, NANSW
     20     FORMAT(25A1, 25I1)
     C      TEST TO SEE IF DONE
            IF(NANSW(1).GE.3) STOP
            IRIGHT = 0
            IWRONG = 0
            DO 1 I = 1, 25
            IF(NANSW(I).NE.NCODE(I)) GO TO 5
            IRIGHT = IRIGHT + 1
            GO TO 1
      5     IF(NANSW(I).NE.0) IWRONG = IWRONG + 1
      1     CONTINUE
            ISCORE = IRIGHT*4 - IWRONG*5
            IF(ISCORE.LT.0) ISCORE = 0
            WRITE(2, 30) NAME, ISCORE
     30     FORMAT(//, 10X, 25A1, 5X, ' GRADE = ', I3)
            GO TO 2
            END


5.          DIMENSION LETTER(3)
    300     READ(1, 200) LETTER, NUMB, ITEST
    200     FORMAT(3A1, I3, 73X, I1)
            IF(ITEST.EQ.9) STOP
            IF(ITEST.NE.0) WRITE(2, 400) LETTER, NUMB
    400     FORMAT(//, 10X, 3A1, I3)
            GO TO 300
            END


7. (a)      DIMENSION TENS(18), ONES(18)
            DATA ONES/3HONE, 3H  , 3HTWO, 3H  , 3HTHR, 3HEE  ,
          13HFOU, 3HR  , 3HFIV, 3HE  , 3HSIX, 3H  , 3HSEV, 3HEN  ,
          23HEIG, 3HHT  , 3HNIN, 3HE  /
            DATA TENS/4HTEN  , 4H  , 4HTWEN, 4HTY  , 4HTHIR, 4HTY  ,
          14HFORT, 4HY  , 4HFIFT, 4HY  , 4HSIXT, 4HY  , 4HSEVE, 4HNTY  ,
          24HEIGH, 4HTY  , 4HNINE, 4HTY  /
            READ(1, 1) N1, N2
      1     FORMAT(2I1)
            IF(N1.EQ.1) GO TO 110
            NEWN1 = 2*N1 - 1
            FIRST1 = TENS(NEWN1)
            FIRST2 = TENS(NEWN1 + 1)
            IF(N2.EQ.0) GO TO 100
            NEWN2 = 2*N2 - 1
            SND1 = ONES(NEWN2)
            SND2 = ONES(NEWN2 + 1)
            WRITE(2, 51) FIRST1, FIRST2, SND1, SND2
     51     FORMAT(10X, 2A4, 1X, 2A3)
            STOP
    100     WRITE(2, 101) FIRST1, FIRST2
    101     FORMAT(10X, 2A4)
```

7. (a)—continued

```
        STOP
  110   IF(N2.EQ.1) GO TO 111
        IF(N2.EQ.2) GO TO 112
        IF(N2.EQ.3) GO TO 113
        IF(N2.EQ.4) GO TO 114
        IF(N2.EQ.5) GO TO 115
        IF(N2.EQ.6) GO TO 116
        IF(N2.EQ.7) GO TO 117
        IF(N2.EQ.8) GO TO 118
        WRITE(2, 120)
  120   FORMAT(10X, 'NINETEEN')
        STOP
  111   WRITE(2, 121)
  121   FORMAT(10X, 'ELEVEN')
        STOP
        .
        .
        .
```

and so on for Statements 112-118

(b)
```
    C PARTIAL SOLUTION
    C ASSUME ALL WAGES ARE OF FORM AB.CD
            DIMENSION EMPL(29)
            READ(1, 1) EMPL, WAGE
      1     FORMAT(29A1, 1X, F7.2)
            IF(WAGE.EQ.0.0) STOP
    C ABOVE TEST TO STOP PROGRAM
            NX = INT(WAGE)
            N1 = NX/10
            N2 = (NX - N1*(NX - N1*10)
            CENTS = (WAGE - FLOAT (NX))*100.
            .
            .
            .
```

Now do the same as in part (a)

■ Exercises 11 (page 281-282)

1. (a) Invalid   (b) Valid   (c) Invalid   (d) Valid
   (e) Valid   (f) Invalid   (g) Valid   (h) Invalid
   (i) Valid   (j) Valid

3.
```
    C ONE WAY
            DOUBLE PRECISION FUNCTION ROOT(Z)
            DOUBLE PRECISION Z
            ROOT = Z**.5
            RETURN
            END

    C ALTERNATE WAY.  THIS IS NEWTON'S METHOD
            DOUBLE PRECISION FUNCTION ROOT(Z)
            DOUBLE PRECISION EPS, ROOT1
            EPS = 1.0D - 12
```

3.—continued

```
            ROOT = Z
     20     ROOT1 = .5DO*(ROOT + Z/ROOT)
            IF(DABS((ROOT1 - ROOT)/ROOT).LE.EPS) GO TO 10
            ROOT = ROOT1
            GO TO 20
     10     ROOT = ROOT1
            RETURN
            END
```

5. (a) (4.0, 6.0)   (b) (1.0, -1.0)   (c) (-4.0, 0)
   (d) (-1.0, 0.0)   (e) (0.0, -1.0)

7.
```
            SUBROUTINE POLY(A, Z, N)
            COMPLEX A, Z, POLY
            DIMENSION A(N)
            KK = N - 1
            POLY = A(N)
            IF(KK.EQ.0) RETURN
     20     POLY = POLY*Z + A(KK)
            KK = KK - 1
            IF(KK.GE.1) GO TO 20
            RETURN
            END
```

9.
```
            COMPLEX FUNCTION POLE(Z)
            COMPLEX Z
            X = REAL(Z)
            Y = AIMAG(Z)
            R = SQRT(X**2 + Y**2)
            THETA = ATAN2(Y, X)
            POLE = (R, THETA)
            RETURN
            END
```

■ Exercises 12 (pages 325-326)

1. The deletion card would be treated as an addition. One way to
   deal with this is to test for a deletion card in the addition
   procedure and to ignore this card if it is a deletion. After
   Statement 20 of the final program for Example 2, replace the
   WRITE statement with

```
        IF(NOP.NE.1) WRITE(4, 11) NUM1, NAME1, PAY1, NSS1
```

3. Insert in routine for adding a record just before the WRITE
   statement.

```
    C       STATEMENTS 25 TO 99 NOW READ AS FOLLOWS
       25   IF(NOP.EQ.1) GO TO 5
    C       IF NOP IS 1, RECORD IS DELETED
            IF(NAME(1).NE.10H              ) GO TO 27
```

3.—continued

```
        DO 26 KKK = 1, 3
     26 NAME1(KKK) = NAME4(KKK)
     27 IF(PAY1.EQ.0.0) PAY1 = PAY4
        IF(NSS1.EQ.0) NSS1 = NSS4
        WRITE(4, 11) NUM1, NAME1, PAY1, NSS1
        GO TO 5
C       END OF FILE1 REACHED
        etc.
```

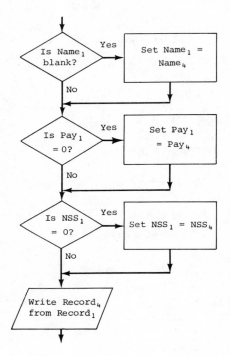

```
5. C    IF NDATED IS DATE DUE IN THE FORM MMDDYY
   C    AND NDATER IS DATE RETURNED, IN SAME FORM,
   C    THEN FINE IS
        DAYS = JULIAN(NDATER) - JULIAN(NDATED)
        IF(DAYS.LT.0.) DAYS = 0
        FINE = .05*DAYS
   C    JULIAN IS A FUNCTION WHICH RETURNS
   C    THE JULIAN DATE – YYNNN WHERE NNN
   C    IS THE DAY OF THE YEAR FROM 1 TO 366.
        FUNCTION JULIAN(MMDDYY)
        DIMENSION MONTHS(12)
   C    MONTHS(I) = NO. DAYS BEFORE FIRST OF MONTH I
   C    (NOT COUNTING LEAP YEAR)
        DATA MONTHS(1) /0/
        DATA MONTHS(2) /31/
        DATA MONTHS(3) /59/
        DATA MONTHS(4) /90/
        DATA MONTHS(5) /120/
```

5.—continued

```
            DATA MONTHS(6)  /151/
            DATA MONTHS(7)  /181/
            DATA MONTHS(8)  /212/
            DATA MONTHS(9)  /243/
            DATA MONTHS(10) /273/
            DATA MONTHS(11) /304/
            DATA MONTHS(12) /334/
            NYEAR = MOD(MMDDYY, 100)
            MONTH = MMDDYY/10000
            NDAY = MOD(MMDDYY/100, 100)
            JULIAN = 1000*NYEAR + MONTHS(MONTH) + NDAY
C           CHECK FOR LEAP YEAR
            IF(MOD(NYEAR, 4).EQ.0 .AND. MONTH.GE.3)
           1JULIAN = JULIAN + 1
            RETURN
            END


7.          SUBROUTINE SAME(L, M, N)
C           READ FILES M AND N, IN UNFORMATTED MODE.
C           RECORDS CONSIST OF L RECORDS EACH (L.LT.500)
C           IF FILES ARE IDENTICAL, PRINT MESSAGE
C           ELSE PRINT ERROR MESSAGE AND STOP
            LOGICAL EOF
            DIMENSION MREC(500), NREC(500)
            IF(L.LE.500) GO TO 10
            WRITE (6, 501)
      501   FORMAT(' L GREATER THAN 500 ')
            STOP
       10   NCOUNT = 0
            READ(M) (MREC(I), I = 1, L)
            IF(EOF (M)) GO TO 1001
            NCOUNT = NCOUNT + 1
            READ(N) (NREC(I), I = 1, L)
            IF(EOF (N)) GO TO 2001
            DO 20 I = 1, L
       20   IF(MREC(I).NE.NREC(I)) GO TO 3001
            GO TO 10
C           AT END OF M, SHOULD BE AT END OF N
     1001   READ(N) (NREC(I), I = 1, 2)
            IF(EOF (N)) GO TO 4001
            WRITE(6, 502) N, M
      502   FORMAT(' MORE RECORDS ON ', I2, ' THAN ', I2)
            STOP
C           END OF N REACHED TOO SOON
     2001   WRITE(6, 502) M, N
            STOP
     3001   WRITE(6, 503) NCOUNT
      503   FORMAT(' RECORD NUMBER ', I6, ' DISAGREES. ')
            STOP
     4001   WRITE(6, 504) NCOUNT
      504   FORMAT(' FILES ARE IDENTICAL ', I6, ' RECORDS. ')
            STOP
            END
```

■ Exercises 13 (pages 346–347)

1. (a) Valid (blanks ignored, variable IJK) (b) Not valid
   (c) Valid   (d) Valid   (e) Not valid

3.
```
        DO 1 J = 1, 5
        IF(I.EQ.NN(J)) GO TO 2
   1    CONTINUE
        J = 6
   2    GO TO(5, 10, 15, 20, 25, 30), J
  30    Next Statement
```

5.
```
        SUBROUTINE SOLV(A, B, C)
        DISC = B**2 - 4.0*A*C
        IF(DISC.LT.0.) ASSIGN 10 TO K
        IF(DISC.EQ.0.) ASSIGN 20 TO K
        IF(DISC.GT.0.) ASSIGN 30 TO K
        GO TO K, (10, 20, 30)
C       COMPLEX ROOTS
  10    WRITE(6, 51)
  51    FORMAT(' TWO COMPLEX ROOTS ')
        RETURN
C       ONE MULTIPLE, ROOT
  20    WRITE(6, 52)
  52    FORMAT(' ONE REAL MULTIPLE ROOT ')
        RETURN
  30    WRITE(6, 53)
  53    FORMAT(' TWO REAL ROOTS ')
        RETURN
C       STATEMENTS CAN BE INCLUDED ABOVE TO
C       COMPUTE THE ACTUAL VALUES OF ROOTS
        END
```

7.
```
        EXTERNAL POLY
        CALL EVAL(POLY, 1.0, 2.0, .2)
        STOP
        END
        FUNCTION POLY(W)
        POLY = W**3 - 3.0*W
        RETURN
        END
        SUBROUTINE EVAL(F, A, B, DX)
        X = A
  10    Y = F(X)
        WRITE(6, 11) X, Y
  11    FORMAT(1X, 2F15.6)
        X = X + DX
        IF(X.GT.B) RETURN
        GO TO 10
        END
```

9. The program sets B(1) = 1, B(2) = 1, B(3) = 1, ..., B(10) = 1.
   This is caused by the equivalence statement, which makes each
   element of B the same as the previous element of A.

INDEX